A Keen Eye

Fact and Folklore on Scottish Highland cattle

"Suil a ghleidheas sealbh"

(A keen eye keeps the cattle)

Author/Editor Ùna Flora Cochrane
Photographer Tom McLatchie

First published Busdubh Publishing in 1996

Designed by Almond Design • Edinburgh

Reprinted 2023 using the text and illustrations
of the first edition, with corrections.

Sections on cattle health and disease have been left unaltered from the first edition,
but reference to changes in UK government regulations inserted.

by Stenlake Publishing
54-58 Mill Square Catrine, KA5 6RD
01290 551122
www.stenlake.co.uk

ISBN 978-1-84033-921-5

Printed by
Claro Print, Office 26, 27, 1 Spiersbridge Way,
Thornliebank, Glasgow G46 8NG

CONTENTS

VISUAL GUIDES

The Visual Guide offers photographs which illustrate the text and encourage a discerning eye for the Highland Breed. There are two sections, the first offering general observations and the second offering judgement of breed standards.

Variation in photographic colour reflects the different sources of photographic material used and also the range of natural lighting effects the Scottish climate presents. Several photographs were taken in rain but no standardisation of colour has been attempted.

Selection of the most apposite photographs was challenging. The final result combines along with some of my own efforts and additional sources, a substantial number from the collection of Mr Thomas McLatchie, Millerston.

PERSONAL DEDICATION

Loving thanks to my mother
for my connection with the land,
to my father for teaching
analytical observation,
to my husband for making possible
the task of writing *A Keen Eye*,
to my daughter for initiating it.

Clan crests by: Gillian Waugh and Dennis Booth

FOREWORD

Ùna F Cochrane's book 'A Keen Eye' is the culmination of many hours of careful research into Highland cattle – one of the most famous cattle breeds in the world.

Compiled by a genuine enthusiast of the breed, *A Keen Eye* is a unique publication which has been thoughtfully arranged to be of enormous interest to any reader – no matter what level of experience they may have.

Basic stockman-ship, breed characteristics, breeding and breed history, together with the special feature of photographic sections portraying an accurate representation of the breed, and a highly informative glance into Scotland's agricultural past, all help in the making of a book which will give pleasure to all who read it.

I am delighted and honoured to endorse Ùna F Cochrane's truly original publication which has a place on any enthusiast's shelf.

A McARTHUR
President Highland Cattle Society 1994 – 1996.

ACKNOWLEDGEMENTS AND SOURCES

Warm kindliness, patience, friendship, and shared knowledge have been extended to me from the many people whom I approached in the course of my preparation of *A Keen Eye*.

Scottish Farmer

Glasgow Herald

In particular Mr T McLatchie, Millerston, and Miss Campbell of Kilberry, rank highly for their unique blend of pertinent, informed and sustained support:
Tom imparting advice when I sought it, never propounding biased views, unstintingly on the photographic alert and available for consultation; Marion most charmingly exacting scholarly standards in my assembling of researched material, fully respecting my chosen path, generously offering information from her own researches;

also to:
Mr A W Howat, Rigg; the late Mr T Muirhead, Corriemuckloch; Mr Angus MacGillivray; Mr & Mrs J P Ramsay; Mrs P Egglestone, Cliburn; Mr & Mrs D J MacMillan, Achnagart; Mr Duncan Buchanan, Shenavallie; Mrs P Knox and Mr W Knox, Mains of Glentruim; Mr A Buchanan, Gallin Farm; all of whom gave welcome information and encouragement trustingly at the very beginning of my research, and especially the intrepid A Hamish G Wilson, Highland Cattle Society Secretary who risked approval of my endeavour, my sincere thanks.

For access to folds for photography and discussion:
in addition to those already mentioned, I heartily thank Mrs J Nelson, Achnacloich; Major W G Gordon DFC, Lude; Miss L M D Robertson, Balinoe Croft; Mr & Mrs D Fellowes, Cladich; Col M P de Klee OBE, Auchnacraig; Mrs M M Edwards, Applecross on behalf of Major Wills; Mr A Anderson, on behalf of Mr J P Grant of Rothiemurchus; Mr C K M Stewart, East Bridgelands; Mrs J Bowser, Auchlyne; Mr E A Cameron, Glen Nevis; Mr E C Ormiston and Mr Fergie Ormiston, The Birches; Mr A J M Gibson, Edinvale; Mr C Macdonald, Auch Estate; Mr D Newton, Otter Estate; Mr D J Campbell, Keilbeg Farm; Mr H Finlay, Achtriochtan Farm; Mr D F F Bryant, Ardmore House; Mr P McDonald, Kilmore; Mr J Cameron-Manson, Buccleuch Countryside Service; Lady J H S Macpherson, Craig Dhu House; Mr D Anderson, Barnakill Farm; Mr D Hunter, Manager of Balquharn Farm; The Murrays, Balhearty House; Mr W Robertson, Ardoran; Mrs E W Cameron, Benouhr; all of whom contributed valuably to my research, in some instances even providing vehicles more suitable than mine for access over rough terrain to the cattle.
In a variety of venues from home hearth to sales ring, on telephone and in correspondence, fruitful discussion time was readily given to me from:
Mr & Mrs A Morrow, Mr B J Elwood, Miss R Dalgleish, Mr A McArthur, Mr & Mrs Eric Barr, Mr D E Darroch, Mr John Keay, Mr & Mrs Ken Headspeath, Mrs E Campbell Shaw, Mr R W Shaw, Mr H M MacPhail, Mr & Mrs B H Dawson, Mr M P Moy, Mrs I E Cameron, Mr & Mrs A R Mackay, Mr I A Mackay, Mrs Ena

McNeill, Mr & Mrs W A N Thomson, Mr & Mrs K W W Brown, Mr W Steele, Mr Robert Dixon, Mrs M Park, Mr D McDiarmid BEM, Mr J C H Ball, Mr M Moore, Mrs Hayter, Mr A Christie, Mr Donald Cameron, Mr J M McFarlane, Mr J Hughes, Mr & Mrs W J Harper, Mr J McKechnie, Mr A MacCuish, the late Mr J B Miners, Mr & Mrs Coghill, Dr E Ramand, Mr C Etough, Mr D Stewart, Mr J Crilley, Mr P Heard, Mrs J Redpath, Mr J Wright, Mr D McKinnon, Mr G Menteith, Mr A M Torrance, Mr J Watson, Mr Puck Ross, Mr Mark Brown, Mr Allan Macdonald, Mrs M McInnes, Mr D J MacGillivray, Mr Doug Shewan, Mr R Beale, Mr G Scott May, Mrs Dixon (Snr), Dr M Newton, Mr T C Farries.

G Scott May

Among veterinary personnel special thanks to:
the enthusiastic Dr Geoff Simm, Mr D A Ferguson, Dr A J F Russell, Dr S Adalsteinsson, Dr M Stevenson, Dr M L Ryder, Dr I Wright, Mr A Sykes, Mr G L H Alderson, Mr W Robbie, Mr C Moir, Mr H Coulthard, Mr A Greigg, Mr Redpath.

Librarians, archivists, and all, who either delved on my behalf or lent precious books:
Sally Harrower, Margaret Davies, Mrs S E Allsopp, Mr Murdo Macdonald, Mrs A A Park, Mrs C A Goodfellow, Mr T Cowie, Mrs M Ramsay, Mr A Whitehouse, Mr Scott Mitchell, Mr C K M Stewart, Mr T McLatchie, Mr D Douglas, Mrs M M Edwards, Mr D B Paterson, Mr S Watt, Mr J Richmond MBE, Mr A W Howat, Mr A R Mackay, Mr A H G Wilson, Mr A Thompson, Mrs K Deasington, Mr & Mrs J Scarlett, Mr D A Hirst, Miss Campbell of Kilberry, Father B R MacDonald, Mr W Storrie, Mr W Steele, Miss R Dalgleish, Dr Gifford, Mrs C Hunter.

Many more voices, and offers to take me round folds which sadly my time-scale did not permit, have added validity and authenticity to the material selected for this publication.

The cheerful ever ready help from Highland Cattle Society staff Nesta van der Wheilen, Susan R Campbell, and Jean Byass eased and hastened on my research.

With the patient expertise of the Almond Design team this book actually did emerge from my researches into print, designer Linda Hardwicke stylishly arranging order in the motley array of material for illustrations, for the covers and text.

The skilled experience of Stenlake Publishing made the Revised Edition possible. They coaxed the original files into working order; edited the book; corrected mistakes I had overlooked in the first edition; and Lewis Hutton completed the mammoth task of compiling a valuably comprehensive Index.

I am pleased to acknowledge my lasting appreciation in a heartfelt thankyou to all.

ÙNA F COCHRANE B.A., FSA Scot

INTRODUCTION TO FIRST EDITION

The purpose of this book is to make conveniently available wide ranging information on Scottish Highland cattle in Scotland. It combines literary research with practical advice in a collection of contemporary and historical facts, statistics, and humorous stories. My role has been to gather and present researched findings.

A *Keen Eye* focuses attention on the breed, its behaviour, appearance, and management, from the time of its origin to the middle of the twentieth century. References to individual supporters of the breed, and to Highland cattle outwith Scotland, play a secondary role.

The contents deal with the breed primarily in Scotland simply because its charisma has spread so far worldwide that fuller coverage in one text would be unwieldy. The information gathered has, however, something for all enthusiasts wherever domiciled.

Since information about the breed in the second half of the twentieth century can be traced through the Highland Cattle Society of Scotland, Highland Cattle societies in other countries, and current breeders, there is not so great a need to cover that recent period in detail in this publication.

Motivation for this study stems from an introduction by the infectiously enthusiastic Gideon Scott May in my childhood to his Strathtummel fold of Highland cattle on the hillside of Loch Tummel. His laughter filled voice, puzzling over the unpredictable arrival of black calves in a breed with scarcely a black cow or bull to be found in the 1950s, stayed with me until opportunity to investigate the breed came my way. The impetus which catapulted my energies into this work came from my daughter's need of information on Highland cattle for her school project on Farming in Badenoch. In general libraries seem to hold very little about the breed.

Many live interviews and visits to folds provided vital insights. Much of the first chapter is drawn from frank discussions with breeders whose experience with Highland cattle ranges from a lifetime to a year. Their generosity in imparting for the benefit of others their hard earned wisdom makes this book of practical value to active breeders. Photographs supporting the text – whilst being no substitute for experience – have been selected with the intention of heightening awareness of the benefits of informed and keen observation.

For all who have an interest in Highland cattle I hope the ensuing pages offer some answers to questions about this beguiling, endearing, vexing, and most enigmatic member of the bovine species, and that my selection of information is sufficiently comprehensive to compensate for omissions necessary to comply with printing and publishing requisites.

Ùna F Cochrane 1996

INTRODUCTION TO SECOND EDITION

Readers of this second edition of *A Keen Eye* have Mr Terry Clemans of Hideaway Farm Highland Cattle, Illinois, to thank for initiating its preparation and release. His solution in November 2020 to his difficulty in securing a copy of the long out-of-print publication was to urge me to prepare a second print-run. The unprecedented range of complications caused by the viral Covid 19 global pandemic along with the original content having been created and stored in a long obsolete digital format made the task unusually protracted and challenging. However the generous commitment of the Stenlake Publishing team prevailed to bring the project to fruition.

The content remains unchanged except for corrections and the useful inclusion of a detailed index, thanks to the inspired work of designer Lewis Hutton. Spare extra pages occasioned by that allowed me additionally to offer fresh relevant comment as follows and a few more photographs.

My childhood in the Highlands of Scotland in Kingussie, Pitlochry and Inverness nourished a love of the countryside, livestock, and all aspects of nature. Farmers and veterinary practitioners among my close relatives and friends increased opportunity for easily gained familiarity with varied aspects of livestock and wildlife, such that caution when among them, as distinct from fear, was instinctive. With an uncle who was a keen photographer and a father whose profession included taking and reading X-rays of oral conditions a belief in the lasting value of photographs and illustrations took root. The subject of my first attempt at photography when at 9 years old I had ventured alone up a hillside at Croft Douglas, Strathtummel, was a Highland cow.

Photographs can be of considerable support in acquiring a quick and more complete understanding of the subject matter. The implications in saying that at 9 years old I enjoyed an afternoon walk up Ben-y-Vrackie are more instantly generated if accompanied by this photograph.

To a discerning eye the commendably quiet but alert attitude of the grazing cow is immediately evident in this photo of my cousin Cath Urquhart being introduced to a Highland cow in Skye in the 1930s.

Explanation of an old method of inhibiting untethered cows from bolting during a new experience of awaiting a judge's assessment is aided with this photograph. Securing something heavy that would bounce or flap uncomfortably on the forehead restricted the distance covered in any attempt to make a hasty exit of the location, and reduced the likelihood of any further escape urges.

Highland cattle are predominantly a breed of whole-coat-colour, but although white markings do occur they may be difficult to envisage prior to seeing an example of it, such as this red & white steer from the early 1900s.

"Herd boy on duty c.1905" might be a better caption for this photograph yet a single glance at it conveys much more information than the words. The stance and garb of the little lad and his proximity to an active bull in the presence of a calf and two cows of the long nose/broad muzzle type once favoured is a quickly assimilated record of earlier times.

Artist George Rankin records with accuracy the business part of bygone cattle fairs in Scotland. A bowler hatted gent and two agents, wearing fore-and-aft caps, negotiate with blue bonnet wearing Highland men and a lowland cattleman wearing a shepherd's cap. The central bull has level horns, well set tail and a head and neck as stipulated in the breed standards set in 1885 by the Highland Cattle Society.

Perthshire artist Scott Rankin (1868 – 1942) depicts a more domestic scene in bygone times of a barefooted woman and child with the family milk cow. Under the woman's arm is a typical 'coggie' pail for collection of the milk.

This image is more than an advertisement for beef. It uses the Scottish friendship toast "Guid Health" to suggest that for good health beef is the answer if from Highland beef bred and reared in the Highlands. The depiction of a MacGregor clansman deliberately invokes folklore and the historic fact that Highland cattle were the key to the health and wealth of the nation for centuries.

In considering updating some of the original text, and duly discovering that an obituary column would be necessary for a large number of contributed articles, in addition to referencing many advances in veterinary science along with changed obligatory regulations since 1994, my conclusion was to leave the original text unchanged other than to improve clarity with some minor adjustments and corrections. Therefore I hopefully leave updating of material on this alluring breed of cattle native to Scotland to a younger writer. Perhaps the following pages may inspire an author with an enthusiasm for the breed equal to mine.

Ùna F Cochrane 2022

Gideon Scott May with his cattle in the 1950s. My parents took me with them on a memorable visit to Gideon and his wife Irralee at Croft Douglas. After Irralee's impressive Winifred Atwell style rendering of a ragtime melody I wandered outside. There I met the Strathtummel fold of Highland cattle. There my keen interest was kindled.

CHAPTER 1: OBSERVATIONS

CHAPTER 1: OBSERVATIONS

MAKING A START

Interested in Highland cattle? Where to see them is one thing, where to buy another.

Some cities, castles, stately homes, country hotels, deer parks, farmers with caravan sites, keep small numbers. The cattle are a popular item with visitors many of whom are keener to photograph them than other attractions on offer.

Prior to buying however, the best way to educate your eye for Highland cattle is to look at them in their natural conditions. This is easily achieved by contacting the Highland Cattle Society whose office personnel will be pleased to give you names and addresses of a variety of breeders not only in Scotland but worldwide according to your needs.

In addition to viewing Highlands by arrangement with their breeder it is of value to visit the official sales of pedigree stock. In Scotland these have traditionally been held at Oban in February and October, although from time to time Highland cattle appear at the Inverness, Perth, and Stirling cattle sales. The Society office will always advise if asked where the nearest and soonest sale is likely to be, as the 1990s has seen an increase in the numbers of sales venues.

At these sales can be found a range of quality from fully pedigreed Show winning standard to meagre beasts intended not for breeding but for fattening for the beef market.

Agricultural Shows are useful if one bears in mind that:

1. the animals shown represent no more nor less than the best stock such breeders as are competing have available to put forward at that particular time;
2. Show stock are not necessarily the best breeding animals in the country;
3. award-winners at one Show may vary in type from award-winners at a different Show.

The beautiful smooth shining horns, feet, and clean freshly combed coat are a feature of Shows. Highland cattle do not look like that all year round. The Agricultural Shows in mainland Scotland which most regularly embrace Highland cattle entries among the cattle breeds are those at Edinburgh (Ingliston), Ayr, Perth, Doune, Stirling, Dalmally, Black Isle.

Breeders of pedigree Highland cattle and general cattle dealers are both usually prepared to negotiate sales of stock privately at any time to suit pocket and purpose.

Choice of stock should relate to the purpose for which the beasts are destined. It would be a sad loss to the breed if top quality pedigree animals are bought only to add charm character or novelty...which they do magnificently...to parklands, the grounds of residential premises or exclusive restaurants, rather than to perpetuate high quality stock as breeding animals.

Animals intended to survive on sparse feeding in mountainous terrain need adapting time to do well if accustomed to lush southern pastures and supplementary feeding; buying an old cow or an unpedigreed cow with a view to breeding Show quality animals could prove in practice a slower road to success than in theory had been planned.

So in selecting animals to suit your circumstances it is wise to enlist the help of someone with a sound knowledge of Highland cattle built from years of experience with them.

Perhaps worth considering before purchase is how important coat-colour is to you. Bear in mind that Highland cattle may take from nine months to two years or more to settle into the full bloom of adult coat-colour. Yellow calves may turn red or black, red may turn yellow, dun or brindle, brindle may turn black, and of course many jet blacks are born brown or brown with yellow hair tips. A parti colour adult coat growing in where the calf had been whole coloured has yet to be recorded.

In deference to Northern Scottish people, frequently spoken of as Highlanders, I choose to refer to the breed of cattle indigenous to the Scottish Highland regions as "Highlands" in keeping with the plural form for other regionally named breeds like Galloways, Ayrshires, Aberdeen Angus. But enthusiastic Highland cattle breeders when talking of the breed are likely to use the term Kyloe at some point. The word Kyloe embodies an element of the mystery of the breed for mystery prevails where facts fail. Views abound on the meaning and derivation of words once familiar to the Northern Scot before his natural language in 1609 was banned by King James VI creating a legacy of linguistic confusion, although a common language between nations is a sensible policy. There being no letter K in written Scottish Gaelic if 'kyloes' meant 'the cattle which have to swim the kyles (narrow sea channels) between the islands and the mainland, ' the word might be a distortion of the gaelic 'caol' for narrow or a phonetic version of the local word for ferries which sounded like 'Kyloes'. Yet it could also have developed from anglicisation of the Celtic word 'coille' for wood meaning the cows of the wood. Wooded areas in Argyll embraced the word 'coille' in their name, and since a district in Ayrshire was formerly known as **Kyle**, also written as **Coil**, it is easy to argue that cattle from that area were called Kyloes. The dictionary of *Gaelic names of Beasts Birds and Fishes* compiled by Alexander R. Forbes states simply "...Ky, kye, kylo: drove."

Today though, Kyloe is generally taken to mean the breed of cattle native to the Scottish Western Highlands and Islands which was described in the early nineteenth century as small shaggy-coated, horned, and usually black or dark brown occasionally with white flecks or white bellies. In these days the cattle from the north mainland area of Sutherland and Caithness, were called Norlanders but were considered by many to be an inferior type to the Kyloe.

Another word encountered in Highland cattle talk is 'Fold'. Current fashion encourages the use of the collective term a 'fold' of Highland cattle rather than a herd perhaps as a reminder of connections the breed has with former times when livestock were driven into a stone or turf walled enclosure, the fold, at night and sometimes also at midday. The procedure was known as folding the cattle. Night folding was at one time for protection from wolves. The last wolf in Scotland died in 1743, according to one source while another states that Sir Ewan Cameron of Lochiel killed the last one in 1680 which seems too early, but many districts have their own 'last wolf' story. Daytime folding was to prevent the cattle from browsing the crops on un-enclosed farm land. Use of the term 'Fold of cattle' may have become widespread after the Scottish Parliament passed The Winter Herding Act in 1686 stating that cattle horses sheep and goats had to be kept in folds, enclosures or houses; a difficult law to enforce. Folding is also explained as a system of enclosing cattle on ground to be manured.

Whatever the linguistic facts the practical facts are that it is quite possible for many twentieth century folds of Highland cattle to trace Kyloe connections in their ancestors.

BEHAVIOUR

Informed observation is the secret of success. Knowledge of animal behaviour is necessary to interpret what you see, while understanding every little movement in your individual animals makes for greater safety and comfort all round.

Never let up continued scrutiny whenever your animals are visible until you are automatically assimilating information from them. Learning to interpret with some degree of accuracy the signals your own cattle are giving is a powerful aid in successful breeding, a skill more readily acquired by those with a deeply genuine interest in the animals. When you first acquire livestock watch them as much as possible and ask experienced persons to explain action or interaction you have noticed. Certainly make provision for someone 'to keep an eye on them' for at least the first three weeks of their being in new surroundings.

Give your new stock plenty of opportunity to identify their new handlers.

It is probably helpful in speeding along the adjustment process to wear the same outer garment for the first few visits to them and to bear in mind that heavy perfume or tobacco odours might delay a little their complete acceptance of you. Without considerable co-operation from the cattle they would be completely unmanageable. Colour of clothing seems to trouble them less than if it flaps about in the wind or with the wearer's movement, for they find unfamiliar movement distracting. Cattle unaccustomed to the required white coats for persons leading livestock in Show rings occasionally seem to react with untrusting wide-eyed suspicion. It could be the 'colour' white which spooks the inexperienced or unprepared Show animal but more probably a combination of factors cause the reaction only one of which is that the animal has difficulty in accepting its usual handler when dressed so differently. Yet the question of how meaningful colour is to cattle does recur in trying to understand unexpected behaviour such as for example that of a two year old heifer which despite comfortable disregard for whatever ropes, hose piping or cable it had to step around in its home territory took great offence at blue nylon rope lying on the grass across the entrance to the Show ring. Later the same animal calmly stepped over the same blue nylon rope entering the same Show ring. In discussion with the breeder it was put to me that anything remotely snake-like can stir a deeply rooted instinct to take evasive action. When checking photographs of the occasion it was noticeable that when the heifer had been difficult the blue rope lay loose in wavy curvy twisting shapes and later when she stepped easily over it the rope was taut and straight. One deduces then it was the shape and not the colour of that rope which caused the problem. But was it shape or colour that made experienced Show cows toss heads and roll eyes at Boys' Brigade youths in dark navy uniforms perched up on the scoreboard rostrum in the Show ring at the Royal Highland Agricultural Show? *(pic 18 p38)* Further observation might provide an explanation. Several lifetime breeders do believe that Highland cattle distinguish vehicles by colour. Their belief is drawn from noticing the cattle responses to their vehicle in weather conditions which would make it unlikely that the cattle were able to hear or smell the particular engine and noticing also the responses when the usual vehicle had been replaced by a different one.

Apart from the immediate need to deal with unexpected atypical reactions of the moment, as instanced above, it is sensible to recognise the possibility of long-term effect on an animal which can harbour the memory of a bad experience indefinitely. So preparing animals adequately for the circumstances you expect they will have to face calls for understanding of both general-to-the-breed and specific-to-each-animal behavioural characteristics. For instance one animal which would quietly walk up the ramp into the transport lorry and travel well evidently disliked walking down the ramp and required space to leap the length of it, and recover balance. A bit unnerving if you chanced to be face on to the leap unaware of the animal's non-aggressive temperament. Then there is the animal which registers its recognition of having been bred and handled by women by being less co-operative with men, or vice versa; in other words there is the occasional beast one might come across with a preference for either a male or female handler. In time they will adjust, but not without trying bullying, for example if their robust over six-foot tall stockman has been replaced by a neat five-foot stockwoman. In such circumstances it can be advantageous to have trees to dodge behind until the adjustment period is over!

Every experienced breeder will have met many instances when highly individual responses had to be taken into account during fairly routine manoeuvres of stock. So although there is no shortcut to the wisdom of experience the more mention of examples of idiosyncratic behaviour the novice can draw out of skilled breeders the easier will be the anticipation of the needs both of the cattle and their handler.

An age old method of bringing cattle from a distance to you is simply to call them by voice. I am reliably informed that the Gaelic call was 'Trobhad, Trobhad' pronounced **'Tro-ott'** meaning 'come along'. But any long vowel sound which carries well over a distance will do, such as 'Coo-oop lassie, Coo-oop, ' or 'Come on' extended into a long 'Kmaw...nnow.'

Of course free-ranging hill cattle which could be miles out of earshot require a different method of collection, perhaps combining manpower, vehicle power, and dogpower. Wherever they are Highland cattle are highly sensitive to sound. They easily distinguish different engine sounds and become very responsive to known, and on the alert with unknown, voices. This behavioural characteristic could in part be due to the fact that whilst the profuse hair on the forehead protects the eyes it does sometimes restrict vision thereby throwing the responsibility of the self preservation instinct more heavily onto the senses of hearing and smell. It follows that quiet calm moving among them (minus indulgent use of anti-midge spray, aftershave or perfume) will cause less disturbance than brusque activity with strong voice.

This was evident when on several occasions I wandered through free-ranging hill herds, camera at the ready, hoping for a good photograph. The animals were so unperturbed at my quiet slow moving presence that even as I clicked away three feet from their horns they would not bother to lift their beautiful heads to give me my prize shot. One black bull and two black cows actually lay down to chew cud in front of my hopeful camera. But throughout my manoeuvres I was unceasingly on the alert for any little signals of agitation in the animals. Noticing details like: a momentary break in an individual's established rhythm of browsing, a tense stillness in the way the head is held, how often an eye peers through the dossan (forelock), how much testing of the new smell of my presence is happening, how much ear flicking is due to flies or preparation for sudden flight or alternative action such as putting **you** to flight, which calves belong to which cows and avoiding getting between calf and mother – makes the difference between sensible and irresponsible human behaviour among bovines.

Once a young calf has suckled it settles down to sleep often lying deep in rushes, long grass, or nestled into a dip in a gulley or river bank *(Pics 6, 7, 8 p34, 35).* The mother will then graze some distance from her calf making it easier than you might think to find yourself between her and her offspring. When calves are a few days old they are likely to play together usually within the grazing herd rather than round the perimeter. Obviously approaching these calves as I did when out photographing placed me between offspring and dams. On one such occasion I heard behind me the snort which usually heralds matriarchal concern and precedes her action to remove any threat to her calf. At once without turning to face the cow I eased sideways out of the direct line between her and calf and strode off downhill gradually gathering speed jumping from tussock to tussock avoiding bog. But whilst appeasing that calf's mother my turn of speed offended a three year old heifer whose few menacing steps towards me were a sharp reminder to move calmly among cattle whenever possible. An instant change of direction to a diagonal away from her at walking pace fortunately reduced her attitude to one of poised watchfulness.

Not once did I approach stock in a direct confrontational way, nor did I stand directly in front for any length of time. If you march straight up to a cow which stands its ground and remain for too long staring at it 'head on' you could be inviting the animal to remove you from its grazing space. Consider that you and the stock share the same space, act accordingly, and it is less likely that the stock will feel threatened or challenged. Watch them and let them watch you before you stroll casually in a diagonal approach seeming to look elsewhere than in a sustained stare at them.

It is important to mention that permission for my access to the folds was in every instance requested beforehand and very generously granted to suit my available time rather than what may have suited the fold management schedule best. But I would hope that should I whilst hill-walking ever come upon Highland cattle my behaviour would not send them in flight twenty miles across the hills as was the case for one breeder who allowed me access to his inby cattle whilst attempts at tracing the whereabouts of his hill stock were made. Whoever the hill users were who so disturbed these cattle they were ignorant of how to conduct themselves in the presence of hill stock and must have made some effort to scare the animals since even young stock with little experience of handling are unlikely to go so far unless considerably upset. It is not unusual for stock which see little of man to take off suddenly with remarkable speed for a short distance, which in hill districts might take them out of sight. But twenty miles was inconsiderate of them when their owners can not be held responsible for the behaviour of the public at large.

Public behaviour towards Highland cattle does give reason for concern. So fascinated are they that wandering into the midst of herds, particularly those with calves, hoping to touch one or at very least video or photograph them happens frequently. Permission is rarely sought, and in general tourists are oblivious to how disturbing the family dog can be to a species once preyed upon by wolves, and still exposed to prowling foxes.

HIGHLANDS WITH DOGS

The more you can find out from the seller about the cattle you buy the better. Some folds use collie dogs to help with hill management but many do not. Incidentally there is a strain of collie dog thought to have originated in Skye which takes to working cattle more readily than others. A distinguishing feature about this cattle dog is the much shorter tail which grows naturally to just above the hock *(Pic 9 p35)* and therefore lacks the curving brush so typical of sheepdogs. Accustom cattle to dogs gradually, rather than discover too late the effect of thoughtlessly having gone to look over your purchases with the family labrador bounding frenetically about.

Make your first few visits to your new stock without the company of even the quietest of dogs. If you are normally accompanied by a working dog when checking your livestock it is likely that the new animals put in amongst them will take note of the prevailing attitude to your dog and behave in line with that but one cannot assume this will be the case. If you see a dog and its owner strolling among a field of Highlands whose strongest reaction is only to lift their heads momentarily, they are evidently used to seeing that particular person with that dog and know that the dog leaves them alone *(Pic 10 p36)*. These same cattle however, on seeing that same person wander among them but with an unfamiliar dog would show concern. In fact a not unknown response is that of a heifer attempting to clear the threat of the unfamiliar dog off her ground then setting about clearing off the accompanying person too. A breeder of long family involvement with Highlands considers that of all dogs small white ones such as West Highland and Jack Russell terriers are the most disliked and may prompt even the quietest of cows to take action. Despite their usually quiet appearance Highlands are at all times very alert. I watched a calf at a major Agricultural Show lie down, rest its weary chin on the ground and close its eyes within twelve inches of a constant parade of feet all sizes stopping and starting about it. Suddenly its eye opened wide. The calf otherwise was still. A minute later the eye closed again for some much needed rest from the strains of a Show. Behind the row of treading feet a free-running young Springer Spaniel had loped silently past and for the duration of its brief proximity the calf's eye was watching. What instinct had alerted that calf...exceptional hearing? sense of smell? or a bovine sixth sense? Whatever the answer that instance is a good example of how aware Highland cattle are of all that goes on around them. A resting Highland is far from asleep. Most cattle are uneasy in the presence of dogs but twentieth century Highlands are thought to have retained a greater measure of mistrust because they are still exposed to prowling foxes in many areas of Scotland. One breeder recounted seeing a fox pulling at an afterbirth before it had been fully discarded. Such boldness is clearly a disturbing challenge to the most deftly used horns, and shows good reason for maintaining the anti-canine instinct. Canadian breeders have said that Highlands defend their calves from wolves with great success.

Many breeders advise putting new stock in a field adjoining existing stock for a few weeks acclimatisation before introducing them to the established group. Don't be surprised if a Highland cow put in with other breeds remains aloof well beyond any reasonable integration period. Highlands are selective and choose their grazing companions carefully, preferring their own kind. I have heard comment that despite their horns they seldom bully other cattle and if in the minority actually tolerate being bullied a bit into accepting a low position in the 'pecking order'. This is disputed by those who have noticed how a Highland among polled breeds or other livestock very deliberately uses the threat of horns to gain dominance, usually for access to choice feeding. But to distinguish between bullying and the Highland's normal method of establishing and maintaining the rank of boss cow is probably only worthwhile if stock are being adversely affected by horn aggression. Horn damage to stock is rare.

HIGHLANDS WITH HORSES

Be vigilant about mixing horses with cattle. Some folds happily accept a horse in their midst (*Pic 93 p63*). Some cattle and horses tolerate each other well enough provided the grazing space is large enough to allow quite separate browsing (*Pic 12 p36*). But disturbing results can occur from unmonitored mixing of horse and cattle. One such case was in a field with only a few young stirks which were challenged relentlessly to chase games by the Shetland pony until panicked to fatal stress levels when one stirk collided head on with the stone wall and broke its neck. Seemingly though, some horses are fearful of cattle and can show edgy behaviour if brought too close, which in turn can make the cattle jumpy. Cattle which have had no opportunity to acclimatise to the presence of horses can exhibit considerable agitation if for example in the clamour of Shows they are suddenly shoulder to shoulder with sharp stepping horses.

If you are intending to show Highlands start broadening their life experiences as soon as you can. Prams with fringed sunshades, escaped balloons and flapping flags can be a menace. Highland cattle will quietly adapt to considerable change provided they are thoughtfully introduced and allowed adjustment time. They are least disturbed by new circumstances if with a known person they trust. They remain essentially the animal which used to share a plough yoke with horses and share the roofed shelter of humans, their working dogs and domestic fowl, often with only a slight partition between them and an open smoking fire. Cattle would not naturally choose to share their space with dogs, horses, smoky peat fires, and so when we expect them to do such things it speaks volumes for their tolerance levels. On occasion I have witnessed controlled tolerance in Highland cattle, and yes in horses too, whilst constrained either by crush or rider when thoughtless cigarette smokers lit up and exhaled in their faces. The animals pulled a face twisting nostrils, screwing up or rolling eyes and registering dislike with their ears and tail swishing.

Sadly the people concerned were indifferent to such signals and had these animals made any violent move such as a toss of the head merely, I am certain a punitive punch or jab would have been sharply administered.

FEEDING

Try to find out **how** your stock have previously been fed. Competitive secrecy about what makes for success may preclude your learning WHAT feeding was given prior to the sale so if your purchase seems to go back a bit...that is lose condition...initially it is possibly a reaction to a sudden change of diet. But knowing what method of feeding was used saves you working out gradually what the animals are familiar with; e.g. troughs, hayracks, individual buckets, indoors, outdoors, morning, evening, once weekly etc. If possible get the food ready first and then let the cattle in to it rather than carry feeding into a park or wherever before you know what to expect of the newcomers. Once Highland cattle know when and where extra food is offered it can be difficult to stop them from approaching it at the gallop. Although Highlands are acutely aware of the precise size of their horns and can manoeuvre them with amazing delicacy, if you are encircled by a group who are competing with each other to get at the food supply you are carrying, there may be no room for you to dodge a sharp jab intended to restrain another animal or to help establish a new pecking order. Hayracks seem a sensible source of feeding in some circumstances but many breeders favour dropping adequate hay for one feeding time in separate lots on the ground *(Pic 87 p61, Glen Coe picture p32).* This allows all the animals to feed at once rather than waiting their turn in the inevitable hierarchy within the group at a hayrack. They clear the food then move off. The circular free standing tubular steel racks seem to work quite well but make sure they are well secured or weighted to avoid the loss that befell one breeder whose two cows both broke their neck... in some way one had caught its horns and panicked, lifting the whole feeder in such a way that it tipped, hanging one cow in the air and pinning the other on its knees.

A method of quietening cattle for catching or haltering being tried by a breeder of only five years experience is to hand-feed them during a walkabout in the field. From a store of cobs in your pocket offer one directly to each animal as you approach it. A need to nose punch, however, when the stock crowded in with this method was admitted.

PETTING LIVESTOCK

If you have started your fold with the purchase of two calves do not make the mistake of petting them too much while they are young. They become too enthusiastic about getting attention and in general do not learn to adjust their adult weight and strength to the frailty of the human form. A bull who always behaved impeccably well during handling unwittingly nearly crushed his handler to death while waiting in the restricted space to enter the sales ring at Oban Market. Last minute brushing and titivating caused the bull to arch his back in pleasure which brought his head against the handler's chest with enough pressure to prevent intake of breath to shout out. Two things saved that breeder who told me *"the bull's horns touched the wall behind me and I managed to bring the fingers of one hand round to close his nostrils, which made him throw up his head. At this moment the doors opened and the bull and I floundered into the Ring."* The breeder concerned in no way blamed the bull. But who could have worked out what had happened had the incident proved fatal?

Over-petted animals may develop a habit of rushing to their petting benefactor and obviously the older heavier animal will have more difficulty stopping precisely when conditions underfoot are wet and muddy. I remember one hill farmer recounting a story in the 1950s in which he told of realising almost too late that his friendly bull careering enthusiastically downhill to partake of goodies in the food bucket would not be able to stop in time. The farmer threw himself full length on the ground and hoped the bull could jump over him. It did, quite competently, and danger was averted. It was very evident the bull was not charging the human merely rushing keenly towards him in eager anticipation of finding something tastier than his grazing. It made an exciting story in the telling, yet a cautionary one about the risks inherent in the solitary nature of the livestock breeder's work. Worrying though is the behaviour from the animal near caravan parks, holiday homes, or restaurants which has become accustomed to the public offering titbits, for all too quickly it develops a taste for 'junk-food' and learns to express its annoyance at inadequate supplies with aggressive horn use.

Although it may be tempting to the novice breeder to try the convenience of conditioning cattle from cuddly calf-hood to come running for tasty cobs or cakes it is probably rather safer to condition the cattle to accept quietly your approaching them in their field without any titbits. My first 'hands-on' contact with a black bull happened in this way, when the breeder took me into the moorland grazing area and quietly approached his bull who was running with a sizeable fold of mixed ages of Highlands. I was invited to prod around the rear end to get an idea of the musculature of a good working bull in natural conditions, i.e. no supplementary feeding, no extra shelter or bedding. The bull took notice of me (but no offence at the tentative inexperienced prods) and made no effort to nudge around searching for food. Clearly he was used to this form of human behaviour for he did not mistake the proddings for a signal to move on but patiently stood whilst I received valuable instruction. Having had more to do with horses than cattle I am always surprised how few cattle kick out at the succession of people who stand behind them and poke and prod at their fleshy bits. But there is always the exception !! I watched one for some time in Oban, as follows.

KEEPING ALERT

A good looking cow of quality was tethered on her own in the middle of a kind of through way across the myriad open air pens at the old Oban Mart. Stockman after stockman had to cross through carrying various items from full straw bales to rope halters and tickets. The cow kicked out with lightning speed, great force, and for a considerable distance whenever anyone was directly behind her. Some stockmen were taken by surprise since in between the kicks she exhibited no signs of agitation and could quite reasonably be regarded as another example of the normally docile and tolerant Highland cow. It pays never to assume animals will behave in a particular way although you may hope that they will. Remain always on the alert for the unexpected. I am told the closer in you stand to a kicker when handling her the less damage her kick will do. A breeder who arranged to have three different ages of Highlands brought into the yard for me to scrutinise had to warn me that I could be inviting a kick from some cattle if I continued with the particular 'hands-on' pressure I was trying at the time. I had assumed that Show animals stood quietly for any amount of prodding, and was trying to trace the outline, somewhat obscured by hair, of the upper reaches of the hind leg between it and the flank. Action from the hock down to the hoof is clear to see but the rest of the leg is not so obvious and I had wanted to check the lie of the upper hind leg which I did by rippling my hand up and down several times. Apparently cattle less ably prepared for Show procedures would have been tempted to kick at such ticklish handling. Grateful for the guidance I had received I was more observant at the next Show I attended where a judge, mid-judging, had to leap nimbly aside to avoid a deft kick. Scottish judges when in the Ring usually make contact with the animals to be clear about what precisely lies under the immaculately styled hair. It can be difficult to assess the actual conformation of an animal with only a visual appraisal.

BULLS

His escape from the field is something you might experience when you take on a Highland bull. Interestingly in all cases recounted to me there was more worry over the costly repair of fencing, iron gate, or what to do about the neighbours' cows who had been visited, than about the bull's temperament. The practicalities of retrieving the wanderer were looked on as of more nuisance value than of danger. Bullocks can prove astonishingly nimble at leaping fences or gates of about five feet high if badly disturbed and frightened. So don't put them in a field bounded by a public pathway used for exercising Bull Terriers and Dobermans. The mature heavyweight bull may have a powerful wanderlust long after you feel he should have settled into his new territory and is more likely to try first pushing his way out than jumping. But since he is capable of both, if you don't have the traditional walled or iron barred bull court, electric fencing is strongly recommended. Even if you intend running your bull with the fold there will come a time when you need to separate him so be prepared with an appropriate enclosure. A fold of eight cows may not stop a bull's eye from a-roving where a fold of some twenty cows may well contain him. (It stands to reason that if all the cows drop their calves within a week or so of each other then an active bull will have completed his work long before his working energies are depleted and hence he will become bored.) Keeping fences and boundaries in good condition clearly is important. Additionally it is necessary to understand that a daily check on livestock is a worthwhile habit to adopt since even when the bull is obediently keeping to his own territory heifers ready for bulling have occasionally astonished their owners by leaping over all obstacles between them and the bull. They have been known to make a night time visit and having returned to their field by the morning nothing is suspected by the stockman until signs of being in calf cause consternation. Animals which have contacted an electric wire fence nose first retain a lasting fear of the wire. But some Highland cattle have been seen to push under a single electric wire letting it spark along their back, unperturbed presumably because Highlands have thicker skin than other breeds, until free from it and into the forbidden territory. Remedy?...two electric wires.

The use of a permanent ring through the nose of bulls is not common in Scotland. The humbug, a heavy duty sprung clip with ring to take a leading rope, leather or chain, is used for all occasions when a Highland Bull is to be led among the public. The bull must be penned and tethered in order to fit on the humbug. When it is in place it should be free enough to slide up and down a little but not slack enough to allow any side to side play. A well fitted humbug is not uncomfortable. Sometimes a humbug may have rough edges, or be too tight on the nose cartilage which will cause painful pinching and bleeding. The bull will be seen to make wild head movements including lowering his nose a lot and will not forget the ordeal of being shown with a painful humbug in place. A bull which has had one bad experience with a humbug may be better with a permanent ring fitted but most breeders find no need to ring their bulls because the quiet co-operative nature of the breed generally does not merit that procedure.

Displays of irritable temper towards handlers in a young bull rarely (some breeders say never) improve with age and handling. Bad temper in a bull usually worsens with age. But generally

Highland bulls when kindly treated are quiet, tractable, and seldom charge. If cornered they may rush for an escape route, which is of course different from an aggressive charge at a person. Mature bulls have an awesome power should they wish to use it. A reminder of this lies in the story of a docile Highland bull which did not take to the Limousin bull put into his field. The Highland bull simply heaved the newcomer right over the fence, quietly!

Ticks are widely known to cause Red-water Disease (blood evident in urine) from which recovery is rare and affected animals cannot thrive. Infected ticks can spread a viral infection known as Louping Ill which is an acute illness with 50% mortality. Less often mentioned is that tick infestation can also cause temporary infertility in bulls, a fact to remember if placing a new bull into tick territory. In most breeds a bull's working life is between 3 and 10 years of age but Highland bulls can work well much longer. Several specials have sired good calves when 18 years old. A few 20 year old sires are known to have perpetuated their strengths albeit through a reduced crop of calves.

Take into account when choosing which bull calf to keep that it takes up to four years for proof of stock-getting qualities. If he is put to work at 2 years old his progeny need to be at least 18 months old before discriminating judgement is made. Remember that added complications of inbreeding will arise from keeping your bull more than three years without arrangements to keep him separate from his own daughters. Current thinking maintains that 1 in every 7 calves from a crop ear bull has crop ear, an unsightly but unharmful condition *(Pic 63, 64, 65, 66, p53, 54).* Inbreeding shows up hidden traits.

How does one value a bull? Milk cows are judged by their milk record, race horses by races won by parents. How highly should one value awards to bulls made entirely on visual assessment on one day and in comparison only to whatever other bulls appear in the Show ring? Where a bull finds himself the sole competitor he is awarded first in his class and may even end up with a championship according to the rulings of some Agricultural Shows. A judge who felt obliged to place a poor quality sole entry bull first in class but who disallowed it receive the championship aroused intense feelings such that the judge resigned his position over the row which followed. He was not again invited to judge there. His stand went a long way towards drawing attention to the fact that Show placings tend to be made to relative standards rather than to a set breed norm. A bull's appearance on turn out at a Show has little relevance to his true purpose as a reliably effective sire of sound progeny. Some highly awarded Show bulls have proved to be disappointing workers. There are many instances where the second or third placed bulls commanded much higher sales prices than the champion because the buyers were applying their own judgement to the long-term potential they expect from an expensive animal rather than to the impressive display of a skillfully prepared one expertly handled in the Show ring.

Showing a working bull may not always go smoothly if the Show comes at the wrong time for the bull. Some bulls do not feed well when lying with a cow. This makes it tricky to bring him into high condition for the Show. Another unpredictable circumstance is that there could always be cows at the Show coming into readiness for bulling which could unsettle your bull.

Bulls more often than cows seem to lie outstretched on their side from tail to nose looking rather dead *(Pic 49 p49).*

Cattle divide their day equally between grazing, resting, and ruminating. A resting Highland may lean the tip of one horn on the ground to take the strain off holding up the full weight of horns and head. But a head and neck stretched out flat is always worth a second glance, as this position is not normally held for any length of time in a healthy animal.

The older the cow the lower she will carry her head naturally when standing or moving due to the increased weight of horn carried by aging neck muscles.

While resting lying down cattle in fact rarely sleep more than a few minutes at a time. If you suspect something is wrong look at the breathing rate. M Stanfield in *The Herdsman's Book* quotes the normal breathing rate for resting dairy cows as being between 12 and 20 chest movements per minute, which is a reasonable guide for Highlands too.

Highland cattle exposed to too much heat will start fast shallow breathing. If continuous exposure to hot conditions is unavoidable the cattle will try to combat the problem by not eating, since that would cause the heat producing activity of getting and digesting food to stop. An animal suffering continuous heat stress over several weeks may retain its winter coat due to activation of abnormal increase in adrenal secretions. Yet if the heat stress is from long hours of exposure to the sun with no shade anywhere the winter coat is likely to be shed fairly quickly because the amount of daylight is what regulates the growth of the coat; i.e. thick and long in reduced winter daylight and the reverse in the extended daylight hours of summer.

HEALTH

Breeds differ in their ability to sweat, but it is thought that red coat-colour reflects more solar radiation than does black. At different Agricultural Shows I observed that the black Highland cows were noticeably more stressed than the red from hours of standing in fierce sun with no shade. It would have been a useful comparison had I deliberately compared the state of the black Galloways and Aberdeen Angus tethered in the same exposed and shadeless Showgrounds, however that must await a later study. But the only animal I saw collapse from over exposure to direct sun at a Show was not of the Highland breed. Red Highlands may sweat more readily than the dark colours and that along with their lesser absorption of sunrays makes them more resilient to hot conditions. One breeder finds that the blacks in the fold are always first to make for the cool shade of trees when the sun rises high in full summer. In another fold it was the black cows which monopolised the high knolls in hot sunshine in order to maximise the value of whatever slight breezes might circulate the hill.

Sweating is often a problem with housed Highlands. A converted haybarn offers plenty of air space while protecting from the continuous wetness of Scottish winters. Those most frequently housed today are calves in their first winter away from the dam. One lot offered a humorous moment when they were released from their winter barn. Tasty cattle cakes were being spread on the ground to coax them well into the field. They ran willingly after their familiar farmer treading all over the cakes noses high. They had been late calves whose only feeding since weaning had been in troughs and hayracks. They had now to learn to look to the ground for sustenance.

The twentieth century climate in Scotland is less severe than for the four hundred years ending about 1800 which historians call The Little Ice Age. The traditionally low roofed cosy cowshed therefore is no longer a necessity, if ever it was for the cattle, and does produce sweating problems in Highlands. Provided they have windbreak cover it seems they survive well enough as this description of Kyloes in 1578 suggests: *"In the mountains of Argyll, in Ross likewise, and sundry other places, are fed ky, not tame, as in other parts, but like wild harts, wandering out of order, and which through certain wildness of nature, flee the company or sight of men as may be seen in winter, how deep so-ever be the snow, how long so ever the frost lie, how sharp or cold how ever it be they never their head sett under the roof of any house."*

Another cause of sweating is fear. Excessive sweating during transport can be the result of fear caused by unnecessarily harsh herding to hurry the livestock to keep to an unrealistic time schedule involving fast driving of the vehicle. Hard whacking with sticks is mostly done by those ignorant of the co-operative but independent nature of Highland cattle. Though capable of remarkable speed of action and reaction Highlands resist being forced to hurry into the unknown. Cows under great stress from fear may produce toxic milk which poisons the calf.

All Highland cattle whatever their colour are renowned for their picturesque habit of standing in water. Not only is the water cooling parts immersed in it the general temperature surrounding the water is usually lower than away from it. Highlands enjoy such cooling down with less risk, thanks to their very thick skin, than some other breeds from biting flies often found in the vicinity of water. Standing belly deep in water also deters blowflies or warbleflies from laying eggs on the legs and oxters whilst also relieving itching from lice concentrations around the fetlocks.

Standing in water is not to be confused with standing in rain. The one is sought the other is not. Cows in waterlogged territory during prolonged periods of wet windy weather will not lie down and when near calving can become exhausted from lack of adequate rest. The unpractised eye may see one cow standing in the rain looking much the same as any other cow standing in the rain, but if a cow which calves in these circumstances does lie down she may be too tired to rise again with harmful consequences for the calf. Tough though they are Highland cattle are captive livestock and need responsible care.

Ensure a plentiful supply of fresh drinking water with easy access at all times, but particularly in hot weather. Fouled water will cause ill health. In normal conditions a cow on lush grass will drink about 15 gallons or so of water per day but on dry feed or in continuous hot dry conditions will need upwards of 20 gallons per day.

Healthy animals have clean dry hind-quarters and tail unless too much rich grass is being eaten without enough fibrous fodder intake to help the digestion, in which case scouring (diarrhoea) may be evident *(Pic 95 p63)*. It is not uncommon for a touch of scouring to affect healthy stock at both the beginning and the end of the grass growing season as they adjust to the differing quality of the grass. Scouring often occurs in suckling calves when the dams first get to new grass in the Spring but should cease in about 48 hours. Since scouring can also indicate more serious health problems keep a close check on the duration of the condition and also on behaviour. Repeated or continuous arching up of the back, moving head or limbs awkwardly, not feeding or chewing cud for a long time, not stretching on being quietly raised from lying, are all indications that something is wrong and experienced attention is required.

Note what trees and shrubs are within browsing reach as Highland cattle will happily tackle birch, willow, oak, hazel, beech, larch, elm, bog-myrtle, whin (gorse), rushes, which are excellent roughage but inexperienced sampling of bracken or acorns could have serious results. Animals transported from their home territory where they learned from older fold members what, when, and how, to eat can make fatal mistakes from feeding unwisely when suddenly placed in a very different environment. Young bracken shoots and juniper have a slow acting poison. Bracken is cancer inducing but trouble may not show until a cow is well aged. Beware buying an old cow from bracken territory. Potentially fatal within a matter of hours for calves are yew, laburnum, ragwort, laurel, and some species of rhododendron. Yet it is reported that cows in Lewis some 250 years ago relished the fodder brought to them during milking comprising *"nettles, dockens, ragworts, chickweed, common rushes and bulrushes."* (*Carmina Gadelica* Vol. 4)

Chopped or cut ragwort can have a special attraction for young steers maybe running in Forestry Commission land where cutting or trimming of scrubland could have taken place before the stock owner realised there had been tidying activities. Similarly, newly cut bracken fronds seem irresistible to young stock which should be kept off cut bracken areas until plants have withered. Any plant trimmings or prunings seem to merit favourable attention from browsing

Highlands. Two year old bullocks seem particularly susceptible to munching their way through anything attainable even if it turns out to be newly-knitted kilt hose for Colonel Campbell of Kilberry. The story goes like this: *"Colonel Campbell was having wool specially dyed to match a new kilt-coat, and went to ask the dyer/knitter when his new stockings would be ready; she led him to her door and gestured down the field to his Highland stirks, "Yonder's your hose, Kilberry, walking the field!" The dear creatures had devoured the newly-dyed wool, hung to drip on the whin-bushes along the field boundary and a fresh lot was having to be dyed and then knitted up."* (Marion Campbell of Kilberry)

However even bullocks find fully grown stargrass unpalatable and no use for roughage. Broom is not poisonous but Highland cattle do not favour it. I have seen them browsing whin blossom but not broom *(Pic 40 p46)*. They will eat rushes only as a last resort to avoid starvation. Where heather is available for browsing it is claimed that in addition to its usefulness in providing roughage the condition of staggers (magnesium deficiency) is unlikely to occur. Research on heather found young leafy ling heather to be relatively high in minerals but that cross-leaved heath and bell heathers are of little nutritional value. Poisoning from meadow saffron and bracken will cause difficulties in breathing, weakness in hind-quarters, diarrhoea and passing of blood in urine and droppings. Ergot of rye, a fungus which attacks the flowering heads of grasses and rye can cause aborting. Buttercup *Ranunculus* if taken in quantity will poison but cows prefer to leave it. They also leave marshmarigold although sheep and goats will eat it. Mastitis (painful inflammation of the udder and teats) is seldom really serious in Highland cattle but it is wise to be on the lookout for early symptoms from June to September when grass can be so rich it could help to induce the condition.

The value of daily checking of cattle is reinforced with the knowledge that should mastitis go undetected a severe type of the condition, udderclap, could go unnoticed and time for saving the cow is limited. In udderclap, caused by a different bacterium from that of mastitis, part of the milk vessel hardens, gangrene can develop, and poisons released into the system can be fatal. Avoidance of this nasty condition is dependent on good husbandry. Fortunately udder problems are not too common in beef breeds.

Implicit in good husbandry is an acute awareness of the feeding value of grazing areas used. Weather conditions quite apart from any land treatments can alone vary the quality of feeding yearly.

Sparse grazing such as may be on some hill land or in overgrazed meadows makes cattle work so hard that they are exhausted before enough intake has been achieved for their needs. Hunger will make cows break through fencing hedging or old walls more than any homing instinct, although if the bull is at home when the cows take the notion to visit, as mentioned earlier, that can provide a powerful incentive for breaking out.

If you suspect your animals are on inadequate food supplies seek appropriate advice before giving supplementary rations of foodstuffs. If there seems plenty of grass but in an area of known acidic soils as is much of Scotland, there is possibly a lack of minerals and trace elements in the diet which will in time give rise to a number of deficiency problems, one of which could be a poor conception rate. A variety of mineral lick blocks are available commercially and widely used with good results, but the correct balance of mineral additives must be understood as for example an imbalance of calcium to phosphorus can cause infertility. Too much magnesium over some two weeks causes horns and feet to go rubbery soft. This previously unknown reaction was discovered by John Keay early on his remarkable droving journey from Skye to Crieff in 1981. All concerned with this venture were keen to keep to the minimum any possible stress reactions in the cattle. Accordingly the livestock received a booster dose of magnesium prior to setting out. The firm supplying cattle cobs, however, who inadvertently were not informed of this booster precaution, had commendably added magnesium to the prepared feed. Fortunately no lasting damage from the high magnesium diet occurred, thanks to alert observation of the animals and early identification of the problem. Balancing the additives in rich feedstuffs clearly requires specialist knowledge and skill, sometimes beyond that of the commercial salesperson. There is always the danger that extra feeding, given to achieve goals in weight and conformation in time for Show dates, may sacrifice the formation of sound feet needed to last a lifetime, for the sake of a few short-term Show appearances. Over-rich concentrate feeding towards the end of pregnancy is known to cause some cows to develop swollen and inflamed udders much in advance of calving creating difficulties for the cow, her calf and their management. Too much haste in producing a big well fleshed shiny-coated Show heifer may make her infertile due to the inhibiting effects of fat deposits on the ovaries. With regard to general health, though, Highland cattle have retained their long-standing reputation for being a relatively troublefree breed with considerable resistance to disease. Many in the veterinary profession consider the relatively disease free status that Highlands enjoy is largely explained by their being farmed extensively rather than intensively. The breed characteristics do not lend themselves happily to known methods of forced growth, and test trials to prove whether farming methods or inherited disease resistance is responsible for sound health in the breed have not been conducted.

COWS AND CALVES

Should your first purchase of the Highland breed be a cow in calf, plan in advance where you want her to drop her calf, particularly if it may be due before the cow has settled to the new territory. Grazing area where a river with a steep bank forms one boundary could be a hazard for the uncontrolled early frisking of a newborn calf from a dam on unfamiliar ground. Calves are fearless of water. Select a place with a mind to the least stressful gathering in, in the unlikely but possible event of either cow or calf needing attention. All going well keep a watchful eye from a respectable distance (the distance will vary with each cow) to check that the calf is suckling well and thriving.

An experienced breeder found the following system worked well in a herd with the heifers expected to calf from February to March: '*when heifers came near calving time we used to bring the whole female herd into the byre for an evening feed in stalls, and keep the calver in next day or at least check how near she was before letting her out, repeating the procedure until she calved – this ensured opportunity to help if needed and a chance to see the calf was all right.*' Calving time calls for the greatest of care among stock. One never knows when twin calves may arrive. A cow which hides her twin calves 50 yards apart and goes to feed them separately obviously demands expert knowledge of behaviour from her stockmen, if they are to avoid coming between the cow and her calf in such circumstances. Fortunately twin calves are not common in the Highland breed so associated problems such as insufficient nourishment or the possibility of an infertile female calf (if the twins are one male and one female) are not frequent. One manager of a fold which produced several sets of twins is convinced that some cows cannot count, for as long as one calf was around the dam she was content and did not look for the other. Feeding silage before calving produces too much milk which can be almost as much a problem as not producing enough. Views on twinning suggest that twins are possibly more likely from lines that have had cross-breeding in past generations or that the kinder and richer the environmental conditions the more able the cows are in producing twins.

If your calving cows are to have the freedom of extensive hill and moorland acreage without trees or shrubby windbreaks they are likely to seek a sheltered spot along a river bank, or a shallow gully at calving time. This place could be up to one and a half miles from the grazing herd. Be particularly alert in such a case to weather changes because some cows, sensing worsening weather, will move to a better place perhaps before the calf is strong enough to follow her through the river or marshy moorland, resulting in one healthy calf drowned. Breeding cows kept in this type of territory have a tendency to return each year to the same calving spot, which habit can shorten your search time when it is noticed a cow due to calf has left the main herd.

Don't panic over newly born calves if they have crumpled noses, oddly shaped mouths, short forelegs, very soft feet, or seem lame in one leg. Give them a few days to 'unwrinkle' as it were from the strictures of the womb.

If you had established a regular time of looking your stock over, perhaps when offering some tasty feeding, the newly calved dam is likely to resume her approach to you when she is ready to trust that no danger will come to her calf in so doing. Cows vary in their tolerance of curiosity from other cows towards a new calf so if you are in among the stock be on the lookout for sudden tiffs erupting causing them swift wheeling around and dodging. Be careful about running heifers with calving cows, or having widely different calving dates for heifers in first calf as too much interest from them in a new calf can cause the dam to reject it. Penning the dam and coaxing her to accept her calf again can take two or three days of unwelcome demands on the stockpersons.

By the time a newly calved cow is mingling again with other stock there should be no signs of the afterbirth which is normally completely expelled within seven hours but can take longer. The afterbirth is rarely found since the cow will eat it. It has been known for a cow to tidy her calf too vigorously by eating the umbilical cord up to the navel after having cleared away placental membrane. Any bleeding from the calf's navel must be stopped quickly. The same cow may behave very differently with her next calf. If you suspect anything is wrong seek assistance in getting the cow and calf into a byre, stall, pen or handling space. Remember that an animal under stress will react unpredictably. One breeder described for me how she had taken a cow and calf into a pen to await treatment and how she had gone into the pen as usual when suddenly her ribs were broken by a distraught dam tossing her against the bars. The breeder had forgotten that the presence of a stranger, in this case the vet, could upset an animal which only minutes before had allowed all the customary close handling by its known and familiar owner. In no way did she hold the animal responsible for her considerable injuries.

Occasionally a calf may be reluctant to lower its head far enough to suck from the dam. This is more readily understandable if the cow is aging and has a low vessel. But the newborn calf's instinct to raise its head repeatedly too high in search of nourishment sent me asking explanations. A vet experienced with Highland cattle thought it possible that during early development of the species newborn calves suckled from lying down. A breeder who had grown up with Highland cattle in mountain territory wondered if the high head lift derived from newborn calves being on the downhill side of their dams when needing to suckle. Equally possible is the idea that while centuries of domestication has reduced the leg length of the cattle somehow the evolutionary process forgot to reprogramme calves not to search so high for their sustenance. Whatever the answer it is a curious problem and one must make sure the new calf does suck well.

Some cows more than others produce a firm wax seal on the teat which unless the calf sucks strongly enough is not removed and therefore although appearing to suckle the calf is not actually taking in any milk. Sometimes a calf may be sucking at hair...not too nourishing! or in time with constant tongue action around the teats hair can tightly entwine one, blocking milk flow completely and if not removed will tighten to the point of cutting the flesh *(Pic 53, 54 p50).*

A calf may develop a habit of using only one teat if for example the vessel and teats are constantly mudcaked, or it may learn to avoid one teat if touching that one provokes a kick from the dam.

Neither situation is good for the cow or calf. Permanent damage to the udder can result unless suckling problems are noted and dealt with early. Sometimes heifers can be late with their first calf and the udder may become seriously swollen. One stockman recounted his amazement about one such heifer when she was seen to lie down and massage-lick her painful udder until the milk flowed out a little, thereby easing the problem until the calf was ready to arrive.

It is a mistake to assume that a cow with large teats will automatically be a good breeder. The newborn calf may be unable to suck from too coarse a teat. It is possible however that her next calf sucks well. There are few absolute certainties in breeding livestock. Although it is desirable to have all calves suck within 6 hours of birth, the will to survive in Highland calves is so powerful that there have been exceptional instances recorded where newly born calves had lasted three days without sustenance yet refused to die. With expert care after discovery they actually made up normal weight gain so that at twelve months old they were indistinguishable from others born in the same season. It is sad to contemplate that severe weather has been blamed for calf mortalities when in actual fact the calves had died from undetected lack of nourishment in their first few days of life.

A few cases of an unusual and perplexing condition began to appear in the 1980s of newborn calves which lack the sucking reflex. They are time-consuming to look after and risky to breed from. If this baffling reluctance to suck is genetically transmitted, the more outspoken breeders are the more information will be available for veterinary analysis and the quicker occurrences of the condition will be eliminated.

A breeder of long experience helpfully reported this account in 1989: "*On March 1st one of my older cows had a bull calf. It didn't suck. We brought the cow and calf to the steading and put him below the cow – nothing happened. Out came the bottle, still no interest. For 28 days that cow was milked and the contents of the 4 bottles per day more or less poured down the calf's throat. He picked at silage – not very good for him, we didn't think. He chewed hay. But drink in the normal way? No. I called him Dopey and on the evening of the 27th day of his life, I gave him a good swearing while squeezing the milk down his throat.*

The 28th morning dawned and down on his knees went Dopey and sucked his mother dry. Happily he is now quite a different chap and able to fend for himself. I wish I knew the answer to his behaviour!" (HCS *Newsletter*)

It can happen that a dam has insufficient milk for twin calves and a foster mother may be needed. Silage after calving, with a little oat straw and hay before it, has been found successful in increasing the milk supply. But avoid feeding silage before calving as this can produce a surfeit of milk with attendant problems.

On seeing a calf suckle from the rear putting its nose between the dam's hocks, I asked an explanation and was told that it was likely either the mother kicked forwards at the suckling youngster usually only when there is pain with the sucking, or that the calf was hungry and had learned how to thieve from other dams with the rear approach as cows are not given to regular visual checking of their suckling young. Not much of the calf could be seen by the cow easily in that position anyway! If the dam's own calf is sucking she seems to take no notice of additional sucking at the same time. In fact if at any time you must draw milk from the dam the best time to do so is while her own calf is sucking, and I have been told that the rear approach for milking is worth remembering because in general cows find it harder to kick to the rear than to kick forwards. If however the dam's own calf is fully in her view and therefore not sucking she will normally kick strongly at any calf attempting to sneak a drink from her on its own. Calves which have needed to learn how to thieve have discovered that if they wait until the cow's own calf goes to drink and then move in quickly to share the full sucking time all is well...satisfied tummies and no kicks.

Sometimes though, rear suckling is simply the most direct route to nourishment as is obvious when watching calves tethered at Agricultural Shows where the secured end of the calf's rope may be some way behind the dam.

A big heavy cow is not necessarily the best breeder. A small cow might be a heavy milk producer which means her calves grow well and fast. Lean cows (not starved) settle to the bull quicker than fat ones which may be infertile due to the results of excessive concentrates feeding in early life. In addition to jumping each other less than dairy breeds Highland cows may stay on heat a shorter time than other breeds, which could explain why selecting the right time for Artificial Insemination is tricky and a follow-up procedure called for by some breeders to ensure conception. It is unfortunate that somewhere over the years the breed was criticised for being unreliable as a regular yearly calver when poor management through lack of indepth knowledge was more likely to blame.

CONCLUSION

Some of the examples here presented are of course the exception rather than the rule, but are included in support of the theory that constant vigilance can make the difference between troublefree and troublesome stock rearing. The more acutely informed and sensitive your observations grow the more you will avoid unnecessary delays in achieving your desired goal as a breeder of Highland cattle and the more useful will be comment from the experienced.

Guidance on market trends must vary with the market demands. Therefore written advice on that is quickly dated. Reliably applicable, however, is information on behaviour of Highlands which, deriving partly from inherited patterns, modifies so gradually that words of wisdom handed on from experienced Highland cattle handlers is of inestimable value.

A worthwhile appeal for informed attitudes to breeding policies came from James Macdonald in 1811...*"Strangers on visiting the Western Isles cry out against the folly of the people in keeping cattle of a small breed; when by changing it for the Irish, or the Lowland Scotch, they might greatly enlarge the carcasses of their stock. But this is a rash opinion. The great question in Hebridean grazing and rearing is what breed will best answer the land and climate, and what size can be most easily and securely raised at the smallest expense? Heavy cattle cannot seek their food in bogs and marshes, leap over ravines, rivers, and ditches, or scramble through rocks, and in the faces of cliffs and precipices, like the present breed, which is almost as active and nimble as a Chamois goat; nor can the poor Hebridean tenant afford to breed any stock which is not proof against the inclemency of his rains and storms all the year round. It is infinitely safer for him, therefore, in the present imperfect state of his agriculture, and perhaps even at all times, and in all circumstances of his country to rear too small, than too large a breed of cattle; and to improve his indigenous, hardy, excellent species, than to import from other districts such breeds as may be indeed profitable for their circumstances and climate, but, which would probably perish in the Hebrides, without more attention being paid to them than, in his situation, he can conveniently afford. A moderate size is accordingly preferred by all skillful graziers; this rule no doubt admits of considerable latitude of application..."* (from *A General View of the Agriculture of the Hebrides.*)

REFERENCES

Source Book of Scottish Economic and Social History, Campbell and Dow 1968
Statistical Account of Scotland Volume 15
The Highlands and Hebrides in 1786, John Knox, Reprinted 1975
Scottish Farming Past and Present, J A Symon 1959
The Development of the West of Scotland 1750 – 1960, A Slaven 1975
Sheep and Man, Dr M L Ryder 1987
A General View of the Agriculture of the Hebrides, James Macdonald 1811
(a Board of Agriculture Survey)

Highland Cattle have proved to be the most ideally suited breed to thrive well in territories such as these. Their presence actively supports biodiversity.

Finding Your Cattle and Calves

1. Heather moorland.

2. Pine trees shading eight animals.

3. Moorland burn.

4. Mountain grazings.

5. Juniper and gorse.

6. Day old calf hidden in rushes.

7. Potential camouflage for two black calves among cone patches (one extreme right).

8. Day old calf on riverbank nearly matches the earth colour.

Alert Tolerance

9. Cows calmly obliging a familiar collie (rare collie breed *see page 18*).

10. Watchful but unperturbed by a familiar dog.

11. Distracted by assessing an unfamiliar dog.

12. Watchful deference when sharing with ponies.

13. Despite alert tolerance from both calf and dam, be aware that can change suddenly.

14. Adapting to new sights and sounds.

15. Note tense ears while calf accepts yet another head pat.

16. Face to face with strangers (unknown cattle) can be disturbing.

17. Proximity of flapping white coats may unnerve.

18. Dark uniforms and white coats may be strange.

19. Uneasy but tolerant. Good temperament is vital, and fortunately common in this horned breed.

20. Standing still for judges is not a natural pursuit.

21. More grooming for this Show business. Some cattle find it calming

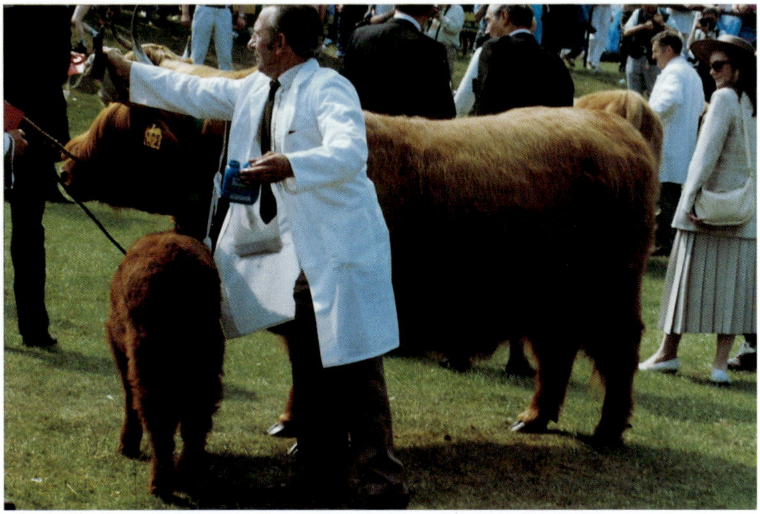

22. Grooming for show, polishing horn.

23. Polishing hoof.

24. Goading away boredom.

25, 26, 27. Examples of hands-on judging.

28. Listening to the judges approach.

29, 30. Change of ownership means sales pens, such as these at the old Oban Mart, outdoors and covered. This mart closed permanently in 1991.

31. Waiting for sale or grooming.

32. The necessary hose-down.

33. Brush-up after blow-dry.

34. Old Oban Mart Show-ring.

35. Old Oban Mart auction ring.

36. Parting company for both.

Change of Environment

35. Rich grass and cooling sea breeze.

36. Abundant coarse grasses.

Robert Dixon

37. Seeking seaweed.

40. Tackling sparse fare.

41, 42. Windbreaks are welcome.

Ensure Food Supplies

43. Supplementary feeding is a good plan.

44. Regular feeding time is advisable.

45. Stealing hay while the stockman is away.

46. Day old suckling well.

47. One week old copies mum.

48. Hopeful six month old.

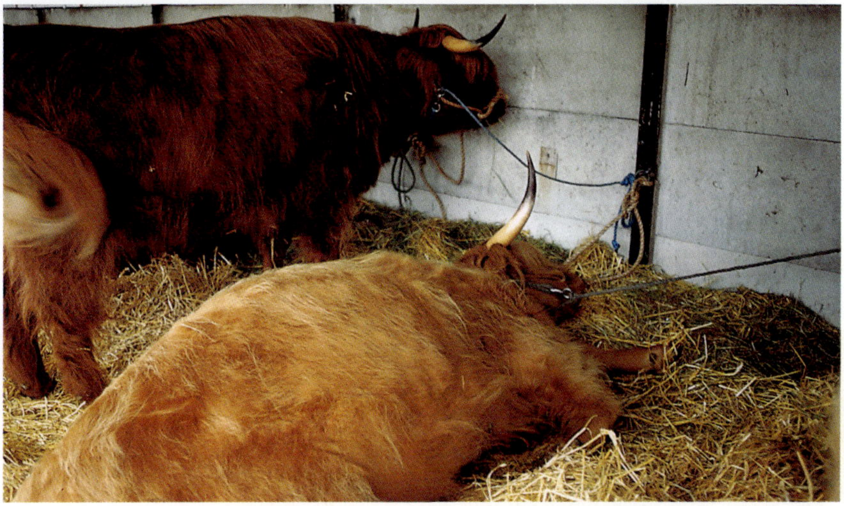

49, 50, 51. Always check when a head is down.

52. Underfed, exhausted or just resting?

53. Hair twist forming.

54. Hair twist removed.

55, 56, 57. Bad stance and tail swishing heralds a problem – udder, lameness or both.

58. Heat stressed in-calf heifer.

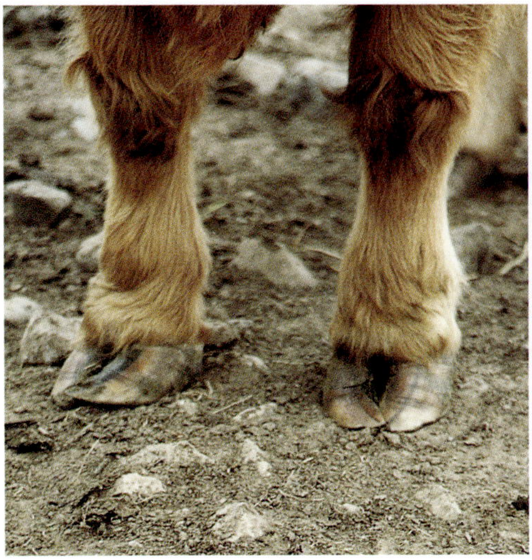

59. A trim needed.

60. Broken clit from untended hoof.

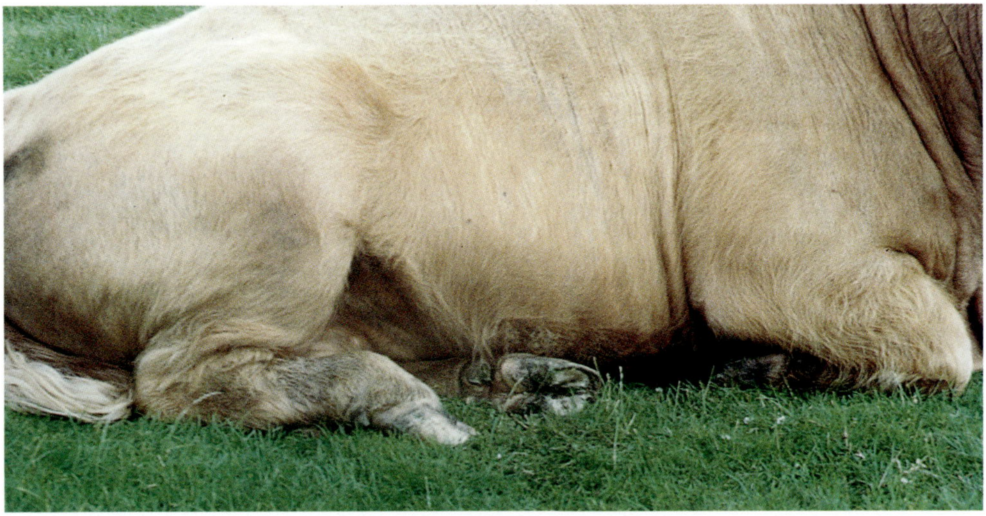

61. Long hoof will need attention.

62. Attention picnickers – calf about to sample your discarded poly-bags.

Crop Ears

63. The calf standing has crop ears giving it the 'toy teddy' look.

64. Defective ears on all.

The Scottish Farmer

65. Twin calves with crop ears.

Not for the Show Circuit

66. Crop ear busdubh.

Robert Dixon

67, 68. Poor conformation.

69 Good cow dehorned.

70. An unimpressive bullock, but useful in a fold to indicate which cows are ready for AI or bulling.

71. Good cow, but recovered from a broken back.

Horns

72. Symmetrical horns on this good cow in summer coat.

73. The heavy horn growth typical on steers.

74. Good cow but developing heavy horns.

75, 76, 77. Examples of good horns on cows.

78, 79, 80, Examples of good horns on bulls, including typical yearling horns braving barbed-wire to reach discarded poly-bag.

81, 82, 83. Asymmetric or lop horns, like these examples, can result from a blow to the head in calf-hood, but genetics and diet can also influence shape.

Behaviour

84. Bulls sparring, can be playful or serious.

85. Be wary of a bull which exhibits an unfriendly attitude like this to your presence.

86. Cows fighting; often to establish rank.

Erica Cochrane

87. Separate feed lots largely avoid horn damage from jostling at feed containers.

88. Protective dam (centre) on the alert. If she is aggressive her calf will learn that.

89. Calves learn behaviours.

90. Friendships and disputes arise without adverse outcome, but behaviour may be unsettled if the dominant matriarch is removed.

91. Calves peacefully eroding a river bank to relieve itchy noses.

92. A plentiful clean water supply is essential.

93. Old friends – it is unusual for Highland cattle to so accept as an equal a horse in their midst.

94. An effective working bull.

95. Spring grazings can be over-rich. A regular check on your stock is beneficial.

Branding

96. Once a common practice, regulation ear-tags now identify animals. By 2022 UK government regulations consider horn branding to be an illegal procedure.

97. Heating the irons.

98. The new brand.

99. Departure.

CHAPTER 2: HORN AND HAIR

CHAPTER 2: HORN AND HAIR

HORNS

Cattle horns are hollow, grow continuously, have a core well supplied with blood, and are present in both male and female Highland cattle. In a healthy animal the horns should feel warm to the touch.

Because the shape of horns is a breed characteristic a glance at the horns used to be sufficient to distinguish between breeds, either at a distance or when in mixed groups. But the cross-breeding of cattle continued to grow in favour from the early nineteenth century until by mid twentieth century herds of pure-bred cattle were unusual rather than the norm and horn shape was no longer a reliable guide in a visual assessment of the purity of Highland cattle. Predictably the shape girth and length of horn has occasioned much discussion ever since increased knowledge first tempted man to create his own "improved" design of bovine.

The combination of long horns and long coat of Scottish Highland cattle makes them an instantly recognisable breed. No other British cattle have both these features. The mature shape of Highland horns can be considered in four categories *(Pics 72-83 p56-59)* the first three of which all come out of the head level and wide spread.

1. Up and outwards; symmetric; cows and steers.
2. Up and backwards swirling; symmetric; cows.
3. Bull horns; thicker shorter less complex sweep, symmetric
4 i. Asymmetric,
   ii. Damaged,
   iii Irregular type,
   iv. Steers.

Considerable variety is to be found naturally. Individual animals are often readily recognised by their horns. Width of spread, degree of curve, amount of upward twist, extent of tapering, sharpness of the tip or point, are all heritable. Hardness of the horn, rings of shading near the base, cracks around the girth, flaky dry roughness lengthwise, and thickness or girth at the base are all considerably affected by diet, climatic temperature changes, and age. One learns very quickly to estimate the age of Highland cattle by the length and girth of their horns. Although there have always been instances of the nursery rhyme 'cow with the crumpled horn' and the probability persists that the one-odd-horn look can be inherited, many cases of uneven horns can be the result simply of a side blow to the head sustained at a time of crucial early horn development between birth and 18 months old. Perhaps they are most susceptible to damage when about 1 inch long. Such a bump can occur unremarkably in normal herd conditions, for example from crowding at feeding troughs, uneven collisions in playful sparring, or from a kick by an authoritative matriarch. Round the clock observation may reveal possible causes for squint, uneven or irregular horns but is hardly worthwhile when one considers they might have been destined to grow that way irrespective of injuries. A check in early growth caused by severe weather or ill health in the dam...even before the calf's horn bud is noticeable...can result in a withered tip to an undersized often dry horn which may slant backwards. It is apt to signal general poor stamina. Such horns are permanently impaired.

A belief in genetic transmission of uneven horns was expressed to me by a breeder who also considered that there may be a link between uneven temperament and lopsided horns....an interesting opinion.

A report from 1720 suggests that the typical horn shape of cattle in Kincardine was the 'handle-bar' type instanced above in the category 1. It reads: "*the Excise Officer's family was the only one in Johnshaven that made use of tea; when the tea kettle was carried to the well to bring in water numbers of both children and grown people followed it expressing it to be 'a beast with a horn'. By 1790 all had a tea kettle.*"[1]

Highland bulls have shorter horns than the cows which may account in part for nineteenth century observations that they had "*hair like goats and horns like buffaloes*" and the horns were "*high and crooked*" (curved).[2] But bull horn tips then generally turned up not down-tilted as had become more prevalent by mid twentieth century.

A breed description in 1805 reads "*Kylo...black, brindled, dun, brown, red; in form flat and deep, like the short and middle-horned stock; very small and hardy, with small upright or middle length horns.*"[3]

Further indication that Highland bull horns turned upwards comes from the rumour that a black Highland bull was used in Ayrshire herds to try to breed upturned horns after many serious accidents from the Ayrshire horns which came straight out of the head.

The following comments about Ayrshires in 1866 were in part echoed a hundred years later about Highlands.

"*Horns are merely dangerous ornaments, and as breeders well know, can be moulded to any form to suit the taste of the times. It may be hinted that if the members at their meetings would devote more time to the discussion of agricultural improvements, and comparing notes on farming matters generally, talking less about the special make of such a bull's horns, or the flowing outline of such another cow's tail, one principal object in view of these clubs when started would be higher attainment.*"[4] Clubs meant farmers' associations or societies at a local level, many of which began during the Agricultural Revolution which in Scotland advanced rapidly once initiated.

The relatively new Highland Cattle Society in 1885 wrote "*In the bulls, the horns should be strong, and come level out of the head, slightly inclining forwards and also slightly rising towards the points. Some, however, do not care for this rise, though any drooping is considered to be a very bad fault when between the crown and the commencement of the curve, as this is generally accompanied by a low weak back. Some, too, are of the opinion that the masculine appearance is slightly detracted from when the horns rise directly from the crown. This however, can only readily be detected and commented upon when particular animals are brought before experienced judges, as within a Show ring.*"

This ruling was intended to reinforce breed characteristics at a time when the popularity of beef Shorthorn was influencing judgement of "improved" Highlands to the extent that a renowned fold occasioned the remark "*Some of the animals shown are said to possess many of the valuable characteristics of the shorthorn as to shape, size, and general contour. A Highland three year old ox of this stock, shown by the Duchess-Dowager of Athole at Perth in 1871 was considered by eminent judges to be a perfect model of its race.*"[5]

The size and shape of Highland bull horns in the last 150 years was the subject of some recent research by the noted breeder and photographer Mr Tom McLatchie, Millerston, who is now convinced that the short length and downwards curve seen in many Highland bulls today (1990s) is the result of much Shorthorn cross-breeding when the cross-breds were more profitable than pure-bred stock. Perhaps less Shorthorn infusion penetrated strains of black Highlands for Mr McLatchie noted he has seen very few black bulls with horns as well down tilted as is the fashion in many award-winning reds and yellows.

By 1905 after years of indiscriminate use of Shorthorn bulls on Longhorn cows it was realised not only that extinction was near but that the original Longhorn animal had had more merit as a breed admirably suited to the hilly Fell district of Northern England than the Shorthorn. Too much crossing with the Shorthorn caused an attempt to restore hardiness (to the Longhorns) by using West Highland bulls intermittently.

By the 1950s there was cause for concern that Highlands too might be cross-bred out of existence. The small group of breeders nationwide intensified their efforts to increase the numbers of pure Highland cattle and within forty years achieved an encouragingly healthy demand worldwide for pure-bred Highlands. Many new buyers seek information about the breed and so it seems likely that the threat of obscurity from over much Shorthorn blood is, for the time being, unlikely.

An intriguing memory comes from the daughter of a former Highland cattle breeder in Skye who recalled that in her father's time at the turn of the century shorter smaller horns were always associated with the brindle Highlands. Possibly they were the result of the first wave of enthusiastic introduction of Shorthorn crosses with the black Highlands, because the pedigree brindle bulls and cows I checked after hearing that observation all carried the accepted standard weight and shape of horn for the breed.

This 1904 advertisement for Molassine suggests somewhat confusingly that bull horns were maybe more steer-like than is generally believed, since the illustration used depicts horns that would most readily be associated with cows and steers yet also shows a ring in the nose, an item usually reserved for breeding bulls.

Steers are castrated bulls normally destined for the prime beef market and often also dehorned. Those *"adjusted bulls"* (as my 12 year old daughter on first seeing steers called them) which are selected for a life as a tourist attraction at various castles and stately homes do get to keep their horns. Steers grow an amazing weight of horn with the thick girth of bull horns yet more than the spread and length of cow horns. A twelve year old steer is an impressively big animal guaranteed to cause a second look. It is interesting to note that the size of Ox horns from the Neolithic period found in Orkney suggests castration was used in very ancient times.[8] A horn spread of 5' or more from tip to tip is not unusual for a good steer today. This is very close to the 5'10" spread of horns, thought to be of Wild Ox, which were found preserved in peat moss in two locations in Caithness. Both finds were of two heads locked together by the horns as if the animals had died fighting.[6] If you look at a group of Highlands whose horn shapes do not readily fall into category 1, 2, or 3 (on page 66), it is likely that they are either steers or beef heifers, since horns of neutered animals show more irregularity in formation than do those of cows and bulls.

Horn colour varies but generally is pale with black tips in black also brindle Highlands, pale with deep brown sometimes black tips in red Highlands, and an even spread of pale tone from base to tip in the yellow to white range of coat-colour and also frequently in steers. Some describe horns as *"a deep waxy colour" "creamy yellow"* but neutral, stone, buff, beige, would do just as well. *"Examining an animal at close quarters mellowness in horn counts for much. A waxy or yellowish tinge in a brindle or red is reckoned to be a sign of kindly feeding. Still some very good animals are unduly white of 'hard' horn."*[7] Early writers usually noted that they were black tipped. But the ivory white colour with jet black point is seen more in the Welsh Black than in Highlands.

Highland cattle use their horns most commonly to scratch with great precision itchy body areas along the back, towards the tail head, flanks and fetlocks and to rest the weight of the head on when in a recumbent position. Cows use their horns to maintain rank within a group of Highlands but rarely, according to some sources, to establish rank in a herd of mixed breeds. Others say that Highlands always dominate mixed groups with threatening use of horn power. Among like kind, however, a dominant cow can usually be seen asserting her right to the choicest feeding by merely threatening to horn away any other approaching cow which has chosen to ignore the first warning of a potent eye roll glare. Actual horn contact is infrequent. An effective method used last century in the Hebrides to restrain bullying of this sort was that of tying a horseshoe to the horns of the troublesome cow in such a way that it dangled in front of her nose (*p10 middle pic*). A humorous account of this can be found in C MacDonald's *Life in the Highlands and Islands of Scotland*. Curiously though, the Highland cows and steers I watched sharing hayracks in fields with Highland and Shetland ponies always deferred to the threat of horse teeth or hoof, in that the horses were allowed their choice of hay first with not a horn tilted in menace towards any of them. Horses it seems are treated with more deference than fully antlered red deer stags, for it has been noticed in Jura that where farmed red deer and Highland cattle are fed in hayracks on the open hill the lead cows dominate the stags without even engaging in horn to antler contact.

Individual Highland cows and bulls have been known to learn specific problem solving use of their horns such as to loosen and scatter baled hay or straw, to lift the drag of a loose halter rope in an Agricultural Show stall, to lift barred gates off the hinges, to insert in a one inch opening of an improperly closed barn door to push it fully open, or to pull up fence posts-and-wiring in order to step out rather than leap out of a field. Theories have been presented that although horns were primarily developed for fighting they may also help with heat regulation and balance on rocky terrain, and that the size of horn acts as a social ranking system.[8] Seriously aggressive horn use is unusual. In general it has to be provoked, for example as in cows with young calves to protect. I watched a cow with calf try repeatedly to horn in the belly two intruding heifers when the dividing bars between pens at a market broke down. At another market a Highland cow with calf showed her objection to the proximity of my back to her pen with a deft silent jab from one horn between the bars which on hitting my back pitched me away a couple of steps. One breeder I spoke to had experienced horn assisted airborne flight into a clump of nettles because of failing to heed signals denoting an unprecedented change of mood in a normally placid and friendly dam due to her just having given birth. This fearless protection of offspring is appreciated by breeders in countries where there are predators more dangerous than any in Britain.

Like the cows, Highland bulls enjoy a well-earned reputation for being docile and easily managed. There are exceptions of course to every generalisation and wise breeders dispense with livestock of bad temperament, recognising easily that wildness from lack of handling is a different issue. One way of preparing hill stock for halter training involves 'cowping' the animal suddenly as it runs on a long rope. This causes quite a heavy fall incurring risk of horn damage, so young stock destined for Showing should be handled thoughtfully.

A bull lowering his head to charge out of the corner stockmen may have had to manoeuvre him into is not necessarily using his horns aggressively, but of course any doubt about his temperament must be acted upon. Indeed I have marvelled at the tremendous care both bulls and cows take... even when in a state of high excitement and fear during the sales ring process...to avoid accidental horning of persons standing in the narrow passageways along which the livestock are being driven with stick whacks on the rump. At Inverness Auction Mart a cow with horns almost touching each side of the passageway was being forced on at such a pace she was slipping onto her knees. She rounded a corner and came face to face with an eight year old boy and his father casually looking at the pens as one might on a trip to the zoo. The cow froze. The father and son looked at her and waited. Her persecutor roared behind. She tilted her head until her wide spread of horn was almost vertical and lunged past the boy leaving plenty of space between him and herself whilst bumping along the bars on her side of the passageway.

Bulls are most likely to use horn aggression on other bulls due to mismanagement, such as for instance, the removal of one bull from a field of three for even a few hours after which he is returned to that same field. On his return fighting will probably ensue.

In the context of food foraging there is a reluctance to apply the potential force of these big horns. For example Highland cattle are more likely to wait beneath apple trees for the fruit to fall than to apply force to shake the tree as a tusked animal might do. One hungry bull was observed on a bitterly cold day waiting beneath a tree for a solitary leaf to fall, chasing away any others from the herd who came near. Possibly the horns are too sensitive to use as daily tools, being reserved primarily for defensive use when there is no alternative. However, there is a report from Canada that a Highland cow was seen using her horns to pull a tree branch into browsing reach for her calf. Well done mother Highland...and do your sisters do that too? Behaviour is transmitted through families. There may be more frequent instances than noticed of Highlands horning branches into browsing reach but only one example came to light in this research. A Dibden bull deliberately selects hazel branches in the height of the richest grazings season and deftly pulls twiggy branches into reach by hooking a horn into them. He handed on this behaviour to one of his sons.

Some bulls like to indulge in a bit of power display when the spirit moves them by slashing at shrubby wayside bushes. Highland though they are, they tend not to toss the caber or log look-alikes!

Cows and bulls which have been wrongly handled can quickly learn effective horn aggression against humans. With almost imperceptible head movement such stock can induce remarkably agile horn-dodging activity in their handlers. This provides entertainment, even spectacle, for crowds at Agricultural Shows but obviously is an undesirable acquired behaviour pattern, which is probably irreversible and is definitely dangerous. Sometimes a preliminary lowering of the head from its habitual position may precede dangerous horn thrusts, sometimes a momentary intense stillness, but these signals are so minimal they can go undetected unless you know the animal well. Safe animal handling requires an alertness to changes in their behaviour, no matter how slight, and aids one's self-protective skill of interpretative anticipation of their likely action. *'To be forewarned is to be forearmed'* is a saying which comes to mind. Assessing a cow's level of stress at being penned can help avoid unnecessary bruising of, for example, a hand resting over the top bar of her pen. A cow which may resent the reduced space of a pen can easily swing an accurate horn point to remove the intruding fingers. Highland cattle possess an excellent sense of space awareness which many humans do not. This lack of space awareness accounts for accidental bruisings to some cattle handlers who may, while grooming an animal, have been standing too close to a wall or fencing to allow dodging space necessitated by natural movement in the livestock.

Serious accidents from Highland cattle horns are exceptional rather than commonplace yet they invoke strong criticism against the breed. Apart from reports of damaged hides in the Dumfriesshire droves, due to horns in the cramped jostling when Irish imports swelled the numbers towards the end of the eighteenth century, accounts of the breed do not include references to bad or dangerous temperament. This absence indicates the generally docile and tractable nature of Scottish Highland cattle over a span of time during which reports of dreadful accidents with horned Ayrshires or Ayrshire crosses were many. Despite the amazing advances in the science of genetics there is still uncertainty about quantifying how much, and which, behaviour is transmitted genetically as opposed to by example and environment. Many second- or third- generation breeders are emphatic that temperament *"runs in families"* and *"is in the blood"*. Their opinions are too rooted in the practical experience of the breed to dismiss lightly. Responsible breeders are continuously on the look-out for inherited rather than acquired aggressive behaviour although community retribution today would not be as severe as implied in the rules set out in Exodus in *The Bible*. *"If an ox gore a man or a woman that they die then the ox shall be surely stoned, and his flesh shall not be eaten; but the owner of the ox shall be quit. But if the ox were wont to push with his horn in time past, and it hath been testified to his owner, and he hath not kept him in, but that he hath killed a man or a woman, the ox shall be stoned and his owner also shall be put to death."*

From observations at several major Agricultural Shows I consider that some animals are encouraged into aggressive responses to humans well before the first little horn bud is clearly visible, because the general public at these Shows seem unable to resist a compelling urge to tousle young calves on the forehead. A pat on the back, flank, or allowing it to sniff or lick a proffered hand is rare. It's straight for the forehead they go, ignoring the felt tip penned notice "**Please do not touch livestock**" Two or three days of relentless tousling is more than enough to awaken a head butting instinct. The calf petting public seem unaware of the difference between a calf's head lowered with ears pulled well back in tense resentful anticipation of yet another forehead-scratching and a head lowered from exhaustion, neither of which positions signal a good time to pet the animal.

In any case it is inadvisable to transfer to horned animals the head stroking beloved by cats and dogs as part of their preening behaviour. Young bulls whose owners were pleased to tell me *"just loves a good scratchy tickle on the forehead"* as though this was proof of good temperament, I would be very cautious about handling in two years time.

One young stockman left in charge at the Royal Highland Agricultural Show astonished me with his demonstration of the "fun" he participated in which consisted of getting onto his hands and knees and engaging a young Highland calf with a head to head trial of strength.

A few unscrupulous cattle dealers in the south of Scotland last century used to saw off horns prior to market time in an attempt to disguise old cattle as young Galloways. Their activities may well have led the Scottish Society for the Prevention of Cruelty to Animals to notify the directors of the Highland & Agricultural Society of Scotland in 1893 of their proposal (later withdrawn) to have dishorning of cattle in Scotland declared an illegal act. By 1963 there were laws stipulating that anaesthetics were to be used in all horn removals. Clearly this vet's story shows scant sentiment about horns from the farmer fictitiously named Mr Gray, who was insistent suddenly that some Highland bullocks lose their horns. As the vet with helper McGregor arrived to dehorn the bullocks they first rescued Mr Gray from his own bull which had taken ill and had gone crazy. The vet recounts the story: *"Mr Gray's men had the Highland bullocks in a small pen. Each one was driven singly into the catching crate, and given a local anaesthetic, after being roped by the horns to the side bar of the crate. After the anaesthetic had time to work, I sawed off each horn in turn, a painless but messy operation. Soon the job was finished, and the twelve magnificent horns lay in a heap at my feet.*

"What a waste," I said to McGregor...

"Not a bit of it" said he. "We'll just put them in your car, I made a bargain with auld Gray...to driving off one bull: twelve Highland cattle horns."

"And what'll you do with them?" I asked.

"Och, I work away at making horn spoons and so on, and I use bits to tidy up the cromachs I make from the Blackface rams' horns in the winter evenings. I'll make ye a right fine one as a wedding present."[9]

The story goes on to reveal that Mr Gray had won the six bullocks in a bet and wanted their horns removed so that the crofter who had lost them. . virtually all he owned...would not be able to recognise his animals and try to reclaim them.

Every so often someone decides to try dehorning their Highlands. No one seems to continue dehorning their stock. Different points of view are regularly aired as is evident from the comment printed in the *Herd Book of 1955* (Vol. XXXIV) *"I do think there is profit and sense in dehorning bull calves when cutting if these animals are likely to find their way into courts"* Commercial ventures following that advice with steers found that dehorning within the same week as castration was so traumatic for the animals that their normal growthy phases were lastingly reduced thereby negating the whole idea of programming forced and fast-finished Highland Beef.

Removing mature horns is unpleasant for vets and stockmen to the point of being upsetting, and those who have dehorned cows have admitted later regretting it once they had discovered how little cause there is for fear of horn initiated problems. Dehorned behaviour remains the same as with horns. It is both sad and comical to see a mature dehorned cow about to enter a byre or cow-shed door pause to tilt and manoeuvre her now denuded head in her once necessary ritual of entry, or a hornless cow unable to scratch loose her winter coat or ease other itchings because there are no low branched trees or posts at the right angle for her in her grazing area. One breeder reflected that dehorning three or four year olds when pregnant perhaps results in barrenness after rearing the first calf. Nevertheless breeding polled Highlands is raised periodically for discussion usually by people new to handling the breed. To date the Society has considered that it is more acceptable to disbud young horns in whichever animals owners choose than to interfere with the genetic stability of the horned characteristic.

For centuries cattle were the main draught animals pulling both ploughs and carts. Old paintings and tapestries depict yokes which were designed to be attached to the horns. These old style wooden yokes were easier to put on, much less expensive than the late eighteenth century leather collars modelled on those used for horses, and were unlikely to have caused breathing restrictions the way badly fitted collars could.

The old method of branding a horn to identify individual cows is still practised in some folds. It is a skillful business which fortunately is demonstrated every so often by special arrangement with the Highland Cattle Society. Show stock are not usually branded, nor calves nor heifers. Horn growth slows enough by three years old to make horn-branding cows after their first calf worthwhile. It is a fast, painfree, efficient method of identifying stock. There is no pungent burning odour and the cows are more taken up with having their horns held still for a few seconds than with any whiff they might detect of the little puff of smoke when the hot iron makes horn contact. The procedure begins with whichever takes longer. . . collecting the cattle or heating up the branding irons. With a race that takes two animals at once the task is quickly completed. Skill lies in judging the correct temperature of the hot iron, the degree of pressure on the horn, and selecting the best position on the circular surface of the horn. The method of inserting irons into burning coals through a side opening in an open-top metal drum burner has the advantage of hiding live fire from the livestock whilst also being a small manageable unit. Too great a heat can damage the branding irons and burn too deeply through the horn. Testing the iron on a piece of wood gives some help in judging when it is ready for use on the horn. Horn brandings when correctly done last the animal's lifetime but any indistinct brands can easily be redone *(Pics 96-98 p64).*

It was common practice in England in times gone by to help shape the horns of Longhorns by either binding or weighting them to produce the shape most in demand for the making of hunting horns (i.e. a primitive bugle), drinking cups, or musket powder holders. Probably a certain amount of horn-shaping was also applied to Highland cattle horns but it seems that the unmodified natural shape was widely used for many purposes.

However "helping" a horn into symmetric alignment with its neighbour by applying weights or heat is more likely a temptation today to those who covet awards in the competitive Show ring than to those who craft the horns for practical purposes. Lack of expertise in methods of coaxing horns to grow a specific way can have unsightly effects yet information on techniques successful in modifying horn shape seems hard to find.

There are still craftsmen working with horn. Their source of horn has to include varied foreign breeds because availability of supply of Highland horn is too irregular. They tend to produce novelty goods rather than such daily necessities of former times as inexpensive spoons, ladles, drinking glass, comb, and buttons. Horn heads on shepherd crooks and walking sticks are practical rather than novelty but the majority today are made with sheep or deer horn. Few horn-crafts workers are listed in Arts Council registers and many do not take a stall at craft fairs because their produce is available on a small, irregular, or commissioned basis which is marketed privately.

An interesting use of Highland horn in the making of a reed-blown instrument called the Stock-and-Horn was described by the poet Robert Burns... "*I have at last gotten one; but it is a very rude instrument; it is composed of three parts; the stock, which is the hinder thigh-bone of a sheep, such as you see in a mutton-ham; the horn, which is a common Highland cow's horn, cut off at the smaller end, until the aperture be large enough to admit the stock to be pushed up through the horn, until it be held by the thicker end of the thigh-bone; and lastly, an oaten reed, exactly cut and notched like that which you see every shepherd boy have when the corn stems are green and full-grown. The reed is not made fast in the bone, but is held by the lips and plays loose in the smaller end of the stock, while the stock with the horn hanging on its larger end, is held by the hands in playing. The stock has six or seven ventiges on the upper side, and one back ventige, like the common flute. This of mine was made by a man from the braes of Athole, and is exactly what the shepherds were wont to use in that country*". (1794) [10] The Stock-and-Horn was never in great demand as a musical instrument. It became of more value as a collector's item.

Horns used as drinking vessels were often ornately worked with silver. One fine example dated 1493 is the Dunvegan Cup. Tradition requires it to be filled with claret...it holds nearly half a gallon. . to be consumed in one draught by each new Chief of the Macleod Clan as part of his investiture in Dunvegan Castle. The horn is believed to be the one taken by Rory Mhor from the black Highland bull which he single handedly slew when it had attacked him on his way through Kintail. Authorities on Gaelic folklore say several clans claim to have had a legendary figure of remarkable strength who defeated a wild black Highland bull in solo combat – which may be so – but there is only one Dunvegan Horn.

A replica of the Dunvegan Horn called The Skeabost Horn, is a beautifully crafted award for prowess in Shinty first presented in 1926 from Duncan Macleod of Skeabost, and still competed for annually. What a link with the past.

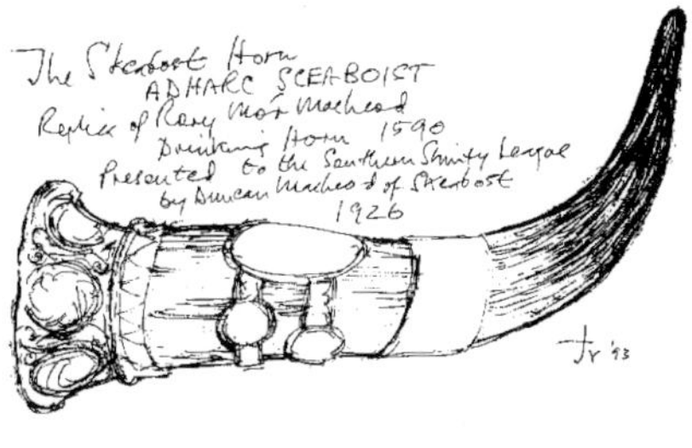

Mr J Richmond MBE

A much earlier reference to horns as drinking vessels makes no mention of decoration... "*the northern peoples*

Pen and ink sketch by UFC after RBK Stevenson 1959 pl VII VolXCII of Proceedings of the Society of Antiquaries of Scotland

drank out of Urus horns which were so large as to contain an urna."[10] This comment is attributed to a Roman scholar and likely to have been made before the fourth century. It seems that six centuries later the 'northern peoples' had not relinquished their horn vessels if the artist who sculpted the Bullion Stone represented an image of his time. The Bullion Stone is a large slab of grey sandstone bearing a sculpted picture of *"a horse plodding uphill, more or less on its own, while the warrior it carries drinks from a large drinking horn which has a bird's head at the tip staring down at him beak to eye as it were."*[11] The stone, found in Invergowrie Parish, Angus, is thought to date from early tenth century.

Another common usage was by herders looking after cattle in times before farm policies were enclosed. Then of course the cattle could stray beyond the distance over which a herd's own voice would carry, so a blast on the horn would call the cattle into eyesight if not all the way home. A marvellous example of a herd's horn from perhaps as early as the sixteenth century inscribed with circles and zig zag patterns is on display in the public library in Darvel. It is owned by Kilmarnock and Loudoun District Museum, now part of East Ayrshire Council Museums.

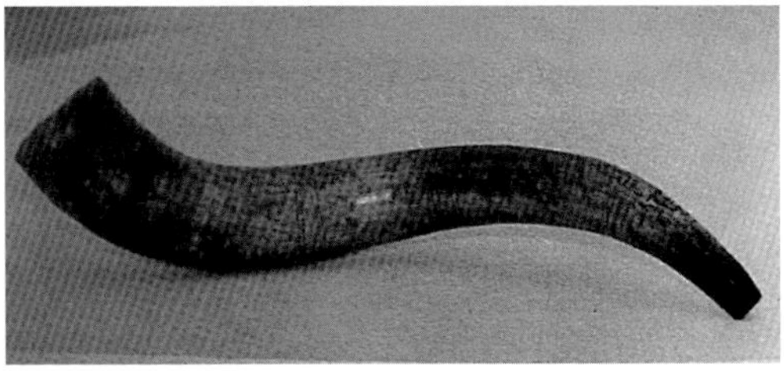

T McLatchie with permission from East Ayrshire Council Museums

The seventeenth century found horns being used to hold a personal supply of gunpowder slung from the waist belt by leather or other thong. Prestigious powder horns were pressed into a flat sided shape which was elaborately carved, often including a message. One belonging to the National Museum of Antiquities of Scotland has inscribed on the inner side *"A man his mynd should never sett upon the thing hee cane nott gett."*

Cattle and sheep horns have been used well into the twentieth century as a Drench for the administration of medicinal liquids to livestock, far out-lasting another early use as an implement for sowing seed.

HOOF

Highland cattle are about as individual with regard to their feet as they are with regard to their horns. Black hoofs go with black coats and often are neatly compact. Black perpendicular streaks down the dark beeswax hoof colour are often to be found with brindle coats. Some hoofs are wide and spreading, some set high like a horse hoof, but all keep growing. Where natural habitat does not keep wearing down the hardened outside edge, paring will become necessary. Some animals require much more frequent paring than others. When hoofs are allowed to grow too long the front points of the clits often cross over each other which throws the weight onto the back (heel) of the hoof and inhibits free walking. There is risk of infection when long hoofs break off or when unattended hoofs are given severe paring. Harsh paring even when done by expert farriers can cause bleeding and temporary lameness or a short-stepping style of walking. Animals intended for Showing should be given time to recover from paring but of course it is an advantage in stock management if you have a strain of cattle which require minimal foot dressing.

Strong hard hoofs are important in Highland bulls which may have a working life of 18 years in varying terrain, and in cows to take the weight of the bull and annual pregnancies for perhaps 23 years. Arthritis does afflict cattle but in instances of lameness check the feet for foreign objects jammed between the clits. A goodly space between the clits is desirable and no undue flatness which throws the weight too far back. However an animal which stands too high on its toes may lack the necessary flexibility at the pastern to cope over many years with the demands of hill country. Calves reared naturally rather than programmed on intensive feed systems are the more likely to grow good hoof, yet even hard hoof will soften in time if exposed only to soft wet ground with no hard tracks for respite.

HAIR

In their hairyness lies much of their survival. Whilst performing a vital protective role, the long haired look also has tremendous aesthetic appeal, perhaps because the bony hips knobbly knees and fleshy reproduction organs so typical of most cattle are less obvious, and the attractive hairy-calf-look is not entirely lost in the mature animal.

Underneath the profuse long coarse outer hairs which protect from rain, snow and wind, is a dense very soft short undercoat which maintains body heat. Calves have an endearing cuddly appearance particularly in the growth phase when both the outer and undercoats are all the same length giving an impression of rough velvet with a very deep pile. Their outer coat grows rapidly until by about 6 to 8 months they often look rather messy, as the coarser adult coat pushes out the softer calf coat which can linger on in scraggy tufts and matted strips for some 3 months.

The adult outer coat is thickest and longest in winter. It should be cast for the summer months. Rubbing off matted winter hair is greatly aided if suitable tree trunks rocks or posts at an angle are available...horn tips can't reach all parts. Complete casting of the winter coat takes many weeks. But in order to have profusely long haired animals displaying that so distinctive breed feature at the various summer Agricultural Shows, mid-twentieth century breeders very nearly succeeded, by breeding selectively, in producing animals which never cast their coat at all.

With such animals vigilance about sweating and over-heating became necessary. Then the appearance at a Fatstock Show (early 1990s) of a Highland steer clipped and shorn to avoid heat stress, stirred up such controversy over the 'hair or no hair in summer' issue that judges, breeders, and the public will perhaps once more come to understand the qualities of the breed whether clad in its summer or winter attire. The summer coat in many of the Highlands I visited exposes a tidy well muscled conformation normally completely hidden by the thick winter coat (*Pic 72 p56*). It is at first a strange contrast to see the real shape of the animal when one is more familiar with the shaggy haired appearance.

Currently there are families of Highlands around to support the belief that some black-coated strains produce the longest and thickest hair, that dun-coated strains produce the shortest hair, and that many yellow coats have softer and finer guard hairs than the darker colours. Without conclusive evidence that the black hair is coarser than the lighter colours or that hair texture relates to flesh texture it is a pity if breeders' judgement of sound stock was ever seriously influenced by the saying *'the finer the texture of hair the finer the grain of the flesh.'* Research by Dr M L Ryder and others on sheep wool, involving precise laboratory measurement of each hair of thousands of samples, has revealed that black wool is longer and coarser than white wool.[12] This difference might apply also to Highland cattle hair on which no detailed research has been conducted to date. Those who are convinced of the 'denser longer' hair on black Highlands will be interested to learn that in Iceland *"there is a tradition that moccasins made from black-haired cattle skin lasted longer than those made from skin with paler hair."*[12]

Whether the hair is curled, wavy, or straight is largely dictated by what is most fashionable in the Show ring as the genetic potential for variety is already there. Presumably genetic heritage to some extent is responsible for the results of 1990s methods of shampoo-wash and fast blow-dry which can produce a distinctly un-Highland look of tightly curled hairs all over. Too hot a 'blow-dry' probably intensifies what happened naturally with rain and sun but the following comments suggest fashion above function.

Mr Grant of Corriemonie in Inverness-shire, known in the 1770s for the high quality of his Highland cattle, searched throughout the Highlands and Skye for *"fine well proportioned shape of the bull or cow, a fine horn, and a soft skin, covered with a close coat of hair, rough and well curled."*[13]

Advice given in Mr Grant's time to a breeder in Ross and Cromarty who had tried unsuccessfully to use lowland and new breeds of bulls on his Highland stock was to find *"a fine bull from Skye with curled jet-black hair."*[14]

A century or so later this was published *"The hair, while it is silky, unctuous, and free from harshness, should be abundant and curling."*[15] Yet within one breeding cow's lifetime from that suggested ideal the first official guideline from the newly formed Highland Cattle Society reads: *"the hair should be long and gracefully waved, very much as in what dog breeders denote wavy-coated retrievers. To have a curl is to possess a decided fault, one which has of late years become unfortunately too common in some folds."* What did the Skye breeders make of this, one wonders, in the very first Herd Book for the breed. Were the breeders whose stock had the "correct" coats the only ones to join the new Society? Were only cattle with *"long and gracefully waved"* coats entered in the Agricultural Shows after 1885? Clearly it is possible that Shows could be detrimental to a breed. As early as 1867 concern was to be heard among Highland cattle breeders that Shows were encouraging too much attention to handsome form and colour and not enough to function in terms of high yield.[3]

Anyone seeking information about the breed quite sensibly turns to the Breed Society for guidance. So it is no surprise to find that subsequent writings such as the following example in 1910 reflect the Society stance. The coat of Highland cattle *"should be of a healthy, glossy growth, thick, and in parts long. It should not be curled, but should slightly wave. When the animals are fed outside the hair is more abundant, and in better order than when they are housed."*[16] The writer goes on to suggest that, when selecting stock, breeders should place more value on the attributes of being regular breeders and good milkers than on the appearance. Sound advice this for those who might listen. But there is still considerable dismay among many breeders if interested parties wish to view their stock when the bull may have cast his dossan (forelock) or when prize cows are in their summer coat with only the vestiges of a long coat showing in a wispy mane.

The length of the dossan is also subject to fashion, or definitions over the last three centuries would not be so at variance, some stating the dossan should not obscure the eyes others that the longer the better. Surely it is a bit excessive to allow a bull's dossan trail in his feed! Cats are not the only animals to suffer from hair balls.

Highland cattle hair does felt well with the cold water method, producing a very soft fabric which sheds hairs rather too readily. A blend with sheep and goats wool produces a more hard-wearing felt fabric. The felting properties of Highland cattle hair is no surprise to breeders who are used to seeing the outer coat form matted felt on the flanks and back of their grazing animals in wet windy weather. No history of a felt industry connected with the breed, though, is readily to be found.

When both the soft undercoat and the long outer hairs are given to spinners a coarse yarn can be hand spun as readily as from other wools. Garments such as pullovers and hats made from pure Highland hair are very warm but somewhat itchy if next to the skin and require care during cleaning to avoid felting. Such a yarn apparently is also less pleasant to knit with than more conventional 'wools.' As with the felting process, spinners have suggested that a blend of sheep or goats wool with the cattle hair would produce a more serviceable yarn.

An old method of stripping hair from the hides made use of lime in the process. Probably the residues from that led to the inclusion of cattle hair in a type of rough plaster made with slaked lime and tallow.

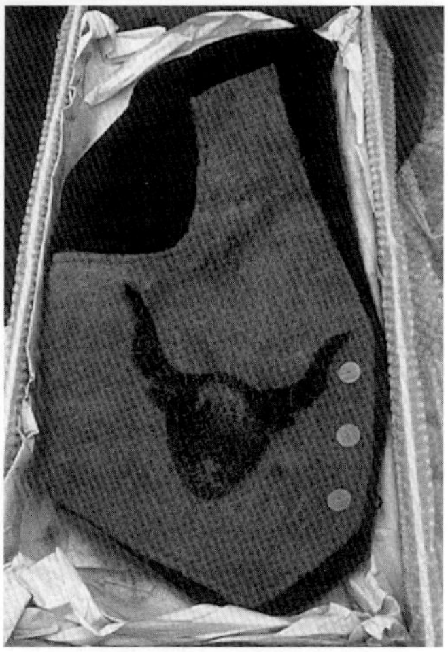

Photo T. McLatchie

T. McLatchie's Highland hair blend waistcoat by Christina Sargent, Wheems, South Ronaldsay.

Indication that long hair may have been shorn for making rope comes from the discovery in 1934 of the remains of an old boat found in Loch Laggan when the Lochaber Power Company caused the water level to drop by about 16 feet. Some matted fibrous caulking was still attached. About 2 feet 2 inches of matted hair yarn was examined in the Zoology Department of Edinburgh University by Professor James Ritchie who believed the hair to be from Highland cattle and that the formation of the rope caulking suggested the hair had been shorn and that the discovery could not be dated more precisely than to say it came from between 700 AD and 1500 AD.[17]

REFERENCES

1 *Statistical Account of Scotland* Vol 15

2 T Farrall in *The Transactions of the Highland and Agricultural Society of Scotland*, 4th Series Vol VIII, 1876

3 A Sturrock in *The Transactions* as above, Vol I 1866 – 1867

4 *Highland Cattle Society Herd Book* Vol I

5 Source mislaid – possibly early *Scottish Farmer Album*

6 Dr J A Smith in the *Proceedings of the Society of Antiquaries of Scotland*, Volume 9

7 J Cameron in an article reprinted in *The Highland Breeders Journal* 1988

8 Dr M L Ryder in his *Sheep and Man* 1983; also Taylor (1966) on heat regulation, *Sheep and Man*

9 R Stevenson in *Highland Vet*

10 L G Langwill in Vol LXXXIV of *The Proceedings* as above

11 Vol XCII of *The Proceedings* as above

12 Dr M L Ryder, personal letter 1996

13 and 14 in Survey IX 1772 – 1782 in *Reports to the Commissioners of Annexed Estates*

15 D Low in "*Domesticated Animals of the British Isles*"

16 Professor R P Wright in "*Standard Cyclopedia of Modern Agriculture and Rural Economy, 1910*"

17 S Maxwell in *Proceedings of the Society of Antiquaries of Scotland* 1950/51

Scottish Highland folklore of the 18th century, found in Gaelic song from earlier times, included mentions of white markings on Highland cattle of old bloodlines. By mid 20th century white socks or splashes in what was then deemed to be a whole-coat-colour breed was considered to be evidence of cross-breeding. But recessive genes can be transmitted for a very long time through many generations before surfacing unexpectedly to astonish those who fix breed standards in the various breed associations - standards designed to maintain breed purity. There is no quick route to wisdom.

CHAPTER 3: WISDOM FROM EXPERIENCE

CHAPTER 3: WISDOM FROM EXPERIENCE

ADVICE ON STORE CATTLE - EARLY TWENTIETH CENTURY

"A man must get to understand animals instinctively through long experience and intimate connection with them, to be able to judge of the possible outcome from the appearance at any time. In buying, one ought to learn how the beasts have been kept for some months previous to the time in question, and never take those from a better climate, or which have been accustomed to better food, than is to be had in their new quarters. Cattle moderately fed, and not kept too warm in winter, are generally acknowledged to have done better when the end of the grazing time comes, than those which have been well fed but kept in close byres; in the latter, the hair tends to fall or rub off too early in the season, leaving too little of their natural hirsute protection when turned out to grass in spring. Those that lie out all winter often in the end do best, if not too lean at the beginning of the season; the extra constitution gained by being out and living under more natural conditions enables them to make up more than the winter's loss of flesh. To those not fed on cake during winter, a few pounds per day, given for five or six weeks before they go out, affords a good start, and "comes out" afterwards in "extra condition". Cattle at three or four years old arrive more quickly at maturity than two-year-olds, and "kill better" than they look, having more internal fat, and being "better made up, "though they lay on a smaller amount of beef in a given time during the period of their existence." Professor R Wallace.

CONVERSATIONAL ADVICE - LATE TWENTIETH CENTURY

In looking for a good quality animal remember *all must be in proportion...that is all parts must relate one to another in proportions specific to the breed of Highland cattle. An awareness of what is disproportionate has to be learned from practising a critical eye on many animals in the company of knowledgeable persons. Photographs can at best only offer an additional learning approach to the live experience. A beautiful head if small on an animal of sizeable frame, or if large on an animal of small compact frame can seem ugly because the overall proportions are unbalanced.* T McLatchie.

Never outclass your bull. A W Howat

Lead your cattle, don't drive them. L M D Robertson

You can't breed good Highland cattle by computer. J P Ramsay

If a cow usually produces heifer calves her bull calf may sire more heifers than bulls. M M Edwards

Patience is vital. A Mackay

Breeding potential in a bull cannot be decided entirely from visual appraisal. J Bowser

Our breed is necessary. It is a cornerstone of the Scottish Cattle Trade. D D Cameron (in HBJ)

Highland cattle are the athletes of the bovine race.
Prioritise your criteria and act on that. K Headspeath

Stockmanship and breed lines are all important, and both show up in the offspring. J McPhail (in HBJ).

Beware the fat animal...there's a lot can be hidden with fat. E McNeill

There is no merit in registering or even propagating purebred animals just because they are purebreds and eligible for registration. J E Lawson (in HBJ)

Native breeds are superior. M Gibson

Remember there can be a lot of change between the age of 12 months and 2 years.
Fretting causes scouring and sweating. Plan transport to avoid fast driving with a loaded cattle float.
A Morrow

If you want to see how a beast walks get it in the cobbles. (poor feet cannot walk well on cobblestone roads) B Coutts in his book *Highland Air*

Creation of fat uses four times as much food energy as does the creation of lean tissues. V. Porter in *Practical Rare Breeds.*

Five Gaelic sayings are appropriate here for although collected before 1905 they still make good sense to those who will pay attention.

Bo aonaich...a cow fattened for market...one of three things not to be judged by appearance.

Is duilich bo a chur air laogh 'us a gaol air gamhainn...a cow won't take to her calf when her darling is a stirk.

Seachain mo chluais's cha bhuail m'adhorc...avoid my ear and my horn will not hit.

Is minig a bha droch laogh aig deadh mhart...many a good cow has a bad calf.

Millidh bo buaile. . . one cow will spoil a fold. A R Forbes in *Gaelic names of Beasts Birds and Fishes, Insects and Reptiles.*

Also from the Gaelic oral tradition is this contemplation about the balance of genetic hand out from sire and dam. Passed on to me by the acclaimed Piper from Glen Uig, Moidart, Allen Mac Donald, I chose to present it in this English rendering:

One autumn evening two old friends were viewing their cattle. With a casual swing of his cromach towards his latest buy from market Macallister was heard to say, "*Well now is that not a fine cow there!*"

McKechnie impassively leaning on the gatepost gazing over the cattle, remarked, "*Aye. But she's fairly got the look of a bull about her.*"

"*For sure,*" said Macallister resting on his cromach and still gazing over the cattle, "*That'll be because her father was a bull.*"

COMMENTS FOR COMMERCIAL BREEDERS

Privately conducted studies by a team in commercial Highland cattle breeding produced the following considerations:

Highland cattle differ from other domestic breeds in more than appearance. It is said generally that the breed has changed less than other domestic 'improved' breeds of cattle. What does this mean?...that they are less manageable? It means that one will succeed best when an effort to understand behaviour intrinsic to the breed is made. The loudest criticisms of Highland cattle are made all too frequently by individuals ignorant of why the Highlands do not submit readily to the convenience methods of late twentieth century rearing by computer. Here are some interesting factors to consider.

1 Highland cattle are seasonal growers. They gain rapidly from birth to weaning then slowdown until during their first and each winter their growth gain is arrested. (This survival technique is known in red deer and some rare breeds of sheep.) Their appetite lessens to survive the winter months during which time even if extra concentrates and hay beyond their needs are consumed such feeding is not reflected in any weight gain. Therefore do not winter Highlands on high concentrates when their growth potential is "on hold" then summer them on poor rough pasture without any supplements when their metabolism is in "high gear" and condemn the breed as difficult to manage.

2 Pregnancy overrides the winter slowdown so bulling two years old heifers does not seem to affect adversely their natural growth to full maturity.

3 With herds of wild ungulates females generally come into season around the same time. There may be an element of this behaviour in Highland cows since if you mix one lot with a strange lot prior to bulling it can lead to many not taking the bull. This could be due to their need for more time to adopt a herd instinct of cycling at the same time.

4 Highland cattle are capable of surviving periods of extreme deprivation but one of their survival techniques is to avoid breeding until both their condition and those of their habitation improve.

5 When a Highland cow calves late in the season...whether due to harsh conditions, bad management or a lazy bull...she may well take the bull soon after parturition in order to calve the following year at a time of optimum nourishment and survival for her and her calf such as April or May. Many suckler cows are culled after producing four or five calves because of long calving intervals. The Highland cow will easily produce upwards of ten calves when adequately nourished throughout conception and pregnancy.

6 During periods of natural growth and weight gain it is very difficult to overfeed bulls.

Research on red deer suggests that castrated stags are less seasonally affected in growth pattern than whole stags, but Highland steers seem to adhere to the seasonal 'slow' pattern followed by rapid weight and growth gain shown in Highland bulls.

Commercial breeders of Highland cattle will do well to recognise the intermittent growth pattern of the breed, recognise that the optimum fattening time for Highlands cannot be readily manipulated to suit unseasonal production of offspring, and recognise the economies possible in going **with** the breed's survival strategies rather than striving to make it into a different looking Charolais, Hereford or Murray Grey.

KILBERRY WAYS
BY MARION CAMPBELL OF KILBERRY, 1993

For the first eight years of my life 'the Highlanders' were of constant interest; both my parents went to look at them, feed or handle, and discuss them, daily, and I was taken as soon as I was mobile (if not sooner! we had an aged pram kept for going to the shore.) Incidentally I never heard them called a 'Fold' – 'the Herd' meant breeding cows plus calves; the Herd Bull was either 'with the Herd' or 'in his park'. The big stots were two years old bullocks, occasionally three years old.

The herd was kept in as natural conditions as possible. The cows summered on rough grazing with access to the excellent machair – grazing at the shore, usually with the bull; the mature cows calved by themselves unless any difficulty was expected. This though had the disadvantage that one could seldom see the calf for the first two days, except through field-glasses, as the cows hid their calves in rushes or whins, and charged anyone who approached. But there was no risk of infection with this system.

The heifers were bulled to calve in Spring, when the whole herd was held overnight in the byre and a heifer near the drop was kept in the stall when the others were turned out to the grass. An early memory is of the sound of the other cows roaring in sympathy when a calving was in progress... "that must be Baravalla Bhuidhe – I thought she'd be early".

Over the winter months though the breeding cows were byre fed every evening. In severe weather – seldom encountered here – the whole herd was held in the byre and only turned out for an hour or so to water.

When the grass was scanty in early spring or autumn but the cattle were out through the day, they were fed sheaves of oats put out whole from a cart – in those days sheaves were mostly tied with straw bands, not twine, so there was no risk of a cow carelessly swallowing a yard of binder-twine, and none of the bother of taking the twine off first. They seemed to enjoy the mixture of grain and straw, and tossed the straw about on their horns. One often saw young calves 'nested' in the spread straw as well – something that can't happen now that it's all combined!

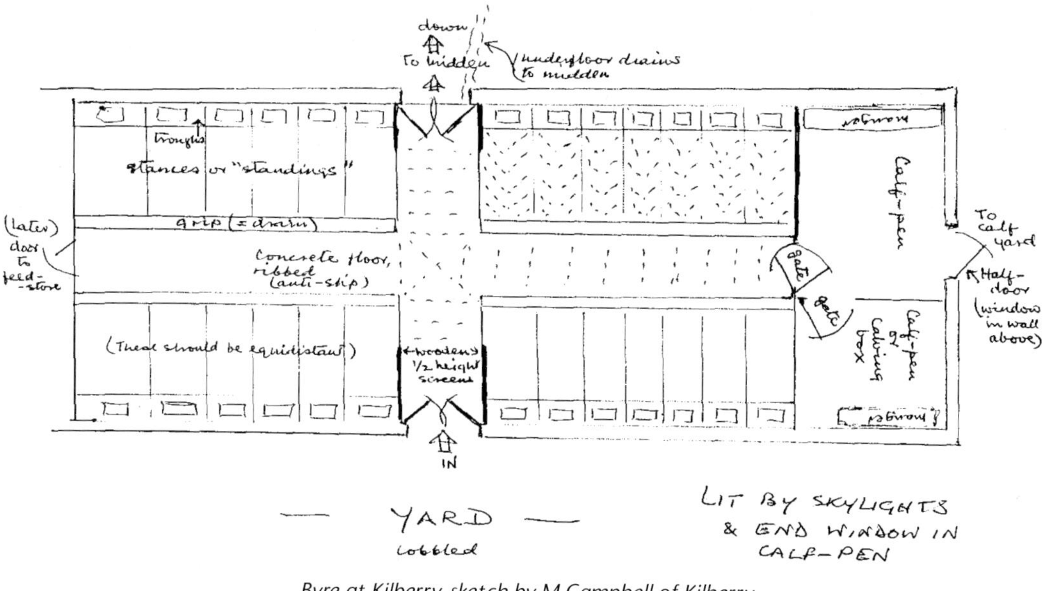

Byre at Kilberry, sketch by M Campbell of Kilberry

Our Byre for the Highlanders was (is) a long building with a central door, another door opposite it to the midden, a calf-pen and calving box at one end; the calf-pen had a gable door leading to a small grass-paddock where young calves could be let out on mild days. When the cattle were to come in, the byre was prepared with hay and chopped turnips in the mangers and the cows were then called from the field – it was seldom necessary to drive them. Each cow had her own stall and rushed into it; heifers had to be steered into their places for some days, and were given smart jabs in the ribs by their seniors if they blundered; calves who had been kept inside, in cold weather, were released and steered by a hand on the rump to join their mothers, once all had settled in the right place. The stalls each had a wooden yoke called a Trevis, like a modern metal yoke – one fixed and one moveable upright, through which the cows inserted their horns very delicately – the 'gate' was then closed by a crosspiece at the top. Chains were never used, because they might catch on the neck hair. The stalls were just far enough apart to prevent horning or food stealing.

Throughout the time I can remember, the herd leader was a senior cow called Cannach. She was the Boss and it was she who was called by name and led the others to the yard. I have watched her being called up from the shore, by a man on the top of the raised-beach terrace some considerable distance from the herd. Cannach would raise her head, slowly turn towards the road up the bank, and set off, immediately followed by everyone else. As the man went up through the two fields between the shore and the steading, the procession strung out after him, a few quiet lowings to straying calves the only sound. No dog was ever used, to the best of my knowledge. As they got nearer the farm it was essential to have all the gates opened ready, for the ladies began to speed up and might come into the yard at the trot, if the evening was chilly and they wanted to get into shelter and be fed.

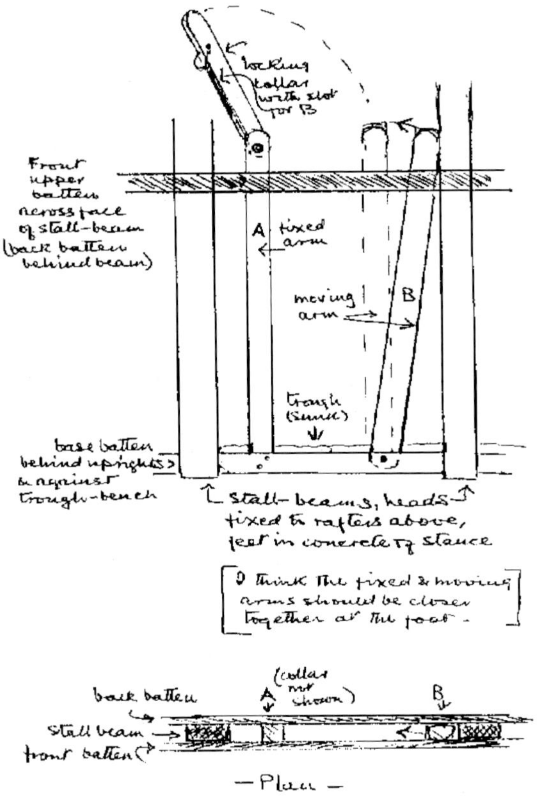

Trevis yoke, sketch by M Campbell of Kilberry

Usually before the herd came in the stots and stirks were into their 'boxes' – smallish covered courts where they had hecks of hay ready. (hecks are hay mangers set high on the wall) In hard weather they were also fed chopped turnips in moveable troughs on the floor, or rather on the manure for the boxes were not mucked out very often because the strawy dung underfoot provided some heating. The beasts' feet were not damaged because they were outside for part of every day unless in times of snow (exceptions here). None of the byres or boxes had water laid on in those days – few people's houses had either, for that matter – but all the fields had, and have, fresh water drinking troughs.

The bull had a 'bull's hoose' opening to a small grass-field, the Castle Park, behind the steading. This was a long narrow shed with an open end which could be closed by drop-in bars; a line of troughs was fixed to one wall. Sometimes when the bull was out with the herd, a couple of bull stirks might be put into the bull's hoose so that they could become accustomed to handling, feeding and grooming – but we never did very much with 'bringing out' bulls, and those we did bring out did not do particularly well. It was said that 'the Baravallas don't run to bulls' although we did have a Reserve Champion in 1917. But whatever the truth of the matter we did on the whole bring out more good females than males; it may have had more to do with my father's interest in them – I really don't know. I think the feeling was that young bulls took a great deal of work and might not repay one for it. My grandfather certainly had the same idea, and I found it true when I was on the job too.

I did bring out one young bull; while he was being trained for Showing he blossomed amazingly, coat and horns gleaming – just from daily brushings and rubbings? It seemed impossible. Then one day the manager's wife tracked down a hen who was 'laying away' and found her in the bull's hoose.

The hen rushed out cackling, the wife seized the newlaid egg – and a warm breath at her back informed her that the rising star had arrived to collect his daily treat. Mrs Manager thought it best to leave the egg in the manger; it speedily vanished, shell and all.

We never milked the Highlanders, though an Ayrshire cow was put to the Highland bull to breed a cow kept for the nursery. Her name was Primrose and I was immensely proud of her as My Own Cow. But I know that the McKechnies in Jura...the Craighouse Herd...did milk some of theirs. The only reason we didn't was that the milk went into the calves, some of whom even got a pail of Ayrshire milk as well, from the other byre.

The Highlanders went, like much else, after my father died, to my mother's immense grief. Long years later, in 1944, I came home from the war (partly unfit, partly on compassionate discharge to look after my mother) and took over running the estate from the old Factor. I had several schemes for improving the cattle-stock on the three farms in hand, and decided to put Highlanders on one of the outlying ones which had only sheep when I took over. In Autumn 1945 I persuaded Mother to come to Oban with me and help buy the first stock. I think there was only one Baravalla in the sale, and she was far beyond my touch, but I did acquire a few pedigreed beasts. One which must have been mishandled at some time was very wild and eventually broke her neck over a cliff when panicked by unauthorised sightseers who only wanted to take a photograph. I think I could have managed to quieten her if I had had some of the old experts of my youth around, but as it was I had to inform the farm people all about Highlanders from scratch, and some of them didn't accept that I knew anything. Gradually however I did put my ideas into practice, with

a a grade A Tuberculin Tested Dairy Farm;

b the outlier with the Highlanders;

c the Home Farm with crossed beef stock, including offspring of non-pedigree Highlanders, an Ayrshire or two and Shorthorns; eventually this mixed bag was put to an Aberdeen Angus bull and we began to collect red tickets at Oban Stirk Sales.

By the time I went out of farming in 1956 the Home Farm had a good even herd of Blue-greys with rough coats and breeding lines to tax anyone's memory.

Our pure-bred Highland bulls were memorable characters. Agamemnon, a large red bull instantly comes to mind.

He allowed small children to ride on his head with their feet on his thick dossan and would walk about the park like that, with apparent pride and pleasure. He was very sociable. Thirty years later the iron gates with bent rails that the blacksmith had been unable to straighten completely are a visible reminder of Agamemnon's recurring need of company and conversation. He approached a gate crabwise, placed his large rump against it, and attempted to sit down. When the gate buckled, he reversed, stepped through the mess, walked off to find my father. Several times he was found encamped on the bowling green by the front door, where at least once he remained while my father played the chanter to him. On another occasion screams were heard from the path to the Laundry where two hysterical maids carrying a basket of clean linen towards the Castle were being 'assisted' by Agamemnon who felt baskets should contain food for bulls, and had put his nose in to investigate. Possibly the best Agamemnon story happened one summer Sunday when the Farm Manager took his usual Sunday walk to the edge of the raised beach to 'look the cattle' without disturbing them. The Herd were, as expected, lying along the sands or standing in the shallows, but the bull was not to be seen. However a few moments' search revealed Agamemnon comfortably ensconced among the cattle on the next farm, while this side of the march-fence which runs into the sea, was a sabbath-breaking mob of 'the Tenants' (persons to whom the Castle and shootings had been let) shrieking and splashing and Tch! Tch! bathing on the Sabbath!!

As he watched, Agamemnon strolled to the shore and set off on his homeward way, swimming comfortably with a powerful stroke and head held well back out of the bow-wave. This was no time for the manager to move – he folded his arms on a strainer post and waited. The sounds of tumult reached the swimming bull; he checked, got a forefoot on the low reef that shelters the bathing bay, and hove himself up to see what was happening. A burst of much shriller screeching ensued, as the bay was abandoned, scantily clad bodies hurtled behind rocks into the thistly scrub, anxious voices called children to safety and the trampled sands were cleared. Satisfied, Agamemnon continued his route to his planned landing-place and trod up the sand leaving Enormous Hoof Marks. *"And I'm telling you thon lot didna bathe on the Sabbath again."*

The stories which follow featuring other memorable Highlands from different folds all provide further insight into improving one's management skills. They all come from current folds with the exception of Bottle-Boy from Skye who was a contemporary of Agamemnon.

SMILIE BODACHAN

Smilie Bodachan eases an itch.

Take for instance Smilie Bodachan. Having wandered around his expansive heather clad grazing grounds in search of a suitable loofah, he discovered the ideal scratcher to be the large upright wooden pole carrying electric power cables across his land to the local community. What satisfaction after a good heave and rub against this pole. And why not? After all, he was only behaving naturally for a shaggy-coated Highland bull whose ancestors had had their choice of tree from tasty Birch to spreading Oak or massive Caledonian Pine. But here there was no tree available and the only ones in tantalising sight were densely packed and firmly protected all the way around by Forestry Commission fencing. So the pole would have to do. It was not for Smilie Bodachan the loss of dignity in the midst of his herd that would ensue from the contortions necessary to scratch the needy parts on a crumbling stone wall.

Curiously though, he came to notice that after his best scratching sessions the farmer was often late with the extra hay and cobs supply. How could Bodachan know that only something as disruptive as an electricity power cut would interfere with the normal farm routine?

Then some strangers came and worked around the pole one day much to Bodachan's interest. He saw them construct a network of barbed-wire all around the base of the pole. When they had gone he inspected their work. What a great idea, what helpful people. They had provided him with a much more satisfying scratcher, one with little sharp bits that really reached the itchy parts on his hide when he pushed against the pole.

What that friendly placid Highland bull never knew was that every time he scratched at that pole the action so rocked the electricity cables they bumped together, causing short circuiting with consequent loss of power to the surrounding community, a circumstance usually associated there with winter blizzards. Once this new cause of power failure was known neighbours would phone the farmer and tell him it was time to delouse the bull again, assuming their power cut was due to an itchy Bodachan at the pole. Yet by that time Bodachan was standing smiling in his quiet dignified way to a different community many miles north west.

MARIE BHANN

Marie Bhann rolled a wide kindly eye to greet Doug on his usual afternoon visit to the livestock. Her head followed more or less her line of gaze nodding gently, her sweeping horns weaving slow motion patterns through the air.

Something odd about Marie Bhann today.

Doug watched her try to rise to come for her feed. With some effort up went the hind-quarters swaying a little unusually, while strangely weightless hoofs repeatedly searched for a more secure position. Peculiar action this on the level part of the field. There she remained half up, her raised half quietly tilting and recovering, first in one direction then another, her head all the while doing a separate balancing act. Then down she went in a floppy heap. Her wobbly head floated around to catch Doug's eye momentarily, seeming to indicate through a dazed look that she would try again any minute to get up if he would just be patient. Up went the hind end. Again the swaying. Again the collapse. Again the unperturbed dopey reaction.

In spite of the alarming appearance of her behaviour the animal was not exhibiting pain stress or suffering. This was not part of any behaviour known to Doug even allowing for pre-calving antics so he called in the vet.

After a thorough checkover the vet remained baffled. He pronounced Marie Bhann's condition to be a great mystery, said he would return in the morning and suggested Doug keep a close watch until then. Marie Bhann seemed to hiccup and effect the nearest thing to a bovine smile these men had ever seen.

Puzzled, Doug decided to search the field for clues. The high end of the field covered in specially lush grass held the answer. Over the fence from this hilly corner was a storage unit for hay and other foodstuffs. A large drum full of glucose syrup which had passed its "use by" date had been discarded and lay behind the building near the fence. But before complete removal by lorry the container's sticky contents had leaked out, dribbled downhill, and well and truly fermented around the grass roots in the nearby section of the field. Clearly Marie Bhann had browsed this area.

No wonder she was not showing stress. She was in the merry stages of alcoholic intoxication. Relief and amusement spread a smile across Doug's face as he left to phone the vet with the news that he had discovered the source of the trouble... it was a case of RBI, that is Recent Bovine Inebriation.

Last thing that evening was a check on Marie Bhann. There she was, up on all four feet at last, but with her newborn calf well licked and suckling.

Doug fancied the wee hoofs were merry as well.

BOTTLE BOY
BY MARJORIE W MACINNES

Bottle Boy was our pet Highland cow. In addition to our main dairy herd my father had in the 1950s about twelve Highland cows and various bulls. But Bottle Boy was special.

One spring time all the Highland cows were due to calve soon when one of them, a big light coloured cow with a long shaggy coat that my father appropriately called Shaggy, met with an accident.

She fell over a cliff, rolled down a steep grassy bank and was found lying at the bottom luckily on grass and not on rocks. However she would not make any attempt to stand so she was made comfortable and for many days food and water was carried twice daily the long mile from the farmhouse. Eventually my father thought that Shaggy was strong enough to try to stand and he erected a large tripod over her, put straps of sacking round her body and gradually pulled her upright by block and tackle. This was done daily until she was strong enough to take her own weight and eventually walk. Then began the long slow walk back to the steading and there her heifer calf was born.

Shaggy was quiet and gentle and used by this time to being handled and my father thought that she would be better inside so she was tied in a wooden stall in a byre along with other cattle.

But she was unused to being inside and tied, and during the night she tried to jump out of the stall, her rope became tangled and she hanged herself.

We were all very upset and disappointed about Shaggy, particularly after the prolonged work and worry of getting her well and home and our joy in her remarkable recovery. Now we had her orphaned calf to feed.

The dairy calves were all taught to drink straight from a pail, but because this calf had got used to suckling she was fed from a bottle and teat and this became my job three times a day. And so she came to be called "Bottle Boy".

Bottle Boy grew into a good looking cow with a splendid set of horns and won prizes at the local cattle Show. She also became part of the dairy herd when required and was quite happy to be hand milked. I don't recall any of our Highland cows being milked by machine like our dairy cows.

Bottle Boy was a law unto herself. She didn't always choose to stay with the rest of the

Highlanders but she was always very aware of what was going on. My father used to go to the local distillery for a week's supply of draff every Monday morning. From wherever she happened to be on the farm, Bottle Boy watched and listened for the lorry returning home and was in the yard waiting when my father drove in. Then she would help herself to still hot fresh-from-the-mash-tun draff until we got to shovelling it into the pit in the barn.

When she wasn't needed as a dairy cow, which was most of the time, Bottle Boy lived outside all year round with the other Highlanders. In the winter time they were fed sheaves of corn – oats with the ears still on the stalks. They usually got one sheaf a day each. Their coats grew very thick and long in the winter time and they were able to live outside quite happily. Their coats always looked best in winter.

We had three bulls that I can remember. First Calum of Glenfalloch, then one whose name I cannot recall and lastly Braes of Greenock, and he was different! We never forgot him! he didn't believe in staying with his own Highland cows and a gate was no deterrent. He just put his horns through the bars, lifted it off its hinges, laid it on the ground, stepped over it and on to the next one! Even gates that had no hinges and that were held up with string and wire were no problem. More than once Braes of Greenock was found miles away striding out for the next village and the local bovine talent! He was not always easy to turn back and my father generally needed help from a neighbour. So a solution had to be found and eventually Braes of Greenock was tethered – a rope round his horns, a long wire, a swivel and a strong iron pin driven into the ground. His wandering days were over.

Braes of Greenock was our last Highland bull. After him my father decided not to buy another bull and instead shared our neighbour's Department of Agriculture bull – usually an Aberdeen Angus. So the year after the departure of Braes of Greenock all our Highlanders had cross-Aberdeen Angus calves and to our delight Bottle Boy had twins. They were only the second set of twins born on the farm so it was quite an exciting event. They were black and not quite as hairy as pure-bred Highland calves which usually look like big teddy bears. Of course Bottle Boy taught her offspring all her tricks. Before they were very old she had them eating draff off the back of the lorry while my father shovelled it into the barn.

Bottle Boy was nine years old when she had her twins and unlike the rest of the herd she was not sold but allowed to stay on the farm to enjoy a peaceful retirement.

EVER JOCK

What a loveable rogue was Jock the Highland Bull. Yet much exasperation did he cause.

He was well disposed to humans and had so mastered the art of appealing to their compassion with a seemingly penitent look of apology for his wrong doings that disposal of him elsewhere was repeatedly deferred.

At two years old Jock left his breeder and home territory to go to earn his keep. He quickly established that he was an inveterate escape genius able to travel freely whenever the notion came upon him. The difficulty for his owners was guessing when that notion might strike. Sometimes he would get a far away look in his eye standing high on a knoll gazing into the distance but mostly he gave no clues about his intentions to roam. Day after day he would be found contentedly grazing where he should be then suddenly he was gone. Finding him was rarely a problem since concerned neighbouring farmers, villagers, or astonished tourists would raise the alarm. When faced with his determined farm manager Jock passively submitted to an amicable amble home.

To begin with he used the usual methods of escape such as leaping over five-barred gates or leaning into wire fencing until it gave way. In fact the latter became his preferred method. Repairing wire fencing and loosened strainer posts spoiled by Jock soon formed a regular task for the new owners. Finally patience was tried too far when only hours after a particularly wet and cold fence repair had been completed Jock was seen to launch himself half over the repair, land astraddle the top wire, then proceed to slither back and forth as though this was a novel way of enjoying a belly scratch before he scrambled his hind legs over the now sadly sagging fence and set off. It was to be lock and key for the wayward bull now. Into a pen he went.

His new enclosure was at the gable end of a large byre which had been divided into sections such that Jock's was through three tubular steel gates each with a push-bar and snib locking mechanism designed to be stock-proof.

At last no need to keep a constant vigil; peace to get on with the daily demands of running cost effectively hill farming territory; no time consuming interruptions to collect the wandering hero. Not for long! Jock let himself out!! How he did is still a puzzle. Two hands are needed to open these gates. If animals can think then Jock was a thinker. Yet to see him cavorting around in a field of 4-hundredweight round bales of barley straw, casually tossing one high in the air for sheer fun and putting maximum spin on it for good measure, suggests more a type of exuberant mindless instinct than cool logic. But maybe his hugely enjoyed horn slashing of wayside rhododendron bushes could arguably be his deliberate way of helping with the control of their spread...if he was a thinker. Whatever his reasoning powers there was no doubting his instant affectionate recognition of the breeder of his calf-hood days whom he had last seen more than a year ago.

How hard it is to be ruthless about such a personable character as Jock. What are his progeny perpetuating one wonders. On reflection it is not surprising that Highland cattle remain a breed of individuals.

THE FINAL STRAW

Do you know anyone who was in Glenetive Forest in the 1940s?

They might have come across large shaggy beasts with massive horns. Highland steers with horns spreading eight feet from tip to tip had been running free there for nearly three years before they were gathered and put into pens in the Oban market.

Twelve of them were hustled into the sales ring, the auctioneer's hammer hammered, and they set off at speed along the only route from that ring, which led them straight into railway trucks. Soon another 163 cattle were loaded onto the railtrucks all bound for the same farm an overnight journey away in the south of Ayrshire.

The next morning the train duly pulled up at their destination. The truck doors noisily slid open. Bright daylight dazzled them after the rattling, rolling, tilting, rocking, smoke and cinders filled darkness of their night journey. There was a momentary pause whilst men and beasts waited. Then a great flurry of hoofs took the animals headlong into the station pens. The Oban buyer was there watching, ready to collect his cattle, all one-hundred-and-seventy-five of them.

In one large herd they began in orderly fashion to progress out of the station and onto the main road through the village. Man and beast were to be congratulated. Maximum co-operation was evident in this less than customary occurrence.

But a huge monster came snarling round a corner to block their way. Few of that herd would have seen a bus before, least of all these Glenetive steers. One-hundred-and-seventy-five cattle panicked, wheeled around, raced back to the station, and careered into the trucks they had just left. No safety there though since the railway porters who had to hose down the trucks in a specified time unceremoniously hunted and chased them out of the trucks and away from the station.

Panic gave way to raging terror. An awesome roaring and bellowing filled the air as cattle fled fast in all directions. Never had the main street cleared so quickly. Children were grabbed to safety. People ran for cover. Shop doors slammed shut. Shocked faces peered through windows at the sudden mayhem. They saw a bicycle complete with rider soar through the air to land on a roof. The merest flick of these Glenetive horns had freed the tips from the cycle wheels and sent the bike and rider well out of the way. The stricken cattle thundered on and in a moment were gone.

Astonished villagers thronged the street sharing their shock and assessing the damage while the farmer went for helpers to find and bring home his scattered Oban purchases, no doubt cursing under his breath at the bus driver's timing.

All but nine of that large consignment were recovered that day. The nine had cleared every obstacle they encountered in their bid for freedom including the fenced-off railway line and were last spotted well on their way to the sky line of the nearest range of open hills. Day after day search parties went out but returned with only stories that these Glenetive steers defied all known tactics of gathering and that each encounter with them showed an increase in their active aggression. A deepening fear was spreading round the community that the mere whiff of a human brought snorts and bellowing whilst the sight of one instantly provoked a full blown charge. And so it was that a week after their escape a saddened farmer summoned the guns and these Glenetive warriors met their eternal freedom.

The gathering, penning, auctioning, rail journey, and herding at their new destination they had tolerated remarkably well. But the last straw breaks the camel's back. In this instance the bus was one stress too many and animals which lack cunning can resort only to aggression, the great killer of trust, if escape is not an option. So the sadness of this story lies not in the death of those mighty horned steers but in understanding the rapid growth of a characteristic normally alien to them... total intolerance of another species. Yet they caused many people to consider how much humanity depends on co-operation. Co-operation takes time, in unquantifiable doses, irregularly and unpredictably required. The advancement of technology would do well to integrate that fact in all programmed activities. No matter how computerised and pre-programmed our lifestyle, tolerant co-operation between interactive life forms remains the way forward.

MEMORY IN FOCUS

The gusting gale force wind caught at her breath and rendered her loudest call insignificant. Visibility was poor due to mist swirling on that high exposed moor but the farmer's wife battled on calling intermittently to the cattle, hoping to bring them to the extra hay waiting for them by her pick-up truck. The wind buffeted her in the back again and again and her ears ached from the noise of the gale. Sensing there was more than the wind behind her and with rising superstition of some other presence she spun round to look. She came face to face with the force that had nudged her back...a two year old Highland heifer. This must be the heifer she had bottle fed as a calf. It had left the farm precincts more than seven months ago and of course had grown and changed considerably. Yet it resumed the close friendship with the farmer's wife immediately on hearing her voice. That evidence of memory, that recognition. . . make coping with the commercial aspects of the relationship between man and beast difficult.

ROPING TECHNIQUE

Jamie was a chubby wee calf, square in frame and sound in wind and limb. Although he had been calved rather late in the year to stand much chance against other pedigree bull calves in the Oban Show ring he was given a few weeks of "training" before being put into a field of cross-bred stots at about one year old. His training had amounted to the once weekly experience of having a pony head collar fitted and being lead to a barn to munch at an oat sheaf while his coat was combed.

Some weeks after joining the stots Jamie was missing from the field. He was discovered among the heifers nearby. He was roped and led to join the cross-bred stots in a different field. "Training" paid off! Some hours later he was again roped and returned to the stots. The following morning with the dew on the grass, he was yet again in the wrong field and this time he set off before he was properly roped.

The roping procedure consisted of approaching the desired animal behind the near side shoulder carrying about three fathoms of light rope, with a running noose at one end. After a brief preliminary stroking of the animal's back, the noose is placed over the offside horn and drawn tight up to the head, making sure not to enmesh the animal's ear. The rope is then looped, twisted once and placed over the nearside horn, and again drawn tight. Should the animal disapprove of the first manoeuvre, it will usually turn its head away from its persecutor and provided the persecutor is reasonably nippy. This presents the nearside horn in an ideal position for the second manoeuvre. On this occasion, however, Jamie set off at a gallop between manoeuvres one and two, and succeeded in getting the rope between his shoulders and straight down his back. This presents the persecutor with a straight choice, let go or be pulled. I opted for the latter alternative and to increase stability – mine – sat down on the wet grass. Some two hundred yards later, Jamie stopped at the shore, fortunately. If you have only crawled out of bed half an hour previously, this exhilarating experience can be recommended to anyone wishing to live a short life and a gay one. More spirit! (*An extract from the story In Lighter Vein, by "VWP" in the Highland Breeders' Journal 1977*).

OSSAN THE BLACK BULLOCK BY ENA MCNEILL MACDONALD

There was always something appealing about Ossan the black bullock. Every autumn he got a reprieve from the knacker because he was so happy and we wanted him to enjoy yet another summer. However, we decided it was time for him to go as he was now five and we needed some decent beef.

Ossan was driven to Lochmaddy abbatoir at lunch time and I must admit my heart was sore and I wished we could all be vegetarians. Even my mother who has always been very practical said, "*Surely you're not killing that beautiful beast?*" Well, what else can you do with a five year old bullock? I wish I had trained him to pull a cart and maybe he would take the peats home or carry bales of fodder in winter.

Late afternoon I fed the cattle. As I counted the sheaves of oats I sadly returned two to the stack and went on my way. I fed them all and as I drove back I felt sick thinking of poor Ossan. How he would like to be digging his teeth into the golden corn. I arrived home and my neighbour waved to me – there's a phone message. "*Your bullock ran away.*" I thought she was joking. "*You've to go to Lochmaddy.*" I then drove the fourteen miles to Lochmaddy to see what was happening.

Poor Ossan had jumped over the pens, swam across a loch and ran across a muddy field. I called him and I felt guilty that he still trusted me as towards me he walked and came toward the gate and cattle grid. He looked around and took his bearings and then leaped over the cattle grid heading north to the Kyles. There was no stopping him but it was near dark (February) and the ferry traffic would soon be coming. I drove past him and when he realised I was driving the familiar pick-up he followed. Sometimes he would stand and look across a loch and I would frantically shout, "*Ossan, Ossan, crios ort!*" (Gaelic for Hurry) He would then walk behind while I kept the Subaru in very low gear. A few cars passed and we must have looked strange walking in the middle of nowhere. I stopped a familiar car and the driver promised to phone one of my crofter friends to bring help.

Slowly it got dark and the traffic thickened. The black beast was very vulnerable in the darkness but he still kept following me. About five miles from Lochmaddy my friend appeared with his Landrover and box. Now, it was fine Ossan knowing my voice, but Ossan had never had a rope near him since he was a calf and that was a long time ago. I threw the sheaf on the road and while Ossan bent down to eat I lassoed his wide horns and then both of us tied him to the passing place sign (we still have passing places on the roads in North Uist). He went berserk and almost pulled the sign post out of the ground. Iain hurriedly drove the box as near as possible, all the traffic stood still and help was at hand. We tied a long rope on his horns and took the end of it into the trailer. While my helpers and I put a strain on the long rope, Iain cut him loose from the signpost, then we pulled hard and he was dragged inside. What a relief! If Ossan had left the road he would have landed in a bog in the dark and I would never have found him alive again.

It was great to see him again frolicking among the sand dunes along with the other bullocks.

The story of Ossan doesn't really end. On Friday 22 April Ossan will start his long journey to Germany. Herr Dill has offered him a permanent home. He left North Uist in mid-March to join other Highlanders destined for Germany. Mr Dill has promised me he won't kill him so if any of you sentimental readers ever visit Germany spare a thought for Ossan. I think he would like to hear a Scottish voice and especially a Gaelic one." (HCS Newsletter 1988) with kind Permission of the Highland Cattle Society

CHAPTER 4: HARDINESS

CHAPTER 4: HARDINESS

HIGHLAND V LOWLAND BULL

'Tis on the heather ridge I was born, 'tis on the heather ridge I was born, 'tis on the heather ridge I was born, And on the milk of a beloved cow was reared, said the Highland bull.

'Tis on the floor of the big house I was born, 'tis on the floor of the big house I was born, 'tis on the floor of the big house I was born, And on honey and beer and wine and grasses was reared, said the Lowland bull.

The Highland bull turned on the Lowland bull and killed him.[1]

LOSS OF HARDINESS

Mutterings that too much protection from the elements and an absence either of need or opportunity to forage would be the downfall of the breed were to be heard even before the new methods of intensive farming were first taking hold in the 1840s. Politics and commerce might underlie some of the worry but not all of it.

Writing about the great Falkirk market mid-nineteenth century Thomas Farrall said of the Highland cattle: *"every one of these animals had its predestined course; the choicest duns, creams, the reds and brindles were bought up by agents to grace the parks of English nobles, where the great variety and contrast in colour had a grand and imposing appearance. Many dealers preferred the black type, as being more hardy, so that there was generally a sufficient demand for all colours. The young six-quarter was destined to clean up rough pastures and eat a little straw in Clydesdale, Dumfriesshire, Cumberland and the neighbouring districts, and well it throve on such fare; the older of the small cattle were taken to Brough Hill in Westmorland, a very important fair with dealers, because it was said to be attended by more gentlemen's bailiffs than any other in the United Kingdom; the finest West Highland heifers found their way into Yorkshire and the Vale of the Tees, where the short-horn had its origin; and what steers were not required by graziers in the home districts of Argyll, Perth, Dumbarton, Ayr, and Fife, were usually consigned to Leicester, Northampton, and Buckingham."*[2]

Evidently there was a genuine demand last century for the animals on account of their aesthetic appeal.

"From their very high feeding they lost some of those qualities which are esteemed in Highland cattle yet they still maintained their full beauty and symmetry." reported an early issue of the *Scottish Farmer Album*, later printing *"The closing of the Herd Book and the consequent in-breeding which followed has, despite the more beefy formation attained, deprived the breed to some extent of its hardy characteristics. Colour of coat, which in former days was mostly dark brindled, is getting lighter every year, to suit the parks and policies in which the breed now has its habitat. This change in coat is not all for the best. With all these harmful influences at work the Highlander now seems to be an irregular breeder, and the rearing of the calves is a much harder task than it used to be."*

In fact the Herd Book was only suspended during the war years, not closed, and there is now better understanding of how both overfeeding and underfeeding affect regularity of breeding.

The 1937 issue of the *Scottish Farmer Album* printed "*Too much favouring the yellow Highland cattle has resulted in coats getting too soft. Coarse longer hair as on the darker cattle gives better protection from the wind, rain, cold and wet.*"

Controversy persists today over how best to ensure that the all round hardiness of the breed is retained in full measure. Had it not been for the extra numbers in the parks and Stately homes habitat the breed might not have survived a hundred years of low commercial standing no matter what colour or texture the coat.

Preserving the quintessentials of the breed is likely to prove difficult were total stock levels ever reduced to the count of head found only in the protected environment of parks. The older farmers mid twentieth century reflected that even those in farms were being fed differently, as the increasing mechanisation of land management was unsuited to utilising awkward rough land often next to the machairs, which when worked manually, had yielded a course meadow hay with rushes intermixed. This hay was believed to be flavoursome, hard, and good for the digestion of the bull at the start of his working season.

Overfed underactive Highland cattle of leisure will lose their hardiness if by hardiness is meant their semi-wild metabolism with its seasonal variability along with a high sensory alertness and individual ability to forage. These features will decrease in time if the breed is reared continuously in a protected highly comfortable domestic environment on a rich concentrates-full diet. It is no secret that bulls reared to win Show awards are more accustomed to being looked after than to faring for themselves. Consequently if put to the hill they take some time to adapt to the harsher conditions where they may not be reliable stockgetters. "*To match the Show bull to the truth – the breed standard – may I, as a novice breeder suggest one modification to the Oban Spring Bull Sale? It is that all entrant animals be brought to Oban five weeks earlier, and that they be turned out on to the surrounding hillsides for a month – perhaps, if local farmers cared to cooperate, they could be fed the odd bales of hay – and then brought in, to be pampered to their hearts' content for the week before the Show. Nobody could then doubt that they would be fit to bear the coveted title of the most splendid cattle in the world – the Highlander.*"[3]

Undoubtedly the sensory alertness in Highlands is largely due to the hard environment in which they generally have been maintained. The need to find for survival what advantage they can from natural wind-breaks, vegetation, and source of water, has retained keen levels of instincts, long memory, and a strong sense of direction. The sense of direction may well come from a combination of sensitive olfactory system with memorised associations.

ADAPTABILITY OF 20TH CENTURY HIGHLANDS

Contemporary breeders tell credible accounts of Highland cattle memory spanning two years, and more. Even today when cattle are transported in vehicles which give them no chance of seeing where they are going their homing instinct seems every bit as strong as it was reputed to have been in droving times. Drovers' accounts agree that great vigilance was necessary over the first few days and nights of the journey so that no cattle were lost due to their strong homing instinct which was accurate within about a twenty mile radius. Recently a few Highlands which were sold locally and transported by float (livestock lorry) to the new farm decided after a fortnight or so, when the new owner thought they were well settled in, to make their way home over 7 miles of railways, rivers, and ploughed fields. The question arises how might they have fared over 20 miles.

The last drove out of Knapdale was on tarmac road in the 1920s and the worst problem came not from unfit cattle but from cars forcing the cattle off the road. Marion Campbell of Kilberry recalls that the last drove she knew about took place in 1939 when her brother's farm manager, the late Donald Gilchrist, walked a drove of cross-bred cattle 57 miles to Oban with two overnight halts. The day after their leisurely three day drove the cattle were sold in good condition. It was not unusual for cattle bought at Oban in her grandfather's time, she reminisced, to be shipped to Kilberry and made to swim ashore.

In 1965 three Highlands swam the quarter mile of sea from the Island of Ulva to the mainland to attend the Mull and Morvern Agricultural Show where they took first place in their class. It was considered that swimming caused the cattle less stress than being loaded on and off a boat.

In 1981 thirty Highlands walked some 200 miles from Skye to Crieff in John Keay's reconstructed drove. Although the animals had the advantage of specialist feed stuffs, which pleased the officers from the Society for the Prevention of Cruelty to Animals who kept an eye on the venture, these modern animals took the journey easily and *"waded burns and swam rivers without objection."*[4]

To conclude these few examples of twentieth century adaptability and endurance in the breed, none of which were from 'Parks habitats', Pibroch of Achnacloich speaks out:

"I spent my youth at Achnacloich then was sent to Appin to earn my living. This was tough terrain and you had to be fit to survive in those hills. Next I was taken to Oban and imprisoned among a large number of bulls like myself. I didn't enjoy my day at Oban. There was lots of noise among these humans. Many stared at me so I just stared back. The following evening I found myself on board a ship beside a lovely brindle heifer. I fell head over heels in love with her but when my new human friends saw what was going on we were separated. The journey lasted nine and a half hours through that night and eventually I got to walk on dry land by midday. I was in a field in Kyles North Uist with about twelve females all looking shyly at me. This place was very different to any other I had seen. There was the sea, masses of sand, long hard marram grass, no trees, and no high hills.

My first meal was a strange one. We got sheaves of corn full of oats and rye and I really enjoyed that and I got as much as I could eat. Life in the Hebrides was very different. I had to get used to the strong winds, and luckily my dossan gave my eyes great protection. Lots of humans came to see me. My kind hadn't been on the island for a long time and the young generation had never seen a bull like me. One little boy got scared and shouted rudely that I was a monster without eyes, and another one called me a buffalo.

My only unhappy time was the spring and summer of 1986. Food was scarce and none could be bought from the mainland. Some hay came from Canada, I heard at £200 a ton. We didn't like it and it made us feel a bit sick so we had to survive on the hill. The month of May didn't have one dry day and that was when Chernobyl exploded. My female friends were very unhappy, they were trying to feed their calves and no way could any concentrated foods be carried to us. We all ate lots of wet grass and heather and our coats were wet for five weeks. It must have been mid July before there was any decent grass. The ploughed fields were so waterlogged that the mallard ducks swam there feeding on the newly planted oat seeds. Lots of the island cattle were miserable, one herd tried to survive on the moor but they kept getting stuck in the mud and their Simmental Sire had to be brought home and rehoused. Many calves died throughout the island. Three of my own cows died. Fionnghail jumped a fence hoping to find better grass and she got caught on the hind leg. The biggest tragedy was Lady Ruadh. She got tangled in wire and my mistress cried for three days. Nobody looked happy. The lightning struck and Proiseag died instantly.

In the autumn of 1986 I met Myra of Balure, my shipboard sweetheart. We knew each other immediately and since then I have hardly left her side. In May 1987 she gave me a handsome son called Marrival. Marrival is a Norse name and is also the name of the hill where we spend most of the summer. All the hills in North Uist end with 'VAL', evidence of Norse occupation.

I have spent four years in North Uist so now feel I must move on."[5]

CATTLE CIRCUMSTANCES IN FORMER TIMES

Let us now cast a comparative glance at cattle circumstances in former times.

Climatic conditions throughout Britain spanning roughly from the 1400s to the end of the 1700s were so cold and wet that winter feeding of livestock seems to have been more difficult then than previously. Consecutive poor summers hardly allowed crops to grow and famine frequently threatened the human population too. For much of Scotland wintry weather had scarcely lifted before setting in again. Consequently over centuries of scant feeding Highland cattle reduced in size and productivity. Their survival, as with wild animals, depended on an ability to maximise the value of any available feeding, particularly in the non-winter months. When too undernourished reproduction was suspended. Plentiful supply of appropriate feeding allows growth to full potential and regular breeding. Too much artificially rich feeding also inhibits breeding ability but recovery seems slower and less certain than with undernourished animals back on adequate rations. But the increased size and productivity of 1990s Highlands compared with those of 300 years ago cannot be disputed. Clearly the breed responds to favourable conditions by increasing in size. Return to a stature greater than that of both today and 'the lean centuries' however, will take more than a few generations of well-fed animals, but the possibility remains that genes controlling optimum size from the ancient larger wild forebears of the 'little Kyloe' might surface again resulting in massive bulls and longer legged cows, were the environment to remain steadily suitable for a few hundred years.

About 200 years ago the shape of steers, oxen as they were called, was bigger and beefier the more plough and cart pulling they did. In the nineteenth century it was understood that for an ox to attain his full size he needed to work for at least two years after having started at about 24 to 26 months old. At the Dumfries Agricultural Show in 1830 a bull drew a waggon with more than two tons of coals about 12 miles even up a 1 in 8 hill with a broken axle-tree preventing wheel turn. (breed of bull not known) Many nineteenth century farmers continued to favour their oxen for ploughing rather than horses because on stony ground they were more steady in their pull, they cost less to feed and sold well for beef at the end of their ploughing years. "*Better a dead Ox than a dead Horse*" was a saying of these times. Oxen can "*work 2 hours longer in yoke than horses without ill effect, cost less to keep and are not temperamental like a horse being driven by the whip.*"[6] Further advantage was that when the plough stuck, oxen would stand still where horses were more prone to struggle. "*Two pairs of well trained oxen could plough a whole acre of summer fallow in one day*" in 1793.[7]

In Midlothian late eighteenth century when "*An acre of whins could keep six horses for 4 months on twenty minutes bruising daily*"[8] what was fed to cattle one wonders. The following notes answer to some extent. They refer to farm husbandry in Scotland before the new methods of agriculture were widespread or fully operational and productive.

18TH CENTURY CATTLE CONDITIONS

Unless otherwise indicated notes on eighteenth century conditions for cattle are drawn from the *Statistical Account for Scotland.*

In the 1770s Highland bullocks were slaughtered about their fourth or fifth year and even on a small farm there were likely to be four or five cows and their followers i.e. a calf, a one year old, a two year old, and a three year old for every cow. Cows were sometimes under shelter in very severe weather but much livestock remained out all winter. By the end of the winter cattle were so starved they followed the plough to eat any upturned grass roots. Very little feeding was available for the cows in shelter although the practice of making hay was beginning to spread and some farms sowed corn on exhausted land to make a winter feeding called 'rush'.

From the account books of a Badenoch farm it seems that about 50 lbs of rush hay was all that could be offered per cow over the whole winter. Less 'well-fed' cows had to be helped out of the cowsheds to spring pastures so weak were they from starvation. Being bled regularly to help feed crofters in times of scarcity to make the blood and oatmeal puddings known as black puddings further drained their strength.[9]

A five year old bullock was said to be no bigger than a Guernsey but the sweet and succulent quality of the beef was probably due partly to the fact that it was largely new flesh made up from the richness of summer pastures after long months of deprivation.[9]

In 1744 one laird in the Glenorchy area lost *"510 hides of black cattle"* when they were housed over winter with no *"provender"*.

In Moray half-starved black cattle, sometimes tied to a stake, broke free and damaged the corn.

In coastal communities of the North West Highlands cows in the byre might get raw or parboiled seaweed, kale, cabbage stalks, dried fish bones.

Of an estimated 2,000 cows in North Uist no more than 300 were exported annually due to death from starvation and 'distempers'. Their winter and spring fodder was corn straw and seaweed cast up on the shore by storms.

In the Trossachs when the snow covered the ground the cattle were fed with "hay of the natural grass produced on the bogs and cut down in August". They had plenty of shelter in woods of oak ash and birch.

The mortality rate in Lewis rose as high as 1 in every 5. Many cows calved every second year while heifers did not have their first calf till about 5 years.[10]

In Skye if the cows calve before 1st March it's sometimes 4 to 6 weeks before they have sufficient milk to feed the calves.[11]

In the Dunkeld area calves were often fed hay tea...
5 pounds good hay, 6 pints water, boil till about 4 pints of decoction. Give hay-tea and 2 pints of milk approximately for Highland calves per day.

Wet hay and lack of water can make calves ill; so also does too much cold and wet for too long; and a remedy for both that and passing blood in the urine was offered by Duncan Stewart (Kintyre) in the *Transactions of the Highland Society of Scotland 1801... "Old Highland remedy was to prepare a gruel thickened with mashed greens to which was added a quantity of tallow. This mix was called* ***Brochancal****. It more frequently killed than cured!"*

Late in the eighteenth century one method of rearing calves in Ross-shire was to allow them one calf to a cow (not as in some areas one calf to two cows) then keep them in herds of 80 to 100 in a grass enclosure getting turnips in winter and hay and straw in frost. In early summer they went 40 miles to their summer hill pastures until October. They were sold at 4 years.[8]

In Ross-shire in the summer the custom was to send off most of the cattle to remote glens for grazings *"where they lose many of them"*.

Summer in Stirlingshire: many tradesmen and manufacturers who still kept cows sent their children to take their animals grazing along the roadside. *"These milk cows in general are the breed of Highland bulls."*

Before the discovery of making hay, feeding livestock in winter was a recurring problem. *"Those which survived starved through the winter on mashed whin and coarse grass; the others were weeded out in the Autumn slaughter and the carcase salted for preservation. The need to have sufficient livestock to make up the winter losses and to provide power for ploughing and cartage encouraged overstocking and this in turn perpetuated the winter killing."*[12]

19TH CENTURY CATTLE CONDITIONS

Severe starvation in winter could be avoided if the coarse grasses were made into hay wrote Rev. Dr. Walker in 1801. *"Cattle avoid the following when green but will if driven by great need take them well dried as a coarse form of hay:* ***Scirpus cespitosus*** *(Deer's Hair),* ***Nardus stricta*** *(Bent),* ***Aira coerulea*** *(Fly Bent),* ***Juncus articulatus*** *(Spret),* ***Juncus squarrosus*** *(Wire Bent), and many species of* ***Carex*** *(One-pointed grass). Cattle will eat these when very young spring shoots are beginning to rise but leave them in summer.*

Whins brought from England and Ireland make useful fodder and windbreak, while broom, a native of Scotland up to 600 feet above sea level can be eaten and also gives shelter. (*Transactions of the Highland Society of Scotland*)

In Kintail Ross-shire grass was *"cut in August and made into ropes 2 fathoms long, twisted two fold; thus compressed it requires less room in barns and is easier to transport to glens in stormy weather for weak cattle.* (*Statistical Account for Scotland*)

To let clover and rye grass grow in the fields winter herding on the common in Lanarkshire was adopted. Then it was found more advantageous to tether cows on their grass fields than to send them to the common. An acre of sown 'tethering grass' could be let for a good price.
When fern is cut green and properly dried both horses and cows eat it. Chickweed was washed and fed to the cows.[13]

In Lewis by the second half of the nineteenth century fewer cattle were kept and most were housed over the winter months. They were given more food such as straw, boiled chaff, occasionally a sheaf of unthreshed corn, potato peelings, herring bones and dried cod bones, crabs, and water from boiled fish.[10]

In 1850 Captain Mathieson of Shinness lost 200 cattle in Spring and Colonel Sutherland of Culnailly buried 18 milk cows and one bull because of starvation.[14]

"Herds of Highland cattle passed this way and when the far travelled animals showed signs of fatigue it was no uncommon thing to see one of the men who carried a bagpipe play some lively air as he marched in front of the drove. The animals seemed to enjoy the music and evidently appreciated this relief to the tediousness of the journey, by walking, as they often would, with a brisk step, whilst some of them that had lain down in the road would quickly rise at the novel far sounding strains." [15]

Six a.m. North West Coast of Scotland about 1850:...sixty cows and sixty calves were all bellowing their hardest after having been separated for the twelve hours of the night...assisted by some twenty herds and milkers screaming and howling, they made uproar enough to alarm any stranger just waking from sleep. This was a twice a day arrangement.

"There was a dyke about one hundred yards long between the entrance-gates at the bottom of the lawn and the Allt Glas burn which kept the cows and calves separate, to the great indignation of both parties, who bellowed out their minds pretty plainly.

Domhnall Donn (Brown Donald), the head cowman, brought his wailing friends the cows to the west side of the wall, and his subordinates brought the calves from their woody bedrooms where they had passed the night on the east side. And then began an uproar of '*Are you there, my darling?*' '*Oh yes, mother dear, wild for my breakfast.*' Then the troupe of milkmaids entered among the mob of bawling cows by one of the small calf-gates in the wall.

They carried their pails and three-legged little stools and buarachs (hobbles) of strong hair rope, with a loop at one end and a large button on the other. The button was always made of rowan-tree wood, so that milk-loving fairies might never dare to keep from the pail the milk of a cow whose hind-legs were buarach bound.

All was soon ready to begin. A young helper stood at each gate with a rowan switch to flick back the over-anxious calves till old Domhnall sang out, looking at a cow a dairymaid was ready to milk, named, perhaps, Busdubh (Black Muzzle), '*Let in Busdubh's calf,*' who was quite ready at the wicket. Though to our eyes the sixty black calves were all alike, the helpers switched away all but young Busdubh, who sprang through the wicket; after a moment's dashing at the wrong cow by mistake, and being quickly horned away, there was Busdubh Junior opposite to its Mother's milker sucking away like mad for its supply, while the milkmaid milked like mad also, to get her share of it. The calf, I suspect often got the lesser half, for the dairy people liked to boast of their heaps of butter and cheese, leaving the credit or discredit of the yearly drove of young market cattle to Domhnall and his subordinates. I have seen young Busdubh getting slaps in the face from its enemy the milker, who thought she was getting less than her share of the spoil; and then calfy was dragged to the wicket and thrust out, and perhaps Smeorach's (Thrush's) calf halloaed for next. This uproar lasted from six till nine, when, justice having been dispensed to all concerned, Donald and company drove the cows away to their pastures, and the junior helpers removed the very discontented calves to their quarters till near 6 p.m. when the same operation was repeated.[16]

Opinions varied about rearing calves. Veal production was never widely practised in Scotland. The two main approaches to calf rearing were:

1 calves separate from dams and allowed to them for a short time 3 times per day until old enough to be at grass themselves.

2 dams and young together...but both dam and young become very wild especially when allowed full liberty. Milk dries with failing pastures so weaning is easy in October and the cows seldom suffer sore udders since temperature in October is low. [2]

A report of wild habits of kyloes in old birchwood on the edge of Ettrick Forest, Roxburghshire 1850s:

"Here the kyloes remained for many months together, sometimes followed by their calves, seeing nobody but an occasional shepherd, and got almost like wild animals, acting exactly like these Chillingham cattle when they caught sight of us, and we were glad to beat a speedy retreat before they came close enough to make their final rush; which indeed they had done some time before, knocking down a man and endangering his life, had not his cries speedily brought the much needed help, which happened most providentially to be at no very great distance."[17]

Special arrangements were often made for wintering Highland bulls used by crofting communities.

"Bulls were supplied from the big-farm folds, of which in those days there were some very good ones. No money passed. The farmer loaned the bull to the township in return for a specified number of days' work to be provided by the crofters at harvest, peat-cutting, sheep-shearing etc.

The wintering of the bull was also an obligation on the township. At the end of harvest a meeting was held to decide whether the crop that year was a big one, a poor one, or a middling one. On that decision depended the daily ration of the bull throughout the winter: he was fed in accordance with the bountifulness (or otherwise) of Providence.

The exact measure of the bull's big, little, or medium ration was governed by the ***Sugan.*** *The* ***Sugan*** *was a short rope made of pleated bent-grass. It had a loop at one end. Towards the other end there were three knots, each about six inches from the other. The obligation to provide the day's ration for the bull fell on each crofter in the township in turn. Each evening, today's supplier would pass on the township* ***Sugan*** *to tomorrow's supplier. The ration was in the form of sheaves of* ***Coirce-Beag****. The* ***Sugan*** *was stretched on the ground. Sheaves were laid on it to the number which would allow of the burden being tightened by the* ***Sugan*** *to the appropriate knot for that year. But, as everyone knows who has tied a burden in that fashion, the degree of security of the load will depend on the degree of tightness of the rope. Therefore, when loop and knot met, if the burden was still loose – in other words, if you hadn't put enough sheaves in (or more plainly still,* ***if you were trying to cheat the bull)*** *– the chances were that some of the sheaves would fall out before you reached the bull-house with your burden. What clearer evidence of mean dishonesty and disgrace:* ***you had lost sheaves from the Sugan****.*

And so to this day in the island a man is well spoken of (or not so well) according as his forebears were honest (or not so honest) with the feeding of the bull.

"Now, " concluded the old man, (who gave the story to the writer) "you will understand my answer to your question about Norman: 'Och! he may have his good points and his bad; but indeed I never heard that one of his kind ever lost a sheaf from the ***Sugan****."*[18]

In some areas in the past the Highland bull was shipped to a nearby island and left pretty much to fend for himself until next required. That he remained manageable in such circumstances surely points to the natural docility of the breed. The following story suggests a fairly obliging animal but perhaps highlights more the hardiness of the crofter than the bull.

Certain Lewis landlords underestimated the strength of feeling they disturbed by trying to remove the township bull from summer grazings which had been used by the community for centuries. Instead of building special bull parks many crofting communities shipped their bull to a nearby island.

"In 1885 Lewis landlords chartered a steamer The Norseman of Glasgow to remove crofters' livestock from small off-shore islands that had for generations been used for summer grazings.

A landing party of six (two gamekeepers, a river-watcher, two shepherds and a crofter) removed the Brenish township bull from the island of Mealista. With bull on board, the Norseman steamed north to the island of Pabaidh Mor where nine cattle and nine sheep were removed onto the steamer. It then proceeded to the island of Vuia Mhor to remove the Aird Uig township bull but by then the alarm had been raised and the Lewis crofters from Valtos and Kneep successfully intercepted the raiders and recovered their animals. They also 'captured' the occupants of The Norseman, and took them to a point near Valtos where the captives were released to find their boat (small one from the steamer) lying a quarter of a mile inland."[19]

"The island of Berneray in Loch Roag is cut off by a deep channel some hundreds of yards wide, through which the tide runs rapidly and strongly. Over this channel the people of the island swim their cattle at high or low tide in order to avoid the worst currents. The calves are generally carried across in boats; but the calves are in a hurry to follow their mothers, and the mothers are in a hurry to be over the sound and on the moorland, and despite all precautions they dash into the sea and are out in the current, the calves rushing after them and struggling bravely with this new element. The masterful strength of the tide gives full scope to the strong experienced cow, the weak inexperienced calf is swept away like a leaf. Now is the time for the men in the boats – they pursue the calves over the stream and either draw them into the boats or lead them to land. Calves and cows having reached the shore safely, they shake the water from their shaggy backs, rush up the rocky beach, and are off to the moorland and their own pastures."[1]

20TH CENTURY RESPONSIBILITY

How well would today's Highlands cope with that? Those that would manage as well as their forebears are likely to belong to the breeders who believe it is vital to maintain hardiness in the breed and who therefore avoid easy feeding methods in convenient parks or roofed cattle courts. The harshness of circumstances in bygone times provided a regular and natural cull of weak stock which, distressing though it must have been to the economics of the breeders' livelihood, does not happen today. Instead the cattle breeder must cull poor stock.

The advance of genetic science places increasing responsibility on individual breeders to understand the full extent to which behaviour, conformation, colour and all characteristics of future Highland cattle depend on their procedures of stock management today.

REFERENCES:

1 *Carmina Gadelica* Vol 4
2 *Transactions of the Highland and Agricultural Society of Scotland* Volume VIII fourth series
3 *Highland Breeders Journal 1977* extract from article by VWP
4 *Highland Drove*, by J Keay
5 Condensed from a story by Ena McNeill
6 *Statistical Account of Scotland* Volume 3
7 *Statistical Account of Scotland* Volume 14
8 *Scottish Country Life*, by A Fenton
9 *Everyday Life on an Old Highland Farm*, by I F Grant
10 *Lewis – A History of the Island*, by D Macdonald
11 *Report on the Hebrides 1764 – 1771*, by the Rev J Walker
12 *Development of the West of Scotland 1750 – 1960*, by A Slaven
13 *Scottish Farming*, by J A Symen
14 *Source Book of Scottish Economic and Social History*, by Campbell and Dow
15 *Romantic Richmondshire 1897*, by H Speight
16 *100 Years in the Highlands*, by O McKenzie
17 Dr. J A Smith in *The Proceedings of the Society of Antiquaries of Scotland* Volume 19
18 A condensed extract from Colin Macdonald's *Highland Journey*, by kind permission of his family, Dr M Newton and Mr W Y Macdonald, reprinted by Mercat Press in *Life in the Highlands and Islands of Scotland*
19 Extracted from *The Crofters' War*, by Dr I M M MacPhail

Courtesy of Joan Faithfull

About as unpredictable as the weather is the specific allocation of genes from the possible dominant, recessive, incomplete recessive, and potential mutant, combined random package inherited from both parents. Glorious uncertainty is a feature of breeding livestock.

CHAPTER 5:
THE LUCK FACTOR IN BREEDING SCHEMES

CHAPTER 5:
THE LUCK FACTOR IN BREEDING SCHEMES

APPLY SCIENCE WITH CAUTION

Scientific aid in strictly controlled breeding schemes can go some way towards eliminating the chance or luck factor. Total predictability of progeny types though is still beyond our grasp.

As veterinary science probes ever deeper into biological mysteries the language used to describe its findings can seem remote to those engaged in the everyday practicalities of rearing stock. Some terms relevant to recurring queries on breeding for specific traits – whether cosmetic like coat-colour and horn shape, or commercial such as fast growth and heavy muscling – follow, presented as the result of having fused discussions with contemporary Highland cattle breeders, geneticists and veterinary research personnel, general practice vets and the findings of various documented research programmes. The information here which is far from comprehensive seeks to highlight merely a few of the complexities involved when one sets about trying to breed consistently a particular type of livestock. Unexpected results in breeding schemes can be very disappointing and uncomfortably expensive, so the more understanding of the essential processes one has, the more realistic will be one's expectations. Specialist advice on genetics from professional sources is increasingly necessary for the average livestock breeder to keep pace with new reproduction methods which of course force choice. Even the widespread use of artificial insemination, available from Highland bulls since 1964, invites speculation and concern as to how clearly understood the long-term implications are of relying on the convenience and reasonable predictability of repeated use of too few sires. Variety of sires is important from many points of view and Animal Breeding organisations continue to work towards improving what semen banks can offer.

"*All breeds of cattle are changing all the time and it seems a good idea to preserve the genetic variation that exists so that at any time in the future we can go back to it. We can never be absolutely certain that we are breeding the right type of cattle*" (Dr. K. O'Connor in 1969...quoted in *The Ark* 1992).

"*In a breed with a small population there is an increased chance of the loss of genetic material by selection of preferred types by breeders, by inbreeding, and by genetic drift. These effects can be reduced by using a very high ratio of males, or possibly by random breeding, but such policies are not acceptable to breeders. Thus it is essential to complement the maintenance of live populations with the storage of frozen semen and embryos. These serve as an insurance, both against a change of type or function within the breed, and against the possible extinction of the live population.*" (Dr L Alderson in *The Ark* 1992, magazine of the Rare Breeds Survival Trust).

VETERINARY TERMINOLOGY

GENES carry the characteristics (traits) of the animal. Genes dictate the functioning of the entire animal, a task so immense that thousands (over 200,000 in cattle) of genes are needed and delegated specific jobs such as for example controlling the growth of the lower jaw, the length of the back, the density of the coat, the angle of the joints, fertility, muscle distribution and so on. Genes are found in particular arrangements on tiny structures called chromosomes, present in every cell nucleus.

CHROMOSOMES Each different chromosome complete with clusters of genes is found in like pairs (30 different pairs in cattle) in all body cells but singly in the sex cells (gametes, i.e. sperm and eggs). At fertilisation the single chromosomes in the sperm team up with the corresponding single chromosomes in the egg to form the normal like-pairs of chromosomes for the body cells of the embryo calf.

MUTANT GENES Normal genes can undergo a permanent chemical change in composition which causes a change in whichever characteristics they control. The changed gene is called a mutant gene. Mutant genes can cause an animal to look different from expectations or to function differently. Such animals are called sports, freaks, or mutants. Sometimes the presence of a mutant gene is not evident from the outward appearance of the animal but may account for its disappointingly different progeny.

GAMETES When the sex cells (gametes i.e. sperms & eggs) are being formed they receive only single sets of chromosomes...not pairs as in all body cells...but occasionally this process (called meiosis) malfunctions in a way which scrambles the genes forcing them to assemble on their chromosomes in a new order from the predetermined one. If fertilisation of such sperms or eggs takes place the resulting calves may appear to lack some of the expected parental characteristics yet still have the potential when mature to produce offspring endowed with the missing traits, since the scrambled genes are entirely normal.

ALLELE is the name for a gene when there are alternative genes present for the same trait, e.g. three alleles (genes) for coat-colour, two alleles for horn/hornless.

RECESSIVE GENES can be thought of as 'lazy' because they will only do their delegated job of control when there is no other gene to do it for them. In other words where there are two or more genes (alleles) allocated the same task the genes which function are called **Dominant** whilst those which remain inactive are called **Recessive**.

Research has identified many dominant and many recessive genes along with the traits they control. A straight-forward example often quoted is that when both an allele for 'horns' and an allele for 'hornless (polled) ' are present the polled gene functions while the 'horns' gene does nothing. The polled gene is said to be dominant. The 'horns' gene is said to be recessive to the polled.

Progeny from a mating of a polled parent and a horned parent would be polled with a recessive gene (allele) for horns.

Some Recessive genes can be **Incompletely Recessive** which results in partial expression of its trait. Since only one gene dictates the horns-or-no-horns outcome, and not hundreds of genes as is the case for most traits of economic value, it is easy to predict with reasonable accuracy when horns will or will not appear from matings of known pedigree stock.

Where (a) several or (b) hundreds of genes deal with one task such as for example (a) coat-colour or (b) efficiency in food conversion rates, precisely which dominant genes are likely to dominate is more difficult to determine, (see Blending under Heritability p112) consequently accurate predictability in breeding schemes is less reliable.

Add to this the possible hidden presence of a mutant gene...that is a recessive mutant gene, and the potential for variations in progeny becomes more clearly understood.

To look at your best livestock and realise that they can have any or all of unknown recessive, mutant, and 'scrambled' genes is to understand why the most experienced cattle breeders insist that no matter how much pedigree and performance information is computerised, analysed, assessed, there will always be an element of luck about achieving consistently high outcome of the desired type of animal.

The cost of laboratory analysis of the genetic content in each of your selected animals, even were such readily available and affordable, would not offer a quick elimination of all chance elements in the whole reproduction process.

Currently the only known and practised route for the average livestock breeder towards predictable breeding is to develop a homozygous (see below) and BLUP Recorded herd (see p116). If you are setting out from the start to do this by buying a nucleus breeding herd from compatible bloodlines at sales it is likely to take a human working-lifetime perhaps two, even when aided with maximum pedigree records traceable, and a lot of luck.

GENOTYPE This refers to the genes 'package' your animals carry and can not be seen with a look at the livestock in their fields. Their physical appearance is the outward expression of their genetic inheritance (package) and is referred to as **Phenotype**. So phenotype you can see, genotype you can't.

PHENOTYPE This refers to the physical appearance of genetic inheritance. If several of your stock have long backs and very deep ribs, they are phenotypical for these traits.

HOMOZYGOTE An animal which has two identical genes for the same trait, such as two for horned or two for polled, is said to be homozygous with regard to that trait. The single chromosomes in the sire's sperm and the dam's egg must have their allocation of genes for the homozygous traits arranged in exactly the same way so that at fertilisation the paired chromosomes have those genes at exactly similar places. Animals with homozygous traits breed those characteristics predictably. Clearly the time-scale in achieving homozygosity in breeding cattle, where only one calving is usual per cow per year, is long-term particularly if many homozygous traits are being established. Disasters such as major disease nationally or company financial collapse can wipe out a lifetime's work in one breeding season. More simply small-scale setbacks in the programme can arise because either cow or bull might have defied the fencing system and mated elsewhere causing the breeder to discard from his breeding herd all progeny ensuing from such unplanned activity if the resulting unknown quantity of variability is to be kept to a minimum.

HETEROZYGOTE Heterozygote animals harbour unseen potential for variability due to the fact that they carry two genes that are different for the one characteristic. The heterozygote in regard to horns has both one gene (allele) for polled and one gene (allele) for horned. When two heterozygotes mate their progeny multiply their possible but not visually evident factor of recessive and or mutant genes. For example if a heterozygote bull and a heterozygote cow are successfully mated eight times they will produce;

A: four animals with genes of unknown potential;

B: two animals which will breed true to the male parent;

C: two animals which will breed true to the female parent.

Which of these eight calves belongs to A B or C will possibly only become clear when they produce many of their own offspring. Even if one known homozygous parent was used the predictable genetic makeup of the eight will remain obscure.

HYBRID VIGOUR This is sometimes called **Heterosis** and refers to the fact that when two very unlike parents are mated lots of pairs of unlike genes occur and all the dominant alleles from both parents show in the progeny. Huge variation results if breeding from such progeny.

SOME BREEDING METHODS

INBREEDING A short-cut, fraught with risks, to developing a homozygous herd is the deliberate use of inbreeding with the intention of concentrating good qualities and exposing weak ones. Great care is vital however because prolonged inbreeding can cause degeneration which may show first with poor mothering, reduced milk production, low fertility, weak calves or slow growth in the young. Some genotypes respond better than others to inbreeding but identifying which of your own stock these might be is difficult. Inbreeding can and has been used to good effect in concentrating particular qualities, but the process usually requires ruthless culling.

The order of closeness is:

1 Full brother to full sister; parent to offspring.

2 Half brother to half sister: grandparent to grandchild.

3 Nephew to aunt; niece to uncle.

4 First cousins.

Inbreeding will show up recessive mutation. Most recessive genes will have appeared by the fourth generation of this process although instances of 'throwback' characteristics can appear from as far back as 20 generations ago (throwback is sometimes called **Reversion**). Reasonably fixed genetic change takes on average about ten generations.

The first inbred generation can be expected to show considerable variation due to the recessive genes gaining opportunity to express themselves. The second inbred generation should produce the true breeding type.

"*We have been conditioned by moral attitudes to reject incestuous breeding methods, but the danger that we should be more concerned to avoid is the increase in homozygosity resulting from inbreeding, which reduces genetic variability and so leads to genetic wastage. It is essential to maintain each breed in sufficient numbers to minimise the risk of genetic wastage and genetic drift.*" (Dr L Alderson in *The Ark* 1992.)

"*If crossing inbred lines use an inbred male on a female out of crossed inbred lines rather than vice versa; a male inbred for good qualities will breed better than he looks, whereas an outbred male is less likely to breed as well as his looks suggest.*" (Sir J Hammond in *Hammond's Farm Animals*) This is worth considering when looking at bulls in the competitive Show-ring as opposed to 'working bulls'. It is a curious circumstance that no meritorious award assessment exists for working bulls, which have established beyond doubt their prepotency for traits of importance both to the wholesome maintenance of the breed standards and to the competitive maintenance of the breed's economic value, unless they are also prepared, trained, and entered for the Show ring circuit.

LINE BREEDING is inbreeding based on a single common ancestor such as a SIRE whose sons and grandsons continue the blood line. Success is largely due to the exceptional qualities of the source animal also to the fact that uniformity of type is achieved (see diagram p199).

Small folds are more likely to produce more homozygous animals than large folds. "*To best avoid disturbing the achieved fold type yet bring in new blood find a bull with 50% outside blood by tracing where you had sold a good bull and buying one of his male offspring out of an unrelated cow. Alternatively buy some new heifers to use with your fold bull and select from their offspring the nearest to your desired type.*" (Sir J Hammond)

Be cautious about placing too much value on animals well back in the pedigree. The genetic input from the ancestors of seven generations back is a 128th of the whole genetic makeup of a calf under scrutiny. While it is unwise to place high hopes on the appearance of a desired trait from ancestors seven generations back it is important to remember that hidden genes from beyond ten generations back **can** show. (See Parti Colour Chart, Chapter 6) The more pedigree information you have the better.

HERITABILITY is the frequency with which inherited characteristics are transmitted to offspring. Heritability factors are affected by environmental conditions...**size** is adversely affected by the variation in quality and quantity of feeding normally associated with mountains and high rainfall regions where natural supplies of calcium and phosphorous are low. Cattle from such areas tend to be small. Good **growth rate** and **early maturity** depend on a good milk supply. Very poor nutrition can cause **Winter Sterility** in heifers. Inadequate food intake can alter the body **conformation** to a marked degree. Even a young bull if underfed and overused will produce very **poor sperm**. Starved animals with low fat reserves prioritise the maintenance of the brain at the expense of general growth, while coat-colour, hair pattern, shape of horn, are relatively unaffected by the environment.

The belief that the maternal line exclusively transmits certain traits which the sire's line does not is difficult to establish scientifically as correct. Genetic inheritance from parents is 50% from each with the one factor known to be transmitted by the male being the sex of the calf. Which traits make up the 50% genetic hand-out from each parent at each conception remains unpredictable.

BLENDING Complex characteristics controlled by many genes are inherited not on a dominant or recessive basis but on a blending of those parental characteristics. For example **size, weight, body-dimensions, milk yield** of parents differing in these traits will endow their calves with these traits at mid-way between the parents.

MATERNAL INFLUENCE The prenatal environment provided by the mother particularly affects size. Weight at birth in a calf from a large mother is likely to be limited or determined by the calf's genetic makeup whereas weight at birth in a calf from a small mother is likely to be limited by the lesser nutrition available in its pre-natal condition.

PREPOTENCY Some characteristics appear more often than others, that is they have strong heritability. Bulls known to transmit certain qualities consistently are sometimes said to be prepotent. Strong heritability traits tend to be those which are developed early in life and are not dependent on environmental conditions. For example head width and shoulder height both develop early and have a stronger heritability than the chest width and width of hock. More nutrition than is needed for the head and forequarters is necessary at the appropriate growth phase to develop the hind-quarters to their full potential even if a broad-ended proven stockgetter sire has been used, since a good beefy back-end is transmitted genetically less reliably than the fore-end. "*The higher the heritability the greater the effect of selection. The lower the heritability the greater the effect of environment.*" (*Beef cow and calf Manual*, Alberta Agriculture)

GRADING UP Improvement of indifferent stock by mating them and their progeny for at least four successive generations with vigorous pure-bred bulls is the way breeds in danger of extinction may be helped to maintain numbers. By the seventh generation the blood-line should be 99.22% pure but more reliably so by the tenth generation. It is important to understand that in a long-lived breed like Highland cattle the more calves a graded up female has the wider spread throughout the herd, or breed at large, is the possibility of 'throwback' offspring appearing from sixteen to twenty generations away.

ARTIFICIAL INSEMINATION In folds where artificial insemination (AI) is used and a cow or heifer remains barren the first complaint is often made against the quality of the semen. The Scottish Milk Marketing Board* is responsible for overseeing the production and preparation of straws of semen for commercial use. They thoroughly check all abnormalities which might reduce fertility potential before accepting any bull for their supply. They can readily check how long sperm can live and frankly acknowledge that of the 20 to 30 million sperms allocated per straw (the saleable unit of sperms) at the start of the procedure up to a third can die in the freezing process, and up to a third can die in the thawing out process. But that still leaves up to 7 million live sperms per conception when only one sperm is necessary to do the job. In view of the fact that straws prepared elsewhere in Europe allocate only 5 million sperms at the start of the procedure and not as in Scotland 20 to 30 millions the complaint that poor conception rates are due to too diluted straws is unreasonable.

Although there are many factors to consider in each case of non-conception after AI administration perhaps one less often mentioned is that Highland cows and heifers tend to be quieter than most domestic cattle breeds about showing signs of readiness for conception and consequently offer a greater challenge of stockmanship to those in charge. It is interesting to consider also that the Highland bull retains perhaps an element of the efficiency necessary in the wild state in so far as less semen per ejaculation than for most other domestic breeds achieves the required conception rate and three Highland bulls per 100 cows or one bull per 24 to 30 cows produces an average over 90% calving success.

New obligatory regulations were set and amended in 2002. All semen for AI in Scotland must be quality tested.

SEX DETERMINATION It is now possible to prepare straws with selected sex determination. The laboratory procedure takes three days to make one straw which has a usable life-time span of only 24 hours. Clearly this is not yet a commercially viable proposition.

CLONING Cloning requires Transgenic Techniques to transfer new genes into an animal by direct injection of the DNA into an egg shortly after fertilisation. **Clones** are genetically identical animals created by technological alteration of the embryo.

EMBRYO SPLITTING TECHNIQUE a maximum of four animals results from this procedure.

NUCLEAR TRANSFER TECHNIQUE potential for creating large numbers of animals in a relatively short time.

UNDIFFERENTIATED STEM CELLS even faster multiplication than with the Nuclear Transfer Technique.

---

* The Scottish Milk Marketing Board's responsibilities effectively ended in 1994, its dissolution in 2003. No single entity replaced it.

MOET, FOT, ET Multiple Ovulation Embryo Transfer, Fertilised Ovum Transfer, Embryo Transfer.

To take advantage of an exceptionally good cow she can be injected to release many eggs instead of just one. AI is conducted a number of times within 24 hours to fertilise many of her eggs. The fertilised eggs (embryos) are collected (flushed) from the donor cow and transplanted into the uterus of the foster mother, which has been prepared by injection to cycle correctly to be ready to receive the embryo. In the 1970s *"from an average of 15 super-ovulated eggs collected per operation about 4 progeny are eventually born."* (J B Friend: *Cattle of the World* 1978)

The technique of Embryo Transfer *"has been used in beef cattle mainly in*
1 importing or exporting genetic material,
2 multiplying recently imported breeds,
3 producing larger numbers of offspring from individual animals of high value.
Individual breeders may well wish to rapidly multiply the merits of individual females within the herd. Individual cows may be superovulated (induced to produce several ovulations), inseminated, and the embryos recovered and transferred to surrogate mothers on the farmer's own premises. Breeders might expect a donor cow to produce 3 to 10 embryos." (G Simm and N R Wray, Edinburgh School of Agriculture *1989/1990 Highland Cattle Breeders Journals*)

"Embryos are collected 6, 7 or 8 days after service or AI commenced and transferred that day or stored by culture, cooling or deep freezing depending on the time they are required to be stored for.
***Aftercare of Donor**: It is important that the donor returns to normal cycling as soon as possible from the point of view of future natural breeding or further superovulation. To this end we inject her with prostaglandin at the time of collection and instruct your vet to repeat the injection on the following day.*
***Freezing of Embryos**: Not all embryos we collect will be capable of storage in liquid nitrogen.*
The methods used depend on the stage of embryo development at collection. Some cows produce more suitable embryos for this purpose than others. We have frozen and thawed more than 4,000 embryos to date and our experience dictates a loss of 10% at thawing and a pregnancy rate of 60% of those surviving. However, careful selection of recipients can improve this to over 70% as mentioned above. If embryos are frozen on your behalf, then these will be stored at the collection centre until required or can be sold on your behalf.
***Choice of Recipient**: These animals though not as valuable as your donors, are every bit as important to your success. They can be:*
1 Maiden heifers preferably of a dairy or dairy cross breed.
2 Young healthy cows up to approximately 6 years of age, which have bred regularly and have had no recent problems such as retained afterbirth, discharges etc.
Our results indicate that heifers of the Ayrshire breed, due to internal height of their pelvis which leads to easy calving, have proved to be particularly successful recipients. They are also excellent mothers.
We recommend 6 to 10 heifers or 8 to 10 cows as recipients per donor.
***Embryo Transfer**: is an extremely valuable and profitable tool for you to use in improving your herd in the correct way, if carried out by an experienced team.*
Infertile cows can still give good results occasionally if their problems can be resolved, as we have proved with certain animals with infections, blocked or partially blocked oviducts and certain hormonal conditions, but if the family as a whole, has a history of infertility, then the situation should be carefully considered before use for embryo transfer.

Choice of Donor: *for preference she should be one who:*

1 Is still in the prime of her breeding life, for example, on average below 10 years of age and from a family which has a consistent history of longevity and regular breeding history. Cows below 8 years of age perform best. Those between 8 and 10 usually are satisfactory and animals over 10 years of age decline steeply in their ability to respond.

2 Has no recent history of infertility or complications with her genital tract.

3 Is in good bodily condition and is as near as possible either retaining condition despite milk production or gaining it.

4 Has excellent production and conformation characteristics.

With cows satisfying the above criteria, problems still unfortunately arise, but by and large, we can expect the following results from:

	TOTAL EMBRYOS	TRANSFERABLE EMBRYOS	PREGNANCIES
MAIDEN HEIFERS (over 18 months)	10	5	3
AFTER FIRST CALF (8 years)	12	9	6
8 - 10 YEARS	8	6	4
10 YEARS	4	3	2

To obtain the best results and for our mutual benefit, we examine in detail all prospective donors prior to entering a programme and subject them to certain tests, one of which is to establish patency of oviducts i.e. the PSP dye test.

We also, when necessary can obtain a sterile sample washing from the uterus which is submitted for bacteriology and any organisms found are subjected to a sensitivity test. This test (PSP dye test) can well be curative in itself in cases of infertility and we now have literally hundreds of cows which have been infertile for 6 months or more producing embryos and breeding normally again."

(By kind permission of Harry Coulthard of CattleTech Ltd. these extracts are taken from the much fuller and very clear explanation of Embryo Transfer available from CattleTech Ltd. Leeds Road, Thorpe Willoughby, Selby, YO8 9HL. 1996)

IVM: In Vitro Maturation...eggs are artificially made ready for fertilisation i.e. matured in laboratory equipment.

IVF: Artificially matured eggs are fertilised in laboratory conditions and cultured as embryos until ready for implanting or freezing.

MODERN BREEDING "*...we would argue that the application of modern breeding technology is not at all incompatible with the traditional qualities of Highland cattle and that indeed many of the techniques now available have much to offer the breed as a whole.*

There are five major factors which govern the rate of genetic progress in any animal breeding programme:

1 THE HERITABILITY OF THE CHARACTER (trait) under selection.

2 THE AMOUNT OF VARIATION between animals in the character under selection.

3 THE SELECTION INTENSITY. Applied to males and females. (e.g. selection of top 10% leads to greater genetic progress than top 20%)

4 THE GENERATION INTERVAL. The shorter the generation interval (i.e. average age of parents when their offspring is born) the quicker genetically superior animals come into the herd.

5 THE SIZE OF THE HERD. Breeders have little scope to change factors 1 and 2 and some to change 3 and 4, but the size of the herd is important. With few animals it is very difficult to get accurate comparisons amongst them and this is a major constraint on rates of improvement. Herd size is entirely under the breeder's control, though availability of land and capital will often limit increases. An important barrier to achieving higher rates of genetic improvement in the Highland breed is the small size of pedigree herds. The accuracy of comparisons between contemporary animals (i.e. animals of similar age, etc which have been treated similarly) is very important in any breeding programme. Thus the first priority for Highland breeders embarking on an objective improvement programme must be to increase herd sizes, or to pool resources with other breeders in co-operative breeding schemes. These issues need to be addressed as a group with agreed selection goals." (from *Highland Breeders' Journal article 1989)*

In that article on Modern Breeding scientists from Edinburgh Genetics discuss how the Highland Cattle Society as a whole might look at the overall development of breeding policy and how this might involve the use of modern breeding techniques.

CHOOSING LIVESTOCK

Choosing well needs more than the eye can tell.

To see in the auction ring, Show ring, open hill, or paddock, a healthy sound animal of great conformation moving well tells nothing more than that on one particular day that animal looked magnificent. In order to predict it or any other animal's likely performance or breeding ability the observer has to apply knowledge other than what the eye can detect. All the necessary knowledge cannot be acquired over a friendly dram after the sales agreement, for in addition to information from the selling breeder such as records of performance of it and its forebears and as much extended pedigree as can be traced, trial and error in your own selective breeding programme is also required. (see heterozygote p.110)

When an animal is highly rated as a 'great breeder' what is actually meant is that the 'genetic worth', or alternatively the 'breeding value', of the animal is known. While the actual strength of inherited traits is more obvious in a controlled environment it is known that **Weight Gain** and **Growth Rate** have a 60% heritability factor and that an animal's performance in low heritability factors such as **fertility and calving difficulties** is not a reliable guide to its breeding value. Performance in both weight and fatness, however, can be taken as a guide to how offspring may be expected to perform.

BLUP

A method now used worldwide for accurate judgement of breeding value in farm livestock, developed in the United States of America from scrutiny of performance and pedigree records, is called Best Linear Unbiased Prediction or BLUP for short. It does require breeders to supply a considerable amount of data for computerised analyses and works best with livestock which produce annually large numbers of progeny per animal, but reasonable estimation of the breeding value (EBV) can be made for sires and dams if given the following facts.

1 Ancestors' performance
2 The animals own performance
3 The performance of full half brothers and sisters
4 The performance of smaller numbers of progeny (e.g. as in dairy cattle).

BLUP evaluation recognises that environmental factors such as management, feeding, age of dam, twin or single reared, weather conditions annually, all influence performance and takes this into account. BLUP evaluations become more accurate the more data is available from herds which, while being in very different environmental conditions, share some common bloodlines such as occurs readily with the widespread use of sires on the AI system. The Scottish Agricultural College research unit regard BLUP as the best method available for predicting the likely outcome of selected matings, and encourage breeders to take part in making BLUP advantageous to all by collecting the required information on readily supplied forms. The more folds of Highland cattle submitting BLUP requisites the more these folds will reduce the frequency of the luck factor working against their expectations and hopes.

The Wild Whites have remained intractable and intolerant of man.

CHAPTER 6: THE COLOUR DEBATE

CHAPTER 6: THE COLOUR DEBATE

WHEN COAT-COLOUR BECAME AN ISSUE

In British farming choice of colour in cattle related more, when it occurred, to individual preference than to agreed policy until the Agricultural Revolution gathered momentum from the middle of the eighteenth century in England, and from the end of that century in Scotland. The expectation of commercial gain from the results of practising the new science of selective breeding tempted more and more farmers to try it.

Agricultural Shows flourished, gained more popularity than fairs, and became the focal point where evidence of the results of selective breeding programmes could be viewed, compared, and information disseminated. They became and still are a great shop window for the latest developments in agriculture.

Early attempts to produce cattle with more and better quality of meat per carcase, or with increased amount and quality of milk per lactation, placed little emphasis on colour, but in the struggle to fix new breeds, or prove that an old established breed had been 'improved', colour began to play a part in representing newly-agreed standards for the carefully bred and recently fixed 'new' breeds which were proudly displayed in Agricultural Shows. Black noses, skin and coat in some came to be regarded as evidence that the old blood was still present and the newly formed breed societies set about excluding such pointers to their breed's origin. Similarly white markings were frowned upon in some improved breeds; also red when it appeared in black herds. But more than two centuries of rigorous selection for colour, in pedigree stock of various fixed breeds, has failed to eradicate one or other of the three basic bovine colours black, red, white, from appearing atavistically where breed standards as set by the breed societies do not permit.

Of the many British breeds Highland cattle have the greatest range of whole colour, yet they produce unexpected and unpredictable appearances of white markings, which leads to sporadic reappraisal of the official breed standards. Controversy regarding the importance of colour in pedigree stock flares up every so often as is illustrated with the following two references:

In 1985 a plea for more moderate thinking about acceptable colour was printed in the *Welsh Black Cattle Society Journal* with the main thrust of the article being *'don't destroy a good black bull just because he may throw an occasional red calf since less visible qualities like production of high butterfat milk, quiet temperament, regular breeding, good health and longevity are more important than colour.'*

In 1990 The Highland Cattle Society decided to accept for pedigree registration the new colour category of "parti colour", that is main colour with substantial areas or patches of white *(Pics 143-147 p175, 176)*. The decision was implemented on the strength of one voting session at the Annual General Meeting where significantly there was a very slim majority in favour. Many Highland cattle breeders remain distinctly ill at ease over the potential of a whole colour bull standing for Artificial Insemination being discovered to be a carrier of parti colour genes. Their wish for caution until fuller control obtains is well founded. *"...because there is no practical procedure available, apart from progeny testing using black ewes, for detecting heterozygous rams, black and brown sheep continue to occur in white sheep flocks."* (M R Fleet) Much research has gone into understanding the genetics of sheep colour and although what applies to one species does not necessarily apply to another, parallels for coat-colour behaviour in cattle may be discovered.

Naturally breeders are entitled to a partiality in colour but concern about the appearance of white in Highland cattle lies not so much with like or dislike of the colour white as with a determination to preserve the established genetic purity of a breed in which unscrupulous cross-breeding might not be apparent in a first cross except, perhaps, in the degree of white coat in an essentially whole-colour breed. While a determination to maintain for posterity the purity of a distinctive breed and to avoid a return to indiscriminate and unrecorded interbreeding is commendable, it has to be recognised that the appearance of white is a recurring phenomenon and that pied Highlands (pics on p 10, 78, 121, 310, 313, 314) did exist before methods of systematic controlled breeding set colour standards. As far as can reasonably be deduced there never were herds entirely comprised of pied animals until the advent of the fixed breed called Ayrshires, the prevailing colour of the northern, western, and Hebridean beef cattle in the seventeenth century and earlier having been either black or a dark dun, with white marked cattle having been selected for milch cows.

courtesey of Rothamstead, Harpenden Herts.

"West Highland Heifer Kyloe by T Bewick 1823, was the fattest ever seen, with the least coarse beef to its weight."

WHITE IN HIGHLAND CATTLE

"The prevailing colour in the seventeenth century of the Kyloe from the Highlands and Islands was either black or a dark dun shade. White marking, or chaisfhionn, was reckoned a good point in breeding milking cows. Other colours were to be found more in Perthshire than elsewhere. In 1776 a traveller in Scotland recorded that the cattle in the North West of Scotland were mostly black with patches of white." (*Standard Cyclopedia of Modern Agriculture.*)

In 1697 the cattle in St. Kilda were "*small and great, all of them having their foreheads white and black, which is discernable at a great distance, are of low stature, but fat and sweet beef.*" (M Martin)

By 1853 they were larger and "*of ordinary Highland colours, not spotted.*" (Osgood McKenzie)

In the 1760s the "*old Scotch low country*" cattle were described as "*formerly black or brown with white or white flecked faces, and white streaks along their backs.*" (Col W Fullerton)

In the eighteenth century in the Strathkelvin district near Glasgow the unimproved milch cow seems "*to have been of the breed of black cattle or Highlander but some of the cows had white faces and broad spots over their bodies while others were mostly of a dirty dun colour.*" (D E McGuire)

It is likely that the following Gaelic saying predates the northern spread of Ayrshire dairy cattle. "*White backed and speckle-shouldered cattle in your fold together, another tending them while your wife sits in her chamber sewing. A good wish.*"

Crodh druim fhionn, crodh guall fhionn, air do bhuaile mar chambla, te aile ga'n cuallach's do bhean a fuaigheal 'na seonar." (A R Forbes)

Whether these pied and speckled Highlands occurred as a result of inbreeding and poor feeding or because of an infusion of different blood from other breeds remains difficult to establish. Gaelic folksong frequently mentions white speckled or white shouldered milk cows but facts gleaned from an oral tradition are rather difficult to date historically.

A curious appearance of white in the West Highland area of Moidart was recorded in 1860 when, apparently, a pure Brittany cow put to a Brittany X Shetland bull produced several pure white calves with black ears and points. This colouring does not normally occur in either of the parent breeds but is typical of the ancient wild forest cattle (*Pics p118*). Colour in domestic stock tends to more variation than in wild animals although instances of white in fallow, red, and rein deer living in restricted territory is known. Perhaps when cattle were enclosed first in small compounds by primitive man and then in the hedged-in landscaping of the eighteenth century they paralleled the deer in producing occasional white animals. However until veterinary science can better predict the onset of atavism and distinguish that from random instances of rogue or mutant genes, many appearances of partial or whole white in Highland cattle will remain unsatisfactorily explained.

According to wide-ranging written sources the colouring of the Wild Ox in Britain is generally agreed to have embraced black, red/brown, and small amounts of white. All accounts of it scanned for this discussion agree that the mature bull was black and the cow reddish brown with darker head and legs. Most accounts maintain there was a white or light dorsal stripe and paleness round the muzzle of the bull while some writing suggests there was also a white patch between the horns on the bull's forehead. Since twentieth century thinking considers that all cattle derive from a common ancestor in North India or Central Asia and that the Urus (Wild Ox) was the diversified form of it to arrive in Britain it is obvious that the Urus provided the earliest pool of colour genes. (See Chapter 7 on Origin). Whole white cattle with vestiges of red or black on ear tips, muzzles, feet, came later probably through centuries of intensifying inbreeding, as herds of wild cattle became trapped in the ever-decreasing forest territories caused by the expansion of man and his agricultural and feuding behaviour. The firm establishment of this white breed with coloured points would have been given a boost if the Romans during their 400 year invasion of Britain did in fact bring with them white cattle. For in these times of plunder and no enclosed fields domestic stock would inevitably have mingled with wild forest cattle of the dark Urus colouring, which allows reasonable speculation that varied coat-colours would result. It is difficult to believe that a few escaped Roman cattle could account for the widespread simultaneous existence of herds of Wild Whites in forests throughout the length and breadth of Scotland and England. Even allowing for prolific breeding of escapees over the four hundred year period of occupation it is more usual for wild colouring to dominate in crosses of domestic with wild stock. An added confusion arises here when one considers that the white Roman Cattle were reputed to have been polled cattle yet the ancient Wild Whites were mostly horned and it is known that the polled factor is dominant to the horned in cross-breedings. So the argument for the white of the Ancient Wild Cattle being the result of continuous inbreeding lingers as a credible possibility.

Another theory on the possible origin of the Wild White is that the Urus of the interglacial periods in Britain developed Arctic coat-colouring, with its seasonal change potential, in the more northern territories, and over centuries of encroaching and receding ice was repeatedly driven southwards only to spread north again whenever food supplies became available. In the periods when the surviving Arctic Urus was in the south, interbreeding with the dark coloured Urus is likely to have occurred, thereby creating the potential for varied coat-colouring and markings long before the arrival of man. It is interesting to note that the Yak, though also derived from the same progenitor and living in a mountainous environment harsher than that of Scotland has remained black in the wild and only breeds varied colours from black through the range to white in the captive domesticated herds. A rare sighting of the hitherto unknown golden-coated wild Yak first made in 1988, (reported in the 1993 *National Geographic Journal*) reminds one of the fallibility of man's assumptions. Nevertheless, with or without an Arctic Urus in Britain variations in coat markings and colour in cattle evidently happened randomly until specific colour, or combinations of colours, were chosen and fixed by breeders in the eighteenth century as proof of planned breeding programmes now known as pedigree breeding.

Prior to dealing with colour in Highland cattle of the late twentieth century, a look at the colour of several British cattle breeds **before** and **after** pedigree breeding programmes shows how many of the breed societies sought to reduce the range of coat-colour acceptable for registration. Possibly the reduced colour range instantly identified 'improved' cattle possessing a pedigree.

Instances of cross-breeding with Highland cattle are mentioned, also the various regional names commonly used for cattle before Breed Societies were formed.

COLOUR BEFORE AND AFTER PEDIGREE BREEDING PROGRAMMES

ABERDEEN ANGUS

BEFORE: rigged black i.e. black with brown or white finching, black with brown ring round muzzle and brown finching, brindle with white mixed, belted black and white, red/brown, yellow.

AFTER: Herd Book from 1862: black; black tinged with brown; small amounts of white around the udder tolerated.

After these rules the numbers of red animals appearing in pure-bred black herds caused the formation of the Aberdeen Angus Red Poll Society.

SHORTHORN (regional names: Durham, Teeswater, Holderness, Yorkshire)

BEFORE: Black, brindle, yellow, dun, red, white.

AFTER: Herd Book from 1822: Red, red and white flecked, roans and whole white. Nose, palate, lips, eyelids to be flesh coloured.

Black skin and coat was very **un**fashionable.

Light coloured Shorthorn bull X Highland cow often produced a dark grey calf.

AYRSHIRE (regional names: Cunninghame, Kyle, Carrick, Dunlop)

BEFORE: black, brown, black/white native cows were put to Shorthorn and Jersey (also called Alderney) bulls around the 1750s to fix the breed of Ayrshire; Dutch breeds may also have been involved.

AFTER: Herd Book from 1877: red, brown, white, mahogany/white, brown/white, black/white.

GALLOWAY

BEFORE: Black with reddish tinge on hair tips of winter coat, dun, red/brown, (red/browns in the 1750s were considered crosses with Highlands) An almost extinct marking by the end of the nineteenth century was a tan coloured ridge along the back, tan ring round the muzzle and tan ears. White patches on udder, belly, thigh, and white hind foot do occur.

AFTER: Herd Book from 1877: black, with white hairs only in tail whisk tolerated.
Despite attempts to eradicate dun its appearance was so persistent that by 1921 it was made acceptable for Herd Book registration.
A white Galloway herd was founded in 1919 near Newton Stewart and even when black bulls were used a very high proportion of calves were white.
The Dun and Belted Galloway Breeders' Association was formed in 1922. There are records of white-middled calves appearing in a herd which has bred black for several generations...in one case for 36 years. There were two herds of Belted Galloways in Ross-shire in the 1920s.

WELSH BLACK (many regional names e.g. Pembrokeshire, Glamorgan, Dewslands, Castlemartins)

BEFORE: Ancient South Wales literature mentions yellow, speckled, brown, dun, white with red ears, rarely black.
North Wales cattle in mid nineteenth century were generally black or red, with white udders, underline, or tailwhisk; occasional brindles; A brown black approaching chocolate was very popular.
AFTER: Black with small amount white on underline tolerated. (Red does appear but is not accepted for the Herd Book) South and North Wales had separate Herd Books from 1874 and amalgamated in 1905.

LONGHORN (regional names: Lancashire breed, Dishley, Leicestershire, Warwickshire, Lough-horned, Waghorned)

BEFORE: Black and brown with some white on the body and white finching. Colouring in the Fell districts of North England was dark roan with black ticks through it, many with white finching, but noses were flesh coloured due to continuous cross-breeding with Shorthorns. West Highland bulls were used to restore hardiness lost with too much shorthorn blood.
AFTER: Herd Book from 1878: red, brindle, grizzly roan, occasional self coloureds, any of these speckled with white, all with white finching and white mark on thigh.
A mealy red-roan Longhorn type with a broad dorsal stripe was bred for some years from a light roan Shorthorn bull on a West Highland cow at Tulliallan Castle, Fife, shortly before the First World War, but the Longhorn breed was not widely used in Scotland.

WHITE CATTLE (Parks cattle, Wild Whites, Taurus Sylvestri, Wild whites of Caledon, White Ancient Forest breed) (*Pics p118*)

A white breed with black or red points. Small herds of these animals have been maintained by dedicated enthusiasts in Scotland, England and Wales. Several herds were founded in the late nineteenth century and early twentieth century but those at Cadzow, Chillingham, and Chartley, are considered to have more ancient bloodlines than others. The ancient whites are well-documented so presented here is only what is relevant to considerations on colour in Highland cattle.
A Herd Book for White Park Cattle was begun in 1919.
CADZOW; white with black points, black ring round black nose, black ears, knees, hoofs and socks. In 1838 many were polled. Mid 1850s a Highland bull is reputed to have broken into the park and caused the reappearance of horned stock. Until 1880s on average three black calves per year were born. Some bulls develop curly or wavy hair on forehead, neck, and front of shoulder. The Cadzow cattle (1990s) are in Chatelherault Country Park two miles from Hamilton, 16 miles from Glasgow.

CHILLINGHAM; (Northumberland England) in the 1780s Wild Whites were transferred from Drumlanrig, Dumfriesshire (Scotland) to join those at Chillingham. By the late nineteenth century there were fewer instances of black eared or improperly coloured calves appearing since the Chillingham whites were selectively maintained to breed with red ear fringes. (Those from Drumlanrig had had black ears) All calves in Chillingham showing black were destroyed. In 1875 experimental cross-breeding with Shorthorn was begun. The cross progeny retained the white and hardiness but assumed Shorthorn shape and pink nose colour. Chillingham cattle are born pure white but many tend to go cream coloured later. All have red ears and many today have black nose pigment.

CHARTLEY; (Staffordshire England) thought to date from 1248. White with black points as for the Cadzow cattle but not so much black. In 1905 or so some white Welsh and four Highland cattle were put to a Chartley bull and produced typical Wild White progeny with black points. In 1906 Longhorn cows put to a Chartley bull helped restore the breed after extinction threatened from tuberculosis contracted after their grazings had been let to farm stock.

ATHOLL HERD; (Perthshire Scotland) In the sixteenth century the forest of Caledon spread from Stirling to Blair Atholl, and provided great sport for the hunting of Wild White bulls. Sightings of Wild Whites became a rarity as early as the 1530s but it is thought likely that their progeny lingered on to become the enclosed stock of the Duke of Atholl's herd. They resembled ordinary Highland cattle in being short legged, straight backed and in having long silky hair. They were white with black ear tips, black eye orbit, black or striped black hoofs, black nose but without any circle of black hair round it. In 1834 they were sold. Some went to the Marquis of Breadalbane, Taymouth, (Perthshire) and some to the Duke of Buccleuch, Dalkeith (near Edinburgh).

Those which went to Dalkeith were all slaughtered in 1838 except for one bull. This bull was put to six Highland cows all white with black points, to found the Kilmory herd in Argyll for Sir John Orde. In time this bull was exchanged for the Breadalbane bull which also bred well at Kilmory. Next a Highland bull which was white with black points was found to continue the strength of the herd. In 1872 twenty-two of the Kilmory Herd went to start the Vaynol Park Herd in Bangor, Wales, followed by a further thirty-two fourteen years later.

The Atholl wild whites sent to Breadalbane would not breed with the white bull there and both male and female are said to have crossed with Highland cattle. The progeny of these crosses having no whites among them were exhibited as Highland cattle in the Highland Society's Show in probably 1836.

In 1849 the Duke of Argyll gifted to the Earl of Breadalbane a white cow with a little black around the eyes, muzzle and a few black hairs in the ears. Some of her offspring found their way into the Duke of Atholl's herd of Highland cattle in the 1860s and produced at intervals '*swan-white animals*'. (Prof R Wallace)

Scarcity creates new concepts of what is valuable. When the once common Wild Whites of the forests all but disappeared tremendous efforts were made to restore them. Legend has it that centuries earlier some Druid ceremonies involved the sacrifice of a white bull, perhaps because any other colour of bull was commonplace or because the colour black was associated with evil. No religious taboo on breeding black stock in the North of Scotland prevailed by the eighteenth and nineteenth centuries when the Gaels of the Scottish Western Seaboard deliberately selected black stock. But whilst they bred for black, the enthusiastic agricultural improvers of the south were just as busy eradicating black, and creating a demand for red or yellow stock. Cattle had to be saleable in the southern markets, therefore by mid-twentieth century so few black Highland cattle were in evidence that breeding for good blacks once more became the specific goal of several breeders. Success was to prove more elusive than expected. Previous understanding of the laws of inheritance maintaining that black colour genes were dominant to red no longer obtained. Other than recognising that reds were prevalent no formula for reliably predictable colour appearance from breeding stock could be established. When black cows threw more red, yellow, white, or dun, calves than ever they did black, the demand for a reappraisal of the colour dominance theories greatly increased.

Man perpetually seeks control over his environment and is ill satisfied with partial control. Yet there is a long way to go before the wonders of recent research in genetic engineering can be reliably, easily, cheaply, and responsibly pursued in everyday farming. So partial control remains the norm.

Breeders would welcome a greater degree of certainty about the outcome of any particular livestock mating. General understanding accepts that the 'purer' the stock the more predictable the progeny. But, for example, finding a red genotype cow, (a red from only red sets of parents, for at least ten generations back) to be your 'pure' starter along with a similarly 'pure' colour of bull is a difficult and time consuming task. With dedicated patience breeders have built up their genotypes only to lose them when circumstances force dispersal sales. Highland cattle have enormous potential for accommodating variability which can be repressed but not easily removed. The questions of how pure is pure and how can purity be proved have been voiced at intervals ever since the 'improving techniques' first took hold, although agitation is more noticeable with each surge of commercially driven cross-bred beef programmes. Yet the full range of breed characteristics and colour keeps reasserting itself, although not without supportive measures from concerned agriculturalists such as F Fraser Darling. In 1945 he wrote:

"unless we have a carefully controlled system of breeding throughout the West Highlands we are likely to find ourselves with the oddest collection of cattle one could imagine, and that would depress the store market, for buyers like uniformity.

If I were allowed to be completely honest and candid, I should say we are getting well on to that condition now. There is too much whim and fashion in the cattle breeding business. Someone decides to keep a certain breed of cow in a district, come what may, and you find in a few years that many of the cattle in the whole neighbourhood are streaked with this breed. That is the result of one man's whim. Fashion also seems to me to go mad at markets. Dingwall wants blacks and will pay a pound extra for a few blue hairs. Perth and Stirling want Shorthorns and Shorthorn crosses, except for the specialised demand for Aberfeldy blacks. Highlanders were hardly paying their freight to Dingwall before this war, yet Oban was reckoned a dear place to buy them. The layout of railways and the fashion of markets, then, seem to impose the colour and breeds of cattle kept on the western grazings to a greater extent than the conditions in which the cattle are bred. We certainly need a safeguard somewhere to ensure that the breeds are not crossed out of existence in the West."
(F Fraser Darling)

The following sample of references suggest cross-breeding, random or planned, was fairly widespread throughout the previous two centuries.

CROSS-BREEDING 17TH TO 19TH CENTURIES

The cattle itemised in letters about cattle stolen in Badenoch in 1687 (1), and for sale in 1786 in Badenoch (2) hint at the presence of three breeds. Fife, Highland, Buchan (polled Aberdeenshire). Both the Fife and Buchan are now extinct.

(1) *"one dun ox, one dun bull, one black ox and one brown young ox with a white ball in his forehead, one gaired or sprainged cow, red and black, two horns little and cross, and one large black."*

(2) *A din stot and brandered stot, £4. 11s. A rigged stirk £2. 4s. A humle black heifer £3. 0s. A brandered stirk, £2. 4s. A black Humle cow and calf £11. 10s. A rigged cow £4. 7s. A black yell cow £3. 16s. A black tagged cow £3. 15s. A brandered heifer £2. 3s. A din stot and a heifer £5. 7s."*

(both (1) and (2) from I F Grant)

Accepted as a troublesome part of normal Scottish life constant cattle raiding repeatedly mixed up livestock. In (1) above only one animal escaped the thieves and made it back to the home farm. Usually the best and strongest animals were the only ones to survive the raids, thus perpetuating strong bloodlines if any were to be used as breeding stock. Frequently cattle raiding was a sport proving that daring and courageous levels of manhood had been achieved. But many clans were forced into cattle thieving out of dire necessity in times of near famine. Rather less tolerable, though, is the behaviour of those who stole cattle as an act of revenge in which instances the animals were often viciously maimed and left to die. Nevertheless raiding undoubtedly allowed some mixing of breeding stock to occur. Several clans were well-known for their raiding forays. Note is made of Argyllshire men raiding from East Perthshire in 1602 and from Strathspey and Aberdeenshire in 1667; and Lochaber and Badenoch men raiding from Angus.

Such raids drove the cattle from 70 to 150 miles away from the lifting point.

Admiral Sir John Lockhart Ross of Balnagown, Ross and Cromarty, *"was at great expense in procuring bulls and queys from Bakewell and Cowley to improve his breed; but without much success. It is my opinion that neither kind is fit for this country. A fine bull from Skye, with curled jet black hair, and small tapering horns, will, with a good Highland cow, produce a more profitable breed."* (*Present State of Husbandry in Scotland* 1773 – 1782. IX)

Sutherland: *"As the horned cattle in Sutherland are not in high estimation, the Colonel has spared neither pains nor expense for improving the breed. A bull and cows from Galloway, a half-bred bull of Bakewell's kind, and the true Highland bull, were all of them got for mixing with the Sutherland blood; and from these have sprung up an excellent kind. The steers I saw are capital, but I admired most these of the Galloway and Highland blood."* (*Present State of Husbandry in Scotland*. 1773 – 1782. IX.)

Perthshire: *"Athol cows have been long in reputation. The present stock of cows at Athol house are of different kinds; the Holderness short-horned cow; the true Athol breed; a halfbreed between a Holderness cow and a Highland bull; a halfbreed between an Athol cow and a bull got by an English bull on an Holderness cow; all of them remarkably fine to breed from, giving much milk and taking on fat soon. The present Duke has it in view to make further experiments particularly to get a cow and a bull from Galloway; which I cannot approve of."* (*Present State of Husbandry in Scotland* 1773 – 1782 VIII)

Inverness-shire: Mr Grant of Corriemonie took great care to provide winter feeding. . largely hay...for his cattle and also avoided overstocking his land. *"Mr Grant's next care was to make a real improvement on his stock of black cattle, for which he wandered not in quest of bulls or cows from southward; he more prudently searched the stocks of horned cattle in the Highlands and Isle of Skye, for the best kinds he could discover there;"* Mr Grant also frequently crossed his breed with *"bulls brought from distant parts of the country, of the finest form and figure of their kind: size is not so anxiously wished for, because all kinds of bullocks may be raised in size, and their weights increased, by a plentiful supply of good food. A hardy bred bullock if he is not pinched with want, but on the contrary has been regularly supplied with wholesome provender, will always thrive. For this reason Mr Grant does not permit his stock of cattle to be housed."* (*Present State of Husbandry in Scotland 1773 – 1782*. IX)

Some extracts from the 1750 to 1790 *Statistical Account of Scotland* endorse that there were widespread attempts to 'improve' cattle.

Auldearn near Nairn: the cattle were mixed. Lancashire, Dutch, Fifeshire, Highland, with more Highland cattle than other. (vol. 19)

Kiltearn, Ross-shire: the breed of black cattle was various; gentlemen and principal farmers improved their Highlands with cattle from Fife and Moray. (vol. 1)

Anstruther, Fife: cattle recently crossed with Lancashire, Holderness and Dutch. (vol. 3)

Bourtie, Aberdeen: in the 1770s black cattle were brought from Fife. (vol. 9)

Scone, Perth: The Countess of Mansfield introduced a breed of cattle remarkable for their size and shape. (vol. 18)

Inveraray, Argyll: A breed of the best Highland cattle in this country are reared at Inveraray where there are also some good cattle of the Galloway and Lancashire kinds. (vol. 5)

Lasswade, Lothian: in general farmers breed *"the common Scotch kind"* but many gentlemen have cows of the English, Dutch, and Guernsey breed. (vol. 10)

Extracts from mid nineteenth century in the *New Statistical Account of Scotland* reflect continued interest in new breeds and the effects of cross-breeding. Serious concern about dwindling numbers or drop in popularity of the Highland Breed had not surfaced.

Islay: in 1839 thirteen Ayrshires were entered in the Agricultural Show in Islay and by 1871 Ayrshires and Shorthorns were numerous while numbers of Highland cattle were very reduced.

Lewis: There were many Ayrshire X Highland cattle by the 1850s and after 1897 Ayrshire and Shorthorn bulls were imported and crossed with Highland cows until scarcely a Highland was to be seen. (Donald Macdonald)

Inverness 1830s: the breed most common is a mixed one of old Highland, Morayshire, and Ayrshire. (vol. XIV)

Lochalsh 1838: various breeds of black cattle but chiefly the Highland. Those for dairy are Ayrshire and Buchan. Teeswater have also been introduced of late. (vol. XIV)

Kiltearn, Ross-shire: common breeds of cattle are the Ross-shire (small size and inferior and only kept by poorer people), the Argyleshire, and Ayrshire are kept by gentlemen for dairy purposes. Pure Shorthorn introduced to one farm. (vol. XIV)

Crieff, Perthshire: crosses between the Dunlop (Ayrshire) and the Highland or Teeswater breeds. (vol. X)

Blairgowrie: Teeswater shorthorn bulls crossed with native breed of cows. (vol. X)

Dumbartonshire: milch cows on low ground are generally a cross between Highland and Ayrshire. (vol. VIII)

These extracts make it clear why the forming of the Highland Cattle Society in 1884 came not a moment too soon. It strove to keep a value on the pure-bred Highland when commerce was excluding it. But the relentless demand for cross-breds continued, encouraged by articles extolling the virtues of the cross-breds without promoting equally strongly the need to increase numbers of pedigree stock, e.g. *"The Highland cow will cross more or less successfully with other breeds, but there is no doubt that the most successful results are obtained by crossing with the Beef Shorthorn."* The advantages of this were first recognised many years ago. Thomas Bates, of Shorthorn fame, in his earlier years experimented with the Shorthorn crossed with the Kyloe. *"Undoubtedly the popularity of this cross is growing and will grow"* (HMSO). Dr. Alan Fraser in *Beef Cattle Husbandry* states that about 1908 all the cattle coming from Western Ross-shire were of this type. "*The cross with the Aberdeen Angus and the fashion for the black polled calf came later, and was not altogether favourable for the Highland Breed.*"

Unless one understands the very widespread use of Aberdeen Angus bulls to achieve fast beef on hill farms throughout mid-twentieth century Scotland the statement from the President of the Highland Cattle Society reported in its Herd Book Volume 38 can be misleading. By 1959 'black bull' no longer meant a Highland bull as it once had. The president had referred to Aberdeen Angus bulls when he said somewhat confusingly "*We can't have all our breeding cattle in Scotland blacks. We must have some coloured bulls as well.*"

Economic necessity can reject scruples about purity of breeding stock in favour of what may be most advantageous financially. So in view of the foregoing samples of information the survival of Highland cattle as a distinct breed surely must be due to the combined factors of:

1 Genetic assertion of original type after cross-breeding;
2 Committed breed enthusiasts working to save pure stock;
3 Geographic isolation.

Geographic isolation is now of less protection though, since contemporary methods of transport can take any breed of cattle anywhere in the world as live whole beasts, or in embryo form, or in semen straws for artificial insemination. Stark reminder of this in 1992 lay in a remote part of the Torridon Mountains (Scotland), approachable only by a single track road over a tortuous route, where I sighted one solitary Highland cow amidst a scattering of European cross-breeds. She was lying on the top of an exposed knoll contentedly chewing the cud while the Limousin, Charolais, Simmental, or whatever, were lower down still grazing. Were they less competent grazers, or did they need to consume more to convert vegetation to beef? Mr F. Fraser Darling's words of warning "*We certainly need a safeguard somewhere to ensure that the breeds are not crossed out of existence in the West*" were indeed a timely reminder to value the preservation of pure stock. Such advice seems to hover round the Highland breed like some invisible protection triggered intermittently to reverberate in receptive human ears. Eminent agriculturalists in 1884 founded the Highland Cattle Society to preserve the purity of a breed of animal then so taken for granted that its perpetual availability was assumed to be as reliable as the regular appearance of grass and heather on the hills. But their efforts were to struggle against economic depressions followed by two World Wars, and the hazards of ever using coat-colour to help distinguish, on one visual examination, which non-pedigree cattle were pure-bred Highlands and which might harbour genes from another breed. Accuracy in that distinction mattered only in so far as registering with the Society mattered. Committed breed enthusiasts at some personal cost had managed to keep the pure-bred numbers from entering the endangered species lists until fresh energies from post-Second World War personnel actively set about improving the situation. They encouraged interest in owning pure-bred Highlands, and exhorted all who still had pure-bred stock, but who were unknown to the Highland Cattle Society, to join in the efforts to revive the numbers and popularity of the breed.

That impetus launched in the 1950s was successful. By the 1980s the breed was firmly established throughout Britain in sufficient numbers to allay the mid-century fears of pending extinction. With the increase in numbers of pedigree stock and many breeders new to the business, discussions about specifying coat-colour in pedigree animals once more surfaced.

COAT-COLOUR REMAINS AN ISSUE WITH HIGHLAND CATTLE BREEDERS

Variations from pale to dark in every colour category can lead to difficulties in defining the coat-colour for registration with the Highland Cattle Society. To mention a few, pale yellow can be close to white and dark yellow close to pale red, dark red can be close to brindle, black can look dark brindle or brown, and dark dun can approximate chocolate. The various committees serving the Society since 1884 have accepted several descriptions such as reddish, yellow brindle, chocolate dun, medium brindle, yellow dun, yellow and red, brown, russet, silver dun, brown, but the 1990 committee favoured simply black, red, brindle, dun, yellow, white, parti colour.

Apart from differences of opinion about when the shade of one colour actually puts it into another colour category, the issue of changing coat-colour adds to the difficulties. Yellow calves may grow into red or black adults, red calves may grow into dun or brindle adults, a brindle three year old may become a red five year old, and most snow white calves become champagne yellow adults. Surprisingly as recently as 1952, a full 68 years after the formation of the Society to maintain the purity of the breed, the Herd Book Volume XXXI records that the official Highland Cattle Herd Book year was altered to allow more accuracy in giving the colour of the animals to be registered... it having been found that two to three month old calves can change colour after their details had been registered.

At Oban Sales 1996 a stockman put forward an interesting belief that *"Any change in coat-colour that is going to happen can be speeded up by repeatedly applying hot air from a blow dryer."*

Defining coat-colour will remain a recurring issue until more is understood about

1 changing coat-colour
2 if in fact there are merits or faults genetically linked to individual colour.

Even if every breeder believed the maxim *"a good beast can't be a bad colour"* the selection of preferred colour is always going to feature to some extent with many breeders and, for as long as there are less than prolific numbers of the breed in existence, colour bias may not be good for the long-term survival of the full genetic package of the old breed.

COAT-COLOUR IN SCOTTISH HIGHLAND CATTLE

Highland cattle possess coat-colour-changing genes, a feature of the survival kit of some wild animal species.

Two calves demonstrated the camouflage potential in coat-colour by lying near cone patches in the pine forest at Balinoe Croft *(Pic 7 p35)*. Their ancient wild forebears were forest animals. Black adults merge with the shadows in the trees where red-coated adults stand out. But the early months of calfhood coincide with the green spring carpeting beneath the trees where light filters through. Pitch black calves on this would be very exposed were it not for the combined effect of the gold-russet-brown overtones in the calf coat and the patchwork of dark ground spaces where scatterings of cones and rust coloured pine needles lie. The black calf which has inherited the coat-colour changing gene can be anything from a pale gold to a red brown with true black showing only at the extremities. At around six to ten months when much of the fluffy calf coat is being shed and the darkness of the maturing black coat shows through, the resulting coat-colour can be mistakenly called brindle *(Pic 120 p167)*. The full coat-colour change to the permanent adult black can take up to three years to complete but is never as intense a black as that of the black calf which lacks the colour changing gene *(Pic 148 p176)*. It is unusual to see a brindle calf, if indeed there can be such a coat in calfhood. It seems that the brindle coat is the slowest to manifest the mature state and that brindles are red in calfhood or sometimes what might be described as 'brown', until the black and red striping shows often as late as the animal's third winter. Predicting whether a dark red calf will become a red adult or a brindle adult can be tricky in the coats that have no early tell-tale black hairs around the head, tail, or hocks, and no dark striping in the hoofs. Not understanding the coat-colour changing characteristic of this breed has resulted in some good black calves being assessed as brindle and then treated as beef stock instead of breeding stock. Though not proven fact it is probable that all coat-colours in the breed possess the colour changing factor with the exception of a minority type of red coat, and a rare type of black to be found more readily in the Welsh Black breed.

Most calves that are pure white at birth grow into a cream or light yellow adult. Again the coat-colour behaviour suggests an ancient heritage of seasonal camouflage when one considers that calves are often born in the season for snow then lose the calf coat for deeper tones in time to blend better with the yellows of Autumn.

From personal research to date it seems possible that Highland cattle also might carry more genes – or more accurately 'alleles' – for controlling coat-colour than other domestic cattle breeds. They may have alleles influencing coat-colour which are so far unknown to geneticists.

The science of genetics has identified and named six locations on the chromosomes of mammals where alleles governing coat-colour can be found. A total of 26 alleles affecting coat-colour in mammals has been identified. Any six to twelve of these are thought to govern the coat-colour in Highland cattle. The particular colour they produce depends on which alleles are present and in which combination at each of the six locations on the chromosome.

After centuries of the controlled breeding of domestic stock it is likely that there are now fewer than the possible 26 alleles in Highland cattle out of which their maximum of 12 come, but still likely to be more than enough to make prediction of coat-colour complex and difficult.

If additional alleles, and even locations, specific to Highland cattle are discovered, the range of possible combinations of alleles is considerably increased, intensifying difficulties in predicting calf colour.

If you buy a red cow and a red bull which look similar in colour, their individual allocation and arrangement of alleles for coat-colour could be quite different. One or both may carry an unusual combination of alleles at one or more location. The colour of their first calf may not be red and their second could differ from the first and still not be red.

The fact that this happens is not news to breeders of Highland cattle. What is wanted is an explanation of how and why coat-colour is so difficult to predict reliably, and why the permanent adult coat-colour can in some cases take so long to appear. The prevailing system of changing the stock bull every two to four years hinders the validity of observations on coat-colour made in normal farm conditions.

Irrefutable understanding of coat-colour transmission and associated traits in Highland cattle requires long-term study possibly involving initially three colour groups of animals whose homozygosity for their colour has been established beyond doubt: group 1 red cows; group 2 black bulls of both categories of black i.e. a: jet black at birth, b: brown/yellow with black points at birth; group 3 brindle bulls. Only once assessment and analysis of progeny coat-colour from a controlled breeding plan involving black bulls on red cows and brindle bulls on the same red cows had been completed could the research go on to include animals with partial white or entirely white coats. The first phase of such work would take from 12 to

16 years. Unless Highland cattle hair were to become hugely valuable on a worldwide commercial basis costly genetic research on merely coat-colour transmission will not happen, except if funded privately. It is unlikely that historical research might sufficiently value the discovery of detailed knowledge of the genetic heritage held in this ancient breed to set up and fund appropriate research, the results of which may not have commercial application. Animals whose coats are 'big-business' worldwide such as sheep and goat breeds, alpaca, llama, and the fur trade, have occasioned ongoing research on many aspects of animal hairs and coat fibres. This has resulted in there being an elite group of geneticists whose special area of knowledge centres on coat-colour.

One such specialist was Dr Stefan Adalsteinsson of the Nordic Gene Bank, Norway. He agreed that understanding coat-colour-changing is a complex issue but thought his following points might be of interest (the word gene is interchangeable with allele in his text):

"Brindle animals have three colour genes on top of each other. The bottom gene produces recessive black when the others are absent. (Obs. Black may carry the gene for red, see below, but we leave that out for the moment) The brown gene, when present in recessive black animals, will convert the recessive black colour to brown (Kolott).

The calves with this colour are born red, but at the first change of hair coat develop into brown, with light coloured muzzle, red inside the ears and on top of the head, and a red stripe along the back. (Kolott: dark brown characterised by a light muzzle and some red inside the ears, on top of the head and along the back. Some brown animals have red colour more widespread on the body.)

The brindle gene can only manifest itself on brown background. It produces red stripes in the areas which are dark brown or black pigmented in originally brown animals. That is how brindle is produced.

The Jersey cow carries brown in many cases, at least in the darkest types.

The Hereford often carries the gene for brindle, but is unable to show it, because it neither carries the recessive black, nor the gene for brown.

Let us say we cross a Jersey cow to a Hereford bull, and obtain a brindle calf. This brindle calf has obtained one gene for recessive black and one gene for brown from its dam, and one gene for brindle from its sire.

Let us look further at the possibilities of obtaining various colours in the Highland. We could have only dominant black and red animals in some herds of Highland cattle. Then we would obtain only two colours in the progeny, black and red, and neither brown nor brindle.

We could also have herds where all four colours, brindle, brown, black and red are found. Let us assume that all the blacks are recessive black, and that dominant black does not occur there at all. Then we can obtain the following calf colours from the various mating types. We only look at matings of sires and dams of the same colour.

Brindle X brindle may produce brindle, brown, black and red.

Brown X brown may produce brown, black and red.

Black X black may produce black and red.

Red X red produces only red.

Mating together of animals of different colours in a herd of this type may produce a variety of colours, but no colours other than brindle, brown, black, and red should be produced." (Dr Stefan Adalsteinsson 1994)

Even if the 'Kolott/brown' theory does not entirely apply to Highland cattle the information is a helpful step towards fuller understanding of cattle coat-colour. It raises the question of what knowledge lay behind the occasional registrations of 'brown' in the Highland Herd Books and why Brown is not a recognised colour category if it occurs naturally in the breed. Were there actually brown animals or were the breeders indifferent to colour distinctions? Would they have said like many of today's public in my exerience *"No there weren't any black ones, just the usual sort of brownish colour. You know, just brown."* That is how red Highland cattle are often described.

"The existence of brown or ***donn*** *– an approximation to black, with light colouring round the muzzle and along the spinal column – goes far back in western annals, and points to the fact that dark reds were favoured by some breeders. A black-brindled bull mated with dark-red cows is very apt to leave browns, especially if the females are of the dark-muzzled or* ***Busdubh*** *order. But if black be easily retained, there is no special difficulty in causing a sway from medium shades to broken colours, pale yellows and silver duns almost merging into white.*

...far back as any scanty writings and traditions are available, the standard colour of the Hebridean cattle was black; no doubt due to selection. On the mainland variety of colouring has been popular from time immemorial – but streaks and patches of white are not now in special favour." (James Cameron 1899)

Mr Cameron's comments allude to there having been Kolott coloured animals in the Highland breed at one time and also that brindle colouring behaves in a complex way.

Brindle holds the key to maximum option in selection for colour perpetuation. When brindle also harbours genes for white the complexities of predictable transmission multiply.

BRINDLE/WHITE LINKS FROM 1870–1990

Long before the 1990 Highland Cattle Society committee instigated the ruling that "Parti colour" should be used to register pure-bred Highlands with patches of white, some breeders honourably noted in the Herd Book of their time which animal was whatever main colour "and white". Thanks to their attention to accuracy the following chart could be made. It traces bloodlines of Highlands calved in the 1990s to connections with the award-winning Ensay-bred Brindle Bull with white scalloped undercarriage, namely Sgiathanach 489 calved in 1870; or with the highly esteemed Athole cow Rosie also of that era. She was dam of the widely used brindle sire Glentilt 295. These parti colour connections indicate the numbers of generations and span of time through which specific genes, those for parti colour in this instance, may have recurred.

PARTI COLOUR CHART SHOWING LINKS WITH BRINDLE/WHITE

Key: F = Female; B = Bull; C = Calved; Gen = Generations; GG = Great Great (Grand Parent); 489 = Sgiathanach (bull); 295 = Glentilt (bull) out of Rosie

NAME	HERD BOOK No.	COLOUR	PEDIGREE
Chaisfhionn Buidhe of Athole. F. c.1881	24	yellow/white	Sire 489, Granddam **Rosie**
Rhouma F. c.1895 (Ardtornish)	3928	brindle/white	Dam & sire from **Rosie**
Proiseag Sgiathach of Garth F. c.1918 9209's dam was sold to the Board of Agriculture (Scotland) 1920.	9209	yellow/white	Sire 7th Gen to 489 Dam 8th Gen to **Rosie.**

NAME	HERD BOOK No.	COLOUR	PEDIGREE
Casfionn F. *c.*1928 (Craighouse Jura)	11139	brindle/white	Sire 9th Gen to 489 and 10th Gen to 295 Dam's pedigree unknown
Sweetheart of Achnaeloich F. *c.*1931	10392	yellow/pale hind socks	Sire & Dam lines each 8th Gen to 489
Ribhinn Ile Islay F. *c.*1935	10991	red/4 white socks	Sire & Dam lines each 8th Gen to 489 Sire & Dam lines each 11th Gen to 295
Ian Aluinn B. *c.*1940 (Craighouse Jura) Granddam is the brindle/white 11139 above.	4137	red	Multiple links through both Dam & Sire to 489 nearest 9th Gen; 12th Gen to 295.
Sgiathach of Kilbride B. *c.*1940	4235	red/white	12 GG grandparents trace to 489, nearest 9th Gen.
Sheila of Foreland F. *c.*1941	11570	brindle/white	Sire & Dam each 10th Gen to 489. all 16 GG. grandparents link to 489, nearest 6 Gen.
Mairi II of Findrack F. *c.*1954	16552	red/2 white socks	Sire 10 & Dam 11 Gen to 489. 14 GG grand-parents link to 489, nearest 8th Gen.
Of the two GG grandparents not linked one had no connected bloodlines, and the other no traceable pedigree.			
Niall of Douneside B. *c.*1966	5986	red	is 12th Gen to 489.
all 16 GG grandparents link to 489: three are 8th Gen; three are 9th Gen; three are 10th Gen; six are 11th Gen; and one is 12th Gen.			
Bachy of Douneside F. *c.*1966	22000	red/white	is 12 Gen to 489. is 7 Gen to 11139
Is half sister to **Niall of Douneside** both had same sire. All 16 GG Grandparents link to 489: two are 8th Gen; three are 9th Gen; four are 10th Gen five are 11th Gen; two are 12th Gen. **Bachy** is seven generations directly from the brindle/white **Casfionn**: **Casfionn** 11139 gave daughter (1st. Gen) which gave a bull (2nd Gen) which sired a bull (3rd Gen) which sired a bull (4th Gen) which sired a bull (5th Gen) which sired a bull (6th Gen) which sired **Bachy of Douneside** 22000.			

NAME	HERD BOOK No.	COLOUR	PEDIGREE
Coigreach of Inver F *c*.1972	23725	red/white	Is 9th Gen directly from 11139 and 8th Gen directly from 9209; is 14th Gen from '489'.
All 16 GG Grandparents link to '489'; four are 10th Gen; ten are 11th Gen; one is 12th Gen; one is 14th.			
Amy of Brunthill F *c*.1990	34123	part-colour	Is 16 GEN from '489'
All 16 GG Grandparents link to '489': seven are 12th Gen; four are 13th Gen; four are 14th Gen; one is 15th.			

THE BUSDUBH PATTERN

Before methods of registering cattle with the Society were established breeders continued their forefathers' system of pedigree identification by giving calves names which connected them to either dam or sire or which reflected a particular coat-colour or pattern.

An interesting category not confined to any one region, but mentioned only about females, is a distinctive marking called "BUS DUBH" meaning black muzzle.

Jet black short hairs in a well-defined broad band around the nose make a striking image on the yellow to russet coat range (*Pic 64 p54, Pic 150 p176*). It is noticeable on red coats but on brindle, if it can occur on brindle, it might be indistinguishable from the usual dark hair around the muzzle. The Busdubh marking is a precise band whereas the dark hair on a brindle often has indistinct edges.

Many breeders today have yet to see a live example of the Busdubh marking; others treat it unremarkably as being merely a lingering reminder of brindle coats somewhere in the pedigree. The brindle coat derivation seems inadequate when muzzle-ring marking is considered in a wider context. As earlier noted the ancient white Cadzow cattle have a black muzzle ring on a whole white coat and the Wild Ox is believed to have had a white muzzle ring, or partial ring, on a black coat. Coat-colour genes are probably capable of behaving in reverse rather like the negatives for photographic prints. Records from several cattle breed Societies mention the sporadic appearance of a black, brown, tan, or white muzzle ring, also found in semi-wild and wild horse species. When a tan or brown muzzle ring appeared in Galloways and Aberdeen Angus it was usually accompanied by the rigged marking of a tan or brown dorsal stripe. The dorsal stripe, 'finching' when it is white, is associated with genetic throwback to ancient times. The Busdubh marking, if it truly is a distinct pattern, may be further evidence that the genetic heritage in Highland cattle remains closer to that of their wild progenitors than it does in other domestic breeds.

Recent examples of the Busdubh marking are carried by:
Sorcha Ruadh 8th of Torloisk 33648 calved 1990, red;
Phiobaidh 60th of Balmoral 33435 calved 1990, red;
Bhoidheach Riabhach 23rd of Shenavallie 35675, yellow.

In order to check the brindle coat presence in the pedigree of Busdubhs the following summary of seven contemporary cows identified for this study exposes many shared ancestors.

Key: c = calved; Gen = generation.

Busdubh Mackay, calved 1992.

After her brindle sire **Ossian II of Glenquoich** 7643, *c.* 1989, no brindles in the sire line until the 22nd Gen brindle **Victor XV** who leads to the 25th Gen black **Young Prince Charlie** 557 *c.* 1882;
First brindle is 14th Gen through the dam line which includes Douneside, Achnacloich, Duntuilm blood to the red **Robag of Tormore** 6244, *c.* 1894 whose brindle sire **Rossie** 456, was 2nd Gen from **Sgiathanach** 489.

Zoe of Auchnacraig 32066, c 1988.

The first brindle in the sire line is 20th Gen **Victor XV** who leads to the 23rd Gen black **Young Prince Charlie** 557, *c.* 1882.
No brindle in dam line but the 3rd Dam's sire was the brindle **Chieftain of Duart** whose pedigree indirectly traces to sire 557 above.

Lady Ruadh 101st Of Benmore 31975 *c.* 1988

First brindle in the sire line is 7th Gen **John of Fordie** 4959 c 1951, then no brindles until 18th Gen **Victor XV** tracing to 21st Gen Y**oung Prince Charlie** 557 *c.* 1882.
No brindles in the dam line but the 7th Dam's sire was the brindle **Braes of Greenock** 4237 tracing to **Sgiathanach** 489; the 11th Dam's sire was brindle **Lord Clyde** 2034; the 13th dam's sire was brindle **Rob Don** 1280. The dam line ends with **Sally** 863, red, *c.* 1880.

Iona of Benmore 31373 *c.* 1987

First brindle in the sire line is 7th Gen **John of Fordie** 4959 *c.* 1951 who traces to brindle 18th Gen **Victor XV** 1292 *c.* 1895, and thence to black 21st Gen **Young Prince Charlie** 557 *c.* 1882.
No brindles in the dam line through Balliemore, Garth, Castle Grant to the red 14th Gen **Sally** 863, *c.* 1880. The 5th and 9th Dams'sires were brindles, **Braes of Greenock** 4237, and **Lord Clyde** 2034. **Braes of Greenock** traces to **Sgiathanach** 489.

Mollaig 6th of Glenquoich 30150 *c.* 1984

First brindle in the sire line is 16th Gen **Victor XV** *c.*1895, tracing to 19th Gen black **Young Prince Charlie** 557, *c.* 1882.
No brindles in the 7th Gen traced in the dam line, but the 3rd Dam's sire was the brindle **Muillear of Glenfalloch** 5174, *c.* 1953 who traces through many brindles to **Calum Riabhach II of Athole** 1325.
Both **Calum Riabhach II** and the 7th sire in the sire line trace to **Sgiathanach** 489.

Proiseag Ruadh 46th of Achnacloich 33112 *c.* 1980.

No brindles in sire line to 7th Gen. Further pedigree not studied.
No brindles in dam line through Achnacloich to Duntuilm blood to the 13th Gen red **Robag of Tormore** 6224, *c.* 1892 whose brindle sire **Rossie** 456 was 2 Gen from **Sgiathanach** 489. The 5th and 6th dams were black.

Iseabal Ruadh of Cladich 26935, c 1978.

First brindle in sire line is 19th Gen **Victor XV** 1162, *c.* 1895 tracing to 22nd Gen black **Young Prince Charlie** 557 *c.* 1882.
First brindle in dam line is the 5th dam, **Iseabal Riabhach I of Kilchamaig** 10573, *c.* 1929, whose sire and dam were both brindle. Next brindle is 12th Gen **Riabhach Og II of Kilchamaig** 3071, *c.* 1889, out of brindle dam **Riabhach Og of Kilchamaig** 830, *c.* 1876 out of the black dam **Dubh Mhor** by an Urlar bull.

The next chart illustrates how bloodlines from 1859 filtered down, to the early 1990s stock of the Leys Castle fold.

BUSDUBH CHART 2

Key:c = calved; name of dam is followed on the next line by her calf, which is followed on the next line by its calf etc.

The black bull **Lord Macdonald** 345, calved in 1859, sired **Targeal** who produced a heifer who in turn produced **Targeal Busdubh.**
Rob Roy 440 and **Targeal Busdubh** produced **Targeal Busdubh II of Ensay**, 2370, calved in 1879, red.
c. 1879 **Targeal Busdubh II of Ensay** 2370, red.
c. 1887 **Targeal Busdubh III of Ensay** 3002, brindle.
c.? **Targeal Busdubh I of Airthrey** 7239.
c. 1908 **Targeal Buidhe I of Airthrey** 7594, yellow.
c. 1913 **Targeal Buidhe I of Tangy** 8926, red.
c.? **Targeal Buidhe III of Tangy**
c. 1920 **Targeal Buidhe V of Tangy** 10356, yellow. (owned by Lord Invernairn, Flichity.)
c. 1926 **Mairi II of Flichity** 10357, yellow.
(**Mairi II** calved **Domhnull of Leys** 3731, in 1932, red; and **Mairi of Leys** 10795, in 1934; and **Mairi II of Leys** 10997, in 1935.)
c. 1931 **Mairi III of Flichity**, 10441, red.
(owned by Walker of Leys Castle. **Mairi III** calved brindle **Alasdair of Leys** 3797 in 1934; **Maid of Leys** 11078, brindle, in 1936; and further calves in 1938, 1941, 1942, 1944.)

At the Leys dispersal in 1993 several animals had black hairs round the muzzle but none had the decisive broad band of black that characterises the Busdubh pattern. This suggests along with the information in Busdubh Chart 1 that the Busdubh marking is a distinct pattern separate from that of the brindle coat marking, but possibly recessive to brindle, and that diluted brindle coats do not result in Busdubh pattern. The nearest to the Busdubh muzzle band were Lady 65th of Leys 35380, c 1991, and Donnag Sgairtail 50th of Leys 35376 c 1990. One breeder considers that the Busdubh pattern varies in intensity on the same animal, which is why it is more obvious one year than another. Whether this is a seasonal change or not is unknown, but the black muzzle band is most often seen on fully mature animals, rather than as seems to be the case for white muzzle ring, mostly on young pale-coloured calves *(Pic 149 p176).*

PERSISTENCE OF BLACK

As with the gene or alleles for parti colour, the gene or alleles for black coat-colour have persisted for more than a century of breeding programmes intended to by-pass the colour.

"In my grandfather's day no colour was considered right for Highland cattle but black. The great thing then was to have a fold of black cows. No one would look at the reds and yellows and cream and duns, which are all the rage nowadays. Though the blacks have since become unpopular, I have been told by the very best old judges of Highland cattle that there is nothing to beat the blacks for hardiness, and that the new strains of fancy-coloured cattle are much softer, and have not the same constitutions." (Osgood Mackenzie whose

grandfather's time was end of the eighteenth century when no Highland Cattle Society was in existence.)

The next two charts trace, down the maternal line, transmission of black coat by taking a starter cow and listing her female calf, the female calf's calf and so on. Sire and dam are on the same line, their female offspring on the next.

CHART A spans eighteen generations from 1877 to 1986. Of the sixteen bulls which sired successive daughters to continue the maternal line only four were black.

CHART B spans nine generations from 1925 to 1973. Of the eight bulls which sired each successive daughter to continue the maternal line only one was black. Neither the starter dam 9920 nor the starter sire 3252 had any black parents for seven generations prior to 1925, which means that Chart B in fact covers sixteen generations.

CHART A:

DAM'S BIRTH YEAR	NAME, No. & COLOUR	SIRE'S COLOUR & HERD BK. No. (ie. Sire of the next female in line...the successive daughter.)
1870s	**Nodhar** (probably Dun)	× sire unknown.
Pre 1877	**Proisag Bhuidhe** yellow	× black 451
1877	**Proisag Dhubh** 783 black	× brindle 537
1885	**Phroiseag Riabhach I** 1812 brindle	× brindle 833
1893	**Phroiseag Riabhach II** 3852 brindle	× black 952
1898	**Proisag Dubh III** 5313 black	× red 1691
1903	**Proisag Dubh V** 7009 black	× red 2319
1913	**Proisag Dubh VI** 9071 black	× brindle 2923
1920	**Proiseag Dubh VIII** 9535 black	× brindle 2758
1924	**Proiseag Dubh X** 10064 black	× red 3706
1940	**Dossan Ruadh of Woodcote** 10204 red	× black 4136 *
1942	**Dossan Dubh** 12428 black	× red 4245
1948	**Proiseag Dubh of Achnacloich** 13068 black	× red 4591
1953	**Proiseag Ruadh II** 16309 red	× black 5335
1957	**Proiseag Odhar** 18740 dun	× red 5522
1962	**Proiseag Ruadh 8th** 20782 red	× red 6047
1976	**Proiseag Ruadh 25th** 26045 red	× red 7129
1986	**Proiseag Dubh 13th** 31167 black	

* The black bull **Prionnsa Dubh of Achnacloich** 4136 continues the direct link in this bloodline, (his dam **Proiseag Dubh X** 10064 and his sire the red 3706) after which the chart continues through the female line from his daughter **Dossan Dubh** 12428.

CHART B:

DAM'S BIRTH YEAR	NAME, No. & COLOUR	SIRE'S COLOUR & HERD BK. No.
After 7 generations of no black forebears in either Dam or Sire:		
1925	**Dossan Ruadh of Achnacloich** 9920 red	× yellow 3252
1929	**Dossan Ruadh of Woodcote** 10204 red *	× yellow 3566
1933	**Dossan Bheg of Achnacloich** 11445 red	× yellow 3795
1940	**Dossan Bheg 2nd** 11674 red	× red 4245 **
1953	**Dossan Bhaeg 7th** 16301 red ***	× black 5335 +
1957	**Dosan Dubh** 18725 black	× red 5522
1962	**Dosan Dubh 2nd** 20766 black	× brindle 5854
1969	**Dosan Dubh 4th** 22927 black	× red 6047
1973	**Dosan Dubh 5th** 24362 black	

* **Dossan Ruadh of Woodcote** 10204 gave a black heifer in Chart A.

** The red bull 4245 was 16301's sire, and also +5335's grandsire on the maternal side.

*** The red cow 10204 was 16301's great granddam, and also +5335's great granddam.

Did the Dosan Dubh line begin because a touch of inbreeding allowed the black genes to dominate, or because of prepotency of the sire 5335?

Ongoing study of past and current pedigree lines will bring an answer closer.

An example of how the reduction in numbers of black-coated Highland cattle had set in by the 1880s comes from the following record of calves from a good black bull in a typical pedigree fold that had been long established by 1880. Twenty years or so later there were some brindle animals in this herd but no blacks.

CHART C:
REDUCTION IN BLACK BREEDING STOCK

Twelve cows gave 22 calves in two years to the black stock bull.
The twelve cows: six red; four yellow; two brindle
produced eleven females and eleven males:
FEMALE CALVES: three black; three red; three dun; two yellow.
MALE CALVES: eight black stots; two red stots; one red bull.

The two year crop of 22 calves released just three potential breeding females with black coats; two had a red dam, one a yellow. No black males were kept as bulls.

The other eight potential breeding females, whilst not being black-coated obviously carried genes for black inherited from their black sire. If always bred to non-black animals and likewise for their progeny, the likelihood of black offspring diminishes along with the knowledge of which stock carry hidden genes for black.

Concurrent with the decline in numbers of black Highland cattle was an absence of first-placings at Scotland's National Agricultural Show, the Highland and Agricultural Show (later the Royal Highland). In the period from 1863 to the outbreak of the Second World War in 1939 black Highland cattle were rarely placed above second in their category. That the common coat-colour in Highland cattle up to the nineteenth century was indeed black one can argue from the point of view that amid the agricultural fraternity's excitement at being able to create and 'fix' new breeds, few competitors or judges would have wanted to promote the most common example of the oldest breed, the black kylo. It may have been that not many blacks were put forward to the National Show because the Islands' strongholds of good blacks had more curl to the dense coat than the 1884 committee for the Highland Cattle Society considered 'correct'. Perhaps breeders and judges were aware of a growing need to compete against the red or roan Beef Shorthorn with the aesthetically more eye-catching red or yellow Highlands. It is possible that the black breeding stock remained smaller than their finished black steers that did so well in Fatstock Shows, and therefore in the height of the 'improving' zeal which favoured large animals the Highland breed was scorned. Whatever the cause the Highland and Agricultural Show results between 1863 and 1939 record no blacks in first place after the 1900 Show at Stirling where a black bull was awarded a first, and the 1902 Show at Aberdeen when a black cow was awarded a first.

CHART D: LOW FIRST-AWARD RATE IN BLACK HIGHLANDS AT THE HIGHLAND & AGRICULTURAL SHOWS BETWEEN 1863 AND 1939

	1863–1900						1901–1939					
	BLA	RED	BRIN	YELL	DUN	WHITE	BLA	RED	BRIN	YELL	DUN	WHITE
MALES	11	35	36	17	8	0	0	24	41	25	6	0
FEMALES	24	32	13	17	11	0	1	41	20	41	2	1

(BLA = black; BRIN = brindle; YELL = yellow.)

AWARDS BETWEEN 1829 AND 1884 FOUND IN THE HERD BOOK VOLUME I SHOW THE TOTALS: 43 TO BRINDLE – 42 TO BLACK – 34 TO RED – 25 TO YELLOW – 14 TO DUN

Greater numbers of blacks were put forward to Shows then than since but even then they were more frequently placed second or third in their class than first. The stark reality of competition is that only the first place is important. The Showground results were certainly no incentive to breeders to keep blacks.

Findings of research on Merino sheep by Iona Macleod established in 1990 that dark colour (pigment) on the nose, lips, ears, hoofs, line on ram's horn, meant there was a likelihood that there would be coloured fibres in the fleece. Other research found that the recessive allele which causes white spots on coloured sheep *"is absent from sheep with dark or black skin on the nose."* (M R Fleet) It is known that the behaviour of alleles relating to colour in sheep does not exactly apply to goats, so it probably does not exactly apply to cattle. However, it might hold a clue to not only the minority of black coats but the increase of the piebald factor in recent times, since for many years there has been a heavy predominance of pink nosed Highlands with neither dark tips to their horns nor dark stripes in their hoofs. Most twentieth century breeders discriminated against dark pigment on nose skin.

Until the mid-twentieth century drive to increase breed numbers many of the larger establishments kept records only of livestock destined for the Show circuit, whilst many of the small-holdings could spare no time to record uncommercial details. A working knowledge of parentage of animals was gradually lost. With the successful rise of breed numbers towards the end of the twentieth century came an increase in the numbers of animals at each extreme of the colour spectrum...black animals, white animals, and more recently parti colour. The appearance of parti colour is curious in that whereas some breeders persevered over many years in their efforts to recover black-coated Highlands and white-coated Highlands from the predominance of reds and yellows, nobody deliberately set out to recover or create the two-tone creature. It is unlikely that research now can reveal the percentage of parti colour, black, white, and red, distribution throughout Scotland at the beginning of the Agricultural Revolution, but most information points to there having been some black-and-white (Pied) Highlands about mid-eighteenth century and earlier and a lot of black pigment noses until 1914 or so. The presence of the twentieth century parti coloureds (Pied) points to the length of time genes can be transmitted in recessive form or that the frequency of mutant genetic behaviour is higher than generally understood. It is said that the Shorthorn cross often produces white socks and that the first cross between individuals of the different White Parks Breeds is often black with white socks. The next two examples had specialists intrigued:

"In 1913 at London Zoo a white Cadzow bull and a white Vaynol cow produced a black bull calf with long white socks on hind legs and a short sock on off fore-leg with an irregular white shoulder stripe on right side and a white tail tassle.

A white Chartley bull and a black Chartley cow produced at Poynetts a female calf mainly black with left femur and hind foot white, a white blaze, and irregular white patch just behind the withers." (Professor R Wallace)

Recessive genes behaviour is not as random as previously believed. As noted earlier (p109) Longhorn cows were put to a Chartley bull in 1906 to help restore the Chartley Whites and Longhorns have a white thigh (femur) mark. Geneticists of the 1990s have much deeper knowledge than those of 1913 of 'recessive genes of a complex nature' which were responsible for these unusual White Parks calves, but the mechanism of inheritance of colour genes is still not fully understood. Mutant genes are a different issue from recessive genes. It could be that cross-breeding encourages the presence of potentially mutant genes in addition to allowing some recessive ones to manifest their trait.

Standard transmission of coat-colour from whole colour pure-bred Highland cattle in one farm over a period of 40 years is shown in Chart E. All possible combinations of sire/dam coat-colour are not represented here, for example no dun sire, no white sire, no white dam, no parti colour, but the chart is fairly representative of average colour mixes in the majority of Highland cattle folds.

CHART E: COAT-COLOUR IN CALVES FROM BLACK, BRINDLE, RED, YELLOW, SIRES IN ONE FOLD OF COWS OF THESE COLOURS PLUS DUN

SIRE	DAM	CALF
BLACK	black	black; yellow
	brindle	black; brindle; red
	red	black; red; yellow

SIRE	DAM	CALF
BLACK	yellow	black; yellow; red; dun
	dun	yellow
(Black sire/black dam can also give dun, red, brindle; on red dam dun; on dun dam red and black. Other results from black sires are possible though not formally collected for this study.)		
BRINDLE	black	black; brindle; red
	brindle	brindle; red
	red	black; brindle; red
	yellow	black; brindle; red; yellow; dun
	dun	red; yellow; dun
RED	black	black; red
	brindle	brindle; red
	red	black; brindle; red; yellow
	yellow	brindle; red; yellow
	dun	black; brindle; red; yellow; dun
YELLOW	black	black; red; dun
	brindle	black; brindle; red; yellow
	red	brindle; red; yellow
	yellow	brindle; red; yellow; dun; white.

WHOLE COLOUR REGISTERED IN HERD BOOKS VOLUMES I TO 69 (1884 – 1990)

A careful look at the Highland cattle Herd Books yields the statistics shown in Chart F of the totals of whole colours registered each year from 1884 to 1990. These figures must be treated lightly as merely a guide to trends in popularity of colours for the following reasons.

i. Chart F figures are drawn from the only source available, the Herd Books and they only record such animals as breeders elected to register; until mid-twentieth century in Scotland there were considerable numbers of unregistered pure-bred stock and there is now no way of assessing colour predominance in unregistered stock long since gone;

ii. colour is not reliably assessed the same way by each breeder. Black animals have been registered as brindle, brown animals either as dun or red, red as yellow, yellow as white, and many with white undercarriage or socks were registered under their main colour as if whole coloured. These seeming inaccuracies may have been because calves are registered before their final mature coat-colour is evident, or because black was unpopular and cheating the registration form was thought to be the only way to keep some quality bloodlines available, or because the Society was wrong to have excluded brown as a distinct colour category particularly as it may represent genetically, like black, a link with the remote past;

iii: the colour of animals in the Herd Books is sometimes absent. The annual totals in Chart F, therefore, are at variance with totals of registrations given in the Herd Books.

For every suspect colour registration there are, however, many correct ones recorded with meticulous care, and so the Herd Books do offer some idea of trends in the choice of colours considered worth the expense and effort of registration.

CHART F:

The chart presents the yearly totals registered of each of the six whole colour categories Black, Red, Brindle, Yellow, Dun, White, over the period from 1884 to 1990 arranged in two groupings, one for males and one for females. Animals listed in the Herd Books without a colour or with a colour not contained in the above six categories have been omitted. No Appendix A and B animals are included.

WHOLE COLOUR REGISTERED IN HERD BOOKS VOLUMES I – XXIII 1884 TO 1932

	HERD BK	I				V					X					XV					XX			XXIII
	year	1884	1887	1888	1890	1891	1893	1895	1897	1898	1900	1902	1904	1905	1907	1908	1910	1912	1916	1919	1923	1928	1929	1932
MALE	BLACK	200	10	12	23	15	10	7	11	12	5	7	9	6	5	3	3	2	2	0	0	0	1	0
	RED	113	12	21	56	49	36	37	33	41	46	40	37	49	31	39	49	37	64	59	57	35	72	57
	BRINDLE	94	12	24	25	30	39	31	50	51	63	56	53	64	50	55	50	43	82	45	53	40	61	40
	YELLOW	92	17	15	23	23	25	15	32	30	49	45	42	56	41	35	52	28	81	66	73	53	52	41
	DUN	51	6	3	5	5	3	4	2	5	6	4	6	9	3	2	5	4	3	1	3	2	6	0
	WHITE	0	0	0	0	0	0	0	0	0	0	0	0	0	0	0	0	0	0	0	0	0	0	1
FEMALE	BLACK	–	200	73	80	145	86	50	58	85	42	64	72	7	32	19	23	21	25	11	8	10	4	1
	RED	–	279	203	214	249	211	186	162	202	178	192	215	36	180	130	124	159	190	124	111	151	77	165
	BRINDLE	–	131	63	78	107	104	56	72	114	111	107	128	32	126	76	91	113	154	91	78	75	77	88
	YELLOW	–	141	103	82	134	94	68	93	126	105	118	126	38	129	99	69	100	148	120	112	146	92	144
	DUN	–	87	38	47	58	34	20	36	32	16	18	39	7	41	17	24	29	19	15	6	11	5	8
	WHITE	–	1	0	0	1	0	0	0	0	0	0	0	0	0	0	0	0	1	1	2	1	1	6

CHART F CONT: WHOLE COLOUR REGISTERED IN HERD BOOKS XXIII (No. 46) 1937 TO 1967

	HERD BK	XXIV	25					30					35					40					45	46
	year	1937	1940	1946	1948	1949	1950	1951	1952	1953	1954	1955	1956	1957	1958	1959	1960	1961	1962	1963	1964	1965	1966	1967
MALE	BLACK	0	1	2	1	2	1	0	1	2	1	1	1	5	0	0	1	2	0	0	1	0	0	0
	RED	93	81	89	109	104	62	53	67	64	76	30	31	34	25	26	30	39	28	32	21	13	40	35
	BRINDLE	56	64	54	78	57	29	41	28	24	27	20	10	9	16	4	10	6	10	6	4	5	5	12
	YELLOW	47	52	53	56	40	18	27	17	14	16	14	11	9	6	8	15	14	10	7	8	5	12	9
	DUN	1	1	2	1	1	0	0	0	1	0	0	0	0	1	0	0	0	0	0	0	1	0	0
	WHITE	0	0	0	2	5	1	0	1	1	1	2	2	0	0	0	0	2	0	1	0	2	0	0
FEMALE	BLACK	3	7	7	5	9	3	9	12	3	5	5	9	8	7	4	6	3	14	8	7	10	2	4
	RED	255	182	270	513	560	311	302	344	419	453	455	463	416	347	325	300	267	326	253	250	239	241	217
	BRINDLE	114	91	81	167	122	65	80	94	77	82	43	49	52	38	24	34	29	24	27	21	26	25	13
	YELLOW	126	112	157	225	157	125	80	140	109	118	78	82	64	59	55	46	41	39	29	42	43	36	41
	DUN	5	6	4	4	6	0	1	6	4	3	5	3	3	0	0	0	2	1	2	0	3	0	3
	WHITE	1	8	7	4	8	3	2	4	2	2	2	2	1	5	1	0	3	3	2	1	1	3	1

CHART F CONT: WHOLE COLOUR REGISTERED IN HERD BOOKS VOLUMES 47 - 69 1968 TO 1990

	HERD BK	47			50					55					60					65				69
	year	1968	1969	1970	1971	1972	1973	1974	1975	1976	1977	1978	1979	1980	1981	1982	1983	1984	1985	1986	1987	1988	1989	1990
MALE	BLACK	0	0	1	0	2	5	1	3	3	4	3	5	2	2	4	2	8	0	3	6	8	6	6
	RED	27	32	23	24	44	90	66	48	56	36	27	42	30	29	31	26	33	30	26	56	75	80	20
	BRINDLE	7	5	6	7	9	13	17	7	5	3	1	3	6	6	1	2	4	1	2	8	11	15	3
	YELLOW	8	6	5	4	7	24	16	12	14	10	14	6	4	6	8	4	4	4	3	12	15	22	11
	DUN	1	0	0	0	0	0	3	0	1	0	1	0	0	0	1	0	2	0	1	1	1	2	2
	WHITE	0	1	0	2	0	0	3	0	1	0	1	3	3	0	1	2	3	1	2	4	3	6	2
FEMALE	BLACK	2	3	1	4	7	18	9	16	11	25	15	14	30	11	15	17	28	25	25	33	32	46	47
	RED	204	226	179	153	285	436	406	414	470	431	461	352	456	332	350	336	334	313	357	442	498	643	717
	BRINDLE	18	16	9	21	31	27	27	19	12	27	26	13	33	20	21	8	10	8	7	8	9	17	16
	YELLOW	41	49	33	47	49	92	79	130	104	131	71	54	73	41	50	60	40	44	73	69	88	93	110
	DUN	0	2	2	3	2	0	6	5	6	4	5	4	3	3	5	2	9	8	7	8	14	16	7
	WHITE	1	3	0	2	2	2	1	10	9	16	16	14	15	15	7	13	12	8	9	16	13	25	24

Chart G follows showing the numbers of bulls in each colour category which were advertised in the Highland Cattle Society's annual journals 1964 to 1993, *The Highland Breeders' Journal*, as available stock bulls. (British Section only)

CHART G:

COLOUR OF STOCK BULLS ADVERTISED IN THE JOURNALS

year	1964	1965	1966	1967	1968	1969	1970	1971	1972	1973	1974	1975	1976	1977	1978
BLACK	1	1	0	0	0	0	0	2	2	4	3	2	3	6	5
RED	39	26	27	24	23	27	27	32	35	38	36	48	39	42	29
BRINDLE	5	9	5	3	7	6	5	6	4	4	3	7	8	4	8
YELLOW	7	1	5	6	8	5	4	3	3	5	6	11	8	7	8
DUN	0	0	0	0	0	0	0	0	0	0	0	0	1	0	0
WHITE	0	0	0	0	0	1	0	1	0	0	1	1	2	2	1

year	1979	1980	1981	1982	1983	1984	1985	1986	1987	1988	1989	1990	1991	1992	1993
BLACK	5	5	7	1	3	4	5	5	9	10	8	7	12	19	27
RED	36	34	49	25	26	29	33	44	43	66	90	113	125	167	179
BRINDLE	6	3	4	6	4	3	6	6	9	9	13	17	20	23	28
YELLOW	9	10	14	7	8	12	12	15	10	13	19	21	20	31	37
DUN	1	1	1	0	0	1	1	3	1	1	1	1	2	2	3
WHITE	1	1	2	1	1	2	3	5	8	8	6	8	10	14	13

REFERENCES IN CHAPTER 6

Standard Cyclopedia of Modern Agriculture
Martin Martin, *A Description of the Western Isles of Scotland 1703*
Osgood Mckenzie, *100 Years in the Highlands*
Col William Fullerton, *General View of the County of Ayr 1793*
D E McGuire, *Agricultural Improvement in Strathkelvin 1700 – 1850*
A R Forbes, *Gaelic Names of Beasts, Birds, Fishes, Insects and Reptiles*, 1905
F Fraser Darling, *Crofting Agriculture 1945*
I F Grant, *Everyday Life on an Old Highland Farm*
Present State of Husbandry in Scotland 1773 – 1782, Vol IX, Vol VIII
Statistical Account of Scotland 1750 – 1790, Vols 19, 1, 3, 9, 18, 5, 10.
D Macdonald, *Lewis: A History of the Island*
New Statistical Account for Scotland Vols XIV, X, VIII
HMSO Booklet published 1955
Dr A Fraser, *Beef Cattle Husbandry*
Dr S Adalsteinsson, personal letter 1994
James Cameron, article in *The Dundee Advertiser*, 1899
M R Fleet 1985, Paper on Wool Technology and Sheep Breeding*
Iona Macleod 1990, Paper on Black Spots and Pigmented Fibres in Merino Wool*
Professor R Wallace, *Farm Livestock of Great Britain*

* Courtesy of Dr G Simm, SAC

CHAPTER 7: ORIGIN

CHAPTER 7: ORIGIN

1. WILD OX - 2. DOMESTIC OX - 3. DIVERSIFICATION

1. WILD OX

THE WILD OX
(SKETCH BY URC. AFTER CUVIER'S PLATE IV IN)
ANIMAL KINGDOM

Also known as: **Urus** used by Caesar taken from the old Gothic word UR for wild; **Aurochs** in German, plural Aurochsen; *Bos* ***primigenius taurus*** used by Linnaeus; **Giant Ox**; **European Wild Ox**.

"No other event in early history was of such comparably far reaching significance for the development of human culture as the domestication of oxen. The ***domestic cattle*** *(Bos primigenius taurus) made possible the step from the primitive hoeing of the upper Stone Age to highly developed agriculture, and, thus, it became the very basis of the Asiatic-European culture. Therefore, the question of the descent of cattle has interested breeders, zoologists, archaeologists, and historians, and has led to various theories.*

However, the modern zoological research on domestication presently confidently considers one wild form, the Aurochs (Bos primigenius primigenius) to be the one ancestor of all domestic cattle."[4]

The Wild Ox existed in Scotland well before the first known evidence of people. Its remains dating from Ice Age times have been found in interglacial deposits near Crofthead in Renfrewshire. The profusion of skulls and other bones found from Wigtownshire to Caithness on the floor of lakes formed from the melting Ice Cap suggests there were concentrations of herds in the valleys of the Tweed, Tay, and the flat lands of Caithness. These last three regions being in the east of Scotland lends credence to the theory that the Wild Ox spread westwards into Scotland from Denmark across the once dry and forested North Sea Basin, and northwards from England while the Thames was a tributary of the Rhine.

The originating source of the Wild Ox is generally considered to have centred in Central Asia or North India from where it spread northwards. The first evidence of it in Europe comes from Germany dated at 250,000 years ago. Wild Ox remains from some 7 million years ago were found in the Himalayas, Japan, China, North Africa, and some 2 million years ago diversification began into Aurochs, Yak, European Bison, Indian Buffalo, Indian Bison (Gaur), wild cattle of India and Banteng of Burma.[1] The evolutionary process had been in action a very long time before cattle reached the north of Britain, those that did belonging to the diversified species of Wild Ox known as the European Wild Ox.

Several ice advances and thaws were to occur before conditions stabilised enough in Scotland to allow life forms to firmly establish themselves. *"Wild Ox, like all other fauna necessarily retreated before advancing ice but unlike Mammoth, Lion, Woolly Rhinoceros and Giant Deer, survived to return northward as vegetations increased around 12,000 to 10,000 BC."*[2]

Cattle, together with reindeer, red deer, and wild horse, first entered Scotland by themselves colonising the area newly freed from the ice-sheet around 10,000 BC. They were followed in due course by hunting bands of *Homo sapiens*. The North Sea Basin being in its southern region *"a zone of marshes, swamps, river channels, mudflats, sand banks and islets"*[2] made possible considerable traffic until rising water levels permanently flooded land connections with Europe around 6,000 to 5,000 BC creating the British Islands of today.

Studies of refuse heaps left by nomadic hunting peoples in Scotland have revealed that they had successfully hunted the Wild Ox which measured about 6 feet at the shoulder with a span of 4 feet from horn tip to horn tip with a girth of more than 20 inches at the horn base.

"The first skeleton mounted in England in the Science School Cambridge of a Bos primigenius measured 5 feet 3 inches at the withers to which must be added 3 inches for hide and fluff and 1 inch for thickness of the frog which gives a live animal measurement of 5 feet 7 inches at the withers or 16¾ hands.

A complete skeleton mounted at Lund in Sweden measures 5 feet 7½ inches at the withers giving an estimated 5 feet 11½ inches or 17 hands 3½ inches live animal measurement.

Study of size of Bos primigenius skulls suggest that the size of one found in Atholl is atypically large possibly as a result of accidental castration while young.

Atholl skull: 2 feet 5¾ inches long; 1 foot 1½ inches between bases of horns.

Kirkcudbright skull: 2 feet 3 inches long; 10 inches between bases of horns.

Preston skull: 2 feet 4¼ inches long; 1¾ inches between bases of horns.

Other skulls in the British museum do not exceed 2 feet 4½ inches in length of face and 1 foot 1 inch between the horns."[3]

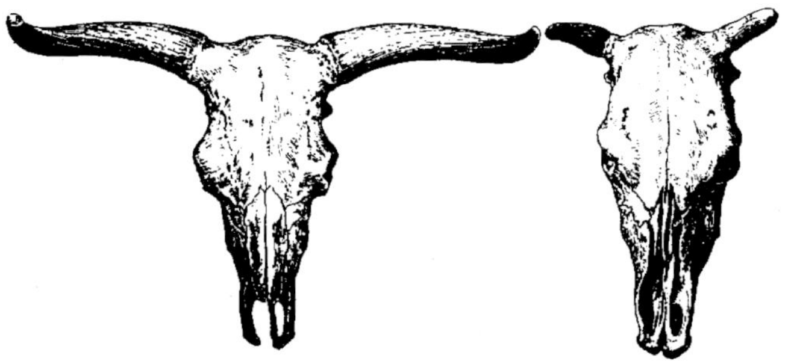

Standard Cyclopedia of mod agriculture & rural economy, 1910

Bos primigenius (Urus) found at Blair Atholl, Scotland

Bos primigenius longifrons (Celtic Shorthorn, Scotland)

"Typical horns of the Urus originate from the skull in a diagonal direction, that is, they start sideways (to the long axis of the skull) but with a decided backwards inclination; almost immediately however as if they had discovered their error in direction, they sweep round, and describe a wide crescent with concave side to the front, and the tips bend very slightly upwards, and a little inwards, so that the tips are not the parts of the horns which are farthest from each other. In the Atholl example, after the normal start outwards and backwards, they proceed almost directly outwards with only a very slight bow until, some few inches from the tips, they turn up, the tips being bent upwards and backwards, and form the parts of the horns which are furthest from one another; each core almost forming a shallow S".[3]

Other reference to the Wild Ox states *"The males and females looked so different that until 1927 some of the cows were thought to have been a subspecies called Bos primigenius minutus. The bulls were about one fourth larger and heavier than the cows and weighed from 800 to 1,000 Kg. They both had a light build with rather long legs, a straight back with only a slightly declining croup, and a deep chested frontal body heavier than the hind part.*

The slender head was long, had a straight profile and long forehead. The horns were up to 80 cm. long, pointed, sturdy, and the crosscut was circular. There are different forms; most grow out to the sides then turn upward and forward, with the tips directed slightly inward. The horns are white with black tips.

The summer coat was short and smooth, the winter one dense and almost curly. The males of Northern Europe were black-brown with a light streak on the back, a white circle around the chin and muzzle, bright curly locks on the forehead, and lighter underside and inner sides of the legs. In Southern Europe they were brown or gray-brown, and in Africa red-brown with a white or pale yellow saddle. The females were plain brown but darker in winter, while the calves were red-brown."[4]

Wild Ox remains excavated from Scottish peat bogs measured upwards of 16 hands at the withers, but other specimens measuring about 18 hands were thought to have predated them.

So reduction in size may have begun even before domestication, a process known to result in loss of original wild dimensions. There is no certainty that the Wild Ox ever was domesticated in Scotland, so scant evidence of ancient stock farming techniques forces conjecture. Some historians do consider it to have been domesticated there too, in keeping with the theory that the Wild Ox had been domesticated *"at several places and at different times under various conditions, and that from there the multitude of the present races of cattle developed."*[4]

Whatever its prehistory involvement with people, plentiful Wild Ox remains yielded from peat bogs in Ayrshire and Berwickshire testify to its well-established presence across Lowland Scotland in addition to its north easterly spread. As ever increasing numbers of various peoples continued to penetrate and settle in Scotland, thousands of centuries of human activities from habitat destruction to hunting drove the Wild Ox to seek safety in the still extensive forests of the remote northern areas. From choice Wild Ox favoured the edge of woodlands in the proximity of open pastures, valleys and water marshes, and light forests which in mountain districts they would frequent up to the timber line. Remains in a mound at Keiss in Caithness and in a broch at Kintradwell beyond Brora in Sutherland suggest the last survivors of the Wild Ox in Scotland died about the ninth or tenth century.

The species had spent at least 6,000 years in Scotland, after the forming of the British Isles.

Specialist study of bones found in Scotland show it to be the same species as the Wild Ox in Europe, the last of which died in Poland in 1627. Records were kept of the only remaining herd there after it had been put under special protection and kept in a game reserve near Warsaw. With twentieth century knowledge of animal husbandry that herd might not have lapsed into extinction. However, before it did an artist from the early sixteenth century made a profile of a bull in oil painting on wood. The painting was discovered in Augsburg by Major Hamilton Smith in the early nineteenth century. He assumed it to be an illustration of the Wild Ox and described it thus: *"It is a representation of a bull without a mane but rather rugged, with a large head, thick neck, small dewlap entirely sooty black, the chin alone white, and the horns turning forward and then upward like the bull of Romania; pale in colour with black tips."*[5]

One twentieth century researcher wrote that the European Wild Ox was of a *"dark reddish brown colour verging on black, with long black tipped horns, and with hair short and comparatively smooth, except on the forehead where it was long and curly."*[5] Another wrote that *"black bulls were long legged, deep chested, curly hair on forehead, white or greyish muzzle, white or yellow stripe along spine, 6 feet or more at humped shoulders, about 2,000 pounds. The smaller cows were dun coloured or red with darker neck and legs, calves fawn, darkening to adult colour by 2 years. Male calves took several years to acquire the deepest black."*[6]

Cave paintings in France dating from about 15,000 BC show bulls which are black or reddish black with a pale line along the back and long upcurved horns.

A description given in the 1875 edition *Encyclopedia Britannica* of the Urus is interesting in that it includes "*a flat or slightly concave forehead.*"[7] Some pedigree Scottish Highland cattle in the nineteenth century showed a dished nose (concave) and similar heads can be found today...late twentieth century.

Scottish Highland cattle also come to mind when reading "*The cattle were Aurochs, Bos primigenius, ranging in colour from white through red to black, the bulls mainly red at birth and turning black in maturity, with touches of white on muzzle, brow, belly and/or spine. Bulls were about 25% larger than cows, standing up to 1.75m (6 feet) at the shoulder. The breed lived in herds, dominated by matriarch cows, with young bulls forming detached 'clubs' and establishing their own dominance, ready to challenge the herd bull some day.*

In such herds the cows, especially the calvers, are the main danger, the bull only showing aggression when roused by his cows or on the approach of a rival. A hunting party of humans would be well advised to pick off well-grown yearling or 2 year olds and keep clear of the adults. Killing the master bull precipitates great restlessness and fighting among younger successors."[2]

Clearly then enough information is available to give a fair idea of the appearance of the European Wild Ox, the progenitor of Scottish Highland cattle. Its decline to extinction was probably due to the combined effects of unfavourable food conditions and intensive hunting by humans.

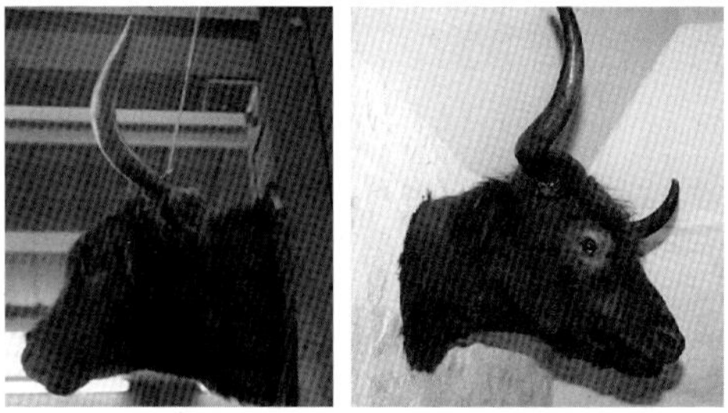

Mark Brown

Profiles of both nose types – dished and long – from the Kilberry Herd 1890s

2. DOMESTIC OX

Also known as **Celtic Shorthorn, Marsh Shorthorn, *Bos brachyceros, Bos longifrons***...this after confusion when Brachyceros was also used for a small-horned, not short-horned, species in East Indian Islands. British writers tend mostly to use Celtic Shorthorn when referring to the early domestic Ox in Britain.

Hunting Man was well-established throughout Scotland before the gradual spread of farming peoples saw a period of co-existence with the growth of barter, begun by the hunters, laying firm foundations of trading.

By 4,000 BC several innovations had appeared more or less at the same time...grain seeds developed from non-native grasses, simple pottery, domesticated cattle and soon afterwards sheep and goats...suggesting such innovations were brought by immigrants, believed to have originated in Eastern and Central Europe. "*They grew barley, wheat, and in addition to oxen bred sheep, goats pigs and dogs. It has been estimated that a 32 feet coracle could have carried over three tons of cargo, including eight rowers, one steersman, passengers and stores, two cows carried thrown, and two calves or six pigs or ten sheep.*"[8] Such a large scale expedition is considered by some to have been less likely than several ferrying journeys made in a smaller craft with a cow swimming in tow, and unless bull calves were carried on board perpetuation of domestic stock would have had to rely on wild bulls. Transporting young bulls in an open coracle is fraught with practical problems. However there is agreement that a race of cattle brought by people to Scotland differed from the Wild Ox in the following ways. Their remains, found usually where humans had settled, showed that "*the bones of the limbs were slender like those of deer, and the skull long and narrow and deer-like carrying two short tapering horns about 9 inches long between which on the forehead was a prominent bony crest. The skeleton indicates that this ox, known as the Celtic Shorthorn, was a long bodied but light agile animal, well fitted to protect itself by speed of limb from the many beasts of prey of the Scottish forests. It probably measured 5' 4" from the nape to the end of the rumpbone, the head about 1' 4" so that the whole length must have been 6' 8"*."[5]

Measurements of an Award Winning Highland Cow in 1992 were:

1 foot 7 inches	from crown to nose;
3 feet 6 inches	spread between horn tips;
4 feet 6 inches	from shoulder/neck to tailhead;
1 foot 10 inches	across hook-bones (torbones);
4 feet 4 inches	high at hook bones

Since the Neolithic peoples along with their livestock were well-established in Britain by 3,000 BC it is misleading that the earliest known form of British domestic cattle were called by later historians **The Celtic Shorthorn** when the Celtic farming peoples only began to arrive and colonise Britain about 400 BC [3]. In comparison to the Wild Ox the Celtic Shorthorn was overall a much smaller animal with a rough long haired coat of a dark red or brownish tint. Red cow hairs found in bog-butter stashes deep in peat mosses in Argyll, Inverness, Banff, Moray, Sutherland, Skye, and North Yell, are considered to be from the Celtic Shorthorn since it is the only race of domestic cattle known to have been in Scotland prior to the Roman invasion. This evidence of colour, though, apart from vagueness in dating bog-butter...anything from eighth to eighteenth century, tells nothing of the colour of the Celtic Shorthorn bull, for his hairs are unlikely to have dropped in at the butter making and he could well have been, like the Wild Ox, considerably darker than the cows, brindle or even black. Jesting aside, the hairs in the butter probably came from the method of sieving the milk through sieves made with hair from cattle hides, or from whisks made from rings of twisted cow hair at the end of a stick. Although bull hides would have been utilised they would have been available less frequently than those from cows and as red cows, according to mainland folklore, were milkier than other colours selection for red may have been practised from earliest times. Conjecture sadly is not conclusive.

By modern stock farming standards the Celtic Shorthorns were more wild than domestic, certainly in Neolithic times. Their lightness of limb suggests that they actively ranged over considerable forest territory which of course they shared with wolves, bears, and wild cattle. The substantial amounts of remains of young animals discovered in bone deposits around human settlements (Scotland) imply 1: that dairy farming was well-established; or 2: that the wildness of the cattle meant that any herding activities must have been virtually a type of hunting which facilitated capture of the young or weak stock.

Whatever the state of wildness a breeding cow would have been more valuable than a calf and only eaten in times of great hardship. So any autumn culling which may have been practised would have resulted in discarded young bones as opposed to adult ones. Such stock as may have been kept in enclosures over the winter were most probably fed on any available straw and leaf fodder gathered from the nearest woodlands. Quite possibly Oak, Birch, Hazel, Beech, Willow, featured largely in their diet.

Domestication of wild mammal species generally results initially in a reduction in body size, brain size, sense organs, usually accompanied by a shortening of the jaws and facial regions of the skull. Less uniformity than in wild species is a general feature of domestic animals. In domestic cattle there certainly is individual variation also quite a difference between the skull of a cow and the skull of a bull.[13] (The bull and cow skull difference might of course reflect the size difference between male and female Wild Ox.) Skulls of the Celtic Shorthorn have always been found in excavations of human settlements and nowhere that would invite speculation that they were ever a wild species. But since most excavations are conducted on occupation sites or graves it would be more accurate to say that as yet no hard evidence has come to light to support the idea that the Celtic Ox was ever a wild species in Scotland. These cattle are believed to have been a domestic variation of the Wild Ox, brought to Scotland in its domesticated form by settlers from Europe.

"Skulls found in Thames alluvium at Limehouse and at Cannington suggest there was a larger species of ox, Bos Frontosus, at least in the south of Britain, at the same time as the Celtic Shorthorn."[9] It had an oval horn core, similar to that found on Scandinavian cattle of the period, as opposed to the round core of the Celtic Shorthorn. At least two main types of domesticated cattle were arriving in Britain from Europe... the longhorned *Bos primigenius* called *Bos taurus* and the shorthorned *Bos primigenius* called *Bos longifrons*...and some argument is put forward supporting the idea that a third major type...polled white cattle...was also brought in these ancient times. Speculation is not out of place, therefore, that random interbreeding occurred, adding to the variety in native types.

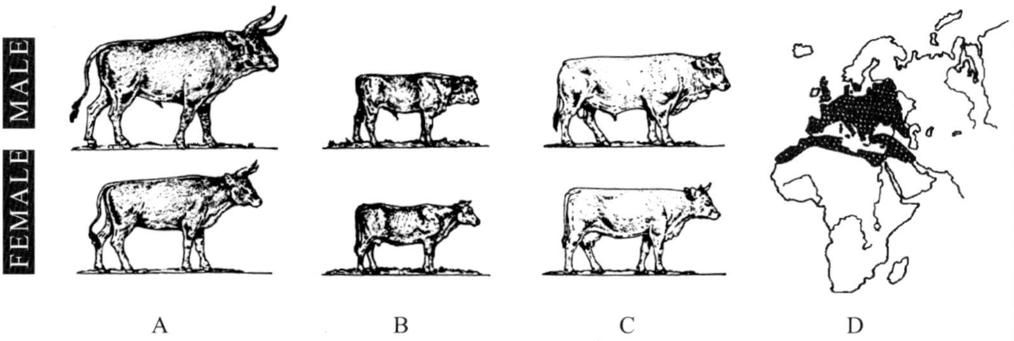

A. Aurochs (BOS PRIMIGENIUS) (WILD OX)
B. Celtic domestic cattle according to fossils found at Manching near Ingolstadt
C. One of the present class Breeds
D. In the shaded region the Aurochs (BOS PRIMIGENIUS) still existed in historic times

In these scale drawings it is noticeable how domestication reduced the size difference between the sexes in the Aurochs

Scale drawings of Wild Ox, Celtic cattle, modern breeds (from Grzimek's Animal Encyclopedia)

3. DIVERSIFICATION

In Scotland any evolutionary diversification of, or involving, the Wild Ox had to take place during the centuries between its extinction in the tenth century and 6,000 BC by which time the rising sea level had separated Britain from Europe. Rain, wind, cold temperature, sparse vegetation, progressive loss of forests, and geological barriers which limited arrivals of fresh stock, are factors governing evolutionary change in cattle in the North, North West and Western Islands of Scotland. Survival tactics may have included reduction in size, growth of thicker hide and longer denser hair. The harsh climate may have encouraged a prevalence of black coats throughout the herd rather than only in males to absorb more efficiently any available warmth from sunlight. This colour change would not have been so vital in the south of England where the climate is consistently milder. Concurrent with that slow adaptive process linked to natural environmental and climate conditions was less gradual change forced by the supreme predator, man.

It seems probable that early farmers supplemented their domestic stock by selecting small or young rather than large mature oxen for ease of handling. Stealing a Wild Ox may have been aided by the breed's habit of dropping the calf in a protective thicket where it lay quietly awaiting the mother's return twice a day for suckling. But given the fierceness of the breed this would have been a hazardous procedure indeed, followed by considerable difficulty in feeding such a calf. Weaned yearlings were more likely to have been caught when wild herds were chased into stampeding out of the cultivated land which they had been browsing. At the same time as taking the young animals man was engaged in hunting the large and well fleshed bulls for his meat supply. This forced the smaller animals to continue the breeding line and could have contributed to an overall reduction in size. But this theory is hardly upheld if one considers that when the black bulls which supply the bull rings of Spain, Portugal and Southern France '*prove themselves to be great powerful animals of immense stamina and resourcefulness in the ring they are not withdrawn to be used to sire similar progeny*'.[10] Either there is a limitless supply of equally endowed bulls or the quality of stock is carried through the female line. It is tempting to deduce that the closer the breed genetically to the Wild Ox the more powerful the female ability to stamp specific traits on offspring. This could have evolved as a survival tactic to combat man's relentless slaughter, begun of necessity and continued for sport, of wild forest bulls much in the way that twentieth century wild female elephants, it has been suggested, may have learned to mate with the lesser bulls because they are more likely to survive the ivory hunters. Such a theory lends substance to the belief some farmers have that the secret of breeding consistently fine Highland cattle lies in the choice of quality females. But since cattle belong to a species which functions in a herd of females dominated by a leader bull who has won his supremacy through successful combat, there is definitely an argument in support of the farmers who believe the quality of their herd sire is the essential factor in maintaining reliably good stock. Perhaps the answer lies not so much in the gender of today's breeding stock as in their relative closeness genetically to the Wild Ox. Could it be that the closer an individual animal's blood type is to that of the Wild Ox the more likely it is to dominate in the transmission of inherited traits?

Nevertheless irrespective of where dominance in genetic transmission lies, continual cross-breeding and interbreeding of domestic stock with semi-wild and wild stock both accidentally and deliberately must have been the norm over thousands of years.

Early invaders such as Romans and Norsemen are thought to have brought with them types of cattle hitherto unknown in Britain.

The Romans may have introduced heavy draught oxen, a red Urus type or a polled white type. Evidence is hard to find and theories abound, but it is likely they encountered in southern Britain various strains of native cattle, the result of centuries of evolving to adapt to their differing environments.

From 80 AD there was a strong Roman presence in Perthshire throughout much of their 400 year occupation of Britain. If they did bring with them live cattle it must have been with provisions bearing reinforcements rather than with the Legions who, *"carried all their equipment and marched at a pace never equalled until the Brigade of Guards broke the record in 1943; hardly compatible with the stately progress of bullock carts."*[2] Yet it is curious that the Highland cattle widely renowned in the nineteenth century for their superior conformation and easy fleshing qualities came from Glenlyon around Fortingall (Perthshire), reputed birthplace of the Roman statesman Pontius Pilate and an area with evidence of heavy Roman presence. These Glenlyon Highland cattle were red. The colour connection with Roman cattle in Glenlyon is a tenuous link because the Plague mid-eighteenth century is said to have wiped out all livestock there except one white cow. However red Highland cattle seem to have been more prevalent in Perthshire than in the relatively Roman-free Western Scottish seaboard where the Highland cattle which proliferated were black, so perhaps the central location of Perthshire permitted a continuous mixing of livestock as peoples moved north/south and east/west through it.

Later invaders, the Angles from Germany, may have brought to England a red and white longhorned type which in due course would mix with local cattle providing further diversity from which the agricultural improvers in the eighteenth century were to select the basis for modern cattle breeds. Not until the 1850s were these "improved" breeds to be found throughout all of Scotland.

A red or dun polled type may have been introduced to the north of Scotland by Norse Vikings who ruled from 794 AD until 1266 and who invaded many parts of eastern England making settlements there too. Norse occupation of Orkney and Shetland is still reflected in place names there deriving from their language. For example their word for cattle-pen was kvi which became quoy as in Cornquoy, Sandquoy, Quoyloo in Orkney. There is a theory that the polled cattle from Buchan in north east Scotland were descended from Norse cattle. Yet the Vikings who invaded and ruled the Western Isles for hundreds of years did not introduce these cattle there too. For if they had, since the polled gene is dominant to the horned gene, few horned cattle could have survived the duration of the Viking occupation. Cattle native to Orkney, Shetland and the Western Isles were horned breeds.

Strictly controlled breeding, such as the careful selection of a particular bull for a particular cow, became widely applied only well into the spread of new agricultural knowledge in the eighteenth century. The main obstacles to selective breeding pre-Agricultural Revolution were lack of enclosed grazings and lack of scientific understanding of genetics.

Archaeological research suggests there were massive field systems in use with stone or turf dykes as long ago as Neolithic times. But these were primarily for crop growing rather than cattle grazing. (Neolithic communities did not require mass production of beef or dairy products from huge herds of cattle.)

It would have been well-understood that the seasonal arrival time of calves played an important part in their survival. However, keeping a domestic bull would have presented many difficulties, since even today bulls have a habit of quietly defying the confines of their enclosure from time to time. *"Very probably it was more convenient and practical to hope a wild bull would sire the domestic cows. Edging the wild herd near when needed could have been achieved by allowing easy access to lush feeding. In South East Asia in recent times salt licks were set out to attract wild Gaur bulls; then domestic bulling cows were turned into the area and left until served and settled. Any Neolithic domestic bulling cows which may have gone off with the wild herd would probably have been driven out in due course by the dominant wild matriarchs to make their way home."*[2]

Then the centuries of repeated invasions with the inevitable plundering and setting fire to villages and woodland must have led to frequent escape of domestic stock which along with semi-wild and wild stock fled from the fires to different territory where their presence swelled the numbers of feral cattle. A theory exists which suggests that domestic bovines gone wild tend to revert to white. In support of this, mention is made of animals which had been running wild in southern districts of the Falkland Islands since 1771 being *"white with feet, whole head or ears only, black"* and wild oxen in the Ladrone Islands *"were milk white except for the ears which were generally black."*[11]

White Wild cattle of similar description were once widespread throughout forests in England and central Scotland where their pursuit provided royalty and aristocracy with a very popular pastime. Early Scottish writers have referred to them as Tauri Sylvestres of the Caledonian Forests. Hector Boece wrote in 1527: *"Caledonian Wood ran from Stirling through Menteith and Strathearn to Atholl and Lochaber. The bulls to be found in this forest were so ferocious great skill and cunning was required to capture them alive. But captured adults died in captivity since they would not eat anything that had been touched or handled by man."*[12] Bishop John Leslie adds a little more information in his reference: *"The forest of Torwood stretches from Callander to Lochaber. This is now the only place to find the few remaining whyte kye. There used to be not only white kye but also oxen and bulls which were snowhite with a thick and long mane like that of a lion. The bulls were so fierce they would attack without provocation. Although once numerous, now through the gluttony of men they are to be found only in the Park of Stirling, and in Kincairney near Dunkeld in Perthshire."* [3]

By the sixteenth century then, the numbers of white wild cattle had so seriously dwindled that protective measures were initiated by the Crown, the great Lords and the monastic bodies which ensured the survival of the species. The surviving remnant of one herd from these times can be found today in Chillingham in the north of England. It is claimed that in 700 years there have been no coloured calves in that herd, nor any twins. No twinning is a trait more associated with truly wild animals than with domesticated ones. However by the time the wild whites were enclosed in parks the ancient Wild Ox had long been extinct and the evolution of differing regional types of domestic stock had stabilised with regard to any intrusion of wild blood. But wild blood was available as recently as 52 generations back in breeding time if one calculates with a cow born in 990 producing a calf at 20 years old which in turn produced a calf at 20 years old and so on to arrive at the birth of the 52nd calf in 1990. These figures are hypothetically possible with the breed of Scottish Highland cattle in mind because the breed is noted for its longevity. Breeders of today know it is quite possible for Highland cows of twenty years old to produce a healthy calf although not every cow gets the chance to prove this. Highland cattle of the twentieth century then, can quite reasonably claim to have a very strong link with Wild Ox blood, since it persisted in the north of Scotland longer than elsewhere in Britain and until comparatively recent times the greatest number of cattle to be found throughout the north of Scotland were of the Highland breed.

In appearance by the eighteenth century it had:

1 the long horns, coat density, black coat-colouring, occasional muzzle ring definition, bull calves born fawn maturing to full black by two years, and frontal body strength, of the Wild Ox which had existed in Scotland before 6,000 BC.

2 the long haired coat, red brown colouring, and small light boned long bodied size of the Celtic Ox which arrived in Scotland about 3,000 BC.

In keeping with changes related to domestication, variation in coat-colour from white through degrees of yellow, gold, dun, brown, red, brindle, to black had occurred, as also had considerable variations in size. Examples of the dished nose of the Wild Ox and the long narrow nose of the Celtic Ox are both still to be found in breeding herds of the 1990s. Variations in horn shape, size, base girth and degree of tapering, aside from known effects of diet and climate, incorporate horn types from both the Wild and the Domestic (Celtic) Ox. The fierceness of the Wild Ox has lingered on only in the protective behaviour of the cow with newborn calf which is hidden away, where conditions allow, from the rest of the herd. The compliance of thousands of years of domestication of the Celtic Ox prevails in the Highland's noted docility and lack of unprovoked aggression. Twin calves, as with wild stock, remains infrequent with Highlands. Both Wild and Domestic ancient oxen had mastered the ability to thrive in bleak conditions with sparse vegetation, which meant slow maturing but very fast laying on of lean flesh and high condition whenever food was bountiful. This behaviour is still a marked feature of Highland cattle in the twentieth century.

Commercial demands and fashion whims over the last 200 years of ever-increasing knowledge in cattle husbandry have caused breeders to select animals for preferred characteristics but overall the breed has altered very little. There are still animals of small and great proportions according to their food supply; there are still black-coated and red-coated animals; they are still a thrifty breed with a remarkable ability to lay on weight in a short time.

It is reasonable to conclude that a blend of Wild and Domestic ancient Ox in Scotland by the tenth century had resulted in a definitive new breed. This new breed known simply as Highland cattle is unique to Scotland and can be called indigenous.

Remoteness and inaccessibility of large tracts of land in the west and north of Scotland had an isolating effect on cattle in these regions, until at least the sixteenth century. Even taking into account mass movement of cattle either by droving to markets or by skillful thieving, less intermingling of varied bovine types was possible there than in the Lowlands and even pressures of change from the Agricultural Revolution throughout the eighteenth and nineteenth centuries did not result in the arrival of meaningful numbers of southern breeds. When the crofting communities were cleared to make way for sheep the numbers of crofters' cattle grazing hill pastures dropped never to return. Attempts were made to improve Highland cattle to compete with the increasing commercial value of southern breeds specialised in the late eighteenth century into milk producers or beef producers. Popularity of the Highland breed declined, numbers reduced drastically, and the Highland Cattle Society of Scotland was formed in 1884 to maintain the purity of the breed. The Highland's traits are transmitted so powerfully to other domestic breeds, however, that diminishing numbers through lack of popularity is arguably a greater threat to its existence than the cross-breeding programmes of the twentieth century commercial beef farmer, since it seems easier to breed back the Highland blood in a cross-bred herd than the other way around. It is hard to lose the Highland element in domestic cross-breds with absolute certainty.

No diversification superseding the original type of Highland cattle has occurred.

Concurrent with the continued existence of the Highland as a pure breed there is, though, a twentieth century deliberately devised 'blend' of Highland and Beef Shorthorn which has resulted in a new breed, the Luing. Instead of taking centuries for the blend to stabilise naturally and breed true to the new form this was achieved by the Cadzow brothers within a 25 year span. (Information available from The Luing Cattle Society Limited.) Their planned programme of breeding to combine specific selected traits from both breeds proved successful.

Perhaps not so successful but worth mention is the breeding programme begun in the 1920s by the brothers Heck in Germany. They attempted to reverse the process whereby the Wild Ox had diversified by breeding back from modern stock to recreate living examples of the Wild

Ox. Their work on this scheme was carried out in two centres. In Berlin the breeds used were Camargue Oxen, Spanish Fighting Oxen, Corsican Cattle, English Park Cattle.

In Munich they used Hungarian Steppe cattle, Scottish Highland cattle, Corsican cattle, gray and brown Alpine breeds, black and white cattle from Frisia.[4]

Although animals resembling the Wild Ox in colour, and shape of horn, but without its massive size were bred most assessments of the experiment conclude that one cannot resurrect an extinct animal species. However an aspect of the experiment might perhaps be interpreted as reinforcing the idea that some domestic breeds more than others have remained closer genetically to the ancient Wild Ox. Not included in the Hecks' programme which focussed on the European Wild Ox were the Gaur and the Yak both of which in the wild today still attain the size and weight of the ancient European Wild Ox. In known instances where a male Yak has sired offspring from Highland cows there has been a preponderance of Yak characteristics. This tends to support the theory that the closer the genetic link to the Wild Ox the more potent the transmission of characteristics.

REFERENCES:

1 J B Friend – *Cattle of the World*
2 M Campbell of Kilberry – *Scottish Cattle in Prehistory*
3 Professor R Wallace – *Farm Stock of Great Britain*
4 Grzimek – *Animal Encyclopedia*
5 Professor J Ritchie – *The Influence of Man on Animal Life in Scotland*
6 R Perry – *Wildlife in Britain and Ireland*
7 *Encyclopedia Britannica* Volume 5, 9th Edition 1875
8 W H Murray – *The Islands of Western Scotland*
9 J G Millais – *Mammals of Great Britain and Ireland*
10 R Whitlock – *Bulls through the Ages*
11 C Darwin – *Animals and Plants under Domestication*
12 Extract from Bellenden's translation of Boece's work condensed and presented in current language by Ù F Cochrane
13 J Clutton Brock – *Domesticated Animals from Early Times*

Evidence of a coat broken with white in a good Argyllshire fold long before the term parti colour was established by the Highland Cattle Society.

VISUAL GUIDE TO BREED STANDARDS

Considerable range exists of coat hue and general conformation completely within the Highland Cattle Society standards for the breed.

The cattle shown here in the colour categories of BLACK, RED, BRINDLE, YELLOW, DUN, WHITE, PARTI COLOUR, range from calf to aged animal, seen mostly in natural settings in varying weather conditions in the 1990s.

Coat-colour can in many instances not only be argued, but if made for registration purposes when the animal is young, can actually be wrong because many Highland cattle possess a coat-colour changing gene which takes varying lengths of time to manifest its potential. Both blacks and brindles can take nearly three years to show the full bloom of their adult coat in its final colour and may have been registered as red. Reds may have been registered as yellows, and yellows as whites. Experienced Fieldsmen will usually be able to predict on seeing a six month old calf what its adult coat will be but the coat-colour-changing potential sometimes defies even their judgement.

The photographs grouped under the heading Breed Standards seek to illustrate that there is not one archetypal Highland bull, not one archetypal Highland cow, but a necessary variety. This is the view of the Highland Cattle Society.

Examples of Bulls Providing Semen for Artificial Insemination Procedures

100. Black Prince II of Rigg

101. Molluag of Tinto – red

102. Gille Coir of Pennygown – yellow

103. Brogach Alex of Glenfintaig – brindle.

Examples of Black Coats

104, 105. Working bulls.

106. Steer, also called a bullock.

107. Bull calf.

108. Yearling heifer.

109. Cow seeking cooling breeze on a knoll.

110. Cow heading for shade in a forest.

111. Cow resting.

112. Young bull in prime.

113. Quiet mature proven stock-getter.

114. Bull calf.

115. Quiet on a halter in field.

116. Casting winter coat.

117. Old but still productive.

118. Red cow with her red calf.

119. Red calf in yellow baby coat.

120. Red baby coat still showing on a black calf.

Examples of Brindle Coats

121. Standing alert for the judge.

122. Content in home field.

123. Yearling bull on halter training.

124. Brindle cow with her yellow calf.

125. Old brindle looking hopefully for something tasty.

Examples of Yellow Coats

126. Young working bull

127. Contrasting coat colours of yellow yearling bull and red cow..

128. Yellow cow standing well on halter.

129. Mature yellow cow.

130. Yellow calf, cow and bull.

131. Yellow cow with her red calf.

132 Yellow baby coat of black calf.

Examples of Dun Coats

133. Strong working dun bull.

134. Dun cow.

135. Healthy dun calf standing well naturally.

136. Dun cow with her black calf.

P Egglestone

137. Dun cow with her white calf.

T. Clemens

138. Dun cow with her twin calves by a dun bull.

Examples of White Coats

139, 140. Good working white bulls.

141. White cow with pink nose.

142. White heifer with dark nose.

Examples of Parti Colour Coats and Muzzle Rings

143. Yellow cow with white patch.

144. Her red calf with extensive white this side and same as her dam on the other.

145. Red and white calf; two white socks.

146. Parti colour cow, red and white; one white sock.

147. Black calf with white undercarriage.

Robert Dixon

148. Jet black calf unlikely to change coat colour in maturity

149. White muzzle ring on both white dam and her red calf.

150. The distinctly defined black hairs on the muzzle called busdubh..

CHAPTER 8: BREED HISTORY

CHAPTER 8: BREED HISTORY

FORMING THE SOCIETY

Highland cattle were well-established in Scotland before any history book was written.

Official recording of controlled Highland cattle breeding in Scotland begins with the forming of the Highland Cattle Society of Scotland in 1884.

The Society immediately set about establishing a Herd Book, the first volume of which was published in 1885. It contained, along with the breeder, owner and such pedigree information as was available from private records and memory, names of bulls calved before the 1st. January 1884. One bull and two heifers with no chance of being registered were those bred at the Inverness-shire farm of Balnagowan and sent to Hudson's Bay Canada in 1813. Other Highlands bred at Balnagowan were purchased for *"the most distant parts of Scotland"* so high was their reputation. (*Inverness Journal* 10 May 1813). Balnagowan stock or progeny may well have been registered in due course but there is no evidence.

The earliest mention in the first Herd Book known as the Retrospective Herd Book, is of a bull calved in 1806, then there are a few from the 1820s with the bulk of entries spanning onwards from the 1830s. Neither cows nor heifers are registered in that first Herd Book. They start in Herd Book 2.

It must be remembered that membership of the Society and registration of animals was and remains a voluntary procedure incurring fees and notifications in compliance with the Society rulings. Many successful breeders of Highland cattle in 1884 were not members of the Society just as today there are breeders who feel no obligation to join. The Highland Breeders' Journal of 1968 mentioned concern over the fact that there were still many breeders who were not members of the Society. It follows that the Society's pedigree records reflect only on members' cattle and of these only the animals which members actively elected to register.

Statistics for the actual as opposed to registered head of Highlands at any given time in Scotland do not exist. British Government records on cattle do not detail presence of specific breeds in each area noting only percentages from the whole of Scotland of beef as opposed to dairy cattle.

However, once the procedure of registration with the Highland Cattle Society was established it took about 50 years to become synonymous with 'good quality'. Some 60 years after that unregistered but indisputably fully pure-blood Highland stock were difficult to find.

The Society was formed at a time when men of vision were concerned at the rapidly diminishing numbers for the first time in history of a breed of cattle once so profuse it was taken for granted as an ongoing integral norm of the Scottish economy. As different types of cattle were being created Societies were formed for each new breed, helping to 'fix' the new animal to breed true to type. Highland cattle were an ancient breed. No deliberate changes had been genetically engineered in them. Nobody had seen any need to form a Society about such an ordinary and old feature of pastoral life. The Highland cattle, the Crodh Dubh, the Black Cattle, quite simply had always been around in plentiful numbers since anyone could remember. Why write or record the old when what was exciting was this new science of agriculture? But the increasing rate of change in agricultural methods very evident by mid-nineteenth century alerted enough people to the significant drop in ratio of natural Highlands to new breeds in time to assess the situation, review the status of the breed, and take action to maintain reasonable prospects for its survival in healthy breeding numbers.

Establishing breed standards for newly-created cattle breeds was surely straightforward compared with the task of selecting one model Highland type out of the variety in conformation, size, coat-type and colour throughout Scottish regions. Differences in opinion about what made some Highland cattle better than others had to be considered, specific characteristics of the breed had to be defined, and those chosen which best favoured the successful continuity of the breed in the fast-changing culture of the post-Agricultural and Industrial Revolutions.

The breed standards were set by members of the editing committee unanimously nominated at the inaugural meeting of the Highland Cattle Society. The members who represented the main Highland cattle breeding areas were:

Mr John McGillivray, Ballachroan Kingussie, for the mainland district of Inverness-shire;
Mr Stewart of Ensay, for Skye and Long Island (Islands chain from Barra to Lewis) district;
Mr Duncan McDiarmid, Camusericht, Rannoch, for Perthshire;
Mr Martin, factor for Poltalloch, for Argyllshire;
Mr W M Malcolm, Auchnacraig, Mull, for Mull district;
Mr McKenzie (junior) of Kintail, for Ross-shire.
Mr Campbell, Shinness, Sutherlandshire, for Sutherlandshire.

These men along with Lord Dunmore of Harris as Chairman, the Duke of Atholl as President, and Mr Malcolm of Poltalloch as Vice-chairman prepared the Breed Standards for publication in the first Herd Book released in 1885 (see Chapter 10 on Highland Cattle Society Publications). One hundred and ten years later these Breed Standards still apply. Yet fiercely propounded views among some breed enthusiasts particularly in Canada on what constitutes "pure-bred" as distinct from "full-blood" are to be heard.

PEDIGREE ISSUES

"Pure-bred" is a term imposed, in the case of Highland cattle in Scotland, on a long established breed which was known to breed reliably to type. The term was unnecessary until new cattle breeds had been created from deliberate cross-breeding and inbreeding of selected cattle types during the fledgling years of genetic discovery in the pursuits of science of agriculture. In these new breeds the description 'pure-bred' meant having parentage traceable to the crossed stock that first consistently produced the desired new type. The record of parentage was called the pedigree so it became interchangeable with 'pure-bred'.

The forming of the Highland Cattle Society with its agreed Breed Standards meant that only the strains of cattle registered by such breeders as joined the Society became the pure-bred stock on record from which future pedigree stock were to derive. But for many many years unregistered and registered Highlands of equal quality co-existed in Scotland without problems. Breeders of fame happily used unregistered or registered stock confident in their own judgement and knowledge that they were perpetuating quality animals pure to the breed. Traditionally sons took over their fathers' land and livestock, knew the breeding lines and continued the process without seeing any need to put the information into print. The term pure-bred with regard to Highland cattle in Scotland simply meant livestock whose parentage was known to be entirely of the breed, while pedigree meant the same but that the information was in print in the Society Herd Book. There were many and there still are a few pure Highlands with no registration numbers whose immediate parentage is known but whose forebears from several generations back are no longer traceable although believed to be pure Highland. Possibly the largest herd of non-registered pure-bred Highlands today runs on Bodmin Moor in England. The evidence of many Pedigrees was lost in the years between the World Wars 1918 – 1939 when prices for pedigree Highland cattle were so low that farmers did not bother to register. Non-registration again featured during the recession in the meat trade throughout the 1950s resulting in a continuance of pure Highland stock with neither registration nor remembered pedigree. Such Highlands are in a different category from those whose parentage was lost due to short-sighted zeal in cross-breeding with other beef breeds without attention to the numbers of pure-bred breeding cows.

Maintaining a permanent source of pure-bred Highland cattle of a wide genetic base in sufficient numbers to withstand any circumstances, from unforeseen disasters to rampant commercial cross-breeding, perhaps ought not to be the sole responsibility of a voluntary organisation like the Highland Cattle Society. The financing and overseeing of a living bank of this ancient native breed, in addition to one of frozen semen and embryos, may be best managed at government level as a national asset. In the meantime the Highland Cattle Society must continue to resource the perpetuation of the breed as best it can.

To some extent the Highland Cattle Society has over the years tolerated intermittent attempts to modify the breed to compete more successfully with devised breeds like the Aberdeen Angus and the Scottish Beef Shorthorn. Thus heavier, beefier, short legged Highlands were encouraged, early maturing forced, and intensive farming techniques tried, with an attitude prevailing of 'anything new breeds can do Highlands can do just as well'. No great success was evident. The breed earned a bad reputation loudly voiced from those who expected them 'to live on air' and then fetch high beef market prices or breed regularly while half-starved. Error lay in not promoting strongly the value of some enduring differences between Highlands and other breeds. Their foraging habits do not spoil grazing areas as badly as the heavy breeds; in fact farmed red deer poach the land around feeders worse than the Highlands. They walk better and for further on rough territory, they are more efficient browsers, work longer, cost less to maintain, and produce a flavoursome finely marbled beef. They also offer a secondary value with their unique ability to improve wild rough territory for other grazing species. Furthermore their seasonal "shut-down" (the reduction in growth phase which happens even when extra feeding is supplied) in the lean winter months, suits hill territory and marginal farmlands, yet failure to understand the no-growth phase and accept it as a benefit of the breed, accounted for financial loss when the costly systems of heavy continuous feeding typical of intensive stock rearing were tried and showed no appropriate weight gains over these months. So great had been the impact of the devised breeds that they flooded the markets for nearly 100 years before there was recognition of the value of the Highlands' winter slow-down which is usually followed by remarkable catching-up in weight gain in the better months of abundant feeding. This quick laying on of new flesh is possibly the key to the breed's merit in producing a particularly succulent and flavoursome beef, especially when finished on good grass, which is absent when fast growth force-fed early cull methods have been tried.

During the years of low popularity the success of the Highland cow in producing excellent fast growth calves to either a Shorthorn or Aberdeen Angus sire created a new beef market, but one which endangered the survival of the breed as the demand for these early maturing cross calves soared to such an extent that too few pure Highland cows to breed them from was suddenly realised to be a serious matter.

The British Government's Department of Agriculture for Scotland as part of its post-World Wars policy to help small-holdings farmers in the Highlands and Islands bought and maintained among other breeds a sizeable stock of Highland cattle. They offered bulls on loan free for a period of three years after which the bull had to be changed, but confusing rules whereby government subsidies seemed to encourage production of the fast maturing cross-bred hill beef did little to recover the lost popularity of pure-bred Highlands. The Highland bull was in less demand from the hill farmers than the Beef Shorthorn and Aberdeen Angus. For example only one Highland bull was requested from The Department Inverness Stud in 1978, 1980, and the last request made in 1983.

In the 1950s before the introduction of continental breeds, some 90 Highland bulls had been hired out plus approximately 40 each of Aberdeen Angus and Shorthorn. As time passed, demand for Highlands fell and for the other breeds, particularly Aberdeen Angus, increased. Comparative figures show that the decline in popularity of the Highland was well-established by the 1970s.

Year	A.A.	Shorthorn	Hereford	Luing	Highland	Total
1973	98	81	4	6	2	191
1976	85	59	33	15	2	195

(figures researched by Mr Robbie, Inverness Office for DAFS 1990)

Changing policy and changing demand saw "The Department" begin to disperse its stock of Highlands from the mid 1970s, selling off its last Highland stud bull from Inverness in 1985 two years after the last request for one. It is thought that no black Highland bulls were available from DAFS between 1946 and 1953 and unlikely there were any after that.

In the 1950s some breeders pressed for renewed efforts to ensure the survival of Highland cattle as a pure breed. Fieldsmen appointed by the Highland Cattle Society encouraged farmers to be more controlled about how they managed their cross-bred and unregistered pure-bred Highlands. It was suggested that their cross-bred herd be kept separate from selected Highland females which were from then on along with their female calves to be put only to pure Highland bulls to raise the stock numbers of known pedigree pure bloodlines. From 1st January 1953 the Highland Cattle Society implemented the regulation that *"females found on inspection to be of pure Highland blood will be entered in Appendix B and their heifer calves will be eligible for entry in Appendix A and the heifer calves from Appendix A animals will be accepted for full registration in the Herd Book. No bulls can be accepted under any circumstances in either Grade B or Grade A registers."*

These measures, along with the support at some personal cost of such breeders as for example the Tysons, Balliemore; the MacLachlans, Kilmichael Glassary; the Nelsons of Achnacloich; Mr A MacEachearn, Smaull; Mr Hugh Morrison of Islay; Lady Congleton of Ulva; Mrs Lees-Milne of Killundine; Lord Trent of Borrodale; Mr A W Howat, Rigg; Major Gordon of Lude, allowed the breed to continue in sufficient numbers to allay fears of extinction. Among others who helped the breed through the danger years were Lady MacRobert, Douneside, Aberdeenshire; Her Majesty the Queen with the Balmoral fold; and a number of large ventures such as the British Aluminium Company, Fort-William; Boots Pure Drug Company, Nottingham; Lord and Lady Home's Douglas and Angus Estates enterprise with Highlands begun in 1927; The Earl of Mansfield, Scone Palace; Sir Francis Walker, Leys Castle; and Lord Margadale of Islay, all of whom held a pure fold in addition to commercial herds.

Highland cattle had withstood the vicissitudes of capricious market trends and two world wars. The breed's continued presence throughout the twentieth century mania for fast-food-products is thanks to dedicated work by individuals smitten by the peculiarly addictive lure that Highland cattle innocently emit. As farm livestock goes today they are a specialist breed rather than an easily marketed high demand commodity. Fortunately though, connoisseurs of beef and supporters of conservation of natural land areas, by late twentieth century, had rediscovered the unique qualities of the ancient breed and created a modest worldwide demand for pedigree stock. Even so there is still cause for concern that after nearly 200 years of anxious opinions over low breed numbers the future of these native animals lies mainly with individualists, special-breed enthusiasts, and part-time and hobby-farmers.

From the 1970s an increasing interest abroad in the breed as an asset in helping to retain or re-establish a healthy balance of plant, insect, bird and animal life in land set aside as nature reserves, raised again the question of what is acceptable as pure-bred. The question arose afresh because after the outbreak of the new disease BSE (Bovine Spongiform Encephalopathy) in Britain in 1986 various nations' government restrictions with regard to disease controls made transfer of live animals between countries difficult, forcing breeders in some countries to risk severe inbreeding, to cross-breed, to simply lose the Highland strain, or to seek alternative measures to maintain their involvement with the breed. Even before 1986 cross-breds had been put to pure Highland bulls (or their semen) until pure Highlands were considered to have been achieved. When this process appeared to be accepted some breeders applied this breeding-up, or grading-up, principle to produce new Highlands by starting with a Highland bull and a different-breed cow such as a Jersey Cow. A pure-bred Highland bull was used with successive progeny until the fourth generation animal from the initial Jersey X Highland having all the outward semblance of a pure Highland was by these breeders referred to as a 'full-blood' Highland. Highland cattle got by this method created disagreement internationally as to how acceptable a full-blood should be for registration as a pure-bred animal of the Highland Breed. A satisfactory solution to that issue had not been reached in 1995 but clearly was desirable so that the expected return to restriction free international exchange of live animals, semen straws and fertilised ova, would not result in some countries refusing to accept Highlands bred by another whilst being delighted to export their own stock.

The question therefore, 'how pure is full-blood or how full-blood is pedigree?' has moved on from the previous issue in Scotland of the purity of unregistered stock. Yet since pure-bred refers only to parentage known for a given number of generations, how many generations are needed to qualify for the status of either pure or full-blood is a contentious issue since who can now prove how many generations of what kind of parentage the animals entered in the earliest Highland Cattle Society Herd Books had? And who can tell with certainty how long which recessive genes from cross-breds can be lurking in breeding stock? History suggests that deliberate cross-breeding programmes were not as intensive with Highlands as with other breeds until well into the twentieth century although inevitably crossing took place. The widespread numbers of the old breed relative to numbers of new breeds was such that cross-breeding was of no real danger until the mid-twentieth century zeal for it had seriously depleted replenishment sources of breeding cows. An answer agreeable to all nations to the purity debate therefore, lacking indisputable scientific fact, will require considerable ongoing discussion to keep pace with new dilemma presented by late twentieth century developments in genetic engineering and, sadly, new disease. The Highland Cattle Society may yet have to define its ruling on the pedigree status of livestock which have by the application of scientific techniques not only been genetically remodelled but brought to term and calved from surrogate mothers of non cattle species. It would be in keeping with the singular dignity of this breed that genetic interference on that level never became common practice.

NINETEENTH CENTURY BREED HISTORY

BREED STANDARDS AND BREEDERS PRE-SOCIETY

Descriptions of Highlands before the Society set standards indicate there was considerable variety within the breed. Dispute if any, pre-Society days, over what constituted a true Highland as opposed to a mongrel Highland has yet to come to my attention. There seems to have been common understanding of the range in type that comprised true Highland cattle.

The earliest breed points I have so far traced come from folklore collected by Alexander Carmichael and are translated from Gaelic to read thus:

Broad she must be on the back
Short likewise from eyes to mouth
Long her hair both black and close
And scarce a span beneath the knee
Her rib both deep and shapely bent
Of tidy form on market day
A gentle swelling to the top
And spirited must her nature be
A long horn either red or blue
Her ear large and tail also
A straight down hough both rough and strong;
It would bitter be if we did not agree.

From writings by Mr John Smith in 1790 about the agriculture in Argyll it seems there were those of the opinion that Skye cattle improved the Argyllshire stock which then through "*superior breeding and greater attention in rearing*" surpassed the Skye stock in size. The ideal to breed for in Argyll in 1790 he wrote was...

"*short in the legs, round in the body, straight in the back, and long in the snout.*" They were black, dun, brindle and brown but black was the most sought after.

Twenty-one years after Mr Smith's report came Mr James Macdonald's definition of breed points published in 1811 in *A General View of the Agriculture of the Hebrides* where he described a Highland bull in the following way:

"*His colour should be black, or dark brown, or reddish brown, without any white or yellow spots. His head should be rather small, his muzzle fine, his eyes lively and prominent, his horns equable, not very thick, of a clear green, and waxy tinge; his neck should rise with a gentle curve from the shoulders, moderately broad at the top, joining full to his chine and chest backwards, and to the vane of his neck forwards. His bosom should be open, his breast broad, and projecting well before his legs; his arms, or forethighs, muscular, and tapering to his knee; his legs straight, well covered with hair, and strong boned. His chine or chest should be so full as to leave no hollows behind his shoulders; the plates strong, to keep his belly from sinking below the level of his breast. His back or loin should be broad, straight and flat; his ribs rising above one another in such a manner that the last rib should be rather the highest, leaving only a small space to the hips or hooks; the whole forming a roundish, barrel-like carcase. His hips should be wide placed, rounded or globular, and a very little higher than the back. His quarters (from the hip to the rump) should be long and tapering gradually from the hips backwards, and the turls, or pot-bones, not in the least protuberant; his rumps close to the tail; his tail itself should be thick, bushy, well haired, long, and set on so high as to be in the same horizontal line with his back. His general appearance should combine agility, vivacity, and strength; and his hair should be glossy, thick, and vigorous, indicating a sound constitution and perfect health. It is unnecessary to enter in detail upon a description of a Kyloe, or West Highland, or Hebridean heifer, as the above, with some very obvious modifications answers for animals of both sexes.*"

The next review of Highland cattle predates by eleven years the launch of the Highland Cattle Society. Here are the main points researched by Thomas Farrall for his historical resume of the breed published in 1873.

RESUME OF HIGHLAND CATTLE BY THOMAS FARRALL in 1873

"The West Highlanders had been preserved in a remarkable degree of purity unlike the North Highlander which had been almost lost altogether due to cross-breeding with the Shorthorn.

Pure Highlanders were then chiefly in the counties of Argyll, Inverness, Perth, Dumbarton, with solitary herds throughout both Scotland and England.

Island Highland cattle produce more hair and horn than any mainlanders but the Mainland Highland cattle were generally superior in bone, frame, and general substance to islands stock.

Farmers prefer black Highlanders but owners such as those of some 20 or so breeding stock at Greystoke Castle, Cumberland, most admire dun, brindle and red. However since the breeding in and in system has not been sufficiently checked there is a decided tendency to drift back to the original black colour, this the owners at Greystoke Castle believe is a significant fact that deterioration is taking place.

Among those who appear to have taken the lead in the improvement of this noble breed may be mentioned Mr McDonald of Monachyle whose bulls were much in demand, Mr McLaren, Callander, Sir Neil Menzies of Menzies, Mr McLaren in Rannoch, the Messrs Stewarts in Glenlyon.

One of the largest herds well-established in the 1840s was that of Mr Malcolm of Poltalloch who paid great care to selective breeding, and careful rearing with shelter and regular feeding.

Mr McIntosh, South Kinrara in Badenoch had a large herd of longstanding but perhaps deficient in hair and horn.

Mr Stewart, Bochastle, Callander was a successful exhibitor noted for good hair and horn.

The Marquis of Breadalbane at the time of his death in 1862 had one of the finest folds in Scotland. Aided by the late Mr John Stewart Menzies of Chesthill the Marquis had selected stock from Rannoch, Glenlyon, Callander, Balquidder and other noted districts. When his stock was dispersed in 1863 the main purchaser was the late Duke of Athole.

Mr Alexander Fraser's father established a large herd about 1830 at Faillie near Inverness with foundation stock heifers from Dunrobin and bulls from Balquidder, Rannoch, Glenlyon, and the best folds in Skye.

The fine little herd of the late Mr R Peter, Urlar, near Aberfeldy which met with great success at Shows are maintained by his trustees. (1873)

Reputed prizewinners in Badenoch are Mr McGillivray, Ballochroan [sic], Mr McPherson, Invertromie, Mr Grant, Inverlaidnan, Mr Davidson, Gordonhall, the late Mr McDonald, Strathmashie.

Several famous mainland herds were dispersed over the years from the 1850s.

Mr McNeill, Lossit has the largest herd on Islay. Mr Webster of Daill Islay who had about 40 to 50 cows used a yellow bull from Jura on mostly black cows and all the calves were yellow or yellow-duns.

Mr Campbell of Jura House had a famous herd on Jura.

Until dispersal a few years ago (perhaps the 1860s) Lord Colonsay had a splendid fold on Colonsay where he used a bull from Rannoch about the 1830s to improve his stock.

In Skye J Stewart of Duntuilm with about 100 head of Highland cattle is difficult to rival... particularly the fine bulls...the herd descended from one of the finest ever which was that of Messrs Donald and Archibald Stewart in Harris who combined the bone and strength of the mainland stock with the hair and horn of the island stock.

Mr McDonald Balranald South Uist also had a large fold of some 100 head dating back about fifty years (i.e. 1820s) His symmetrical, well shaped, pure-bred animals lacked size so in the 1870s Perthshire stock were introduced to increase weight.

The great markets for Highland cattle in 1873 are Dumbarton, Falkirk, Doune, Portree. Choice heifers from Argyll are usually sold in Dumbarton after June. Aged cows sold are between six and ten years old and surplus young stock usually eighteen months old. Crossing Highland heifers with Shorthorn bulls is very successful and very popular."

An informative article published in 1910 both endorses and adds to Mr Farrall's information. It mentions that notable Highland cattle came from Jura, Colonsay, and Bochastle; that Breadalbane, Gordon, Chesthill, Eoligarry were developing a stronger strain with extensive interchange of animals for breeding; that others who worked towards improving the breed in the 1870s were the Duke of Sutherland, the Earl of Seafield, Lord Dunmore, the Duke of Atholl, and the folds of Minmore, Monzie, and Benmore; and that the folds of quality in Argyllshire were Melfort, Ardsheal, Ardanaiseig, Ardtornish, Achnacloich, Canna, Kilchamaig, Rum; with those in other counties being Southesk, Cammusericht, Shinness, Ardross, Airthrey, Dunmaglass, Strathaird, Farr, Garth. (Professor R P Wright in Volume VII of *The Standard Cyclopedia of Modern Agriculture and Rural Economy 1910*)

Professor Wright also commented that recurring dispersal sales had caused, particularly in this long-lived breed, regrettable loss of valuable characteristics carefully maintained through systematic continuity in breeding schemes.

Sadly there is a certainty about the repeated occurrence of dispersal sales throughout the twentieth century. Fold names already familiar to the reader can be found in the following list of sufficient examples to support Professor Wright's view.

FOLD DISPERSALS

1885	McNeils of Barra
1901	Balranald...Macdonald sold 87 head from his Overkellie Fold
1903	Shinness
-"-	Monachyle
1904	Melfort
-"-	Dunlossit
1905	Southesk, private partial dispersal
1906	Duntuilm, Skye, Mr Macdonald
1909	Airthrey, Mr Graham
1912	Grant of Castle Grant, Grantown-on-Spey
-"-	Dunmaglass, Mr Sopper
1920	Scorrybreck, Portree, Mr P D Robertson
-"-	Lady Merrilees of Garth
1921	Balranald final dispersal
1922	Tangy, Miss Grace Hall
c.1924	Balnacraig
1925	Stronvar, Mr J Carnegie
-"-	Netherton, Mr J E Christie
1927	Major portion of the Duke of Atholl's fold
1928	Kilberry
-"-	Farr

1933	Bochastle partial dispersal
-"-	In the 1930s Errol, Southesk, final dispersal of Atholl
1940	Killean, Mrs Macalister-Hall
1941	Kilchamaig in the hands of the trustees of the late Miss L C Turner
1942	Bochastle final dispersal
1945	Kilchamaig
-"-	Quothquan, Miss Dunlop
1946	Fanans, Mrs Chapman
1947	Ardanaiseig, Sir T Ainsworth
1948	Laudale, Mr J A Fletcher
1950	Foreland, Mr W Walker
-"-	Balliemore, Messrs Tyson
1951	Glenforsa, Mr Beale
1959	Scammadale, Mr Macdougall
1961	Duart
1963	Inverernie estate
1965	Smaull, Mr MacEachern
-"-	Glenalmond, Lord Rootes
-"-	Tullybelton Perthshire, Lady Abertay
1967	Braes of Greenock, Colonel Hyde and Mrs Hyde
1971	Nether Pollok estate
1972	Dalquharran
1975	Ardmenish, Jura
1977	Torloisk
1980	Ulva, Lady Congleton

INFLUENTIAL BULLS OF THE 19TH CENTURY

By recording details of all the bulls which nineteenth century breeders considered worthy for inclusion in the first Herd Book of the Highland Cattle Society, assessment of the breeding bulls available in the 1890s was perhaps made easier for breeders of these times.

Here in alphabetical order are the names of some breeders whose cattle were highly esteemed in the 1880s, a few named influential bulls they owned (presumably their stock bulls), the colour of the bulls they owned and chose to register in Volume I of the Herd Book, and the number of bulls registered as bred by them.

It will be noticed that Balranald, Bochastle, Benmore & Glensanda, Poltalloch, Nether Largie, all favoured dark coats to red ones in their stock bulls.

BREEDER	INFLUENTIAL BULLS OWNED	COLOUR OF REG. OWNED	BULLS BRED
Duke of Atholl	Donull Ruadh 144 Calum Odhar 79 Gille Buidhe 228 Rossie 456	of 5, 1 black, 1 red, 1 yellow, 1 brindle, 1 dun	24

BREEDER	INFLUENTIAL BULLS OWNED	COLOUR OF REG. OWNED	BULLS BRED
Earl of Breadalbane	Ossian of Athole 403 Myrtle 379 Raonull 435 Fingal 211 Gille Riabhach of Bochastle 273.	of 6, 2 black, 2 yellow, 1 red 1 brindle	12
J Campbell of Kilberry	Kilchamaig Buidhe 325	1 yellow	–
R D Campbell of Jura	Calum Dubh of Poltalloch 76	1 black	3
R Carmichael, Islay	Donnacha Ban Nan Oran 155 Gille Buidhe of Poltalloch 241	1 black, 1 yellow	1
J Duncan, Benmore & Glensanda	Coirintee 115 Roderick Dubh 451 Glensanda 294	of 5, 2 black, 2 yellow, 1 brindle	6
Lord Dunmore	Guanach I 306 Niseag II 391 Tarragheal 519 Crinan of Applecross 123	of 12, 3 black, 5 red, 4 brindle.	29
Colonel G Gardyne Glenforsa	Fear-a-Bhaile Og 208 Calum Og of Athole Raonull Riabhach 436 Fear-a-Bhaile of Glenforsa 202	of 7, 1 black, 1 red, 2 yellow 3 brindle	5
Alex. Macdonald Balranald	Athole 20 Bochastle III 54 Breadalbane 57 Balranald II 30 Poltalloch II 416/ Duntuilm 178/ Urlar 542/ Largie 337/ Kilchamaig Dubh 326/ Sgianach 485/Roderick Dubh II 452.	of 31, 22 black, 4 dun, 3 yellow 2 brindle	88
A Macdonald Nether Largie	Monachyle Dubh 363 Luskintyre Dearg 348 Camusericht 92 Stewart 509 Kintail 334 Birrie 41/ Giobach 284/ Webster 553/Rum 462/ Priest 417.	of 29, 23 black, 1 red, 3 brindle, 2 yellow	31
D & J Macdonald Monachyle	Fear Buidhe 209	1 yellow	4
Duncan Stewart formerly Monachyle	Gille Dubh 246 Gille buidhe of Monachyle 238	of 3, 2 black 1 yellow	3

BREEDER	INFLUENTIAL BULLS OWNED	COLOUR OF REG. OWNED	BULLS BRED
Allan MacGillivray Gordonhall	Gilderoy 223 Ossian 402 Oscar 401 Wallace of Bochastle 545	of 7, 2 red, 3 yellow, 2 brindle	4
Dr. D W MacGillivray Eoligarry	Alastair of Balranald 6 Donnacha Ruadh 167 Oscar II of Athole 398	of 3, 1 red, 1 yellow, 1 brindle	1
O H Mackenzie Inverewe	Niseag I of Harris 390 Prionnsa Dubh III 425	of 3, 2 black 1 red	1
A & J MacNaughton Kerrowmore, D&W&J MacNaughton Cashlie.	Gille Dubh of Kerrowmore 254 Glenlyon of Kerrowmore 291 Domhnull Odhar 140	favoured red, but used all.	8
J Malcolm & the late Neil Malcolm, Poltalloch	Duntroon 177 Glenlyon 290 Gille Dubh 250 Breadalbane II 58 Balranald IV 32 Calum Riabhach of Athole 82 Oscar of Athole 397 Wallace of Monachyle 546 Donnacha Dubh of Urlar 161 Crinan of Poltalloch 124 Calum-a-Ghlinne 74 Fear-a-Bhaile of Ormaig 204	of 32, 14 black, 3 red, 1 dun, 7 brindle, 5 yellow, 2 unknown	44
The late R Peter, Urlar	Gille Dubh II 247 Braidalbane Og 56 Gille Buidhe of Urlar 242 Domhnull Dubh of Urlar	of 9, 3 black 4 red, 1 dun, 1 yellow.	11
Earl of Seafield & Dowager Countess of Seafield	Bochastle IV 55 Fear-a-Bhaile of Athole 199 Wallace II of Seafield 549 Fear-a-Bhaile of Seafield 205	of 13, 1 black 6 red, 1 dun, 3 brindle, 2 yellow	13
D Stewart, Luskintyre	Tarcal 524 Tarbh Ruadh 523	probably red, and brindle favoured	5
J Stewart, Ensay	An-t-Eilanach 12 Geobach 220 Fear-a-Bhaile of Duntulm Cluasan 113 Sgianach Og 486	of 21, 6 black, 10 brindle, 5 red	37

BREEDER	INFLUENTIAL BULLS OWNED	COLOUR OF REG. OWNED	BULLS BRED
J Stewart, Ensay (continued)	Sgiathanach Og 491 Prionnsa Tearlach II 427 Gille Calum 243 Rob Roy 440 The Gardener 529		
J Stewart, Bochastle	Bochastle 52 Glentilt 295 Black Prince 45 Prionnsa Buidhe 422 Calum Riabhach of Bochastle 83 Donnacha Dubh of Bochastle 160	of 10, 2 black, 4 brindle, 2 dun, 2 yellow	24
Duke of Sutherland	Rob Roy III 442 Calum Ruadh of Athole 86 Gille Odhar of Bochastle 264 Gille Dubh II of Ormaig 258	of 7, 1 black, 3 red, 2 dun, 1 brindle	2
A Turner, Kilchamaig	Calum Odhar 79 Glenrisdale 292 2 red, Prionnsa Tearlach 426 Gille Dubh of Kilchamaig	of 5, 1 black, 1 dun, 1 brindle	6

ASPECTS OF EARLY AGRICULTURAL SHOWS

Reports of the Highland and Agricultural Society of Scotland Shows, begun 62 years before the Highland Cattle Society was formed, offer some information on the breed.

A brief note on the development of Scotland's national annual agricultural display is in order here since after Mr T Farall the next authoritative researcher into Highland cattle facts – Mr James Cameron – in compiling his articles on the breed, relied heavily on the Show results to support his personal interviews with breeders in the late nineteenth century.

The origins of the Show took root as early as 1723 with the formation of The Honourable Society of Improvers in the Knowledge of Agriculture in Scotland. The meetings were disrupted in 1744 by the social and political unrest in Scotland from those who wished to remain a separate kingdom from England. However it reassembled some 11 years later as The Edinburgh Society for the 'Encouraging of the Arts, Sciences, Manufactures and Agriculture'. This society initiated a large public display in Edinburgh representing all four above categories of interest, although the only livestock included in that first display were stud stallions and calves fed for the butcher. This paved the way for creation in 1784 of The Highland Society of Edinburgh, which with considerable vigour set out to stimulate the general populace into an interest in the science of agriculture. In addition to arranging talks by the most enlightened persons of the time and offering awards for instructive essays, it encouraged other districts and counties to form their own societies with the purpose of educating widely by sharing knowledge and holding livestock competitions. It seems that premiums were initially offered only for bulls of the Highland breed and that judges were to *"pay particular attention to the shape of the bulls and not to the size, as it is meant to encourage the true breed of Highland cattle."* (from *History of the Highland and Agricultural Society*). In 1807 competition classes included heifers.

What can be regarded as the first National Agricultural Show of Scotland, held in Edinburgh in 1822, was a meagre affair by modem standards, and exhibits were primarily fatstock. There were awards for *"each of the four most approved breeds of black cattle"*. The general expression 'black cattle' had for long been used and understood simply to distinguish cattle from horses in talk of livestock. The word "black" was dropped in favour of the term 'cattle' in 1829. By popular demand the Agricultural Show became an annual event, taking place in a different city each year. The earlier trial of holding a biennial Show was not favoured.

In 1834 The Highland Society of Edinburgh was renamed The Highland and Agricultural Society of Scotland (HASS) – later the Royal Highland (see p.223). It decided to encourage West Highland, Ayrshire, Shorthorn, polled breeds of Galloway, Angus, and Aberdeenshire, and to exclude from award competitions the Fifeshire breed and the horned Aberdeenshire. Both excluded breeds rapidly fell into decline and are now extinct.

Initially there had been neither large numbers of the breeds exhibited nor many awards offered to tempt breeders to make the considerable arrangements necessary to attend, but the event gathered momentum, expanded, and competitive participation became for many the pinnacle of their cattle breeding endeavours.

The cost of showing Highlands is high when one takes into account that they are a beef breed noted for their ability to thrive in conditions which do not normally require daily handling. Preparation for Show events therefore requires training the cattle to accept with as little stress as possible the many unaccustomed restrictions. The dearly loved family provider, hand milked, friendly and easily handled, and mourned over when necessity forced her departure, was not the cow which appeared in the Show ring last century. Those which did attend were mostly from large commercial herds. The close relationship between man and beast which grew on the journey to the Showground was probably the basis of the control used for the duration of the event; few Highlands were roped or haltered until the middle of the twentieth century. (see middle pic p.10)

As transport methods changed so did methods of preparing Highlands for Shows. Halter training became essential instead of optional. This had to start well in advance of the Show date and obviously had to be included somehow in farm management schedules not geared to daily cattle handling, as was the norm with dairy breeds and intensively farmed beef breeds. Add to that the longevity of the Highlands placing restrictions on the variety of animals a breeder may have with which to compete in any 10 year span and there is room for argument that breeders of Highlands were uniquely disadvantaged with regard to the Show circuit. And the problem of whether to Show Highlands in their winter or summer coat is yet another facet of Showing that does not trouble other breeds.

Undue emphasis by some judges on the importance of long coats in the Show-ring developed probably as a reaction to the known but unproven presence of Shorthorn blood in some animals from the 1920s onwards. A self-styled connoisseur of Highland cattle at an Oban Show in the 1920s was heard to say how greatly he admired *"beasts of the true mahogany colour"*. This rash statement exposed the speaker's ignorance of the admired colour being from Shorthorn blood. Such is the influence of judges that by the 1970s few breeders considered it worth their while to present any animal which had cast its winter coat naturally for the shorter summer one, and agricultural journalists were given to such comments as *"but for the want of coat this animal might have won"* or *"This was a grand animal but lacking in coat"* which helped to spread the erroneous idea that the breed was long haired for twelve months of every year. Apart from the fact that the horns only began to take a downward curve after shorthorn crosses were rife, often the only other tell-tale evidence was in coats which not even in winter grew the full profuse length of the regular Highland animal. But an official preliminary selection process conducted in the height of winter, to sort out the Shorthorn coats from the true Highland coats, was never set up. Dispute about some pedigree stock harbouring unknown amounts of Shorthorn blood was still circulating in 1962 when Mr W Heughan wrote "*Lady MacRobert's noted Highland bull Victor of Gylen evidently liked the look of some Angus-Shorthorn heifers – a kind of natural selection. At any rate, his mind was made up and he went over the fences and a public road, and two of them were served and produced two lovely dark red heifer calves. They became really fine looking animals with short horns, deep bodies and with quite a lot of Shorthorn characteristics. By all means endeavour to stabilise the type, but they cannot be suitable for the Highland Herd Book or the Beef Shorthorn Herd Book.*"

For too many years Highland cattle which did arrive at the Showground were kept in the background almost hidden from public gaze. The 1928 President of the Highland Cattle Society, Miss L C Turner, Kilchamaig, insisted that the Highlands be judged in full view of the Show-going public, since when they have occupied the same Show-ring status as other breeds.

Representation of the breed has varied over the years from a large turnout to no entries at all. Showing at the National Agricultural Show has always been a very expensive business which for the most part excludes participation by the smallholder whose priorities with cash flow may not include the cost of Show competition but whose few animals may be excellent examples of the breed. For them, either as exhibitors or potential buyers, the Regional Shows often appeal. It is worth remembering when perusing Show results that although the early Shows included animals representative of both commercial and selectively bred types, all too soon those most usually entered were bred for the purpose of Showing and could be called Show Types. Many excellent animals never see a Show ring. Sooner or later they are sought out by the Show circuit personnel to revitalise particular breed characteristics or to maintain strength by using fresh bloodlines from other pure stock. Both categories of breeders are important for the healthy continuity of the breed.

Until the Highland Cattle Society was formed some 146 different persons exhibited Highland cattle at the National Show, the then Highland and Agricultural Society of Scotland Show. Considering there were usually six classes in which to enter bulls, cows, heifers, stirks or stots and that even three new exhibitors per each of the 62 years would total 186, it reflects both that the breed was in decline and that a dedicated group were prepared to carry the banner for the breed. The names of those who were awarded for the Highland stock they exhibited at the National Shows are listed at the end of this chapter. Their considerable efforts to reinstate the status of the breed undoubtedly helped its survival.

It is strange to contemplate showing animals which for 62 years of Shows had no Breed Society, no official pedigree, no specially appointed breed judges, no printed guide on the characteristics of a "true" example of a breed which seemed to encompass three breeds...Westlanders, Mainlanders, North Eastlanders. Evidently breeders of that time had an understanding of the native beast and a widely accepted competence in selecting quality stock. Setting criteria for breed conformation, appearance and character for Show purposes has, over 100 years, reduced the variety. Concerns have been expressed that overall quality may also have altered. Early Show photographs indicate variation in types which were awarded. (See articles by Mr McLatchie pages 304 – 314)

The early accounts of the National Show mention the breeders and exhibitors but usually scant information on the animals...hardly surprising when there was no pedigree registration number issued until 1885 to help with details or to distinguish between animals bearing the same name. Names of individual animals began to appear after 1862 but confusingly often changed with change of ownership. Traditionally cattle named with a colour in their name such as Ruadh (pronounced *roo-ah*) for red or Dubh (pronounced *doo*) for black meant that the animal itself was the colour in its name. But the more bloodlines were mixed the more a calf born to a Dubh mother was not black but in the absence of official society registration systems would be named for the breeder's own livestock records as 'Dubh something' or 'something Dubh'. The same happened with red lines producing other coloured calves yet these non-red calves would bear the name Ruadh; so also with Buidhe for yellow, Dubh Chiar for black with white on the undercarriage, Chaishfionn for white marked animals. Colour was a useful instant identity tag often used in comments on award-winning animals as will be seen in two of the Show reports below.

FIRST FIVE YEARS OF THE NATIONAL AGRICULTURAL SHOW (Scotland)

Here is the mention of Highland cattle in the first five years of the National Agricultural Show drawn from an article by Mr James Cameron.

"1822 Edinburgh...a blue or dun 4 year heifer of a beautiful form and great points and a very remarkable brindled heifer of 2½ years with its dam were exhibited by Mr J Dickson of Dunse

1823 Edinburgh...six 4 year heifers bred by Mr Campbell of Islay MP. and Dr. Crawford, and two heifers bred by Mr J Graham (Junior) of Ballagan were shown as extra stock by Mr Graham who was awarded an honorary medal for bringing stock such a distance.

1824...no exhibits of Highland cattle

1825 Edinburgh...a Skibo of 40 months bred by General Dalrymple of North Berwick and a 28 months West Highland heifer bred by Mr Dickson, Dunse were shown by General Dalrymple. (Skibo was the name given at one time to Highland cattle from Sutherland) They won the award for best two heifers of any breed except Shorthorn.

1826 Glasgow...Two 4 year heifers, a Black and a Brindled bred by Mr McNeill of Colonsay and entered by Sir John Maxwell, Pollok, were considered by many judges as the best stock exhibited at the Show. They had been shown as Extra Stock. An Honorary medal was awarded."

AWARD-WINNING BREEDERS EXHIBITING HIGHLAND CATTLE AT THE HIGHLAND & AGRICULTURAL SHOW FROM 1822 TO 1884

1822	**James Dickson**	Dunse, Lothian
1823	**John Graham yr.**	Ballagan, stock from Islay.
	General Dalrymple	North Berwick, stock bred by J Dickson, Dunse.
	Sir John Maxwell of Pollok, Bart	stock bred by Mr McNeill, Colonsay
	Donald Macdonald	Balquidder Perthshire.
	John Boswell	of Kingcausie.
	James Campbell	Roseneath, Dumbartonshire, stock from Islay.
1828	**Moses Buchanan**	Laighpark, stock bred by Mr Malcolm.
	Peter Macintyre	Tynablair
1829	**John Menzies**	Chesthill, stock from the late Mr Stewart, Auch

1833	**Charles Stewart (late of Auch)**	Chesthill, stock bred by Mr Stewart Fasnacloich.
	John Campbell	Ballychewan
	The Duke of Gordon	
	Earl Gower of Skelbo	
	The Marquis of Stafford	
	The Earl of Ormelie	
	Donald Macdonald of Craigree	
	John Stewart	Cashlie
	Robert Stewart	Ardvorlich
	Alex. Anderson	Balnacraig
1835	**Jamieson**	Largs and Arbuckle, Ayr, exhibited cattle bred by Captain Walter Campbell, Islay.
	The Marquis of Breadalbane	Perthshire
1836	**Donald Stewart**	Luskintyre, Harris
	Duncan McLaren	Camusericht, Perthshire
	A & A Stewart	Lewis
1838	**Charles Stewart**	Chesthill, stock bred by J. Menzies, Glengarlandie, Perthshire
	William Cunninghame of Craigends	
	John Macdonald	Inverlocharig
	James Stewart	Edinleachduch
	Colin Campbell of Jura	
	Mr Neil Malcolm of Poltalloch	Argyllshire
	Alex. Stewart	Mains of Dalvey
	Donald Cameron of Locheil	stock bred by Mr Morrison, FortWilliam
	John Campbell	Ballychoan
	Duke of Sutherland	
	A & A Stewart	Inverscuddle
	Dugald Gilchrist of Ospisdale	
1839	**John Cameron**	Corriechoille, Inverness-shire
	William Grant	Ruthven Banff, stock bred by Mr McLaren, Rannoch, and stock bred by Mr Stewart, Harris
	James Grant Duff of Edin	stock bred by C. Stewart, Glenlyon
	George Taylor	Aldroughty, stock bred by the late Duke of Gordon
	Patrick Small	Dirnanean, Perth

1844	A G Morrison	Salachan, FortWilliam
	W A Campbell of Ormsary	stock bred by Mr Macdonald, Monachyle
	Alex Cameron	Invercomerie Farm, stock bred by C Stewart Glenlyon
	Messrs Stewart	Glenfinlass, stock bred by C Stewart, Chesthill
	Donald McLaren	Glenartney, Perthshire
	The Marquis of Breadalbane	stock bred by J Anderson, Braes of Foss
	John Cruikshank	Cloves nr. Elgin stock bred by Duke of Sutherland
1848	D MacNaughton of Cashlie	stock bred by D Macdonald, Craigruie
	William Grant	Ruthven, Banff, stock bred by A Macnaughton, Pubil
	Archibald Campbell of Jura	Messrs. Stewart, Invermeran, Fortingall, nr. Glenlyon, Perthshire
1850	Donald McLaren	Brae Lenny, Callander, Perthshire
1852	Rt. Hon. Duncan McNeill of Colonsay	stock bred by C. Stewart late of Chesthill.
	Allan Pollok	Ronachan, stock bred by C G Campbell nr. Stonefield, Tarbert, Argyllshire
1854	Allan Pollok	Ronachan, stock bred by C Campbell, Ballinaby, Islay
1854	Allan Pollok	Ronachan, stock bred by R Campbell, Jura/Lochgilphead
1856	G&JG Smith	Minmore, Glenlivet, Morayshire
	Alex Stewart	Dalvey, Grantown, stock bred by J Gordon, Ballintomb
	Allan Pollok of Broom	stock bred by D Macdonald, Monachyle
	The Hon. Lady Menzies	Rannoch Lodge, Perthshire
	William Webster	Islay
	Theodore Macrae	Struy nr. Beauly, Inverness-shire stock bred by the late Mr Macdonald, Monachyle.
	Robert Maclean	Gordonhall, stock bred by A Macdonald, Strathmashie
	The Duke of Leeds	stock bred by the late T McKenzie of Applecross
	Robert Anderson	Meikle Kildrummy, Nairn
	Hugh Fraser of Abersky	Inverness
	R D Campbell of Jura	

	Dugald Sinclair	Kilchamaig, stock bred by J Macdonald, Monachyle
1857	**Allan Pollok of Faside**	NewtonMearns, stock bred by Mr Campbell of Jura
	Donald McLaren	Corrychrone, Callander, Perthshire
	William Wilson	Whiteside, Aberdeenshire
	John McLaren	Monzie, Blair Atholl, Perthshire
	Lady Pigot	Cambridge, stock bred by Mr Macfaydyen, Oban
	James, John, & Joseph McLaren	Muirpersie, Kirriemuir.
	Harry Shaw	Bogfairn, Tarland, stock bred by J Grewer, Braemar and stock bred by A Duncan, Cabrach
1859	**Allan Pollok of Broom**	Mearns
1861	**Duke of Hamilton & Brandon**	stock bred by D Sinclair, Kilchamaig
	D Fletcher of Glenaros	Mull
	R Anderson of Lochdhu	Nairn
1863	**Duke of Atholl KT**	stock bred by the late Marquis of Breadalbane
	J Gordon of Manor Keith Hall	stock bred by the late Marquis of Breadalbane
1864	**D Stewart**	Monachyle, Lochearnhead, stock bred by J Macdonald of Monachyle
	Archibald Stewart	Claigan, Skye, stock bred by J Stewart Duntulm
	J Stewart "Bochastle"	Callander, Perthshire
	George Campbell	Ardifuir, Lochgilphead, stock bred by J Malcolm, Poltalloch.
	Robert Lawrie	Fincharn, Lochaweside
	Mrs Ewing	Strathleven House, Dumbarton
	Alex Macdonald	Nether Largie, Lochgilphead, Argyllshire
	G H M Binning Home of Argaty	Doune, stock bred by the late Marquis of Breadalbane
	J L Stewart of Coll	stock bred by Dugald McNeil of Saddell
1865	**Duncan Macpherson**	Kingussie, Inverness-shire
	Robert Peter of Urlar	stock bred by the late Marquis of Breadalbane
	A C Campbell of Monzie	stock bred by J S Menzies of Chesthill
	Alex Fraser	Faillie, Inverness, stock bred by the late Marquis of Breadalbane
	John Stewart	Duntulm, Skye

1867	**Archibald Clark**	Garvie, Greenock, stock bred by D Macarthur, Auchadunan, Cairndow
	D Macarthur	Auchadunan, Cairndow
1868	**John Stewart**	Flodigarry, Skye
1869	**A&A Macdonald**	Strathmashie, stock bred by D Macpherson, Kingussie
	The Earl of Seafield	Morayshire
	J Mackechnie yr.	Glenmore, Oban, stock bred by J Malcolm, Poltalloch
	C Macpherson Campbell of Ballimore	stock bred by A Clark, Garvie
	J Grant	Inverlaidnan Carrbridge, stock bred by Duke of Atholl
	David Carnegie of Stronvar	Lochearnhead, Perthshire
	T Leslie Melville Cartwright	Melvill House, stock bred by D McLaren, Corrychrone
	Commander D Stewart, R N Colonsay	stock bred by Lord Colonsay
	Donald McIntyre	Tighnablair, Comrie, Perthshire
	Alex S Stevenson	Auchanneilan, Lochgilphead, stock bred by D Carnegie, Stronvar
1874	**Cluny Macpherson of Cluny**	Kingussie, stock bred by the late R Peter, Urlar
	William Fraser	Lairg, Daviot, Inverness-shire, stock bred by J B Baillie of Leys Castle
	Lord Middleton, Applecross	
	Archibald Stewart of Ensay	
	Colonel C Greenhill Gardyne of Glenforsa	Stock bred by P. Underhood, Ardnacross, Mull
	Hugh Mann	Meadowfield, Nairn
	James Campbell	Ormaig, stock bred by J Malcolm, Poltalloch
1875	**Lord Aveland**	Glenartney Forest, Comrie, Perthshire stock bred by J Stewart, Duntulm
	P Sinclair	Upper Largie, stock bred by J Malcolm of Poltalloch
	Earl of Breadalbane	Taymouth Castle, Perthshire
	The Master of Blantyre	Scibberscross, stock bred by J Malcolm of Poltalloch
1876	**J Grant**	Inverlaidnan, stock bred by J Macgillivray, Ballachroan, Kingussie
	John Cumming	Killiehuntly Farm, stock bred by D Macpherson, Invertromie, Kingussie

	Alex Aitkenhead	Cowglen, Pollokshaw, stock bred by D McAlpine, Strathmore, Lochgilphead
1877	**John Mackintosh**	South Kinrara, Aviemore, Inverness-shire
	James Duncan	Benmore, Greenock, stock bred by J Stewart, Bochastle
1878	**W H Marshall**	Callander, stock bred by McNeil, Lossit, Islay
	B Irving	Barndennoch, Dumfries
1879	**John Macgillivray**	Ballachroan, stock bred by Earl of Seafield
	Lord Kinnaird, Rossie Priory	stock bred by the late R Peter, Urlar
1880	**Hector A Campbell**	Ardfenaig, Mull
1881	**Duncan McDiarmid**	Cammusericht, stock bred by Duke of Atholl
	J MacNaughton	Braes of Balquidder, stock bred by Duke of Atholl
	P McMartin	Liangarstan, stock bred by the late D McLaren, Corrychrone
	Alex Macdonald	Balranald, North Uist
	George A Cox of Invertrossachs	stock bred by J Stewart, Bochastle
1882	**A Dunlop Anderson**	Ardsheal, Ballachulish, stock bred by the late D McLaren Corrychrone
	George Robb	Glasgow, stock bred by J Stewart, late of Duntulm
	Duncan Stewart	Mollan, Callander, Perthshire
	George Willison	Ardlarach House, Luing, stock bred by Campbell, Cladvale, Islay
	Colonel Greenhill Gardyne of Glenforsa	stock bred by P Underwood, Ardnacross, Mull
	A S Finlay of Castle Toward	Greenock
	John Campbell of Kilberry	Argyllshire
	David McGibbon	Ard-na-Craig, Campbelltown, Argyllshire
1883	**John Stewart of Ensay**	
	The Mackintosh of Mackintosh	Moy Hall, Inverness-shire, stock bred by A Macdonald, Balranald
	Allan Macgillivray	Gordon Hall, Kingussie, Inverness-shire
1884	**P Robertson**	Rahoy, Morvern, stock bred by D A Macdonald, Killiemore, Mull
	J&D Cameron	Roromore, Glenlyon, stock bred by P McMartin, Auchessan
	The Earl of Dunmore	Ruadhal, Harris

THE STEWARTS OF GLENLYON; LUSKINTYRE AND ENSAY IN HARRIS; DUNTULM IN SKYE AND LOCHDHU NEAR NAIRN, INVERNESS-SHIRE

Several generations of Stewarts from Glenlyon in Perthshire bred many generations of fine Highland cattle to equal the best in Scotland. Clearly their expertise was in action in the late eighteenth century when Mr Donald Stewart must have acquired the skills that were to serve him well when he left Perthshire to relocate in Harris.

LUSKINTYRE, HARRIS

Mr Donald Stewart went from Glenlyon firstly to the farm of Park in Lewis in 1802. He was soon joined there by his younger brother Mr Archibald Stewart from Garth, Glenlyon. They worked a policy of using the best of the bulls they knew from Glenlyon and elsewhere in Perthshire with the best of the island stock. Their cattle were much in demand throughout Scotland.

Mr Donald Stewart moved to the farm of Luskintyre in Harris in 1809 from where he continued his cattle breeding. His son John, born in 1825, when of age, transferred some of the stock in 1844 to his own farm of Duntulm (alternatively Duntuilm) in Skye where he kept them until in 1882 he fell heir to the farm of Scorrybreck also in Skye, and to the island of Ensay off Harris, on the death of his Uncle Archibald Stewart. John Stewart then moved his stock to these properties. The best of his stock were:

In ENSAY (Island off Harris)

the Guanachs....derived from a cow his father had bought at Corrie in Skye. His father (Mr Donald Stewart) considered Corrie a source of the finest Skye cattle and purchased from there a stock bull named "Corriechatchan".

Targeals....cows which came off the Glenlyon stock in 1802.

the Donnachs....cows of Western origin.

the Shellays....cows from either Harris or the island of Shellay.

the stock bull Tarbh-Herrach, bred at his father's farm of Luskintyre.

DUNTULM/ENSAY/LOCHDHU

The Herd Book prints Ensay, Portree, which suggests Ensay is in Skye. There is no Ensay on Skye. To avoid confusion references should have read Mr J Stewart of Ensay off Harris, and of Scorrybreck and Duntulm, Skye.

Mr John Stewart's most famous animal in the 1860s was the triple first awards wide-headed Targeal Riabhach 799, a most characteristic and true breeder. Her sire was the black Lord Macdonald 345 who left good stock at Duntulm. In 1871 the brindle Sgiathanach Og 491 sired by black Geobach 220 earned the special prize, and Targeal Riabhach (of Ensay) collected a gold medal.

Sgiathanach Og 491 sired a brindle bull An-T-Eilanach 12 with an unbeaten Show career and considerable reputation as a Show bull. He was inbred in that his sire's sire and his dam's grandsire were one and the same Geobach 220. Another award-winning bull Prionnsa Tearlach II 427 of the Donnach strain was also related to Sgiathanach Og through his sire Rob Roy 440 (inbred to Geobach). Prionnsa Tearlach II was a first class stock bull. He left females of conspicuous merit. (He is not to be confused with Prionnsa Tearlach 426 bred at Poltalloch out of the Ribhinn strain and sired by Gille Dubh of Atholl 250; owned for a time by Mr Turner Kilchamaig, then by the Duke of Sutherland on whose estate he proved a great success.)

One of Targeal Riabhach's best-known Show daughters was Targeal Bheag 797 but she was not a breeder's animal like Guanach III 789 and Ribhinn Lurach 1304 which were good breeders and award-winners. In the 1870s and 1880s the Guanach strain gave repeated award-winners.

Guanach Lachin, a black female calved in 1867 tracing back to the Perthshire-bred Monachyle and Craig-an-righ bulls at Luskintyre, gained a 2nd, a 1st. and a gold medal. She transmitted her quality to the black Guanach III of Ensay 789 who collected four placings, and also to Guanach V of Ensay 791, the beautiful brindle champion of the Centenary Show. Her sire was the three times placed Fear-a-Bhaile of Duntulm 201.

A notable Ensay bull of the 1880s was Ceatharnach 642 first awarded at two years in Glasgow 1888. His dam was the Show winning Guanach V of Ensay 791 and his sire Young Prince Charlie 557, son of the excellent bull Prionnsa Tearlach II 427 earlier mentioned. A fine bull of robust well-knit frame and a handsome countenance, he lacked something in quality. He was not an outstanding success as a breeder at Ensay, Ardtornish, Poltalloch, or Cholderton, but his son Ceatharnach Buidhe 719 reflected well on his sire for he was regarded as a *"perfect representation of lordly Highland grandeur when looking one straight in the face"* and had great massiveness although accompanied by a slight slack waistedness with poor fleshing from hip to plate. Ceatharnach Buidhe 719 duly sired a bull of remarkable scale...Laoich 1260.

Laoich lacked the noble countenance of his sire but was superior in general conformation, depth from shoulder top to floor of the chest, heart-girth, length of frame, cleanness and taper of neck; the balance of parts and quality being altogether extraordinary. The extent of his 'line breeding' to Prionnsa Tearlach II was as next indicated.

Prionnsa Tearlach II 427 sired the following three animals...

1 Young Prince Charlie 557

2 Morair 681

3 Ribhinn Og 795.

Young Prince Charlie 557 with Guanach V gave Ceatharnach 642

Morair 681 with Shellay 763 gave Shellay III 2351

Ribhinn Og 795 with Ceatharnach gave Ceatharnach Buidhe 719

Ceatharnach Buidhe 719 with Shellay III 2351 gave Laoich.

The diagram shows clearly how Laoich inherits more than 30% of the genetic makeup of Prionnsa Tearleach II, four generations away.

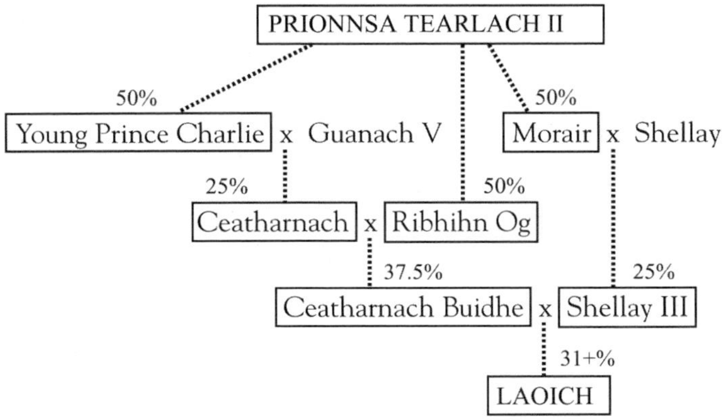

This example of inbreeding to one animal...line breeding to Prionnsa Tearlach II, was by no means unusual practice among the nineteenth century cattle breeders who seemed to understand how to get good results from inbreeding. Perhaps their success seems all the greater when records of the percentages of failures in their breeding schemes are not available and when it is likely that for each quality in-bred animal there were most probably a great many poor beasts bred as well.

Ensay-bred successes spread well into the twentieth century with for example Mr D A Stewart of Ensay's very fine bull An-t-Uramach 3499, 1920 champion, which was bought for Lady Ogilvie-Dalgleish of Errol at the highest price yet paid for any Highland bull. An-t-Uramach of Errol later went to the Douglas and Angus enterprise with Highland cattle where he set the high standard for which that fold is still renowned. The Ensay stock lines were continued by Miss Stewart from the farm of Lochdhu, Nairn. A two year old bull from there given a third place at Oban bull sales in 1939 went to Mr McEachern, Islay.

CHESTHILL STEWARTS

Other leading names in that Perthshire family of Stewarts were sometimes collectively called the "Chesthill Stewarts", hailing from farms at Auch, Cashlie, and Chesthill. Mr Charles Stewart Chesthill and his brother Mr John Stewart, Cashlie, both bred stock which between particularly the years of 1820 to 1840 had far-reaching influence on the breed in Scotland.

A different Mr John Stewart from J Stewart, Cashlie and J Stewart, Scorrybreck and Ensay, but said by one historian to belong to the same family, became known as "Bochastle". When seen at cattle events the word went round *"Bochastle himself is here."* It was said that he bred great cattle but parted with his best too readily.

"BOCHASTLE" STEWART, CALLANDER, PERTHSHIRE

With the Stewart flair for breeding good Highland cattle Mr John Stewart of Bochastle worked his large herd to a high standard of excellence. He purchased stock from Atholl notably the bulls Glentilt 295 and Daibhidh Buidhe, Marie Dubh the black award-winner, and another black of the Dubh Chiar strain, forebear of the Sgiathachs.

A powerful breeding bull and multiple award-winner was the light dun Donnacha-Ban-Nan-Oran 155, bred at Bochastle. He had well-set horns of great quality and a beautiful brow with an attractive dossan. He stood straight on strong legs, his general shape was good, but not specially deep in the rib. He bred beautiful cows and heifers which in turn were remarkably good breeders. But this bull, along with Roderick Dubh 451, a black Nannie strain of cow a dun Sgiathach and several other quality heifers from Bochastle were purchased by Mr James Duncan of Benmore; a loss to the Bochastle stock.

Another multiple award-winner was the black cow Proisag Dubh of Bochastle 783. At 12 years she collected the award in 1885 for best female. Her head and back-swirling horns were strikingly sweet and of intense Highland character; she was full of quality and had exceptionally good hind-quarters. She was slightly narrow in the chest and transmitted this fault mildly to one son Black Prince 45 but in pronounced form to another son Victor V 951.

Victor V however produced female stock consistently of the Proisag Dubh character. Proiseag Dubh's sire and dam, Roderick Dubh and Proiseag Bhuidhe, were two of the best animals which passed from Bochastle to Benmore, and from Benmore to Ardtornish.

Partial dispersal of the Bochastle fold occurred in 1933, after which Bochastle-bred animals carried the name Milton, such as Padruig of Milton. In 1939 a 15 year old Bochastle-bred cow in calf went to Achnacloich and Padruig of Milton went to the Department of Agriculture and Fisheries for Scotland Stud Farm in 1941. Final dispersal after the death of Mr J Stewart "Bochastle" was in 1942.

Fine tribute to the ongoing quality of Mr J Stewart's cattle came from Mrs Bouncer, Fasnacloich, in the 1960s with her comment about a black Bochastle-bred cow that produced fine female calves to the bulls Lasgaire of Canna, and Gille Og of Canna, *"a grand cow that walked with a style and dignity I have never seen equalled."*

BALRANALD NORTH UIST

The Macdonalds of Balranald were another family with a long history of great repute as Highland cattle breeders. Those farming Balranald in 1756 are credited with having introduced the practice of securing winter fodder for stock by gathering hay. A traveller in 1776 wrote that the cattle there were mostly black with patches of white and had horns. The young laird of the properties in the 1890s was the twelfth in succession to farm cattle there. Earlier than the fourteenth century the origins of the fold are not known but the assumption is that Highland cattle were there before that time. According to the *Scottish Farmer Album* of 1922 *"The Board of Agriculture's smallholding policy in the Western Isles necessitated the dispersal of the Balranald Fold in 1922...the oldest herd of cattle in the world."* The report mentioned that yellow, dun, and white animals were sold in that dispersal. One hundred and sixteen years earlier a yellow bull was calved at Balranald from a white marked strain of cows. He was registered as Seillein 481 in the first Herd Book of the Highland Cattle Society. A black son of his, calved in 1810, was registered as Morchius 365.

THE MCNEILS OF BARRA

The powerful clan of McNeil are reputed to have bred a fine quality of black cattle for centuries before the Barra fold was dispersed in 1885 when most of the stock went to Lord Dunmore of Harris and some to Dr MacGillivray, Eoligary, Barra.

Lord Colonsay and his son were famed for their black cattle in the 1750s. The McNeils of Colonsay are descendants of Torquil McNeil, Castle Sween, Knapdale 1449. They owned various estates but in particular owned Colonsay and Oronsay from 1701.

JURA

Highland cattle had been on Jura for so long that in 1764 at the dispersal sale of Archibald Campbell's fold nobody could suggest when they first came to the island. It was rumoured that the stock did first come from the mainland.

Mr R D Campbell of Jura was awarded best bull at the Highland Show of 1857 with the three year old Calum Dubh of Poltalloch 76, a bull whose bloodlines from both parents went to two famous Luskintyre strains...the Guanach line on his sire's side and the Ribhinn line on his dam's.

POLTALLOCH, LOCHGILPHEAD ARGYLL

The herd at Poltalloch was founded in 1790. By the 1840s Mr Malcolm's cattle were noted throughout Scotland for their size and general excellence. Poltalloch cattle were constantly in the Show awards lists for some 40 years.

In 1862 Mr Malcolm won great acclaim at the Battersea International Show with a 6 years brindle bull, Duntroon 177 bred by the Marquis of Breadalbane. Duntroon and two other bulls from Perthshire...Glenlyon 290, and Crinan of Poltalloch 124 who was easily the best in Kelso 1863, sired stock of great substance at Poltalloch. Crinan, a good sized yellow bred by Mr John McLaren at Monzie Blair Atholl, proved to be one of the best sires ever used at Poltalloch. Mr Malcolm paid considerable attention to his selection of bulls and two others in his famous line-up were from the Duke of Atholl's fold, namely, Gille Dubh 250 and Calum Riabhach 82. Duntulm quality was also brought in through Fear-a-Bhaile of Ormaig 204 carrying Monachyle blood and a great breeder.

Duntroon sired the notable Show winner Molachag I 540, Breadalbane-bred but owned by Mr Malcolm, also the Breadalbane-bred Jess of Poltalloch 523 who produced to Crinan 124 the award-winning bull Oscar 399. Mr Malcolm again received awards with the wide-framed robust looking Mhaldag 64, characteristic apparently of Poltalloch cows sired by Fear-a-Bhaile of Ormaig 204.

Poltalloch continued to feature strongly with awards in the 1870s gained by Ribhinn III of Poltalloch, Duntulm Og 182 a grandson of Duntroon, and Bealach 469 a dun heifer sired by Crinan out of the Breadalbane-bred Show success the dun Mhaigdean I 530.

TAYMOUTH/BREADALBANE, TAYMOUTH CASTLE, ABERFELDY, PERTHSHIRE

This fold was established about 1830. The presence of Highland cattle at the castle was to span the time of three of the Marquises of Breadalbane.

The Taymouth cattle, often referred to as Breadalbane cattle, were of *"splendid size and bone, remarkably free from coarseness, soft and rich in their hair; the cows, nearly all through very good milkers, had noble heads, the sweep of the horn in many cases being most majestic."* Two very fine stock bulls had come from the famous breeder and judge Mr John Anderson, Braes of Foss, Pitlochry, Perthshire.

The Taymouth animals were acknowledged to be well ahead of competition for many years and by the 1870s there were few good folds which did not bear the influence of Taymouth lines.

The Marquis of Breadalbane also kept an excellent herd at Luing near Oban and selected bulls from and for the two breeding grounds with singular expertise. Breadalbane stock first appeared in Shows at the Highland and Agricultural Society Show at Perth in 1863.

Mr R Peter, Urlar, Perthshire, owed much of his success to the regular purchase of Taymouth stock; likewise the Duke of Atholl whose stock bull Donull Ruadh 144 has been described as one of the finest Highland bulls ever bred, and as *"the potent force at the base of the Atholl Herd"* was sired by the Marquis of Breadalbane's famous Duntroon 177 out of the great Breadalbane Fassie (Fasaidh) family. Duntroon sired many award-winners and good breeding cows such as Molachag I 540 and Taymouth Jess 523 (Jess of Poltalloch) calved in 1859. Mhaigdean I 530 and Proiseag Odhar were Breadalbane cows of special note as were Rosie I and Queen I by Donald Odhar (not in Herd Book). Despite disruption of the Taymouth herd animals of the old Taymouth stamp continued to be well represented in awards lists to the end of the nineteenth century through such names as Bochastle Mairi Bhuidhe 2321, Atholl Te Bhuidhe 1397, Ruadh Mhor of Melfort 3274, and Calum Riabhach II 1325.

Many of the best stock went in the dispersal sale of 1863 to the Atholl Estate and Poltalloch. A few went to the Duke of Hamilton but they later found their way to the Atholl herd.

Seven years after that dispersal a new fold was founded in 1870 from a dun cow (originally at Taymouth) and her daughter, only to be virtually cleared out again 20 years later. But by 1896 the Breadalbane fold was once more being built up and then comprised ten cows and nearly 20 head of younger stock. The best of the 1896 fold were by the champion bull Rossie 456 from Atholl whose sire was the champion Calum Riabhach 82 of Atholl. Rossie's dam was of Urlar stock. The older cows of the 1896 fold were of Taymouth descent: the yellow Mary strain, short legged and by the sire Gille Bhuidhe of Cashlie 589; the yellow Bell strain of goodly size and the sweetly pleasing yellow Maggie strain, both also from Gille Bhuidhe; a dark brindle of the Mary strain...a fine stylish cow; and two brindled Maysies sired by Rossie 456. One of the brindled Maysies with *"horn well set and of the right quality"* had a beautiful forehead, symmetrical body and flowing hair traced her ancestry to a black cow *"of that strain"* bought from Barbreck (Argyll) about 1872.

Remarks about the 1890s stock seem more fault finding than in the past. The 12 years brindle of the Mary family put to Rossie 456 produced a brindle bull Young Rossie 1071 who had *"weak horn but great body and skin"* A full brother to Young Rossie was a *"sappy well haired black of looser build, to be kept in the herd"* while the brindle would go. The brindle Beauty was *"growthy and good quality but slack in the loin."* The brindle of the Maysie line sired by Rossie was *"a good cow, horns a little back set, and rather long in the muzzle"*, and the rising 2 years black Maysie was a *"thick set and profitable type."* A different judgement of a brindle four years old Maysie whose ancestors were from Barbreck Argyll said *"Her horn is well set and of the right quality, she has a beautiful forehead, a back and quarters to please a Highland fancier, while her flowing hair gives a proper finish to her symmetrical body."*

ATHOLL, BLAIR CASTLE, BLAIR ATHOLL PERTHSHIRE

The Duke of Atholl created a stir in 1863 when his three Breadalbane-bred animals each took first place at Kelso Show. They were six years red Rosie I and three years dun Queen I sired by Donald Odhar, and the two year old red bull Donull Ruadh 144. Donull Ruadh won many prestigious awards, yet notwithstanding his time away at Shows he proved a magnificent stock getter. Latterly he went to the Honourable Lady Menzies, Rannoch Lodge, Perthshire.

His most distinguished son at Atholl was the red Fear-a-Bhaile 199 out of the yellow Lili of soft flowing hair and back-swirling horn. Fear-a-Bhaile did not have great size but weighed well, had good conformation, style and hair, and achieved well at Shows. He went to the Earl of Seafield, Castle Grant, Moray, and sired several award-winning stock.

A well-known Show and stock bull in the 1870s owned by the Duke of Atholl and bred at, Duntulm, Skye by Mr J Stewart was Sgiathanach 489...a dark brindle *"of good size with a handsome head, fairly clean neck, and well balanced body set on short substantial legs, and he had the indefinable 'something' which takes the eye of a judge who is on the lookout for a stock bull."* He left a famous son Calum Riabhach 82 in the Atholl herd and a magnificent bevy of females such as Te Riabhach 35 probably the widest headed cow yet seen, Rosie III 34, Donnag, Donnag II 26, Donnag Og 27, N'Odhar Mhor, all cows of great scale and the grandest breeding properties. Sgiathanach later went to Camusericht, Rannoch, Perthshire, where he worked well for Mr D McDiarmid. His full pedigree was not recorded in the first Herd Book but Mr J Stewart's father said that Sgiathanach was strongly inbred to Monachyle (Perthshire) blood as both his sire and dam came from the Monachyle bull Broken Horn (Gille Ruadh 277) three and four generations back respectively. This connection with a Perthshire strain was thought to be the reason for his great results when put to Perthshire strains.

Calum Riabhach 82 was built on a massive scale. He was a very masculine type of majestic bearing, a long deep and wide frame, sappy skin and *"the bones of the real old Breadalbane model."* (probably large and substantial) His neck was *"not so clean as a modern judge* [of 1890s] *would wish."* He carried himself with a springy step until well on in years. He could not be used much at Atholl because most of the cows were too closely related to him but he did well at Poltalloch where he left many big and true-breeding females. Some of his notable progeny were: Calum Odhar 79, grandson of the Breadalbane Queen I; the famous brindle bull Rossie 456; the lengthy heavy brindle prize winner Iain Challum 667 out of the Ribhinn strain. Iain Challum bred well at Kinnaird Castle, Perthshire.

The award-studded Show career of Calum Riabhach of Athole 82 culminated in the champion cup for best male of the West Highland breed at the Centenary Show of the Highland and Agricultural Society in 1884, pushing his son Calum Odhar of Athole into accepting the cup for second best male of the breed at the same Show.

Calum Odhar was a bull of 'great scale and splendid bone with extraordinarily good back and ribs, very long and even, and deep quarters, practically perfect brows and muzzle. *"His horns could have been better set and he was rather loose in the neck for Show perfection. He was inbred to the Queen strain, his granddam being also the granddam of his sire."*

Rossie 456 sired by Calum Rhiabhach 82 out of an Urlar cow tracing back to Glenlyon stock like his sire *"steadily improved until he was over five years old, and was then a bull of great sweetness and style, with beautifully set, if rather fine, horn, clean neck, and excellent hind-quarters. He wanted spring of fore-rib to some extent, but he proved an admirable breeding bull. His stock at Atholl, Taymouth and Dall have been of very great all-round merit as individual specimens and as breeders."* His most noted sons were Donull Riabhach 875, a most successful stock bull at Shinness and Ardtornish, Adhollach 960, and Duke of Berwick 877 used with excellent effect at Kinnaird Castle, and Blair Atholl 979, a good breeder in the West Highlands.

Among the quality Atholl cows Rosie III 34 merits special mention. One of the grandest cows seen for years she gained many awards. She was *"a red of large, deep, square frame, straight above and below, well set on her legs, she could not stand wrongly. She had a fine head with horn of perfect quality and although she had a natural dock ear, the long fringe hanging from it was pleasing to the eye."* Her sire was the Ensay bull Sgiathanach 489 and her dam Rosie II of the Breadalbane strain.

The Atholl fold usually numbered around 50 animals. Sadly this fold carrying ancient bloodlines was partially dispersed in 1927 and completely dispersed by the mid 1930s.

CORRYCHRONE, CALLANDER

Mr Donald McLaren gained a first place with his heifer at the Glasgow Show of 1855. He became a prominent award-winner throughout the 1860s and 70s firstly with cows and heifers and then with bulls, then with both as at the 1875 Show when he was awarded a first and a third placing to two bulls and a second and a third to two heifers. One of his most noted animals, winner of the first place at Perth 1861 was painted standing with her calf by Gourlay Steell. The painting belongs to the Royal Highland and Agricultural Society.

Another well-known Corrychrone animal was Rob Roy III 442, latterly known as Rob Roy of Sutherland when he went to the Shinness Herd. He *"had unique grandeur in form and carriage, but rather a coarse head with wild horns after 4 years old, a strong frame, mellow hair and good bone."* He won second place when 3 years, took the special prize in the aged class when 4 years and was exhibited at the Centenary of the Highland and Agricultural Society in 1884 where he failed to collect a placing. When he was next shown at 10 years he failed to collect an award. He was not a successful stock bull either. His sire was a proven stock getter but his dam was an unreliable breeder. The best male progeny of Rob Roy III was his grandson Lord of the Isles II 781 by the rather low-horned black bull Glen Dubh 662. It is unlikely that Mr D McLaren knew of these as information written in 1882 referred to the 'late D McLaren'.

ARDTORNISH, MORVERN, ARGYLL

In 1887 Mr Valentine Smith purchased Mr J Duncan's Highland cattle from Benmore. By so doing he acquired many animals which had been bred by "Bochastle". Very quickly Ardtornish became the most remarkable prize-winning fold of the late nineteenth century.

The compact strongly characteristic bull An-t-Iasgair 13 carrying Luskintyre and Ensay bloodlines might have gone unnoticed if left with the smaller western cows; but Mr Smith purchased him and was rewarded with some splendid progeny such as Sgiathach IV 2276 the broken horn female champion of 1891 and 1892, the first prize yellow cow Proiseag IV 2275, and the male champion in 1893 the compact brindle bull Victor VII out of Proiseag Dubh 783. This was the result of putting An-t-Iasgair to large open-framed cows quite unrelated to himself, as he was inbred to Ensay Donnachs. *"He was an out and out Hebridean, short in face, moderate in size, strongly jointed, and with extraordinary wealth of hair. His female offspring so far have proved to be true breeders."*

Ardtornish produced excellent females of the breed and added Bochastle's Proisag Dubh 783 to the fold in 1888, although aged 15 years by then.

Another highly successful stock-getter for Ardtornish was the brindle Donull Riabhach 875 calved in 1889 whose sire Rossie 456 was from the renowned Ensay-bred Sgiathanach 489, and whose dam was Beauty of Athole 21.

Clearly the Ardtornish blend of Bochastle, Atholl, and Ensay bloodlines continued to produce first class stock.

CAMUSERICHT, RANNOCH, PERTHSHIRE

Highland cattle from Camusericht are mentioned in folksongs and stories of Clan MacGregor raids, but once Agricultural Shows were well-established the public recognition given to breeders who had won awards for their stock spread their success faster and further afield than previously.

The stylish brindle bull Ailpean 4, bred at Atholl out of the dam Taymouth Jessie, brought fame to his owner Duncan McDiarmid of Camusericht. Another successful Show bull and a great stock-getter was Fear-a-Bhaile of Camusericht 200 also out of Taymouth Jessie but sired by Sgiathanach 489. Fear-a-Bhaile's daughter produced the award-winning Calum Riabhach of Garbole which went to Taymouth in 1899. Interestingly an agricultural writer of that time suggests that Calum Riabhach of Garbole had Sgiathanach connections through his sire Fear-a-Bhaile of Moyhall 1354 which is at variance with the Herd Book but which would point to successful inbreeding. Fear-a-Bhaile of Camusericht 200, however, left good stock at Camusericht, Bochastle, Gordonhall, Garbole.

THE QUIET CONTINGENT (NINETEENTH/ TWENTIETH CENTURIES)

There were many who quietly perpetuated quality Highland cattle of ancient bloodlines without the public acknowledgement earned and spread from repeated entries at Agricultural Shows. These loyal enthusiasts were to be found throughout Britain but the scale of this text limits specific mention to a representative few in Scotland. Often they were highly esteemed judges whose placings at Oban and the National Agricultural Shows were well respected, their understanding of the breed known to have been assimilated from generations of family involvement with it.

MESSRS JAMES AND ARCHIBALD MACINDEOR were well-known judges of Highland cattle and kept a fold of high quality. Their family had taken tenancy of the farm of Balole on Islay, when the McNeills of Lossit relinquished it in 1854. The MacIndeors purchased Mr McNeill's stock of 25 Highland cows with calves and about 30 stot stirks. These animals had distinguished old bloodlines which the McIndeors continued until retiral in 1947. One of the best Agricultural Shows held by the Islay Jura Colonsay Agricultural Association was that of 1907. By that time Highland cattle no longer predominated in the cattle classes but '*some beautiful specimens and a grand massive bull*' were on show from J and A MacIndeor, Balole, who seldom exhibited, and never at a National Show. Their ground marched with that of Lord Margadale's Kilinallan Farm which gave them opportunity to observe the offspring of Kilinallan stock bulls, and resulted in direct purchases. Lord Margadale, the former Major J G Morrison, bought the entire Balole stock of 30 cows with calves and also all the heifers when the MacIndeors retired. The ancient Balole/McNeill bloodlines were then incorporated into the Ile fold, Islay, and were well-placed when shown by Major Morrison, as for example with Ruadh Bheg II of Balole 12515 and Elit Ruadh V of Balole.

KILBERRY (BARAVALLA)

For several centuries Campbell lairds in Argyll bred excellent "black cattle".

Widely known towards the end of the nineteenth century for the quality of their stock were Lieutenant John Campbell of Kilberry and R D Campbell of Jura.

John Campbell's high reputation was associated with a source of reliably good breeders which he attributed to bloodlines he bred from one or two cows purchased in the 1870s from Dr Campbell's farm of Baravalla. One of the first Kilberry-bred calves from Baravalla cows was named Buidhe 97, apparently not outstandingly beautiful, but a great breeder. The name "Baravalla" came to mean "Kilberry-bred" largely due to the remarkable fecundity that the Kilberry-bred Baravalla 932 (sire Kilchamaig 325) passed on to her many calves. She was calved in 1885, gave good brindles and reds for 16 years and died at the age of 23 years in 1908. Most of her bull calves were red and three of her four heifers were brindle. Her last calf was born in the twentieth century, the brindle Baravalla Og 5489 calved in 1901. At the Kilberry dispersal in 1928 stock went to, among others, the folds of Douglas, Ormsary, Achnacloich, Bunnessan, and Ile.

John Campbell, himself a judge, only occasionally exhibited at Shows, collecting awards nonetheless when he did. His son Lieutenant Colonel John Campbell ably continued the Kilberry lines until his death in 1928 and the subsequent dispersal. Baravalla lines were still in such demand in the 1950s that after her return from the Second World War the Colonel's daughter Marion was unable to purchase any with which to rebuild the bloodlines of the old Kilberry fold. However, she selected stock at Oban intending to establish once more at Kilberry a herd of quality pedigree Highland cattle. In honour of the cow Craig, whose head is mounted at Kilberry Castle, and who was in the old Kilberry herd long before Baravalla, Marion Campbell favoured the prefix Craig-a-rithist which means 'Craig again. 'Craig 88 had been purchased by 'Old Kilberry' from Digby Jones at Kilchamaig in 1876 and from two of her heifers – Craig Og 80 and Geepoch Buidhe 945 – sprang a great line of good breeders. But before fully stabilising the new line of cattle with the old name link, a decision was made to sell complete with livestock the farm which held them. The new owner did not continue to register the cattle so the Kilberry connection was lost.

THE MACNAUGHTONS, GLENLYON

The nineteenth century Macnaughtons of Glenlyon bred sound stock with a skill which survives today in several descendants.

A Macnaughton, Glenlyon, A & J Macnaughton, Kerrowmore, D Macnaughton, Cashlie, W & J Macnaughton, Cashlie, J & P Macnaughton, Dericambus, were better known in the 1880s for the type of animal they bred than for regular attendance in the Show circuit. Their twentieth century descendants however, who have an instinct in the management and breeding of Show winning and strong working stock, can be traced from the late Mr Macnaughton, Kerrera...fold name Gylen, through his widow who continued to breed Highland cattle from Kippen Home Farm, Dunning, his son Donald and his daughters Mrs H Corrigall, fold name Earn, and Mrs Connie Lawrie, fold name Lagg, who frequently collect awards for their Highland cattle. Connie Lawrie is particularly enthusiastic about the breed and has brought out the best in whatever Highland stock she handles, both in the Show circuit where she has had creditable successes and in breeding high quality animals. Her skill with livestock was evident at ten years old since when her continued involvement with Highland cattle has done much to maintain ancient bloodlines.

Influential animals from Macnaughton stock are Victor of Gylen, a power in Lady MacRobert's Douneside fold; his son Victor of Earn, a price record breaker for Mrs Heather Corrigall; Adamh of Glenfalloch; and breeding cows of the Bachy, Bernice, and Conachair strains. Further information may appear in a future publication planned by Mrs Connie Lawrie.

MR MALCOLM TYSON, cattle judge, and his brother kept a pure-bred fold under the name Balliemore. Their stock came from ancient bloodlines bred by their forebears on the farm of Bernice on the shores of Loch Eck. Many of their animals carried the name Bernice, as for example Bernice Ruadh II of Balliemore 12929 who went with heifer calf to Major Shaw McKenzie, Newhall, Ross-shire.

The Tysons kept the breed through times which caused many tenant farmers to sell up, but found it was time to retire from active livestock involvement in 1950. Three years later Mr J J Currie, Kildalloig, gained a second in class at Oban with Bernice of Kildalloig. Previous to that Mr J J Currie had added the three year old Bachy of Balliemore 12875 to his stock. The second in class bull Gaisgeach Ruadh of Balliemore 4591 went to Mr Macnaughton, Kerrera and then to Mr T A Nelson, Achnacloich.

THE MESSRS MCLACHLAN were for long tenants at Kilmichael Glassary in Argyll, and had, like their fathers before them, bred Highland cattle all their days. Few of their animals were ever registered but represented as did the Tysons' stock, many of the old strains and were an ongoing link with the past. Their fold also dispersed in 1950.

BROWNS, KILMORE

Mr John Brown, an experienced judge at all leading Shows was, as were his forebears, brought up with an understanding of Highland cattle. He bred and sold many fine animals, frequently winning at Shows with bulls. Comment was made in 1945 about a particularly good black heifer of his which fetched a high price, that it was a pity he was judging and so could not put his own stock into the Show ring. That much admired black heifer went to the Ardkinglas fold as did the progeny bred at Kilmore in the 1940s from a Fanans bull.

Mr John Brown died in 1946, and the Kilmore cattle were taken over by his son Iain. Time was to show that Iain Brown did not pursue the stock breeding with the same enthusiasm as his father and the Kilmore lines ebbed away.

THE BUCHANANS, SHENAVALLIE & ACHNABA, LEDAIG

The present Mr Duncan Buchanan, Shenavallie comes from a family who have bred Highland cattle on a commercial basis for more than a hundred years. He has repeatedly judged Highlands including the huge entry in 1994 when Her Royal Highness the Princess Royal opened the long awaited new Oban Cattle Mart at Upper Soroba, 1½ miles south east of Oban.

Mr Buchanan's father, D Buchanan senior, took Highland cattle from Eriska near Oban, to Achnaba, Ledaig, where they bred successfully for some time before his first entry in the Herd Book with Gille Buidhe of Achnaba 1524 calved in 1895, grandsire Bochastle Ruadh 1196.

Five years later came the next entry with Gille Buidhe II of Achnaba 1990 calved in 1900, great grandsire Bochastle Ruadh 1196. The third entry was the 1911 calved Gille Ruadh of Achnaba 2968 whose bloodlines through a Duntulm-bred dam traced back through Ensay dams to Gille Dubh of Monachyle.

D Buchanan senior left Achnaba in 1919 for a term of management for the Earl of Dundonald, Lochnell Castle, Ledaig. The estate acquired some Achnaba stock which were registered under the name Shenavallie.

D Buchanan senior along with brother W Buchanan returned to Achnaba in 1928 and continued to breed thoroughly *"good doers and regular breeders"* only entering the occasional animal of special merit in the Herd Book, such as Druimfionn II of Barbreck sired by Iain Buidhe of Atholl 2763.

1937 found D Buchanan senior well-established at the farm of Shenavallie, which passed to the present Duncan Buchanan with every likelihood that his son D M Buchanan will continue the tradition of Highland cattle breeding there.

The stock bull in the early days at Shenavallie was a son of Druimfionn II of Barbreck registered as Gille Buidhe II of Achnaba 3720. Other memorable stock were the Oban top priced Champion Mairi Ruadh II of Shenavallie, sired by Prionnsa of Errol, and the reserve female champion Bhoidheach Bheag of Shenavallie, sired by Niall of Scammadale.

Shenavallie animals are bred for traditional hardiness and are renowned for their reliability as stock getters. The policy has been to rear commercial rather than Show stock yet in addition to buyers from abroad many of the leading Show folds continue to dip into Shenavallie bloodlines to keep the full Highland character uppermost. Shenavallie animals carry links with namely folds of the past as for example in Elspeth out of Baravalla Beothail V 13058 tracing to Poltalloch and Bochastle lines who went to Braes of Greenock fold in 1952.

Duncan Buchanan likes wide, open heads, and finds brindles do well. Buchanan cousins at Cochno and Barbreck Farm (at Taynuilt, and unlike the Barbreck at Lochgilphead not used as a fold name) also bred Highlands with some success but have long since retired.

BARBRECK/LEACHY LOCHGILPHEAD ARGYLL

Mr J P Dalgleish moved from Fife to Barbreck, Lochgilphead, in 1935 taking with him the Highland cattle which quickly became highly regarded representatives of the breed. The foundation stock for this influential fold included animals from Ensay, Bochastle, Southesk, Killundine, Kilchamaig, Achnacloich. Barbreck Highlands took many male and female championships at Oban and won consistently high placings until partial dispersal in 1960. Although turning out cattle for Agricultural Shows was not a marked feature of the Barbreck policy, whereas choosing sound bulls carefully and using only regular annual calvers in the breeding cows was, female stock sired by Barbreck bulls collected reserve female champion rosettes at the Royal Highland Show.

Reminiscent of 'Bochastle' with regard to livestock Mr Dalgleish bred reliable animals which proved their quality wherever they went, both through the male and female lines. He bred stylish cattle with strong bone in a large frame of sound conformation, with good coats and a well set head. Always keen to share knowledge of the breed, Mr Dalgleish conducted a much appreciated demonstration in Oban 1946, on good types of hill cattle. For this he illustrated some points by taking his 1945 Oban purchase, the champion bull Ruaridh Mhor 4262, straight off the hill in working condition. For seventeen years he maintained his valuable support of the breed, handing on his skill and enthusiasm to his family. The Dalgleishes always acknowledged the substantial input from their cattleman Mr George Campbell and were delighted that he was awarded the Achnacloich Medal for bringing out the best junior female at the 1953 Oban Spring Sales in the very first year in which it was presented.

With some 38 cattle in 1959 it was learned that the Barbreck estates were to be sold so dispersal of the Barbreck stock was set for 1960. Rosemary Dalgleish succeeded in retaining some of the Barbreck specials but was required to find a new fold name. So these Barbreck-bred animals were continued under the new fold name of Leachy.

Rosemary continued to apply the policy established so successfully by her father but with even less involvement at Shows. She won admiration and recognition for her own ability to produce high quality stock. Her good natured understanding of the breed is very evident in conversation as is also her readily given tribute to generous assistance from the late Mr T B L Thomson, a former President of the Highland Cattle Society and father of the President elected in 1996. With reluctance she retired from the ranks of active breeders in 1994, taking the last of the Leachy stock to the Highland Cattle Society Spring Show and Sale in Perth that year. The Barbreck/Leachy awards-winning female strain once more took the female championship, this time with Siusan Ruadh 26th of Leachy who was purchased for the Craigowmill fold. According to Rosemary the Barbreck/Leachy Siusans, the brindle Molags and the An Uiseags all transmitted to progeny their good natures and tendency to produce mainly female calves.

The Barbreck stock had gone to the folds of Findrack, Strathallan, Ile, Achnacloich, Douneside, Scone, Benmore, Ballathie, the Department of Agriculture, to name but a few and also abroad to South America. The most notable bulls were Coirneal of Barbreck, a brindle who did well for Major Granville Morrison of Islay, and MacIain of Barbreck who went to Achnacloich. Other bulls of importance to the Barbreck fold were Ruaridh Mhor, Domnull of Benmore and John Severie.

NA COMERICH

The black Applecross herd of fame in the eighteenth and nineteenth centuries might have dwindled away completely after the Second World War had the twentieth century owner Major J L Wills been unreceptive to encouragement from the estate farm management team of Mr A and Mrs M M Edwards to keep some Highland cattle at Applecross. Major Wills acquired the stock along with the estate which he took on in 1928. The Applecross Herd Books make mention some 20 years before the Highland Cattle Society began of an impressive array of mainland and islands bulls from renowned breeders' stock.

Bloodlines of Athole, Poltalloch, Balranald, Urlar, Monachyle, Ensay stock to name but a few had kept the Applecross animals in high repute. From 1856 onwards many of them went south to the Duke of Leeds and were not replaced. Gradually changing emphases on the Applecross estate resulted in dwindling numbers of Highlands and by the 1940s some uncertainty about continuity of bloodlines. Between 1918 and 1983 only three original black family names appear in the Applecross Herd Books somewhat infrequently. They are the Molach, the Cruinneag, and the Morag lines. Unfortunately a gap in the Herd Books makes it difficult to be accurate about unbroken pedigree links between twentieth century and nineteenth century stock. Nonetheless, with persistent enthusiasm Mrs M M Edwards and Mr A Edwards worked more blacks back into the Applecross herd from the 1980s using the bulls Black Prince of Commoncraig, Tearlach Dubh of Balinoe, and Donald of Inver. Further change was to find Mrs Edwards no longer with the Applecross Estate but ready to take some Applecross Highlands into the twenty-first century under her own fold name of Na Comerich which is the name of a black line bred at Applecross in the 1860s from a cow called Comeraich, calved in 1864.

MONKSMOOR (ENGLAND)

After nearly a century in Devon a few of the Monksmoor Highland cattle found their way back to Scotland.

The late Mr R H Jane had brought Highland cattle to his Monksmoor Farm, Devon, in 1904. They carried old bloodlines from Bill Luscombe's herd on Dartmoor, where local historians say there had been Highland cattle for at least 150 years. That means these Dartmoor Highlands were pre-Agricultural Revolution animals and therefore likely to be as typical of the natural old breed as could be found anywhere.

In 1941 Bill Luscombe sold his Highlands to Fred Knapman and Mr R Henry Jane. Later Mr R H Jane bought Mr Knapman's Luscombe cattle which swelled the Monksmoor herd to 200 head.

In 1965 five animals from Lord Rootes' Glenalmond Fold dispersal and six from Lady Abertay's Tullybelton Fold dispersal were purchased for Monksmoor. A bull even further from Devon was selected from Breachacha-bred stock on Coll. Mr R H Jane looked for *"length, size, large hoofs and testicles, and insisted that the bulls must have good bone and meaty second thigh."*

He had a dream of owning a herd of white Highlands but settled for Silver Duns after experiencing too many congenital eye defects in the white cattle. When a black or red calf arrived instead of the expected and hoped for Silver Dun he was given to saying *"It's the glorious uncertainty of breeding."*

Before his death in 1984 Mr Jane had achieved his goal of having a healthy 'white' herd at Monksmoor. Sadly his life's work was not to be continued by his family and the Monksmoor Highlands with their centuries old heritage were abandoned to a commercial cattle dealer. A few of these animals were saved from oblivion when Mr A A Wheelwright, who had a great respect for the late Mr Jane, managed to intercept the commercial dealer's cattle-float loading procedure and purchase a few which he transported to his Longley Farm near Forres in Scotland. One or two found their way back to the Island of Coll to Mr Stewart's Breachacha Fold. When the pedigrees of those at Longley Farm were traced three of the great breeder lines from Monksmoor were discovered: the Henrietta, the Lorna, and the Monica lines. A Monksmoor heifer from the Monica line and one from the Snowball line bred by Mr T F McClung came under the auctioneer's hammer at Oban in February 1996 bearing the fold name of Croc Mhor. Names change faster than bloodlines but with a little perseverance related livestock can often be traced.

EXMOOR (ENGLAND)

Also back in Scotland after family generations spanning more than 150 years on Exmoor is one of a Scottish drover's family.

Mr Philip Heard's ancestors were among the Scottish drovers recruited in 1826 to deliver cattle to Exmoor. *"In October 1826 a Mr Knight proceeded to Falkirk Fair where he bought 450 most beautiful West Highland cattle."* (P Heard) These animals went south primarily as breeding stock for Exmoor and not, as was then so common, to be fattened for sale in the southern beef markets. A few of the drovers settled in Exmoor probably engaged in managing livestock, for Mr Heard believes his family always kept Highland cattle. Mr Heard is in some ways a twentieth century drover for he runs a Hauliers Business and has a lifetime's experience of driving (in the road transport sense) cattle of all breeds. Unlike the old drovers few of whom owned a large head of stock, Mr Heard has today around 100 Highland cattle on his Culfuar Farm, Tayinloan, Argyllshire. Although his father had pure-bred Highlands on Exmoor Mr Philip Heard is a commercial cattle breeder. But since the chance purchase in 1986 at an English cattle mart of two pedigree animals, the white bull Chladan of Achnacloich and the cow Princess 2 of Rum he has sustained an interest in buying and breeding pedigree Highland stock. Having moved his fold from Exmoor to Culfuar Farm in 1990 Mr Heard says they do much better in Argyllshire, because the natural forage is richer than their previous southern grazings.

There is no claim being made here of Mr Heard's stock tracing their ancestors as far back as Mr Heard can trace his, but his story is another instance of the curious reversal of the history of Highland cattle...the breed that once was taken to England from Scotland and 150 to 200 years later was being taken to Scotland from England.

A Yorkshire dealer bought 300 cattle from Jura in 1737, then in 1763 there is mention of a Mr Moorhouse from Yorkshire purchasing 600 cattle from MacLeod of Waternish Skye, and a further 1,000 from his visit to Skye and Raasay before heading south to the Falkirk tryst. The English destination for which these cattle were bought remains unknown, but it is possible some of them could have arrived at Exmoor.

THE DISQUIETING TWENTIETH CENTURY

Amid the restless twentieth century shaken by wars, emergence of new diseases, advancing nuclear and computer technologies, and amazing ventures into Outer Space, the active interest upheld by the British Monarchy in livestock farming, agriculture, and nature conservancy is calming and reassuring.

Biological and veterinary sciences seem poised to render obsolete the term 'natural', but artificial environments are fragile.

If Highland cattle can remain intact as a natural breed, free from genetically engineered remodelling, free from fast growth stimulants, free from cloning, free from embryonic culture in non-bovine species, there will come a time when they are truly necessary. This breed may yet release to science the secrets of endurance. Its survival, however, under threat from the ripple effects of changing technologies needs all the support available.

Royal interest in the breed was noticed in November 1866 during Queen Victoria's reign when *The Oban Times* newspaper reported that purchases at the Doune Tryst included nineteen three year old Highland bullocks destined for Her Majesty's Home Farm at Windsor. In 1878 *"nine two and a half year old white heifers were sent by Joe Brown of Hermitage, Dalbeattie, through Burrell of London to the manager of the Royal Show Farm, Windsor. They were progeny of the Kilmory herd of wild whites."* (Prof R Wallace) (See Kilmory Page 125)

Mr Aitchison, the manager at Kilmory at that time, was quoted in the *Transactions of the Highland & Agricultural Society of Scotland 1878* as saying *"I sent some few years since six heifers to Her Majesty's farm at Windsor; but Mr Tait the manager there, told me that, though the crosses with the Shorthorn bull answered admirably, they had to give them up, owing to its getting wind that they were 'Scotch wild cattle,' and when ladies were walking in the park they looked at them with their black eyes."* (Mr Aitchison was probably not describing the ladies' eyes.)

The potential of the Highland as a beef breed was pursued some years later by His Majesty King George V whose interest led him to Show Highland Steers at the Smithfield and Scottish National Fatstock Shows where the Royal entries won awards. Winning Windsor entries in the 1930s in both steer and heifer classes included stock of Atholl, Kilchamaig, and Bochastle breeding.

King George VI granted his Patronage to the Highland Cattle Society of Scotland in 1938, ten years before the title of Royal was conferred on the Highland & Agricultural Society of Scotland. Among the Highland Cattle Society Herd Book entries in 1940 is one from His Majesty the King, Sandringham.

Following King George VI's reign came the present monarch Queen Elizabeth II who granted her Patronage to the Highland Cattle Society in 1952. Selection of Highland cattle for the establishment of a fold at Balmoral began in 1953 and by 1954 fourteen heifers in calf from Jura,

Islay, Achnacloich, and Strathallan Castle went to found the now famous and considerably larger Royal Fold of pedigree Highland cattle in the Balmoral Estate. Balmoral entries loyally participate regularly in the National Agricultural Shows, and the Highland Cattle Society's pedigree Shows at Oban, frequently achieving top awards. The Balmoral Highlands are mainly red with a few yellows and a persistent brindle line stemming from the 1962 presence of the bull Tearlach of Strathallan.

ACHNACLOICH

Captain T A Nelson founded the Achnacloich Fold near Oban in 1901. Ninety-five years later, Achnacloich stock under Mrs J Y Nelson's ownership were still highly sought after throughout Britain and for the many folds flourishing abroad. The Nelsons believe that continuity of policy is very important and they attribute much to their first manager Mr Peter Bruce who helped establish the enduringly sound fold type over his 34 years at Achnacloich.

The early stock carried bloodlines from Atholl, Southesk, Kilberry, Stronvar, Duntulm, and Ardanaiseig.

The first stock bull, calved in 1902, was Malachi 1870, sired by Riabhach II of Atholl 1325, and proved to be such a good breeder that one of his sons was kept as a stock bull in 1908. The dun cow Corrichean II of Canna 6486 was very long-lived and her progeny were still part of the fold in the 1950s. Capleadh V of Ardanaiseig 7144 bred by S A Ainsworth also proved to be a very valuable animal. Her granddam was the original Capleadh who gave the name to long successful lines in many folds. Dosan Dhearg of Duntulm 6783, Princess Vala II 9055 of Southesk, two Kilberry Baravalla descendants bought in 1923 and two of the Lady White strain from Stronvar are the other stock which stamped the early fold with quality.

Sires worthy of mention were An Spaideil Ruadh of Killundine 3708, Prionnsa Bhuidhe II of Kilchamaig 3795, Corneil Ruadh of Mingary 4771, and Calum Seoladair of Smaull 4245 bought in 1945. The last named sired the now legendary supreme champion Uallach of Achnacloich 4475 (red) who broke the 28 year old price record at his sale in 1948 to Mr Walker of Foreland, and whose influence is to be found through many important folds. MacIain of Barbreck 5522 and Alpin of Douneside kept the Achnacloich standards in the 1960s, furthered of course by Fionn of Achnacloich being loaned to the AI Station in Perth before going to the Department for Agriculture and Fisheries for Scotland bull stud for islands destinations.

Even before the 1960s Highland cattle from Achnacloich had been sold for destinations in North and South America, Australia, and The Falkland Islands. By 1965 Peru, Denmark, South Africa and Canada could be added to the exports list.

The successful black strain stems from a 15 year old Bochastle cow Captain Nelson had bought in 1939 from Mr Fletcher of Laudale. She was carrying the black bull calf Prionnsa Dubh of Achnacloich 4136 whose female progeny formed the black female lines still in evidence in the 1990s.

Achnacloich-bred animals accrued many championships over many years in both male and female entries, and even when management policy no longer included entries at Shows, particularly since the implementation of IBR Regulations (see page 295) the stock held their value.

THE GOVERNMENT DEPARTMENT FOR AGRICULTURE IN SCOTLAND

This government department has held various names. For convenience here DAFS (Department of Agriculture and Fisheries for Scotland) will be used to refer to 'The Department'.

At the beginning of the twentieth century the British Government was aware of continuing depopulation of the Highland and Islands areas of Scotland. In 1913 part of its initiative to stem this process involved setting up some measures intended to attract the crofting communities to stay. One of these was the offer of a bull on loan for up to two years free of charge to any township with adequate grazings for its upkeep. Three stud farms were set up around Inverness and four breeds initially on offer were Highland, Shetland, Shorthorn, and Aberdeen Angus. Care was taken in selecting yearlings from farms known for hardy unpampered stock. Mr J Dean, a Senior Inspector of Livestock in Scotland found that running bulls together kept them docile and tractable. DAFS insisted that a Beef Shorthorn bull be used every so often *"to keep the outcross vigour and stamina". The Scottish Farmer* correspondent reported that DAFS bought 74 bulls in 1935 and 86 bulls in 1936.

Some DAFS Highland cattle purchases were from:

No date	Garth and Flichity.
1921	High price for a bull from Glenbrittle, Skye.
1938	Righ of Quothquan: brindle from Atholl and Killundine lines.
1940	A stirk from each of Fanans, Barbreck, Duchess of Montrose.
1941	The stirk Padruig of Milton of Bochastle breeding and a two year old bull from Douglas & Angus.
1943	Muireach of Barbreck 4058, Bein Dearg 4169 from Douglas & Angus, Benmore of Craighead 4148, and two yearlings from Cuilfail and Ardanaiseig.

In 1944 DAFS noticed that few breeders were rearing bulls.

1945	Seumas Righ of Douglas & Angus, Angus of Balmuick.
1947	A 3 year old from Mr J Cameron, Glenfinlas; a 2 year old from Arran.
1948	Righ Buidhe 4394 from Fanans-bred stock.

To counteract the shortage of Highland cattle DAFS undertook a breeding scheme which by 1951 saw them with stock in Ballinaby, Corries, Glam, Fearns, Killundine, Glen Etive, Knocknagael.

1952	DAFS bought stock from, Ile, Kilmore, Barbreck, Glenfeochan, Auchlyne, Ardanaiseig, Ormsary, Kildalloig, Mingary, Douglas & Angus.
1967	DAFS owned Fionn of Achnacloich on offer to the Islands.

Several farms throughout Argyllshire belonged to DAFS for varying lengths of time during the breeding scheme but the last had been relinquished by mid-1980.

FANANS

Many in Mrs Chapman's well-regarded Fanans Fold came from old bloodlines carried by the largely unregistered stock which had belonged to her father Mr J Currie, Inverawe.

An expensive Bochastle bull went to Fanans in 1927. Noted for leaving progeny with beautiful heads was Righ II of Fanans. The female championship at Oban in 1944 was won by Fanans and also the reserve champion bull there which went to Leys Castle. Fanans had come to prominence in the 1930s and 1940s under the able management of Mr A McKenzie until dispersal of the fold in 1946, when they walked along the old drove road through Glenlonan to the Oban mart. Mr McKenzie purchased several Fanans bloodlines for his new employer Sir J Lithgow of Ormsary and others were bought for the folds of Foreland, Kilmore, Mingary, Strathallan, and Corryarick.

ARDMENISH

Contemporary with the Fanans success years was the Ardmenish Fold on Jura. It was formed in 1914 with the purchase of a cow from the Duke of Argyll's Maam Fold. The First World War interrupted planned progress but in 1928 purchases were made from the Kilberry dispersal and further stock was added from Achnacloich, Foreland, Shenavallie, Ormsary, Leys, Strathallan and others. This fold stayed loyal to the breed throughout the years of downwards plummeting markets but dispersal came in 1975 with some animals going to Sir William Lithgow's Ormsary Estate and some to Norway and France.

LAUDALE

Contemporary with Ardmenish but dispersed earlier Mr J A Fletcher's Laudale Fold was known for its reliably characteristic stock. *"One man buys a bull another buys a pedigree."* Mr Fletcher had a singular skill in buying the best bulls, although *"not necessarily the dearest."* He kept the breed *"through lean times with optimism and foresight."* (*The Scottish Farmer*) His stock carried the best old strains of the breed and represented many of the old lines. He owned the black Proiseag Dubh 10064 bred by Mr J "Bochastle" Stewart which later went to Achnacloich carrying the black bull calf Prionnsa Dubh 4136. In Oban 1939 a dun Laudale cow of unknown pedigree was best of breed and the Oban champion in 1948 was a Laudale heifer which went to the Mingary fold. Laudale made leading prices at Oban for many years. Laudale females went to Strathallan and to Millhills where the cross Highland was favoured.

When Laudale Fold was dispersed in 1948 some went to Ile, Mingary, and thirty-three females went to the Scottish Cattle Company, Beauly, with which Colonel Crabbe of Findrack was connected. Others went to DAFS Ballinaby among which was Black Prince of Laudale. He sired some very good stock to unregistered Dams at Ballinaby. Some of the dams and progeny arrived later at the Rothiemurchus Fold.

GENERAL OVERVIEW OF POPULAR 20TH CENTURY FOLDS

Fold names come and go, maintaining various strains of the breed for the duration of each sustained management policy. The longevity of the breed means that for several years after a fold has been dispersed animals bearing its name continue to perpetuate the characteristics for which their fold was recognised and also to remain in the sales or Show circuit for some time. With this in mind the following overview gives a general idea of when some of the fold names were most in circulation. Most of the folds named in the first grouping were bred from long-established herds of Highland cattle of very old bloodlines, only a small number of which were ever registered or shown.

FOLD NAMES MOST IN CIRCULATION

1900 to 1920

Balranald, Duntulm, Poltalloch, Monachyle, Melfort, Shinness, Southesk, Airthrey, Castle Grant, Inverawe, Ardanaiseig, Camusericht, Ardtornish, Ensay, Bochastle, Farr, Atholl, Garth, Flichity, Kilberry (Baravalla), Balole, Ardmenish, Smaull, Balliemore (Bernice), Scorrybreck, Tangy, Fanans, Killean, Achnacloich.

1920 to 1940

Ardtornish, Ensay, Bochastle, Farr, Atholl, Garth, Flichity, Balole, Kilberry (Baravalla), Kilchamaig, Ardmenish, Smaull, Balliemore (Bernice), Scorrybreck, Tangy, Fanans, Killean,

Achnacloich, Errol Park, Achnaba (Shenavallie), Stronvar, Ballinaby, Cladich, Douglas & Angus, Ile, Leys, Kilmore, Barbreck, Craighouse, Laudale, Killundine, Quothquan.

1940 to 1950

Balole, Kilchamaig, Ardmenish, Smaull, Balliemore (Bernice), Killean, Fanans, Achnacloich, Shenavallie, Cladich, Douglas & Angus, Ile, Leys, Kilmore, Barbreck, Craighouse, Laudale, Killundine, Quothquan, Skipness, Foreland, Auchnacraig, Kildalloig, Rothiemurchus, Scammadale, Barguillean, Carskiey, Ormsary, Ulva, Muckairn, Mingary, Corryarick, Torloisk, Benmore, Glentannar, Ballinaby, Gartlea, Kilbride, Ardkinglas, Scone, Ardanaiseig, Duart, Breachacha, Glenfalloch, Balmuick, Fordie, Glenforsa.

1950 to 1970

Ardmenish, Smaull, Balliemore (Bernice) Achnacloich, Shenavallie, Cladich, Douglas & Angus Ile, Leys, Barbreck/Leachy, Craighouse, Laudale, Killundine, Skipness, Foreland, Auchnacraig, Kildalloig, Rothiemurchus, Scammadale, Barguillean, Carskiey, Ormsary, Ulva, Muckairn, Mingary, Corryarick, Torloisk, Benmore, Gartlea, Kilbride, Ardanaiseig, Duart, Breachacha, Rigg, Scone, Ardkinglas, Strathallan, Severie, Douneside, Glenquoich, Balmoral, Nether Pollok, Braes of Greenock, Dalquharran, Ballathie, Glengorm, Dunach, Finglas, Gylen, Strathmashie, Woodneuk & Commoncraig, Balmuick, Fordie, Glenforsa (new input of stock)

From 1970

By and throughout the 1970s a number of the treasured fold names were finally lost, so reduced they were scarcely come upon, or finally dispersed. Among those were Ardmenish, Smaull, Balliemore, Craighouse, Laudale, Foreland, Kildalloig, Barguillean, Carskiey, Ulva, Gartlea, Kilbride, Ardanaiseig, Duart, Braes of Greenock, Dalquharran, Ballathie. Ile fold from 1979 to be crossed with Shorthorn, Hereford and Simmental.

Some of the remaining well-established folds meeting the 1970s intact were:
Achnacloich, Shenavallie, Cladich, Douglas & Angus, Leys, Leachy (Barbreck) Auchnacraig, Rothiemurchus, Ormsary, Torloisk, Benmore, Scone, Strathallan, Severie, Rigg, Douneside, Glenquoich, Balmoral, Pollok, Glenforsa, Glengorm, Breachacha, Strathmashie, Gylen, Woodneuk & Commoncraig, a few Glenforsa matriarchs formed the nucleus of a new Glenforsa fold named Pennygown.

The 1970s were years of expansion of the breed and many of the strong folds of the 1990s were founded then. The 1980s were characterised by the rapid growth of many small and very active folds.

INTERRUPTED LINES

Some fold names of the late twentieth century which appear also in the earliest Herd Books cannot be assumed to hold direct descendants from these bygone times. Where there is belief that undocumented continuity of breeding stock occurred actual evidence is hard to trace.

The early history of Meggernie, Applecross, Cladich, and Glengorm allows speculation that throughout change of landownership, interrupted management policies, or break-up of estates the livestock continued to thrive and breed, perhaps even in a semi-wild state, and that during such time knowledge of pedigree stock and progeny was lost.

Mull was and is a great stronghold of the breed, having sent stock with the fold names of Glengorm, Duart, Ulva, Torloisk, Auchnacraig, Glenforsa, Wellburn, Pennygown, Callachally, Torosay, Cailaich, well beyond the island shores throughout the twentieth century. There have always been Highland cattle on Mull, yet proof of direct ancestral links between current stock and last century's stock is hard to track down.

Glengorm Estate is an interesting example of the 'interrupted or lost pedigree lines' theory.

GLENGORM ESTATE, MULL

Glengorm in the north east of Mull currently has a fold of 60 pedigree Highlands, and an estate history which includes nineteenth century Highland cattle calved before the Highland Cattle Society of Scotland was formed.

Highland cattle at the Glengorm of the 1870s carried bloodlines from the most acclaimed animals of that period. Glengorm registered females which were calved in 1871 and 1873; the first was a granddaughter of the famous Breadalbane-bred bull Duntroon 177, and the second out of the popular Mhaigdean of Poltalloch sired by the Ensay-bred Duntulm Riabhach 183.

The Herd Book entries from Glengorm in 1890 showed the colour range of seven red, one black, four light dun, three brindle, three yellow, with genetic input from the best Perthshire and Argyllshire folds of long standing – Athole, Urlar, Cashlie (Glenlyon), Monachyle, Bochastle, all in Perthshire, Kilchamaig and Campbell of Jura in Argyllshire, and Duntulm in Skye.

Highland cattle were maintained on the estate until 1912 after which the disruptive war years interfered with documentation on perhaps two to three generations of pedigree livestock.

The bull Gille Buidhe, registered in 1948, sired the stock bull Fauna of Glengorm which is thought to have sired the nine homebred females registered in 1953 by Dr Richard Fawcitt when he took over the estate. He kept the Highland Fold in good shape handing on 16 cows to the next owner in 1962.

In the ensuing eight years of Mr J Carr's ownership fresh bloodlines from Mingary and Strathallan's great stock-getter Viking of Strathallan were introduced, then several good heifers from the next stock bull Alasdair of Braes of Greenock 5735 were retained at Glengorm. By the late 1960s Carn Mairg of Scone Palace 5858 carrying Ile bloodlines and many Show awards had proved to be a wise choice for the Glengorm Fold.

When he purchased Glengorm Estate in 1970, Major R E Nelson took over the established Highland Fold with enthusiasm and kept a very successful female line from Carn Mairg which is still active in the fold. Stock bulls have included Jock of Benmore, Canadian GOF Stepdancer, Loggin of Ardanaiseig, and Coinneach of Pollok 7457 in 1990.

Now under Mrs Janet Nelson, Glengorm Estate is set to take the Highland breed strongly into the next century.

Part of the estate is home to the Headspeaths' fold, The Wellburn, which although independent from the Glengorm Fold is to some extent helping to perpetuate the strongly characteristic Glengorm bloodlines through one of their early purchases which has bred well consistently. Ken and Gracie Headspeath have a great respect for this matriarch of their fold, Furan 7th of Glengorm calved in 1974, still with them in 1995 but retired from active breeding.

BROKEN OR DIFFERENT BLOODLINES UNDER ONE FOLD NAME

Some fold names can be confusing for the researcher of continuity of bloodlines.

For example there have been two Barbrecks...one the Dalgleish fold at Lochgilphead and the other Barbreck Farm near Taynuilt. Unless aware of this it is easy to mistake an entry in the Herd Books. Similarly there have been two Balinoes...one near Oban and long since dispersed, the other currently very active breeding black Highland cattle at Ardgay. The cattle registered under the Benmore fold name in the 1880s do not seem to link with the bloodlines of the current Benmore, and the Ardanaiseig stock of the 1890s is not readily proved to link directly with the Ardanaiseig stock registered in the 1940s.

The two powerful folds of Leys, established 1931 and Douneside, established 1952 were dispersed in the early 1990s, yet confusingly, new stock quite unrelated to those of the old bloodlines of the first Leys and Douneside folds continue to appear under these fold names. This is because new ownership of the policies was permitted to use the original fold prefix in the case of Leys, and in the case of the Douneside fold regulations concerning the Lady MacRobert Trust required that a minimum of five Highland breeding cows be retained permanently at Tarland. The diligent researcher is well advised to cross refer information from the Herd Books and the Journals and the Newsletters, to help piece together the jigsaw of information about breeders' stock in the unsettled years during and immediately after the wars. For instance Mr J J Currie registered Highlands from Cuilfail in 1943, Arnicle in 1945 and Kildalloig in 1950. It is likely that he retained some of his breeding stock as he moved from tenancy of one farm to another, but of course they are registered with different fold names.

Consulting several sources also helps with minor confusions in the spelling of names. Over the years some variations occur in the Gaelic spelling of names of animals. Usually their Herd Book **number** clarifies the situation. Place names also receive the varied spelling treatment largely as a result of the imperfect transition from a Gaelic culture to an English one. Names such as Duntulm, Killundine, Ardanaiseig, Kilchamaig, Muckairn, Corryarick often appear as Duntuilm, Kilmundine, Ardanasaig, Kilmachaig, Muckrain, Corryarrack or Corrie Yarrack.

LARGE COMMERCIAL CATTLE ENTERPRISES 20TH CENTURY

The pure-bred Highland cow produces most economically the best type of fast-growing well-fleshed cross-breds that do well on and for marginal hill land whilst selling well to the butcher. Obviously a steady supply of pure-bred Highlands is vital. Several large concerns in addition to a few individual holdings ensured this by keeping their own pure-bred herd within their programme of cross-bred stock and land management. Clearly these commercial breeders played an important role in effecting the survival of the Highland breed.

However, lack of continuously updated statistics giving an overview of the breed numbers did not allow breeders to make informed decisions about the full effect of their cross-breeding policies and in hindsight it is sad to read reports like these:

"The Duke of Hamilton's herd at Dubhgaradh in Arran in the 1890s were well-bred lines from two famous bulls, Rossie of Atholl and Ceatharnach of Ensay. Fifteen heifers of this herd were sold in 1894 for crossing with white Shorthorn bulls in Lord Camperdown's Home Farm at Lochee, Dundee.

Sir Gerald Ley purchased 31 non-pedigree Highlands in 1950 to cross with Hereford and their progeny to be crossed with Aberdeen Angus. In 1956 he bought 16 more Highlands at Oban to cross directly with Aberdeen Angus."

Inevitably questions arise about how efficiently commercial breeders keep their pure-bred stock pure.

Mid-twentieth century *"long in the snout"* animals may have inherited the nose from encounters three or four generations back with Whitebred Cumberland bulls, whereas long-snout stock previous to the cross-breeding fashion probably were throwbacks to their ancient forebears' mixed origins of 'longnose X longhorn' i.e. the domesticated bos longifrons and the wild bos primigenus.

Certainly the profitable Beef Shorthorn cross of modern times did result in Shorthorn genes straying into Highland stock resulting in animals with a need for richer feeding, reduction in length though not density of hair, downturned horns particularly in bulls, and blockier conformation.

Before the total number of pedigree breeding animals was too low to rescue, the situation had been recognised and, by the late twentieth century, largely corrected with no immediately obvious harm to the essential characteristics of the breed, but with a more limited genetic pool than ideal.

Prominent folds which come into the category of large commercial enterprises are Ile, Scone Palace, Leys Castle, Douglas & Angus, Cladich, Rothiemurchus, Severie. All (first three now dispersed) have made efforts to keep the breed represented at Scottish and, or, English Agricultural and Fatstock Shows, whilst making no pretence of the fact that their pure Highland cattle which featured in the awards lists were maintained to provide good breeding cows, to produce cross-bred beef stock only for as long as the beefstock market is high.

Enthusiasts of the cross-bred Highland beef include:

Lord Margadale Islay *"demand is for the cross-heifers not pedigree herds"* 1960;

Mr A J K Laing, *"the Highlander is, in fact, an improver breed."* (1966) He promoted cross-breeding with Shorthorns in Scotland and with Herefords in America.

Mr D D Cameron, 1961 advocated 50% infusion of Beef Shorthorn blood into the Highland breed.

Mr J Stewart, Dalquharran Castle, bred Highlands from 1957 to 1972 and believed *"the strongest type of hill animals one could wish for"* came from the Shorthorn bull cross with Highland cows.

Mr D M Stewart OBE, an authority on Scottish Shorthorn, strongly advocated the cross-bred for hill beef.

Moray Estates Development Agency, Braes of Doune, bred Highland heifers to Beef Shorthorn bulls.

Cadzow brothers bred the new breed Luing from crossing Beef Shorthorns with Highlands.

Management methods in the large enterprises varied and although undoubtedly there was loss of pure old bloodlines, there was also a preservation of the breed in greater numbers through the unpopular years than might otherwise have remained. Credit must go to the Ile fold for very successful promotion of the breed in England during recession years and for sustained successful presence at the Smithfield Fatstock Show, London, to Scone Palace fold for successfully flying the breed flag at the major Agricultural Shows and for providing the first Highland bull to stand for AI in 1964, and to Cladich for continuous work for the benefit of the breed in the north of Argyllshire, abroad, and at Dalmally Agricultural Show.

RIGG, THE BIGGEST COMMERCIAL HERD OF THE 1990s

Mr A W Howat of Rigg, a deeply respected judge of Highland cattle, grew up with an awareness of the breed firstly through a friend's father who knew the drove routes from Fort William to Aberdeen, and then from observation of the breed on moors in Dorset during a brief period of farm management there in his youth.

Once established in Rigg Farm in the north of Dumfriesshire, he took to rearing Highland Beef steers in addition to other breeds of cattle and sheep entirely on a commercial basis. Several years later, in 1952, he registered female Highland breeding stock of which four were brindle, seven red, and nine yellow. His concern in the 1970s that, for no sound reason, black Highland cattle had been reduced to a rarity prompted his determination to ensure the preservation of a pool of black high quality stock typically characteristic of the Highland breed. Accordingly, from the 1980s, his commercial breeding programme included breeding for blacks. In this he was so successful that ten years later Rigg not only had the largest head of Highlands in Scotland but held the largest number of blacks breeding black progeny. Mr Howat holds the traditional view that registering animals is of secondary importance to breeding prime quality beef stock for commercial sale and that entering stock in Agricultural Shows is not a necessary nor obligatory procedure. So pedigree enthusiasts will find some Rigg lines difficult to trace much earlier than the 1950s, and will also discover that well-bred stock are sought after even without the publicity advantages of the Show ring. Rigg policy of rigorous culling of all but the hardiest and most reliably regular breeding stock, irrespective of market trends, has undoubtedly helped preserve the true characteristics of this native breed. Rigg bloodlines will continue to play a significant role through the numbers of black bulls of Rigg breeding and a few heifers recently released for continuity of breeding in other folds.

HIGHLAND CATTLE IN CENTRAL BADENOCH (20th Century)

The area of Inverness-shire known as Badenoch once was well stocked with both commercial and registered Highland cattle. Award-winning Highlands from the large farms of Ballachroan and Gordonhall and Killiehuntly last century have long ago been forgotten. Killiehuntly Farm lies at the Kingussie end of Gaick of the foreboding folktales (see Chapter 9), on an ancient route through the hills between Badenoch and Blair Atholl, previously used by drovers. Although there are no Highlands at the Game Keeper's Cottage there today the couple or so of Highland milk cows always kept by Shenna (longbeard) the Keeper last century provide a direct link with award-winning Highland cattle of this century.

Shenna was accustomed to walking through the dark pass of Gaick to Blair Castle. His milk cows came from the Atholl fold. His son Ewan, used to milking the cows and tending to Shenna's Highland ponies at Gaick, gained recognition in adulthood for pioneering the leisure pursuit of pony trekking in Britain in the 1940s. Ewan also kept some Highlands as milk cows and in turn was no doubt glad to leave his son E Cameron Ormiston to deal with the milking.

Cameron never found horns were ever a hazard even with first time calvers but said that as with milk cows of any breed one had to be ready to avoid a kick. He reflected that perhaps the wide backward swirling shape of the Highland cow horn evolved in the more densely forested times as a defence against predators that leapt onto their backs.

He graduated from the milking task to driving his father's stirks to their summer pasturing about fifteen miles away at the head of the River Dulnain around 2,000 feet above sea level. The Ormistons never used dogs in their droving, finding control easier mounted on Highland ponies; the cattle seemed quieter and easier to manage when driven by horsemen. But even with ponies there was little way of pacifying Highland cattle making their first ever encounter with reflective shop windows flanking both sides of their route off the hill. These cattle were unregistered utilitarian and commercial from Strathconan, Rothiemurchus and later Leys. They were of all colours with brindle predominating in the 1940s.

When Cameron took on the Strathmashie Estate in the 1960s he decided to start a small pedigree fold. He charged Jimmy Veitch with the task of buying his starter stock from Oban. Jimmy's experience with Highland cattle led him to include a Corriemuckloch cow in-calf in his purchases, which along with heifers off Rothiemurchus stock proved a successful nucleus for the Strathmashie fold.

Cameron's main interest continued to be with Highland ponies so both Highland breeds... cattle and ponies...occasionally shared the same transport lorry to the Royal Highland Show at Ingliston where they also shared top awards.

Shenna's great grandson Fergus Ormiston has inherited undoubted skill in handling cattle and horses, saddling up and riding with flamboyant ease Highland bulls and Highland pony stud stallions. Cameron believes *"a way with livestock is bred in you"* and is now content to let Fergie manage the Ormiston cattle having proved his capabilities with the first of his successes – when he won the Supreme Championship at the Royal Highland Show with his own animal which he had brought out, Dileas 12th of Rothiemurchus 28227, bred by J P Grant (Yr.) of Rothiemurchus.

The Ormistons retained the fold name of Strathmashie when the estate changed hands. In moving to Kingussie they brought the cattle closer to the haunts of Thomas Sinton whose collected poems on Badenoch make frequent reference to cattle (See Chapter 9) showing how the breed was an integral part of the Badenoch way of life.

The Grants of Rothiemurchus have quietly maintained a continuous presence of Highland cattle in Badenoch on a greater scale and probably equally rooted in last century's traditions, although records of the current fold date from the 1940s. The Rothiemurchus fold of around 30 breeding cows is kept to provide heifers for cross-breeding programmes on the estate to produce good commercial beef cattle. The management policy supports local Agricultural Shows such as the Grantown-on-Spey event whilst also providing excellent viewing facilities of the pure-bred Highland fold for the many tourists to the area. Involvement with the National Agricultural Shows has neither been necessary nor important for this fold.

Between Rothiemurchus and Kingussie lies Dunachton Estate which did have pedigree Highlands for a time in the 1950s. The Oban champion in 1953 Morag Ile, of Barbreck and Scammadale breeding, and Annag II of Findrack were two of the carefully selected Highland breeding stock. It was found, however, that the management policy which embraced a variety of estate livestock was not economically compatible with the needs of the Highland cattle and they were sent off once more to the auction ring.

During her residence in Badenoch a keen interest in the history of the area influenced to some extent Lady Jean H S Macpherson's decision to have Highland cattle grazing the precincts of Balavil House and later Craig Dhu House. With fine respect for the breed she chose a black cow of grand scale to complement her reds.

Also careful to represent both black and red Highlands in recently acquired livestock is the Highland Folk Park at Newtonmore, which aims to provide a 'living' example of crofting life in the Highlands from the late nineteenth century. Traditional breeds of animals are kept in the Highland Folk Museum at Aultlaurie Croft which is worked with the traditional methods.

In their remote past Highland cattle evolved from the prehistoric Wild Ox which penetrated the north of Scotland. That in addition to the Highlands being native to Scotland helped them qualify for a presence in the Highland Wildlife Park, Kincraig, Badenoch, opened in 1972, where both black and red steers can be seen.

A little to the south west of Newtonmore and still very much in Thomas Sinton's Badenoch of the folksongs the now well-established fold of Innisard pedigree Highland cattle is to be found.

Further testimony to the suitability of the breed for this sparsely clad hill land when coupled with the evident expertise of the Knox family, is the considerable number of top awards and prices which have gone to the Innisard Highland cattle.

CITY CATTLE

One of the first municipal authorities in Scotland to keep Highland cattle for their amenity value was the City of Glasgow. Dundee, Aberdeen, and Cumbernauld followed but not Edinburgh. The nearest Highland cattle for Edinburgh public to view are those in Dalkeith Country Park which surrounds Dalkeith Palace, designed in 1701 for Anne Duchess of Buccleuch. The small fold there graze probably the same land that the famous Atholl whites with black points grazed in 1834. However, their presence is only for such time as their owner Mr J Cameron-Manson, Buccleuch Countryside Service finds it manageable to maintain them there.

CITY OF GLASGOW HIGHLAND CATTLE

Glasgow Corporation Farms spent 1285 guineas at the 1952/53 Oban sales on seventeen Highland heifers from Achnacloich, Ile, Jura, Shenavallie, Scammadale, Benmore, Severie, and Creity Hall. Their colours were, seven red, three light red, two brindle, five yellow.

Then in 1967 Mr Laing purchased Susan Ruadh with calf, Nighean Buidhe in calf, both sired by Seumas of Glenalmond, and 5 bull calves from the Nether Pollok Estate and registered them with the fold name of St. Mungo.

That same year Mrs Ann Maxwell MacDonald gifted Pollok Park, ancestral home of the Maxwell family for seven centuries, to the City of Glasgow. The Maxwells were known to have bred Highlands in their Nether Pollok Estate in the 1820s.

When the Nether Pollok Estate fold was dispersed in 1971 thirteen cows and four calves and the stock bull Calluinn of Benmore were purchased by the city of Glasgow who were given permission to use the fold name of Pollok. Since then the Glasgow Parks fold has been registered as Pollok with their central base in Pollok Park.

The Pollok fold is run on a semi commercial basis. It sent stock to the safari park in the south of Holland in 1979, it ceaselessly encourages visitors of all ages to appreciate the merits of this native breed, and many prestigious Show awards indicate a successful management and breeding policy.

The cattle still belong to the city of Glasgow. Pollok Park was registered as a country park by the Countryside Commission for Scotland in 1980.

It is interesting that Mr R C MacMillan who introduced Highland cattle to Manchester City Corporation in 1954 had worked at Ardtornish in 1929 and then Glasgow Corporation before moving south. (see Ardtonish p.204)

A connection of wider interest, perhaps, is that between Glasgow Corporation Highland cattle and Millerston, the most continuously prominent fold in the Show awards over the last 23 years.

MILLERSTON

Ten served heifers from Glasgow Corporation's reduction of Highland stock in 1972, with poor prospects of a home, were taken by Mr Tom McLatchie who considered they might be an interesting diversion in his forthcoming retirement from active farming.

Only two were actually in calf so a few were trained for Showing. Of two shown one was not placed, yet it was she who collected eight championships and eight reserve championships in the ensuing ten years. This typifies the Millerston recipe for success...shrewd assessment of livestock combined with tirelessly attentive husbandry.

Millerston success at Oban in 1982 was to play, unintentionally, a significant role in the history of the breed.

Mr McLatchie's policy, with no hint of colour bias, sets out to breed good scale in truly characteristic animals, and accordingly a good animal was chosen to put forward to the Oban Spring Show and Sale of 1982. The coat-colour was black.

The last black to be placed at Oban had been some 27 years earlier when Boichead Dubh II of Braes of Greenock created a stir of colour controversy by gaining reserve champion in 1955. Only one black – Sine Dhubh V of Ballinaby was exhibited at Oban in 1957 after which blacks were scarcely seen until the judge Mr Donald MacGillivray awarded the female championship to the black Una of Millerston, thereby rekindling the issue of colour bias in breeders of Highland cattle. Within two years a broader outlook on colour was evidently taking hold.

1984, the centenary of the formation of the Highland Cattle Society of Scotland, was a memorable year for Millerston. The Oban Spring Show female championship on that auspicious occasion was awarded by the judge Mr Andrew Smith to a black cow, Una III of Millerston, and the female championship at the Autumn Oban Show of that year also went to Millerston to the red Ailleag Og VI. A double success in connoisseur territory in 1984, and what better destiny for Una III of Millerston than to join the Rigg Fold in its efforts to maintain a goodly number of black bloodlines.

Tom McLatchie's considered judgement had selected five of the original ten heifers, Capleadh, Una Ruadh, Una, Ailleag Og, Prionnsa, on which to base the future breeding programmes at Millerston. His fold of winners all descend from these lines.

Whatever is in store for this modest man of focused energies, sought after for his slide talk shows and knowledge of wild flowers, violas, potatoes, bantams, local history, history of Highland cattle, retirement is no longer a word in his vocabulary.

CONDENSED BREED HISTORY

1 From 1780s the educated landowners applied the new science of agriculture to cross-breed to improve their Highland cattle while the crofters kept the original type.

2 From the 1880s crofters had to relinquish a breed that had no longer sufficient commercial value to be economic, while the landowners kept pure-bred Highlands for their aesthetic appeal on sporting estates.

3 By the 1990s men and women from all walks of life and in many countries were keen to preserve the original type of native Scottish cattle and were actively involved with anything from two cows upwards depending on what grazings could be arranged. Landowners had discovered that running Highland cattle on land overgrazed by too heavy a deer population helped redress the balance of plants.

4 Twentieth Century Review.

1920s

Post-war slump/trade picked up very slowly/buoyant by 1937/ slump in 1939 due to the Second World War.

1948 – 1958

Post-war boom highlighted too few pure-bred strains to meet the demand. Several old folds still in business /new folds being formed Ardkinglas/Lochavich/ big enterprises booming like Ile/Luing/Cladich/Muckairn. Much crossing to produce fast bulky beef growth. President of the Highland Cattle Society elected in 1957 was quoted in the Farming News "*Although I am a great supporter of Pure Highlanders it is the crosses I am chiefly interested in.*"

1960s

Slump. Forestry Commission buying farms and putting livestock off...even sheep! in order to plant trees.

1970s

Prices for female Highlands rising /market buoyant/active new and first time breeders doing well in the market and the Show circuit. /low profile concerns maintaining Highland cattle on such Western Islands as Jura, Mull, Coll, Rum, Canna, the Uists, and later Skye.

Articles featuring individual folds can be found in the Highland Breeders Journals held for reference in the Highland Cattle Society Office. Incomplete collections of the journals are in the national libraries in Edinburgh and London. An index to these articles up to 1990 is in Chapter 10. More recent information in the 1995 Journal mentions several of the Scottish folds which were open to visitors during the First International Gathering of Highland Cattle Breeders held in Edinburgh in June of that year; details on the Wenmar fold in the Isle of Man and folds in Bergisch Land Germany are also included. The Scottish folds in that issue of the Journal are: Balmoral, Cameron (Loch Lomond), Pollok, Meggernie, Glenquoich & Lude, Corriemuckloch, Tullachard, Glamis, Invertrossachs, Rothiemurchus, Leys, Glen Nevis, Auchnacraig, Torosay, Pennygown, Glengorm, Wellburn, Achnacloich, Cladich, Inveraray, Ormsary, Benmore, Glenogle, Highland Breeders in the Outer Hebrides, Millerston.

ROYAL HIGHLAND SHOW

FROM AGRICULTURAL SHOW (H.A.S.S.) TO THE "ROYAL HIGHLAND" (R.H.A.S.S.)

Agricultural Shows had been held in many districts of Scotland some time before the first National Agricultural Show held in Edinburgh in 1822 took place. The National Show became a popular annual event on an ever-increasing scale and favoured a different city each year with its presence. The title of Royal had been conferred in 1948 by King George VI and in 1960 permanent grounds at Ingliston, Edinburgh, were acquired. Consequently this nationally-enjoyed Agricultural Show came to be referred to as the 'Royal Highland' and sometimes simply as 'The Highland'. It remains the most prestigious Agricultural Show in Scotland.

ON JUDGING HIGHLAND CATTLE

The whole issue of competitive showing of a 'working breed' is contentious. Judging the work-potential of livestock from a brief visual encounter clearly is challenging to say the least, particularly in a breed where differences in type are necessary in order to thrive well in different environments. True impartiality in judging is virtually impossible whether from a local or foreign judge and in any case would not be worthwhile when what is wanted from a judge is the expression of his accumulated wealth of experience with the breed being judged. Inevitably the Show 'circuit' attracts some, repels others, encourages the pampered product, and excludes the potent breeding stock for whom Shows often occur at the wrong time, but Show results do influence the future of the breed. One needs to interpret the value of a first placing in a large class as opposed to a class of one entry. Top in the Show ring may not fetch top price in the auction ring. Championships and awards made at the Oban Pedigree

Highland Show and Sale in February and October often reveal a completely different range of entries from those attending the Show of the Royal Highland And Agricultural Society of Scotland held mid-summer.

In 1828 instructions to the judges at the Glasgow Highland and Agricultural Show included:

"In forming their judgement, the judges will have regard to the symmetry, size, early maturity, and qualities characteristic of the different breeds they have to judge of; making allowance for age, feeding, and circumstances peculiar to the cases which come before them."

Regulations for the competitors included:

"giving name of breed, kind of food which they have been fed, name and residence of breeder, and pedigree of stock as far as is known.

Bulls must be secured by a ring or a screw in the nose, with a chain or rope attached, otherwise they cannot be admitted to the Show yard.

The Oxen exhibits for the Premium must not have been fed on distillery wash or grains.

The distance each Ox travels to the Show and the date of being put to fatten to be mentioned."

The class for a prize of 10 Sovereigns or plate of that value was: '*for the best two cows of West Highland Breed not exceeding 6 years old and not otherwise fed than on grass for four months preceding the day of exhibition.*'

Additional premiums offered were for:

"The best pair of Highland Oxen or Spaved Heifers fattened solely upon pasture grass since Whitsunday last, not under four years old.

The best small sized Highland Oxen or Spaved Heifers fattened as above and not under four years old." (from an *Account of the Cattle Show and Great Agricultural meeting held at Glasgow on 24 September 1828*)

It is interesting to consider that nearly 100 years before the Highland Cattle Society was formed judges of Highland cattle at district Shows in the West of Scotland were told,

"pay particular attention to the shape of the bulls, and not to the size, to encourage 'true' breeding." 1789.

By the 1840s Lorn Agricultural Society applied the following judging points:

1	CARRIAGE	25 points
2	BACK & RIBS	20 points
3	HEAD & HORNS	15 points
4	HIND-QUARTERS	15 points
5	HAIR	10 points
6	NECK	5 points
7	LEGS	5 points
8	SIZE	5 points

(researched by M Storrie published in *Continuity and Change* 1988)

By the 1880s and 1890s Highland bullocks were great heavy beasts (see photographs page 305). With scant attention after the twentieth century's War years and ensuing economic depression they returned to the breed's more natural scale, only to increase again by the 1980s in response to selective feeding and breeding for that purpose.

Obviously a sound knowledge of the history of the breed adds to the quality of a judge's opinion.

SHOW VENUES H.A.S.S. 1822-1947 • R.H.A.S.S. 1948-1960

1822 Edinburgh
1823 Edinburgh
No Highlands in 1824
1825 Edinburgh
1826 Glasgow
1827 Edinburgh
1828 Glasgow (regulations given p224)
1829 Perth
No Highlands 1830 Dumfries.
1831 Inverness
No Highlands 1832 Kelso.
1833 Stirling
1834 Aberdeen
1835 Ayr
1836 Perth
No Highlands 1837 Dumfries.
1838 Glasgow
1839 Inverness
1840 Aberdeen
No Highlands 1841 Berwick
No Highlands 1842 Edinburgh
1843 Dundee
1844 Glasgow
No Highlands 1845 Dumfries
1846 Inverness
1847 Aberdeen
1848 Edinburgh (Shows now held biennially)
1850 Glasgow
1852 Perth
1854 Berwick
1856 Inverness (International Show in Paris also in 1856)
1857 Glasgow (return to annual Shows by popular demand)
1858 Aberdeen
1859 Edinburgh
1860 Dumfries
1861 Perth
1862 International Show Battersea, London
1863 Kelso
1864 Stirling
1865 Inverness
No Show in 1866 due to outbreak of Rinderpest.
1867 Glasgow
1868 Aberdeen
1869 Edinburgh
1870 Dumfries
1871 Perth
1872 Kelso
1873 Stirling
1874 Inverness
1875 Glasgow
1876 Aberdeen
1877 Edinburgh
1878 Dumfries
1879 Perth
1880 Kelso
1881 Stirling
1882 Glasgow
1883 Inverness
1884 Edinburgh
1884 **Formation of the Highland Cattle Society**
1885 Aberdeen
1886 Dumfries
1887 Perth
1888 Glasgow
1889 Melrose
1890 Dundee
1891 Stirling
1892 Inverness
1893 Edinburgh
1894 Aberdeen
1895 Dumfries
1896 Perth
1897 Glasgow
1898 Kelso
1899 Edinburgh
1900 Stirling
1901 Inverness
1902 Aberdeen
1903 Dumfries
1904 Perth.
1905 Glasgow
1906 Peebles
1907 Edinburgh
1908 Aberdeen
1909 Stirling
1910 Dumfries
1911 Inverness
1912 Cupar
1913 Paisley
1914 Hawick
No Shows during the First World War
1919 Edinburgh
1920 Aberdeen

1921 Stirling
1922 Dumfries
1923 Inverness
1924 Perth
1925 Glasgow
1926 Kelso
1927 Edinburgh
1928 Aberdeen
1929 Alloa
1930 Dumfries
1931 Edinburgh (no cattle entries due to Foot & Mouth disease)
1932 Inverness
1933 Dundee
1934 Glasgow
1935 Aberdeen
1936 Melrose
1937 Alloa
1938 Dumfries
1939 Edinburgh
No Shows during the Second World War
1948 Inverness
1949 Dundee
1950 Paisley
1951 Aberdeen
1952 Kelso (no cattle entries due to Foot & Mouth disease)
1953 Alloa
1954 Dumfries
1955 Edinburgh
1956 Inverness
1957 Dundee
1958 Ayr
1959 Aberdeen
1960 Ingliston, Edinburgh on the permanent site.

HIGHLAND & AGRICULTURAL SOCIETY OF SCOTLAND(H.A.S.S.)

MULTIPLE MAIN AWARDS WINNERS UP TO 1914

M = Bull; F = Heifer or Cow.

M. Duntroon 177, brindle, 1st Perth 1861, Battersea 1862, Stirling 1864

M. Donald 144, red (Domhnull Ruadh of Breadalbane), 1st Kelso 1863, Stirling 1864, Inverness 1865, Gold Medal Glasgow 1867, Gold Medal Aberdeen 1868, Gold Medal Edinburgh 1869

F. Molachag I 540, red, 1st Kelso 1863, Stirling 1864, Glasgow 1867, Gold Medal Edinburgh 1869

F. Nora Odhar 549, dun, 1st Perth 1861, Battersea 1862, Stirling 1864, Gold Medal Glasgow 1867

F. Mhaigdean I 530, dun, 1st Inverness 1865, 3rd Glasgow 1867, 1st Aberdeen 1868, Gold Medal Edinburgh 1869

F. Targeal Riabhach of Ensay 79, brindle, 1st Glasgow 1867, Edinburgh 1869, Gold Medal Dumfries 1870, Gold Medal Perth 1871

F. Ribhinn III of Poltalloch, black, 1st Glasgow 1867, 2nd Aberdeen 1868, 3rd Edinburgh 1869, 1st Dumfries 1870, Gold Medal Perth 1871

M. Fear-a-Bhaile 199, red, 1st Aberdeen 1868, Edinburgh 1869, Gold Medal Dumfries 1870

M. Sgiathanach Og 491, brindle, 1st Aberdeen 1868, 2nd Edinburgh 1869, 1st Perth 1871, Gold Medal Stirling 1873

F. Guanach Lachin 792, black , 1st Kelso 1872, Gold Medal Inverness 1874

M. Sgiathanach 489, brindle, 1st Inverness 1874, Gold Medal Glasgow 1875, Gold Medal Aberdeen 1876

M. Gille Riabhach of Sutherland 276, brindle, 1st Glasgow 1875, Gold Medal Aberdeen 1876, Gold Medal Edinburgh 1877

F. Phroiseag II of Benmore 160, brindle, 1st Glasgow 1875, Perth 1879, Gold Medal Glasgow 1882, Inverness 1883 1st Family Group

M. Gille Dubh of Duntulm 252, black, 1st Stirling 1873, Gold Medal Glasgow 1875

F. Targeal Beag of Ensay 797, red, 1st Inverness 1874, Glasgow 1875, Aberdeen 1876

M. An-t-Eilanach 12, brindle, 1st Aberdeen 1876, Edinburgh 1877, Dumfries 1878

M. Wallace II of Seafield 549, red, 1st Inverness 1874, Aberdeen 1876, Gold Medal Edinburgh 1877, Gold Medal Dumfries 1878

M. Calum Riabhach of Athole 82, brindle, 1st Perth 1879, Gold Medal Stirling 1881, 1st Edinburgh 1884 And Champion Cup

F. Guanach III of Ensay 789, black, 1st Perth 1879, Kelso 1880, Inverness 1883, 1st Family Group Edinburgh

F. Guanach V of Ensay 791, brindle, 1st Inverness 1883, 1st In Family Group, Cup Best Female in the Breed, Edinburgh 1884,

F. Proisag Dhubh 783 of Bochastle, black, 3rd Stirling 1881, 1st Glasgow 1882, 2nd Edinburgh 1884, 1st Aberdeen 1885, Silver Cup Melrose 1889

F. Sgiathach VI 2929, black, Edinburgh 1893, Best Female 1893 in Edinburgh and 1894 Aberdeen

M. Valentine XI 1160, red, HRH Duke of York's Medal For best Highland animal in all classes, Presidents Medal in 1895 Dumfries for best Highland animal, 1st Perth 1896

M. Laoch 1260, yellow, Perth 1896, Glasgow 1897 Medal for best Highland animal, Inverness 1901 Champion (did not leave great progeny)

F. Sgiathach XVI 4223, black, Glasgow 1897, Kelso 1898, Edinburgh 1899

M. Calum Riabhach II of Atholl 1325, brindle, Kelso 1898 Medal for best Highland animal, Edinburgh 1899 Same Medal

M. Victor XVI 1427, black, Glasgow 1897, Stirling 1900

F. Sgiathach XXIV of Ardtornish 4807, black, Edinburgh 1899, Aberdeen 1902 Champion Medal awarded for the first time to a female

M. Calum Buidhe of Atholl 1475, yellow, Edinburgh 1899, Stirling 1900 Champion Medal, Inverness 1901 Best animal in all classes

M. King Alaric 1712, yellow, Aberdeen 1902, Dumfries 1903 Champion Medal, Perth 1904 Champion Medal

M. Fear-a-Bhata of Atholl 1819, brindle, Dumfries 1903, Perth 1904, Glasgow 1905

M. Lord Clyde 2034, brindle, Glasgow 1905, Peebles 1906 Champion

F. Laochag Buidhe IV of Ensay 6584, yellow, Glasgow 1905 Champion, Peebles 1906, Edinburgh 1907 Prince of Wales Gold Medal and Medium Silver Medal

M. Saladin 2067, brindle, Glasgow 1905, Peebles 1906, Edinburgh 1907 Champion

F. Fuinary Queen 7705, red, Stirling 1909 Champion, Dumfries 1910 Champion, Inverness 1911 Champion

M. Calum-Ban-A-Rithist of Farr 2393, light yellow, Dumfries 1910, Cupar 1912 Champion, twice awarded Silver Medal for Breeder of Best Bull

M. Merlin 2589, red, Inverness 1911, Hawick 1914 Champion, Silver Medal For Breeder of Best Bull

M. Morair Inernarin 2788, red, Dumfries 1910, Inverness 1911, Paisley 1913, Gained Two Provost Muir Mackean Awards also one Silver Medal for Breeder of Best Bull

MULTIPLE MAIN AWARDS WINNERS (H.A.S.S.) 1919 TO 1939

(V CUP = Perpetual Victory Challenge Cup)

M. Ossian Ban of Atholl 3176, light dun, 1920, 1921, 1922 Champion

F. Princess Caroline II of Southesk 9400, yellow, 1920 Perpetual Victory Challenge Cup, 1921 V Cup, 1925 V Cup and Champion and the Renfrewshire Perpetual Gold Challenge Cup

M. Iarla Buidhe of Atholl 3650, yellow, 1923 V Cup and Champion, 1924 V Cup and Champion

F. Corrina of Southesk 9824, yellow, 1927 V Cup and Champion, 1928 V Cup and Champion

M. Culnadalloch II of Achnacloich 3441, yellow, 1928 V Cup, 1929 V Cup and Champion

F. Sidonia of Southesk 9827, yellow, 1928, 1929 V Cup,

F. Maura II of Southesk 10513, yellow, 1929, 1930, 1932

M. Merlin IV of Southesk 3640, brindle, 1930 V Cup and Champion, 1932

F. Sweetheart of Achnacloich 10392, yellow, 1932, 1933 V Cup and Duke of York Champion Silver Medal

F. Baravalla Smiorail II 10636, red, 1935 V Cup, 1936 V Cup and Champion

F. Capleadh Ile 11127, red, 1937, 1938, 1939

FIRST IN CLASS WINNERS 1948 TO 1960

The Royal Highland and Agricultural Society of Scotland's annual Show... THE ROYAL HIGHLAND SHOW (R.H.A.S.S.)

1948 Inverness

M. Uallach of Achnacloich 4475, red, V Cup and Champion
F. Blarag of Foreland 12052, yellow, V Cup
M. Coirneal of Barbreck 4371, red
F. Baravalla Smiorail II of Mingary 12859, red
F. Annag Ruadh of Easingwold 12541, red
F. Laochag Ruadh of Foreland 12689, red

1949 Dundee

M. Cuiladair of Mingary 4615, red, V Cup and Champion
F. Blarag of Foreland 12052, yellow, V Cup
M. Alasdair Ruadh 4447, red
F. Barbara Ruadh of Mingary 12855, red
F. Capleadh Ile XI 13207, light red
F. Baravalla III of Mingary 13146, brindle

1950 Paisley

F. Capleadh Ile XVI 13240, red, V Cup and Champion
M. Aodhair of Mingary 4691, brindle, V Cup
M. Calum Og of Ballathie 4489, yellow
F. Capleadh Ile II 11203, red
F. Morag of Mingary 12856, red
F. Sobhrach Og of Foreland 13389, red

1951 Aberdeen

M. Uilleam Buidhe of Glenfalloch 4798, yellow, V Cup and Champion
F. Barbara Ruadh of Mingary 12855, Deep red, V Cup
M. Victor of Gylen 4817, red
F. Capleadh Ile XIV 13235, red
F. Catriona Ile 13724, red
F. Ribhinn Og of Mingary 14179, red

1952 Kelso

Outbreak of foot & mouth disease prevented cattle entries at Shows.

1953 Alloa

F. Catriona Ile II, Vol. 31 Herdbook, V Cup and Champion
M. Uilleam Buidhe of Glenfalloch 4798, yellow, V Cup
M. Padruig Ruadh Ile, Vol 31 Herdbook
M. Ban Righ Alainn II of Douglas, Vol 31 Herdbook
F. Lileas of Glenforsa 14360
F. Capleadh Ile XI 13207
F. Currac-na-Cuthaig of Scone Palace 14180

1954 Dumfries

F. Barbara II of Mingary, V Cup and Champion
M. Gaisgeach of Duart 5051, red, V Cup
M. Viking of Strathallan, 5215
F. Capleadh Riabhach VIII of Easingwold 14025
F. Catriona Ile II 15498
F. Capleadh Ile XXV, 16271

1955 Edinburgh

M. John of Severie, V Cup and Champion and Renfrewshire Perpetual Gold Challenge Cup
F. Capleadh Ile XXIV 15504, V Cup
M. Gaisgeach of Duart 5051
M. Uallach Ile III
F. Currac-na-Cuthaig of Scone Palace 14180
F. Malda Bhoideach of Achnacloich 16302
F. Annag Ruadh Ile XIV

1956 Inverness

F. Lilli-a-Gleann of Douneside 16230, V Cup and Champion
M. Uallich Ile IV 5426, V Cup
M. Gille Coir of Duart
F. Annag Ruadh XIV 16860
F. Sidonia Ile 35th
F. Lileas of Glenforsa 14360

1957 Dundee

F. Capleadh Ile 24th 15504, red, V Cup and Champion
M. Laoch of Douneside 5188, red, V Cup
M. Drumachar 2nd of Scone Palace, Vol 35 Herdbook
F. Corryarrick Shelah 16970
F. Sidonia Ile 35th 17556
F. Capleadh Ile 42nd, 18144

1958 Ayr

M. Prionnsa Bhuidhe of Mingary, yellow, V Cup and Champion
F. Fionnairaidh Ile X 15517, red, V Cup
M. Seumas of Jura, brindle
F. Princess Ealasaid VI of Achnacloich, red, 17575
F. Capleadh Ile XLII 18144, red
F. Baravalla Mairi of Douneside, red

1959 Aberdeen

F. Leannan Og III of Douneside, 19155, V Cup & Champion

M. Gaisgeach of Duart 5051, V Cup

M. Gille Coir II of Scone Palace

F. Deothlag of Scone Palace 17490

F. Capleadh Ile XLII 18144

F. Oighrig Ruadh of Douneside 18673

1960 Ingliston Showground Permanent Venue

F. Morag Ruadh of Mingary 15763, brindle, V Cup & Champion also Edinburgh Corporation Perpetual Gold Champion Cup for best animal in Highland classes presented by the City of Edinburgh to commemorate the Society's 100th Show

M. Rannoch of Strathfillan 5567, V Cup

M. Uallich Ile IX, Vol 38 Herdbook

F. Mairi VIII of Scammadale 18631

F. Capleadh Riabhach XI of Easingwold 18909

F. Corryarick Rhona, 19673

CHAPTER 9: CULTURAL CONNECTIONS

CHAPTER 9: CULTURAL CONNECTIONS

TRANSPORT

Movement of goods is an essential part of all cultures. The method of transport of goods is influenced by and in turn influences various elements of a nation's heritage.

Scotland is no different from many nations in having found cattle to be a source of haulage power as steady draught animals, a source of high protein sustenance from dairy products and red meat, a source of clothing, furnishings, and daily utensils from the hide and horns, a source of celebration expressed in art forms by singers, poets, painters, sculptors and craftsmen, and a vital part of the nation's economy. The aesthetically pleasing breed of Highland cattle makes a unique contribution to Scotland's blend of commerce and culture.

Economic benefits from ownership of cattle requires their being sold. Being sold requires their being transported to a sales point and new destination. Methods of transport have undergone immense change since the days when cattle transported themselves to market by the entirely natural process of walking. Teleportation is far from natural and still only a figment of the science fiction imagination, but the transportation of live cattle from one country to another by air had become an unremarkable procedure by the end of the twentieth century whereas at the beginning it had been unknown. Travel by aircraft suitably prepared to take livestock, is today as normal as shipping or trucking by rail and road was in the 1930s, the major difference being the speed of travel time. Highland cattle, by all accounts seem less affected by skimming across time zones than their human carers. In previous centuries those who cared for the cattle from their home territory to market (tryst) were called drovers. There seems to be no twentieth century equivalent for the "drover" who expertly rolled into one profession the skills of stockman, buyer, seller, route-planner, veterinary attendant, financial investment agent, goods guarantor. Instead, the international transport of livestock involves an array of variously qualified specialists each playing a part in a complex arrangement.

TWENTIETH CENTURY TRANSPORT

Mr Richard Beale, Director of Stanford Livestock International Ltd. has a wealth of experience in the worldwide transport of farm livestock from exotic alpaca and precious stallions to the humblest of piglets.

He described Highland cattle as "*Rustic animals, very beautiful*" adding that they have been taken through the transport routes with no more complications than other breeds, but that handlers need to remember to allow a little slack in the halter lead to permit the dignified head carriage natural to the breed. Too tight a grip on too short a lead causes Highlands to pull and head toss which can result in accidental horn jabs. He also mentioned that experienced handlers know to be ready for the breed behavioural characteristics of alertness, like sniffing the wind and frequent looking all around. Instances of aggressive horn use were difficult to recall due to their rarity, but handlers concede that with or without horns an animal with a bad temperament is difficult.

Mr Beale's business acumen embraces a compassion for livestock that believes training cattle to halter-leading is essential for quiet panic-free loading into transport crates for air travel, or transport stables for shipment. The 30 days quarantine for health checks prior to export are valuable for assessment of temperament in individual animals so that handling of them can be conducted appropriately to create minimum stress.

Large-horned Highlands are all tied facing alternate positions so that each set of horn-points is beside a tail rather than a head to avoid endangering eyes with accidental contact in the course of the journey. Care is taken that any scything or swinging horn action is not likely to damage the aircraft.

Transport far abroad is scheduled to avoid peak temperature times and in the case of Highland cattle when their thickest winter coats have been shed naturally.

Today's shipping across the South Atlantic provides a luxury cruise for animals compared with nineteenth century conditions. Pedigree treasures usually travel in individual stalls in transportable stables, often on deck rather than in the hold, with doors open to allow maximum natural ventilation during favourable weather. How this contrasts with conditions prevailing mid-nineteenth century.

NINETEENTH CENTURY TRANSPORT BY SEA, RAIL, AND ROAD

The steamships which transported livestock from the Western Islands in the nineteenth century were not built for that purpose and were adapted simply by fixing rings round the bulwarks and the sides of the holds. Animals were tethered to these rings.

The holds were dark apartments generally 50 to 80 feet long, 25 to 35 feet wide, and 7 to 9 feet high. There was neither light nor ventilation except from the hatch. Sometimes 50 cattle were packed into such a space. The cattleman "*moves about his own peculiar domain, the hold, with the most absolute power, knocking the animals about, beating and cursing them in the most unlimited manner. Usually a crane hoisted the cattle on board, each in a sling, but occasionally a haltered beast was led on board. Once landed on deck the animal was dragged to be tied by a 6 to 9 inch rope length to the side rings. There were no systematic arrangements for food and water on board. Sometimes shippers sent hay for their beasts but if they did not the ship provided none. Even when hay was sent the cattle were so tied and positioned that they could not eat or drink. Quick breathing and constant moaning of the near suffocating animals was the norm and when the hatches had to be closed in storms it was a wonder any survived at all. When one slipped and fell usually at least one on each side of it fell also and died.*" (George Menzies)

The steamer *Claymore* took two days in fair weather to transport cattle from Portree in Skye to Oban Cattle Mart. There are records of very early trade by sea to and from the Western Islands on routes from Greenock and Glasgow but steamships serving the Inner Hebrides began to replace the sailed vessels in the 1830s and by 1890 a dozen a week were entering West Highland ports. From 1839 there were regular steamers between London and Inverness.

The railway network advanced rapidly during the nineteenth century allowing a combined transport system to develop of shipping cattle to Kyle of Lochalsh and off-loading them from the steamship hold into cattle trucks for railway haulage. Cattle off-loaded at Oban were transported by rail from Dalmally by 1870, and directly from Oban and from Mallaig when these rail lines were completed some years later. The Highland cattle shipped to Poolewe were perhaps luckier for they had to walk south east across Scotland to Dingwall or Inverness markets before being loaded onto rail trucks. Rail from London to Perth had been completed in 1848, and to Aberdeen in 1850 encouraging the development of the heavy beef cattle that could not walk well and reducing the trade there in Highland drove cattle. The Perth to Inverness railway opened in 1863.

As with shipping, where the most usual though not frequent accident was from steers slipping out of the sling when being hoisted on board, there were risks with rail transport.

One accident which shocked the public happened in 1881 near Dava Station on a bleak stretch of exposed moorland, where my grandfather ran a progressive farm, near Grantown-on-Spey. A whole trainload of cattle perished when the train plunged into a snowdrift and was buried.

Railway companies encouraged farmers to use their services with advertisements such as this for the 1859 General Show of Stock and Implements held in Edinburgh *"The Railway Companies in Scotland will carry Stock, Implements etc. to the Show at the usual rates and return them free when unsold. The same privilege will be given by the Aberdeen, Leith, and Clyde, Shipping Company and by the London and Edinburgh Shipping Company."*

In 1902 a popular farming magazine carried this information from the Beaver Line of Royal Mail Steamers:

"Direct sailings every Saturday from Liverpool: November – April to Halifax Nova Scotia, & St. John; May – October to Quebec & Montreal.

Specially constructed to meet the requirements of the Livestock Trade...high 'tween decks, fresh water service, well ventilated, electric light throughout.

Apply to Elder, Dempster & Co, Africa House, Water Street, Liverpool; Montreal, Quebec, or St. John, or Hernu Peron & Co. Paris."

The flourishing shipping and railway transport of live cattle to London was to be short-lived on account of the increasing amounts of refrigerated meat being imported from 1875 onwards.

Road haulage of live cattle and sheep began about 1925 and within ten years large numbers of lorries were being used. Road transport of livestock is still a convenient system and improvements in the structure of truck, often called 'float' are ongoing. Hauliers say Highland cattle are neither better nor worse than other breeds to transport except that they are noticeably calmer when travelling beside known animals.

The twentieth century powered transport of Highland cattle by sea, rail, road and air seems to have appealed less to historians, novelists, and artists than did the droving of earlier centuries.

Perhaps this is because terrestrial transport methods are commonplace and no longer viewed as a spectacular achievement, and also because Scotland is no longer the mysterious, wild and remote neighbour to England. Drovers and droving certainly created some very strong commercial and cultural links between the two countries and provided much of interest to many people.

DROVING

Walking cattle from one place to another was called droving. It means the deliberate moving of the livestock, necessary most commonly to find new pastures and grazings or to reach markets for selling and buying.

There is mention as early as 1359 of the respectability of drovers when the two Scots Andrew Moray and Alan Erskyn, along with their three horsemen and servants were granted by letter safe conduct for travelling through England or the King's foreign dominion for one year. In 1502 surplus Highland cattle in Skye were exported to Inverness market which required a long mainland walk after the boat journey from Skye. (A R B Haldane)

Twenty or 30 cattle can be managed by one man, some accounts say 60 per man, but often droves were much larger, requiring several men on foot while the main drover usually rode ahead to check that rivers were not too swollen to ford or that there were suitable resting and grazings spaces as planned. Distances covered were immense and took weeks to complete.

Highland cattle gathered from isolated glens in the far north of Scotland might be driven at a rate of about 2 miles per hour to cover 20 to 25 miles per day. Not more than ten miles per day avoids serious loss of condition in fat cattle, if allowed food and water once in five hours. Drovers varied in their management of pace to arrive at precise dates in market destinations hundreds of miles from their start point. Some allowed for occasional rest days, others kept a steady slower pace. Cattle snatched mouthfuls of wayside herbage when they could and drank freely when fording rivers. They were rested generally at midday en route and then overnight on the village common which they grazed if the end of that day's drove brought them to a village. Land was increasingly enclosed with dykes and fencings and not only were common grazings no longer available, drovers' overnight stopping places known as stances, became enclosed fields which were rented to the drovers for negotiable amounts per head of cattle.

Drovers are not to be confused with roguish cattle thieves. The only lawlessness among drovers, who were generally non-aggressive, probably occurred immediately after the annexing of Scotland to England which curtailed Scotland's long accustomed freedom in continental export and import trade, and forced her to accept heavy customs dues levied on certain goods bound for English markets. Cattle and hides were taxed. In 1661 the dues on live cattle stood at two ounces of gold bullion for four cows, and the same for three oxen, to be paid at tolls set on selected routes which the drovers were required by law to take. Policing all these routes was difficult. Drovers became adept at avoiding the heaviest tolls and customs. The customs dues were in time lifted, but not the tolls for using roads and bridges. They were continuously raised. The droving trade took the brunt of many initial problems in combining two countries under one government at a time when the larger country had huge debts to settle and perceived the smaller one as a source of revenue. Apart from customs evasion in these early days the regular or professional drover was reliably trustworthy, peaceable, and never a politically active individual.

"...with the Union of the Crowns of Scotland and England (1603), the cattle droving industry, which had previously been discouraged, came into its own and the beasts were sent on the hoof from the remotest Highlands to England, and the whole social life of the North came to depend upon this industry. The numbers of cattle that were raised under the old, hard conditions was extraordinary. The autumn trysts at Crieff (on the borders of the hilly country of Perthshire) became important at the end of the seventeenth century and by 1723, no less than 20,000 cattle are said to have been sold there annually. In that year a traveller visited one of these fairs. He said that 30,000 guineas were spent by English drovers. He wrote more fully of the people at the fair than of the cattle: 'The Highland Gentlemen were mighty civil, dress'd in their slashed short Waistcoats, a Trousing (which is Breeches and Stockings of one piece of striped stuff) with a Plaid for a Cloak and a blue Bonnet. They had a Poinard, Knife and Fork in one Sheath hanging at one side of their Belt, their Pistol at the other, and their Snuff Mill (mull) before, with a great broad Sword by their side. Their attendants were very numerous, all in belted Plaids, girt like a Woman's Petticoats down to the Knees, their Thighs and half of the Leg all bare.'...they spoke an unintelligible Language to the English. (see 19th century cattle fair p.11)

The Principal trysts were shifted from Crieff to Falkirk later in the century to meet the convenience of the increasing number of English drovers who came north to attend them. By 1771 it was estimated that 30,000 head of cattle were sold at the three yearly sales held there in August, September, and October, and the numbers went on increasing until 1850 when 150,000 cattle were sold. After this the droving industry quickly declined." (I F Grant)

"About 1650 a warrior band from Skye pioneered what became the main Hebridean industry by escorting droves of cattle to the trysts at Crieff and Falkirk. These Skyemen were a fighter escort and

opened the routes that became a principal source of Hebridean wealth for nearly 200 years. The drive south was in autumn when animals were in best condition." (W H Murray)

The armed escort was necessary for protection from two main categories of men, 'professional' cattle thieves, and the bands of clansmen rebelling against 'foreign' rule from England. The political unrest in eighteenth century Scotland made woods and glens unsafe for even the best respected drover. Understanding this, the English military leader General Wade issued licences to certain drovers exempting them from the Disarming Acts of 1716 and 1748. History has not disclosed any abuse of these licences by drovers.

Inevitably there were instances of lawless ruffians using for their personal advantage the well earned honour and respect surrounding drovers. Time was to reveal that Simon Fraser Lord Lovat, Chief of the Fraser Clan was in fact a selfish and wicked troublemaker. When he was heading north to muster forces to rebel against English rule he and his party found themselves at the port of Leith (near Edinburgh) without the secretly promised ships. There happened to be about fourteen drovers, of a clan known not to favour the Jacobite cause, on their return journey from cattle sales waiting at the Leith docks to get a ship north. They preferred the risk of a sea journey to facing bandit country on the mainland. Lord Lovat and his men masqueraded as these drovers whenever government forces made spot checks on the ship, and even successfully coaxed Lord Salton into supplying them with horses when they disembarked by explaining that it had been necessary to sell the horses in Edinburgh before boarding the ship bound for Inverness and that was why they (the false drovers) were carrying their saddles. Lord Lovat thus escaped detection by invoking the goodwill held by all towards drovers. Once his party had reached Inverness they stole 28 cows from one source, killing eight for supper in one evening. In a later exploit 200 of his men purloined about 400 cows and 200 sheep for provisions. (Major Fraser)

A comment made to Lord Seafield when he was Chancellor of Scotland suggests that it was more honourable to be a cattle dealer than a politician. When Lord Seafield was suspected of bribing Scottish noblemen to support the plan to unite the English and Scottish Parliaments in 1707 his behaviour drew this remark from his brother:

"Better sell nowte than sell nations." (J A Symon)

Nowte meant cattle. Dealings with Highland cattle in Scotland, then as now, involved all levels of Scottish society from the richest landowner to the landless labourer in prejudice free interaction. The real value of the Highland 'nowte' is nought, however, in twentieth century commerce. The former national economic importance of the breed is unlikely to return.

"Scotland was covered by a network of several hundred trysts and drove roads, all integrated as gathering points and routes for the main drive south in autumn, when the beasts were in best condition. The cattle flowed like rivers down these drove roads, travelling ten miles a day. The two main streams from the north took source in Caithness and the Hebrides, each being swollen by bellowing tributaries from all the hill regions en route to Falkirk. The Caithness and Sutherland herds went for sale first to Muir of Ord, where they were joined by all beasts from Wester Ross between Loch Broom and Loch Alsh, which came by Strath Bran, Glen Cannich, and Glen Affric. They then went on to Kingussie and through the Drumochter Pass, or else down the Great Glen where they were joined by the Skye and Outer Hebridean droves for the crossing of the Corrieyarrick Pass to Upper Spey and Drumochter. The Skye droves crossed Kyle Rhea to Glenelg, and reached the Great Glen either by Glensheil to Invermoriston or else by Glen Loyne to Invergarry. In the North-East Highlands all the great passes between the Spey and the Dee – Lairig an Laoigh, Lairig Ghru, Feshie-Geldie – were used to supply Braemar and numerous other trysts along the length of Dee to Banchory and Aberdeen. From the Dee in turn, all southward passes to Strathmore and Strath Tay were busy with traffic, notably the Cairnwell pass from

Braemar to Glen Shee, the Capel Mounth from Ballater to Glen Clova, and the Cairn O'Mount south from Banchory. All these routes and many more were blocked for days on end by immense herds, sometimes stretching up to ten miles where routes converged. In 1772, 24,000 head were sold at Falkirk; by 1812, 50,000 cattle and 40,000 sheep; and the figures rose year by year until 150,000 cattle were sold annually around 1840. After 1850, the development of steamer services and railways steadily reduced droving traffic." (W H Murray)

THE GREAT LOCHABER DROVER

No doubt very aware of the gloomy prospects for the droving trade was the most acclaimed of Scottish drovers, one John Cameron of Corrychoille, near Spean Bridge, Lochaber. Known as "Corry" after his farm name of Corrychoille, he was a man of powerful independent reasoning, sharp business sense, skilled livestock handling, and astonishing endurance and energies. As a barefoot lad in the late 1780s he saved his earnings from minding drovers' stock while the men refreshed themselves at his father's Inn. As a youth he hired himself to drive sheep and cattle to Falkirk Tryst and by early manhood he was known to be an experienced cattle dealer and drover.

Quick to take advantage of changing land tenure he bought lease after lease of farms as soon as they became available until he could rest and graze droves on his own farm ground for much of the journey to market. His farms in the Lochaber district around Spean Bridge to Fort William were:

"Caonich, Kenmore, Murlaggan, Cailleach, Glenkingie, Glenspean, Monaquoich, North side of Glen Desseray, Crieff, Salachan, Muick, Glen Pean More, Glen Pean Beg, Coull, Glaickfearn.

To give an indication of the extent of his deals and transactions, the cattle which he bought at the Skye fairs and ferried across Kylerhea, near Balmacara, are said to have rested each night on their way to Falkirk tryst on one of his own farms. The daily trek of such droves would probably be in the region of fifteen miles, and this gives an idea of the number of farms he must have rented. I have been told that his droves, particularly in September when getting near Falkirk, occupied the road for a distance of between five and seven miles. When one knows that at the September Falkirk Tryst he always sold no less than 2,000 head of cattle and 20,000 sheep, this appears feasible enough."

Cattle tryst scenes typical of Corry's experience are:

"The cattle dealers of all descriptions chiefly on horseback are scouring the fields in search of the lots they require. The Scottish drovers are for the most part mounted on small shaggy, spirited ponies that are obviously quite at home among the cattle: and they carry their riders through the throngest groups with astonishing speed. The English dealers have, in general, large, stout horses, and they pace the ground with more caution, surveying every lot carefully as they go along. When they discover the cattle they want, they enquire the price. A good deal of riggling takes place, and when the parties come to an agreement the purchaser claps a penny or arles into the hands of the stockholder, observing at the same time it's a bargain. Tar dishes are then got, and the purchaser's mark being put upon the cattle, they are then driven from the field.

...from 60 to 70 tents are erected along the field for selling spirits and provisions. In one of these tents a few gentlemen attend from the Falkirk Bank to accommodate the dealers with the money they require. Many kindle fires at the end of their tents, over which cooking is briskly carried on. Broth is made in considerable quantities, and meets a ready sale. As most of the purchasers are paid in these tents, they are constantly filled and surrounded with a mixed multitude of cattle dealers, fishers, drovers, auctioneers, pedlars, jugglers, gamblers, itinerant fruit merchants, ballad singers and beggars."

"One evening himself and a fellow drover were recalling the past events over their whisky toddy, when the latter remarked to Corry,

"I am of the opinion that you are a greater man than the Duke of Wellington."

"Toots, toots, man, " replied Corry, at the same time taking an extra large pinch of snuff, "that is too much of a compliment, too much by a lot."

But his friend continued to expiate on his great powers in collecting and driving such large droves of sheep and cattle from the most remote parts of the Highlands to the southern markets and finally suggested that the Duke of Wellington could not do it.

To all this Corry remained silent for a while, then he took another glass of toddy and slowly remarked:

"The Duke of Wellington was, nae doot, a clever man, very clever, I believe. They tell me he was a very good sojer, but then, d'ye see, he had reasonable men to deal with – captains and majors and generals that could understand him – plant a company here and a company there at his direction; but I'm no sure after all if he could manage twenty thousand sheep and several thousand of black cattle as well, that couldna' understand one word he said, Gaelic or English, and bring them every hoof of them to Falkirk tryst! I doot it, I doot it very much! But I have often done that."

At the age of seventy-five Corry lived as active a life as ever. He had walked the six miles to look over his sheep before breakfast one day, then rode off to a meeting at Spean Bridge. Leaving there at three o'clock he visited his flock on the way home and had to extricate some goats from danger. He took ill so seriously before reaching home that he had to be helped off his horse on arrival. His condition worsened and before the doctor could arrive Corry had passed away, sharp witted and active to the end.

All the above information and more on John Cameron, 1780 to 1856, can be found in a booklet published by The Oban Times Ltd. Oban, entitled *The Lochaber Drover* written by Alastair Cameron. With their kind permission these extracts have been included in this publication.

Detailed and comprehensive information on droving is thoroughly covered in two major texts, one by A R B Haldane, *The Drove Roads of Scotland*, first published in 1952, the other by K J Bonser, *The Drovers*, published in 1970 dealing largely with droving in England.

It taxes the twentieth century imagination to envisage the scenes of cattle sheep and horses converging at trysts for two to three days in some instances and two to three weeks in others when the following figures are considered.

30,000 cattle sold in Crieff in 1723. 60,000 cattle sold in Falkirk in 1794. 100,000 cattle exported to England around 1800 to 1810 of which 20,000 were from the Hebrides, 2,600 from Islay, 1,200 from Jura, and 2,000 from Mull and adjacent islands. The word chaos comes readily to mind in thinking of the practicalities of watering and feeding and settling down the livestock for each night they were at the market venue.

Two hundred years after the peak of the droving days a diminishing number of inns and public-houses carry names like "The Black Bull" and "The Drovers Inn". These were much needed places of refreshment, revitalisation and rest for those involved in the buying, selling, and transporting of 'the black cattle' of Scotland. Today many proprietors and managers of these premises know little or nothing of the historical connections of their 'pub' with black cattle and in changing the name for something they consider will be more appealing to twentieth century young adults another fading strand of the old culture is finally lost.

Mr Donald Cameron who founded the Glen Nevis fold, told me that in the 1930s or 1940s he drove his cattle over the Carter Bar road on their way to Redesdale Forest where the Forestry Commission were experimenting with using cattle to graze the forest verges and open sections.

One of the farms he passed had an elderly person who told of remembering the old droves going by that way, adding that the old records of a purchase made from these drovers was still in the farmhouse somewhere. The fresh young staff in the Forestry Commission Headquarters were unable to trace anything useful about cattle grazing in Forestry Commission land and without knowing it, further impressed upon me, as I waited on the public side of a glass window in their headquarters' office how imperceptibly a culture is lost.

REFERENCES

George Menzies, *Transactions of the Highland and Agricultural Society of Scotland* Vol 2
O'Dell and Walton, *The Highlands and Islands of Scotland*
1902 *Scottish Farmer Album*
A R B Haldane, *The Drove Roads of Scotland*
I F Grant, *Highland Folkways*
W H Murray, *The Islands of Western Scotland.* The extract is noted as being from A Nicolson's *History of Skye* 1930
Major Fraser, *Major Fraser's Manuscript: His Adventures in Scotland and England His Mission to and Travels in France in Search of His Chief His Services in the Rebellion (and His Quarrels) with Simon Fraser Lord Lovat 1696 to 1737* published by David Douglas in 1889, Edinburgh
J A Symon, *Scottish Farming*
W H Murray, *The Scottish Highlands*, 1976
Alastair Cameron, *The Lochaber Drover, "Corrychoille"*

ADDITIONAL READING:

K J Bonser, *The Drovers*, 1970
S Toulson, *The Drovers*, 1980
J Gray Kyd, *The Drove Roads and Bridle Paths around Braemar*, 1958
D V Arnold, *Scottish Cattle Droving & the Hambleton Drove Road.* booklet, 1982
Dr I Richardson, *Laggan – Past and Present*, 1990
John Keay, *Highland Drove*, 1984
C Macdonald, *Echoes of the Glen*, 1936

FILM AND TV

THE BIG SCREEN

A form of twentieth century entertainment popular since the 1920s is the watching of films on a large screen in the type of theatre designed for film shows, the cinema. The most prolific source of lavishly created films is Hollywood in The United States of America, although there are many other film studios worldwide. The closing decades of the twentieth century found the film industry exploring afresh the entertainment potential of Scottish history filmed on locations in Scotland. To establish a credible sense of authenticity in some scenes Highland cattle were

necessary. So from time to time Highland cattle have made an appearance in such major films as:
Keep Your Fingers Crossed – Kirk Douglas handcuffed among the Cladich Highland cattle.
Women in Love
Chasing the Deer
Rob Roy
Braveheart

THE SMALL SCREEN

From the 1960s television, the small screen system in the home, became increasingly popular because of its convenience and wider choice of what to watch.

Most of the films made for the large screen can be shown on television screens. In addition television offers a wide variety of viewing from daily news and informative documentary programmes to comedy and musical entertainment.

The roving cameras of many television companies have captured shots of Highland cattle for the little screen, slipping in a few seconds here and there of these eye-catching animals, and helping to maintain a public awareness of the breed. Television companies do not permit public browsing through past news broadcasts but are usually prepared to negotiate arrangements for private viewing of their own film footage from feature programmes. Some have facilities to make a copy for purchase if requested.

Scott Mitchell for Grampian TV, Darran Gardner for Scottish TV, Andrew Whitehouse for BBC TV, Carol Hubbard for Granada TV, Martin Armstrong for Yorkshire TV, and Anne G Docherty for Scottish Film Archive, supplied the following information which may interest the enthusiast and stimulate more film coverage of Highland cattle.

GRAMPIAN TV, acquired by STV Group in 1997 became STV North in 2006

Most of the film footage readily traced showing Highland cattle occurs in news programmes from 1989. Early black and white footage is lodged with the Scottish Film Archive.

Ena MacNeill with Highland cattle in North Uist is featured in the programme *CRUINN-CE* Number 13 series 2 September 1994.

SCOTTISH TV (STV), Pacific Quay, 120 Govan Road, Glasgow, G51 1PQ

The following titles which include glimpses of Highland cattle can all be viewed by arrangement.

THE ROYAL HIGHLAND SHOW:

1988 Highland cattle and Belgian bulls.
1989 Farmer nursing collapsed Highland cow with water.
1990 Cattle in pens including Highland cow and calf.
1994 Highland and ordinary cows and cattle.

Glasgow Garden Festival 1988 – feeding horses; Highland cattle.
Glencoe 1991 – Hill farmer Ewan Findlay feeding hay to Highland cattle.
News Rush 1993 – Snowbound farm and farmer feeding Highland cattle and cows in the snow.
Scotland Today 1995 – Glencoe snow; Highland cattle in the snow.
Glasgow and Edinburgh 1989 – Highland cows in Pollok Park.
Highway 1992 Highland cows near Linlithgow.

BRITISH BROADCASTING CORPORATION (BBC), Pentland Place, London, W1A 1AA

BBC TV film footage which can be viewed by private arrangement:

Its a Square World 1964 – 4 seconds of Highland cattle coming out of a train in the Michael Bentine series.

Tomorrow's World 1973 – 12 seconds of Highland cattle on Rum.

Scottish Drove 1981 – full coverage of John and Julia Keay walking Highland cattle from Skye to Crieff, some 200 miles along the ancient drove roads.

New Lords of the Isles 1981 – 30 seconds of Highland cattle on Strathaird Estate in Skye.

Wildlife on One: Return of the Sea Eagle 1981 – 53 seconds of Highland cattle and red deer on Rum.

London Plus Highland Cattle 1985 – 19 minutes 12 seconds interview with Tom Copas.

Breakfast Time Eigg 1989 – programme on Eigg, 51 minutes 30 seconds shows Highland cattle.

Country File 1990 – Judith Bolton talks about grooming a bull for Show; man grooming in Scotland. 86 seconds.

The Tales of Para Handy, Master Mariner 1994 – transporting a Highland bull.

As with Grampian Television various news programmes have included reference to Highland cattle, the earliest noted being in 1952.

GRANADA TV, merged with Carlton Communications to form ITV plc in 2004.
White City Place, 201 Wood Lane, London, W12 7RU

The Land:The North West Highlands 1975 – the effect of the bleak rocky terrain on the lives of the inhabitants. Highland cows and calves...at roadside, in middle of road scratching, grazing and rubbing neck on stone. 19 minutes 39 seconds whole programme.

Village Show: Dalmally 1988 – Ursula Buchan meets breeders of Highland cattle and others at Dalmally Agricultural Show. 25 minutes 41 seconds whole programme.

Graham's Ark 1981 – Graham Thornton visits Stewart Park, Middlesborough, to see their collection of Highland cattle, deer, llamas, guinea pigs etc. 20 minutes and 30 seconds for the whole programme.

YORKSHIRE TV, bought by Grenada Group in 1997 now part of ITV plc.

Lone Furrow – The Far Eastender (Benbecula) 1987 – Highland cattle in pens at the Benbecula sale of livestock, 1 minute and 24 seconds of 26 minutes 16 seconds programme.

Power in the Land – Highland 1988 – 45 seconds of crofter feeding Highland cattle in Glenelg, in film looking at the way forestry methods and fish farming threatens the traditional crofting way of life. (24 mins 5 secs)

Bellamy's Bugle – Beasties 1988 – 30 seconds of Highland cattle during David Bellamy's visit to Glasgow. (11mins 02 secs)

Yorkshire TV coverage of the Great Yorkshire Agricultural Show from 1991 includes some views of Highland cattle.

SCOTTISH FILM ARCHIVE,
now Moving Image Archive, Kelvin Hall, 1445 Argyle Street, Glasgow, G3 8AW

Highland Cattle 1935 – 3.01 minutes, silent, black/white, educational
Land of Invention 1940 – Black/white, rural landscapes include some Highland cows, 1minute 2 seconds.
Harris 1950 – Colour, amateur film, silent, one Highland cow.
The Heart is Highland 1952 – Colour, Documentary, Market pens.
The Enchanted Isles 1957 – Colour.
Introducing Scotland 1958 – Colour.
Song for Prince Charlie 1959 – Colour, Highland cattle and stag on Culloden moor.
Champions in the Sun 1964 – Colour, Royal Highland Show, 84 seconds of Highland cattle in Highland scenery.
Highland Capital 1968 – 33 seconds of Highland cattle in the grounds of Leys Castle.

THE BRITISH FILM INSTITUTE (BFI) ARCHIVES, 21 Stephen Street, London, W1T 1LN

The BFI have been established since 1993 and are hard at work cataloguing and preserving film. Their collection can be searched online from the BFI Archive website.

There are many more television companies operating within Britain each holding or discarding old film footage and endeavouring to update their access or retrieval systems. Border TV, for example, in 1988 showed their film entitled *The Drove*, devised and written by Eric Robson, following a group of cattle walking along the ancient drove routes from the Borders to London. There were only one or two Highland cows in that herd though, in contrast to the all Highland drove from Skye to Crieff by John Keay.

WRITERS

WRITERS AND NOVELISTS

For centuries before writing was an everyday skill Highland cattle had been vital to the economics and social fabric of northern Scotland. They were a necessary possession for every community and continued to be a social link through the changing structure of the benevolent clan system, the rise of sharp distinctions in social ranking, and the multi-layered levels of twentieth century society in Scotland. Highland cattle are extraordinary ambassadors. They impact on the senses when included in novels. Acclaimed writers, both of serious and light-hearted works have crafted images of Highland cattle that stir the emotions with even the briefest reference. When Sir Walter Scott's grandfather was a successful drover it is not surprising to find that one of Scott's works is entitled *The Two Drovers* and makes mention of real happenings such as the tryst at Doune and the superstitions that beset milkmaids. In the nineteenth century novel *The Raiders* by S R Crockett a chapter entitled 'The Great Fight at the Bridgehead' describes a fearful occurrence when a bottleneck of red Highland cattle and black Galloways at a narrow bridge had their backs set on fire to force them to break out of the impasse. R L Stevenson's hero in *St. Ives* joins company with two drovers; Neil Gunn's *Sun Circle* and Eric Linklater's *Magnus Merriman* build on the symbolism of the bull; Tim Severin's *The Brendan Voyage* details the ancient skill of preparing Ox hides for covering a boat; and among short story collections there are many which include Highland cattle. Peter McNab's 1984 publication *Tall Tales from an Island* has the short story *The*

Tale of Eachann's Bull ...a humorous story highlighting how reliably amicable and obliging a Highland bull can be with its known and trusted friend and how unpredictable in the absence of that known person. Drumbuie and Amadan are two red Highland bulls which are mentioned variously in Gideon Scott May's collections of stories *The Kilt for Keeps, The Croft and the Ceilidh,* and *Gideon's Way*. A black Highland bull features in the truly delightful full length story for adults over twelve years of age by Kathleen Fidler, *The Droving Lad* which is about two heroes – Torcull the Black (bull) and young Colin Cameron. (Corrychoille lives again!) The story flows through real place names and real events, cleverly fleshing historical fact to create vibrant situations which feel contemporary yet of last century at one and the same time; G Whittam's pen-and-ink illustrations are excellent.

The adventurer writer and broadcaster John Keay undertook the droving of Highland cattle some 200 miles from Skye to Crieff and wrote eloquently of the journey in his book *Highland Drove* (1984) mentioning much of the history of the breed in a fluid easily read style. Of the powerful photographs interspersed throughout the pages two merit particular mention...a head on view of a steer mid-air as it leaped onto to terra firma off the ferry landing ramp; a street scene of the cattle amidst cars, shops, and people, walking with as much composure as if in the quiet of the remote glens.

A fine collection of stories which were out of print when research for this publication began were republished by Mercat Press in 1991 and retitled *Life in the Highlands and Islands of Scotland.* They were written by the late Colin MacDonald, the first Agricultural County Organiser in the Hebrides, so appointed early this century by the Aberdeen and North of Scotland College of Agriculture. Mr MacDonald's writing is imbued with the kindly dignity typical of Highland people and blends factual details with humorous accounts of practical experiences in the course of his duties. Stories drawn from accurate observation of man and beast may perhaps have taken a modicum of embellishment in the telling, but that of course is the art of the sennachie showing through.

With gracious goodwill Mr Macdonald's son Mr W Y MacDonald and daughter Dr Margaret Newton agreed to several references from *Life in the Highlands and Islands of Scotland* being used in *A Keen Eye* and also to an abridged version of the story of Usgar from Colin MacDonald's *Highland Memories* which is now out of print.

The Usgar story is packed with instances of behaviour characteristic of the breed, as for example when tempted to leap into a field of turnips, when chased out of it, when challenged by the dominant cow in new pastures. However, the condensed core of the story given here reveals primarily the breed characteristic of long memory that amazes Highland cattle breeders when they first discover evidence of it in their own stock.

USGAR: BEING RED LETTER DAYS IN THE LIFE OF A HIGHLAND COW

(Sound the u **not** as in **but**, but long as in **June**: and the word as a whole sounds **Oosscar**).

She was born out on the machair of a township in the Hebrides. It was a bonnie April morning that set the larks acarolling in the sun despite a remnant of winter's chill in the air. She wasn't quite yellow, nor yet quite brown, but yon in-between colour which denotes a hardy constitution. And she was as curly as a toy teddy bear; indeed, that was what she looked like lying in the shelter of the tuft of sea-bent. Her mother (Annag), not content with the thorough cleansing she had already given her baby daughter, was still giving a lick here and there, and softly moaning an invitation to be up and doing at a first meal from an udder that ached with its amplitude of rich warm milk. Suddenly mother sensed approaching danger and whipped round on the defensive!... But it was only her mistress, Kirsty, coming to see if the expected calf had yet arrived. A glance at the little stranger and Kirsty knew that her wish of many years was at last satisfied.

"M'usgair bheag!" ("My precious little jewel!") cried Kirsty, and her gently caressing the curly coat while Annag looked on with a fondly-fatuous expression of eye that was comical in the extreme. Now the reason for Kirsty's great joy was this: Annag's great-great-great-grandmother Morag had come to the croft as a wedding gift to Kirsty's husband's father from **his** father. That was a long time ago, but always since then there had been on the place a descendant of the wedding gift cow. But it had looked as if Annag would be the last of her line. For years Kirsty had hoped that Annag would produce a daughter. But no! year after year it was a great big son she presented to Kirsty; and now, after so many disappointments, there was Annag's little daughter that would one day take up the succession as the favourite cow on the croft. No wonder that Kirsty called this calf her precious little jewel!

...By the time she was eighteen months old, Usgar had grown into a fine stirk and was already showing a pair of horns of great promise...Young Donald was now home from the war. Through the lovely green-grass days of spring and summer Usgar saw him and his neighbours hard at work on the land, sowing and planting, and carting seaware and peats...Late in July there came into Usgar's life another of those days which she would long remember. It was the day of the Agricultural Show. Nearly all the people on the island came to it.

That morning Donald had tied a rope round Usgar's horns, brushed her long silken coat with a brush in a way that she half liked and half didn't, then he led her off to the Showground about five miles away. There they found gathered together the pick of the island's cattle. Usgar was led into the ring by Donald when it came to the time for heifers of her age to be judged – and Donald became the envy of the island that day ! For Usgar, now over three years of age, had developed into a beauty that even in that select company was outstanding. While still retaining the sprightliness and glorious bloom of youth she had acquired some of that stateliness of carriage, that majesty of mien, that was to distinguish her for the rest of her days. Not one moment did the judges hesitate. The first prize red ticket was tied round Usgar's horns; and before the Show was over there was an assortment of championship tickets with it, dangling over her nose. Both for Kirsty and Donald this was indeed a memorable day. Then a thing so dreadful happened that it hurts to tell of it. Ever since he returned from the war Donald had been moody and nervous and not like his old self at all; more than once he had taken more drink than was good for him.

...and his outstanding success at the Show was too much for him: along with several friends he had made a merry night of it. He was never quite sure of what had happened, but was horrified next morning when a drover came to take Usgar away with some other beasts he had bought! So **that** explained the large sum of money Donald had found in his purse! He had sold Usgar! Usgar that was the pride of his mother's heart – and indeed of his own! So their day of triumph was followed by a day of grief too deep even to be spoken about. Usgar and the others were driven off to the pier, and that same evening hoisted in a sling to a most alarming height and then dumped down in the bowels of a ship to be carried far away, and finally forced into the sea to swim to the rough, rocky, uninhabited island which was to be Usgar's home for seven years.

...Only cattle and sheep lived there now, and it might be months before a man came to see how they were doing or to shear the sheep or take away some of them to the sales.

...Every year to the Scottish Highlands from April till October there is a constant stream of visitors to enjoy the peace and grandeur of our scenery. The majority of them keep to the main routes, but always there are some who go searching into all sorts of odd and out-of-the-way places. It was one of this kind who one day landed on the island to which Usgar swam ashore some seven years earlier.

...the owner of the cattle...was paying one of his periodic visits to see how they were doing. Mr Osborne made a complimentary remark about the cattle and made special mention of the beautiful big cow that was so friendly. Mr Stewart agreed they were a fine lot and regretted he must soon sell the big cow, because although she was by far the best, she had disappointed him in that she had never produced a heifer calf: seven bull calves in a row! Now Mr Osborne had often thought of starting a small fold of Highland cattle at his place in England. Here might be his chance – and it was almost certain that a cow which had so many sons would soon have a daughter! In a few minutes a bargain was struck. Usgar – for Usgar it was – would be shipped next week to Kyle and railed to the south of England. And the clattering and rattling of the train and the awful hunger of that long journey remained in her memory for many a day. Another seven years passed

...Donald had flourished exceedingly on the croft, and when they got the news that a favourite niece was to be married in London before leaving for Canada, nothing would do but Donald must go and give away the bride. At the wedding he met a far-out cousin of whom he had little previous knowledge. But; of course, cousins are cousins. This one was manager on a farm a few hours by train west of London. Donald must go to see him before starting for home.

...There were over a dozen very fine cows and a few younger beasts. As the two men stood in the park to have a right look at the animals, there happened to be grazing quite close to them a cow of magnificent proportions, but obviously well up in years. Moving slowly along as she grazed, this cow got right into Donald's "wind" just at the moment when Donald expressed his admiration for so grand a cow: "ille! nach eile i sin math ged a the i aosda?" Suddenly the old cow ceased grazing, raised her head and sniffed into the breeze. Then she came slowly towards the men, with her nose still in the wind. They watched her with curiosity. She came right up and sniffed Donald's Harris tweed plus-fours! – and then looked straight up at him. "Strange! I never saw her do the like of that before," said the cousin in the Gaelic. "Aye, " said Donald, also in the old language, and him fair trembling with excitement and looking closely for certain colourings on the cow's sides till he found what he was looking for. "Aye! it's her right enough! It must be – it is our USGAR!" and, as if in confirmation, the old cow was now licking his one hand while he rubbed behind her ears with the other...

'You are selling her this very day,' said Donald, ...and so it was that Usgar once again found herself in a railway truck on a long, long journey. But she was neither lonely nor hungry this time, for Donald travelled by the same train and had a word with her whenever there was anything of a wait at a station. He also saw to it that she had plenty to eat and drink till they reached Oban. And when it came to getting her aboard the steamer for the Outer Isles there was no need for twisting tail or slashing stick. The old cow walked down the tilted gangway in the manner of one knowing where she was going. Out in the Minch, while the Islands were not yet in sight, Usgar was seen to be strangely excited and kept turning.her head towards the side of the ship where a modicum of daylight showed. At the pier she walked briskly ashore. From then on it was Usgar that led the way – and at such a pace that Donald was hard put to keep up with her. Before they reached home it was dark. She made straight for the gateway that gave entrance to the machair.

Donald let down the rails...."

(heavily abridged version of the Usgar story from Colin MacDonald's book *Highland Memories* first published in 1949 by the Moray Press, Edinburgh and London, now out of print, but available for reference in Aberdeen University library.)

The small selection of books mentioned illustrates how Highland cattle have strayed into literature in the English language. The recent revival of the Gaelic language has put some children's stories, designed to encourage early reading in Gaelic, onto sales shelves in bookshops. One such story features the travels of an individual Highland cow, another a Highland bull.

The popular press of newspapers and magazines find photographs of Highland cattle of sufficient impact to print half to whole page photographs of them from time to time, often in full colour.

The front cover of *Vogue* fashion magazine in November 1991 featured a model dressed entirely in black taking a golden red young Highland Bull for a walk as though he were the latest high fashion accessory.

Earlier that year *Country Living* devoted half a page to a photograph of a red Highland Calf being led to an Anglican Church to participate in a blessing of the animals service.

Various Scottish Tourist Board publications and posters show Highland cattle.

Advertising agents use the image of the Highland to suggest special quality. For example in 1992 Jaguar Motor Cars Limited, (Coventry, England) produced a powerful scene of a Jaguar car racing round a corner to be confronted with the hazard of a Highland Cow standing in the middle of the road.

POSTCARDS

Since the popular press of the late twentieth century, including the postcard business, seems only to show "red" Highland cattle the average member of the public can be forgiven for believing erroneously that is the correct or only colour of the breed. Previously the postcard receiving public were better informed (see back cover). Out of more than 100 recent colour postcards only one showed a black Highland cow and one a white, four had a yellow cow and the rest were red.

Late Victorian and early twentieth century postcards are now collector items because in times with less newspapers, magazines, and few cameras, postcards became a useful historical record of the land and its peoples (see black/white examples over page). Many old postcards made from photographs of Highland cattle show a range of coat-colours and a range in type and size. The changing Scottish culture with increased leisure pursuits and possessions no longer needed postcards as documentary evidence of a holiday venue, but often delighted in a growing fashion for sending humorous cards. So images considered by some to be funny of a Highland bull's nose close-up, or a calf's tongue tip lodged up its nostril competed with the more traditional panoramic view of mountains and cattle for tourist sales.

"TWO OF SCOTCH".

HIGHLAND CATTLE.

Highland Cattle on Trek, Isle of Skye.

6931.

A Highland Trio.

3023 Mother and Child

A HIGHLAND HOMESTEAD.

ARTISTS

NINETEENTH CENTURY

The extensive programme of military road building throughout Scotland in the eighteenth century allowed the seeds of tourism to be sown. The trickle of explorers, traders, philosophers, artists, landowners, curious to discover what lay north of the Scottish-English border land increased steadily. Royal interest in Scotland in the nineteenth century with King George IV's visit to Edinburgh and Queen Victoria's marked fondness for touring remote scenic areas kept a buzz of respectability among the intelligentsia over things Scottish.

Artists' recordings of hitherto unknown places were very important in these times without the regular visual news of twentieth century television. Paintings were a form of pictorial journalism, elevated in some instances to creative masterpieces. A lucrative market grew and flourished for paintings of Highland scenery. The nineteenth century artists were prone to giving romantic overtones to their canvas impressions of Scotland; nevertheless many fine works detailing Highland cattle were created.

Some of the artists best known for their paintings of Highland cattle are mentioned in the ensuing resumé with bibliography substantially prepared by Kate Deasington, textile designer and formerly curator of the Scottish Arts Council Collection.

GOURLAY STEELL 1819 – 1894

Son of John Steell, a well-known wood carver in Edinburgh, he trained at the Trustees Academy and became a successful animal painter in oils. He also painted water-colours of still-life subjects, studies of Scottish characters, and animal studies. He was appointed Animal Painter to the Royal Highland and Agricultural Society of Scotland in 1840. One major work of his, still owned by that society, which has had to sell various important paintings to meet ongoing rises in expenses, is that of the *West Highland Cow and Calf, 1st in her class at the Highland & Agricultural Show in Perth 1861 owned by Donald McLaren, Corrychrone, Callander Perthshire*. An earlier commission by Richard Dennistoun Campbell of Jura in 1857 shows a black bull and a dun cow of the Jura fold at a time when the colour dun was becoming more popular.

Gourlay Steell was a personal friend of the Highland cattle breeder John Stewart of Bochastle. When he had completed a portrait of the famous Bochastle cow Proisag Dhubh he inscribed it *"with the artist's best regards."* A limited edition print of the painting was made by the secretary of the Highland Cattle Society of Scotland in the 1990s.

Gourlay Steell followed Sir Edward Landseer in being appointed Animal Painter to Her Majesty for Scotland by Queen Victoria after Landseer's death in 1873.

The surname Steell is often to be found in print spelt either as Steel, or Steele.

He left a son, David George Steell (1856 – 1930) who studied at the Royal Scottish Academy Schools but whose works are not generally praised as highly as those of his father.

JOSEPH DENOVAN ADAM 1842 – 1896

Adam was a prolific painter of Highland landscapes, animals, and still-life. He established a school of animal painting in 1887 at Craigmill near Stirling and lived there until his death. On this small farm he kept Highland cattle as well as sheep, poultry, and dogs, all of whom were used as models by his students. The studio was situated in a park across the road from his house, and had a 60 foot long glass wall which enabled classes to continue in bad weather. During the summer as many as 25 students could be working at Craigmill, receiving instruction from other well-known artists including John Lochhead and John Roberts.

His son J D Adam (Junior) worked with his father on Craigmill Farm, where he sometimes collaborated with him on large paintings. He became a recognised artist in his own right, with a looser water-colour style than that of his father.

LOUIS BOSWORTH HURT 1856 – 1929

"*Mist-laden mountains and morose Highland cattle*" were the words used by one critic to sum up the works of L B Hurt. This was to underestimate the skills of an artist who was one of the best to meet the great demand for Highland landscapes in the late nineteenth and early twentieth centuries. He has a broad, free style with great ability to capture the variety in cloud formation, whether in thin skeins or in a solid mass. Some critics have pointed out that he may have had problems depicting the hoofs of cattle, frequently disguising them in long grass or heather, but he captures very well the natural groupings that arise in the breed and their attentive awareness of their surroundings. Perhaps these critics had never visited the mountain passes to find out for themselves that hoofs are more often hidden than exposed in these heathery grazings. He often painted in Scotland, which cannot be said for all artists of the time who painted Highland scenes, returning to his home in Derbyshire before setting off to paint also in Wales. Although many of his paintings are of enormous size, he was not an expensive artist; prospective purchasers of his works exhibited at the Royal Society of British Artists were asked to pay between 6 guineas to £60.

Prolific in his paintings of Highland cattle he usually rendered them in several coat-colours; for example his *Through Glencoe* has two black, one brindle, two yellow and several reds; while the one entitled *Highland cattle in a Mountain Landscape* has two black, three red, and one white.

RICHARD ANSELL RA 1815 – 1885

Born in Liverpool he is best known for his animal subjects in Highland settings. He was thought to be more sensitive in his treatment of the animals in his work than L B Hurt and insisted on painting the appropriate breed of sheep or cattle. In his shared painting with W P Frith entitled *Sheep Gathering in Glen Sligachan, Isle of Skye* he has black horned cattle, red horned cattle, and one black calf with a white face.

ALFRED DE BREANSKY 1836 – 1921

De Breansky was a prolific landscape painter, specialising in Highland lochs and mountain landscapes in Scotland and Wales. He lived in and around London and exhibited at the Royal Academy. His brother Gustav painted mainly marine and coastal subjects and his two sons were both landscape painters. In many of his Highland scenes he captures the atmosphere of each place, carefully noting the location on the reverse, and incorporating sheep or cattle in a lifelike, convincing way, so that they really "belong" in each context; the livestock are frequently small-scale within a panoramic view and favour red Highland cattle often with one white as in the works *Ben Ledi from the Pass of Ledi* and *The Banks of the Tay*.

PETER GRAHAM 1836 – 1921

Born in Edinburgh, the son of an accountant, Graham studied under Robert Scott Lauder, and was a contemporary of Orchardson, MacWhirter and Pettie the expatriate Scots who helped popularise the Highlands with their works shown in London. He studied portraiture until 1859, when he started to sketch from nature, and from the 1860s onwards he concentrated on landscape. In 1866 he settled in London and achieved a notable success at the Royal Academy with A *Spate in the Highlands*. This led to a commission from Queen Victoria to paint *Bowman's Moss, Balmoral Forest* in 1868. His attention to detail was remarkable; he kept Highland cattle at his home in Buckinghamshire to use as models, although he visited Scotland each year to paint, and captured superbly some of the brooding aspects of Highland scenery. His works were always popular, and his success such that his dealer had a waiting list of buyers.

His work *Moorland and Mist* 1893 is in Dundee Art Gallery.

EDWARD HARGITT RI 1835 – 1895

A reasonably successful Scottish landscape painter typical of the nineteenth century artist, his Highland cattle have a sense of motion as in *The Drovers Road* 1893 which features yellow, red, black, dun cattle.

HENRY GARLAND 1834 – 1913

An English contemporary of similar standard does not achieve the same sense of movement in cattle as for example in his *Highland Drove Passing the Three Sisters Glencoe*. Rather than emphasising space and distance, Garland often brought the mountains close to the viewer, giving them a dominating presence of their own, so that they are not simply a background to animals. A prolific painter of Highland landscapes particularly between 1870 and 1890 he was a frequent visitor to Scotland, and was commercially a very successful artist.

WILLIAM WATSON (JUNIOR) ACTIVE 1866 – 1921

Son of the miniature painter, William Watson (Senior), young Watson studied under the two leading animal painters of the day, Sir Edwin Landseer and Rosa Bonheur. He lived in the north of England until 1914, and exhibited several times at the Liverpool Autumn Exhibition from 1874. At the Royal Academy in 1872 he showed a painting entitled *Highland cattle, Rowardennan Ferry, Loch Lomond*. He also exhibited several times at the Royal Society of British Artists while living in London where he died in 1921. Watson was an inveterate painter of sheep and cattle in the landscape, the Highlands being his favourite location.

The two most accomplished and influential animal painters in nineteenth century Europe were the English Sir Edwin Landseer and the French Rosa Bonheur.

SIR EDWIN LANDSEER: born in 1802, first travelled to Scotland in 1824. That venture included a visit to the novelist Sir Walter Scott at Abbotsford where he painted the great author and his dogs, later painting scenes from Scott's historical novels. Appointed Animal Painter to Her Majesty for Scotland, Landseer stayed frequently at Balmoral, and was a very popular and famous figure in his lifetime.

ROSA BONHEUR: born in Bordeaux in 1822 is one of the greatest animal painters in history, and the most famous woman artist of the nineteenth century. She made studies of animals at horse and cattle fairs and in the abattoirs of Paris, dressing in men's clothing in order to be less conspicuous. Her work emphasises the nobility, grace and strength of labouring animals, against a background filled with the light and clarity of Dutch seventeenth century landscape painting. During a tour of Britain she made many sketches on her journeys, and enjoyed her visit to the Falkirk Tryst so much that she even bought some cattle. More about her tour of Britain can be found in the book by Dore Ashton entitled *Rosa Bonheur. Life and Legend.*

The decoration of fine china made in England at Grainger's and at Worcester involved a particular skill in painting. An English family remarkable for their talent in painting fine china sprang from John Stinton born in 1829.

JOHN STINTON: specialised in landscapes with figures for Grainger's china. Three of his sons became painters and two of his grandsons also.

JOHN STINTON (JUNIOR) born in 1854, died in 1956 aged 102.

He specialised in ordinary cattle subjects, then from 1903 in Highland cattle landscapes, but also did English cattle and old castles and landscapes for plate centres. He ranks as one of the finest Worcester China landscape painters of the twentieth century and must rank among the finest ever of landscape painters on china.

HARRY STINTON 1883 – 1968 was the fourth child of J Stinton (Jnr) and a distinguished student at the National Art School taking several medals in open competition at South Kensington. He studied for many years under his father and did the same Highland cattle scenes although his palette of colours was different, using more purples. His water colours rank highly among English water-colour painters of the twentieth century.

BIBLIOGRAPHY:

STANLEY CURSITER: *Scottish Art at the Close of the 19th Century*, Harrap & Co. London, 1949

MARCUS HALLIWELL: *Highland Landscapes*, Garamond, 1990

JULIAN HALSBY & PAUL HARRIS: *The Dictionary of Scottish Painters 1600 – 1900*, Canongate Press, 1990

WILLIAM HARDIE: *Scottish painting 1837 – 1939*, Studio Vista, 1976

JAMES HOLLOWAY & LINDSAY ERRINGTON: *The Discovery of Scotland*, N. G. S. Edinburgh, 1978

DAVID & FRANCINA IRWIN: *Scottish Painters at Home and Abroad 1700 – 1900*, Faber, 1975

FRANK RINDER: *The Royal Scottish Academy 1826 – 1916*. Maclehose, Glasgow, 1917

CHRISTOPHER WOOD: *A Dictionary of Scottish Painters*. Antique Collectors Club, London, 1978

TWENTIETH CENTURY

By the late twentieth century most of Scotland had been thoroughly besieged by exploring hill walkers, keen photographers, nature lovers, holiday campers, roving television journalists, tourists and settlers of all sorts. The excitement evoked in the nineteenth century by the novelty of the Highland scenes could no longer be a selling point for the artist of the 1950s onwards. But the very scarcity of Highland cattle has made them now a subject worthy of the contemporary artist's attention where in the past they were an unavoidable natural feature of Highland Landscapes, and added a touch of authenticity to the mist-laden glens and mountains when included.

These aesthetically appealing cattle are today most frequently immortalised on canvas by artists who have been commissioned to paint particular livestock in a specific landscape. But the more commissioned work an artist does the less work is available for exhibition. Private exhibitions often reflect the range of the artist's skill on a variety of subjects rather than a collection of paintings popularising rural images as the Victorian painters did. Schools of art are now more concerned with exploring new concepts of imagery, new materials, new boundaries, than with teaching or promoting techniques which capture a realistic and vibrant image of living forms. Nevertheless there are artists to be found who have combined a successful style with an undoubted talent in painting Highland cattle.

EIRENE HUNTER

Internationally known for her animal portraits in natural settings, an artist with years of experience in creating oil paintings of Highland cattle in groups, individually, or in entire folds is Eirene Hunter.

A graduate of the Glasgow School of Art, her lifelong interest in animals flourished into full-time painting of subjects rendered with such accuracy of individual character that she was continuously in demand. Like the successful artists of the nineteenth century she considers that visits to the animal subjects are an important element of her work, and that a fair degree of artistic license was probably exercised then in choice of coat-colour artists gave the Highland cattle in their landscapes. Her reasoning lies in the fact that groups of black cattle are best given vitality and definition on canvas by being juxtaposed with contrasting coat-colours. She produces any size of painting but finds that the most frequently commissioned size for late twentieth century buyers is 18 inches by 24 inches. Occasionally a limited number of prints are made from selected oil paintings, at least one of which features Highland cattle, entitled *Highland Cows and Calves*.

DONALD AYRES

Donald Ayres works equally well with oils or water-colours on subject matter dealing with Scottish landscapes, wildlife and country sports. He favours oils for works which include Highland cattle, often in the foreground of a mountain landscape, and takes care to represent accurately precise horn shape and typical behaviour.

CHRIS DODDS

Chris Dodd's art is rooted in agriculture and landscapes. After formal study at Leeds and Ravensbourne he completed murals for the Forestry Commission, panels for the Scottish Agricultural Museum, Historic Murals for Edinburgh and Stirling Castles and enjoyed the change in scale of work when supplying a commissioned painting of Highland cattle. The work entitled *Highlanders on a Dunbeath Morning* catches streaming sunlight defining the long hairs of the cattle and fine tree branches very early on a crisp autumn morning. A limited run of prints was made of this painting. A love of light and colour is evident in all this artist's work.

SHARON MACDONALD MA

A graduate of Glasgow School of Art, Sharon MacDonald returned to full-time painting after teaching and lecturing for some years. Working in water-colours, oils, or chalk and pastel, she captures a spontaneous moment of nature on seashores or in landscapes. A genuine love of creatures has resulted in an enthusiastic exploration of painting Highland cattle. Examples of her cattle paintings are in Fitzroy Gallery, Oban; Inverbeg Gallery, Loch Lomond and in Stirling Gallery.

CRAFTS

Today there is no major Scottish crafts industry directly dependent on Highland hides or horns because there is neither reliable supply of these raw materials in adequate quantities, nor a sufficient demand for products other than tourist mementos.

Traditional craftsmen made an item firstly for practical purposes then if appropriate decorated the product. Modern craftsmen make an artistic product for sale in the tourist trade and not primarily to serve a practical function. Individual craft workers and even a small company may flourish for a few years using horn to make spoons, comb & brush sets, table lamps, tumblers, brooches, buttons, crook-heads, shoe-horns, key-rings, whistles, hunting horns replicas, knapkin rings, some of which may bear carved designs or decorations with filigree silver. The horn used is likely to be from a variety of sources abroad only supplemented by the occasional few Highland horns.

Highland hides were part of the survival strategy of mankind in bygone times because they were a multi-purpose material of constant availability. The hide of the Highland ox or cow, usually prepared and dressed at home, gave a 'stout unyielding leather' which was used in preparing simple boats, in making leather thonging for many tasks now completed with nylon ropes, to package salted seafowl and salted 'beeves' for storage or transport, to form a door-flap in seventeenth century turf-roofed crofters' houses, to cover the wooden battle shields called targes, to make shoes which were paid by giving a whole hide to the shoemaker, to make purses, pouches, sporrans, knife-sheaths, to make broad drive-belts and bellows for steam-powered machinery, to make saddles and parts of harness, and no doubt for many other purposes. It is said that leather cured at home was done using the roots of tormentil (*Potentilla erecta*) in the process.

There were large tanneries in eighteenth century active ports such as Inverness, Dundee, Stranraer, Kirkcaldy, and cattle sales venues like Crieff and Lanark. The number of hides used per year for the manufacture of shoes in Perth which were then shipped to London is recorded as 'up to 5,000 plus 500 dozen calf skins' but records do not distinguish between Highland hides and those from other breeds of cattle. Scarcity of oak bark for the tannery processing, reduction in the numbers of hides available, and changing market demands destroyed the viability of the tanneries which gradually closed down.

Twentieth century Scottish leather craftsworkers use hides of the correct strength or pliability for the end products, and although the hides may be imported the finished article may carry a Scottish decoration. Targes and sporrans are examples of this type of leather craft.

TARGE: This type of shield carried into battle by seventeenth and eighteenth century Highland clansmen was circular, about 20 inches across, and made of oak wood covered with cow-hide nailed to its surface with brass studs. The studs frequently formed i) a star pattern, ii) a concentric circles pattern, iii) a central panel with four or six surrounding panels pattern. Leather tool work might also add to the decorated effect which was simple in the seventeenth century and more ornate in the eighteenth century. Replicas of targes, designed to be wall decorations, are made by individual craft workers today.

SPORRAN: Sporrans were originally a simple drawstring pouch which attached to the waist belt. "*By about 1700 a clasp top had been introduced, generally of brass and semi-circular in shape. During the nineteenth century, however, the sporran developed into a peculiar, hairy, and tasselled adornment, perhaps the most debased aspect of Highland Dress.*" (M. Brander)

General David Stewart of Garth, Glen Lyon, when writing in 1822 noted that "*the belt which had been used by the Highlanders was of strong thick Ox leather and three or four inches in breadth, fixed by a brass or silver buckle in front. . . but is entirely disused in the Highlands.*" The Victorian revival of the kilt produced absurd hairy sporrans and even more debased tastes in patterned brogues to be worn with it despite the fact that "*if Highlanders wore shoes at all, which was highly unlikely, they were of untanned ox leather.*" (Michael Brander: *Scottish Crafts and Craftsmen*, 1974)

Highland cattle do feature in a range of artistic products from resin figurines, models in fine china and bronze to hand-carved crystal decanters and glasses.

The soft toy market has tried a variety of models but few are very successful because the horns, so characteristic of the breed, are problematical in a number of ways.

The horns also limit the possibilities in fashioning silver jewellery.

There seems no limit however to the range of artistic representations on the ubiquitous linen tea-towel, which can be found in two tone sketch form, multicoloured picture effects, or repeat pattern styles. As with the other articles there is no single convenient source, nor any guarantee that items will be available indefinitely. One finds the crafts persons at major Agricultural Shows and Game-fairs and commissions products.

Clearly Highland cattle have a presence in much of Scottish culture, but like the animals on the open hill, one has to look for them.

LEGEND AND FOLKLORE

THE SUPERNATURAL

Personal accounts, stories and legend interweaving the supernatural with everyday Highland life are to be found in a variety of publications.

The *Inverness Courier* files this story dated 1828 from John Macdonald who was born in 1721: *"Early one morning while looking after his black cattle, he was surprised by the sight of two ladies, as he thought, winding slowly round a hill, and approaching the spot where he stood. When they came up, they enquired for a well or stream where a drink of water could be obtained. He conducted them to the Virgin well, an excellent spring, which was held in great reverence on account of its being the scene of some superstitious and legendary tales. When they had quenched their thirst, one of the ladies rewarded Macdonald with a shilling, the first silver coin of which he was possessed. At their own request he escorted them to a gentleman's house at some distance; and there, to his great surprise and satisfaction, he learned that the two "ladies" were Flora Macdonald and Prince Charles Stewart."*

When lack of fencing and enclosures necessitated twenty-four hour herding of the cattle, fears of the unknown during the long hours of night-watch gave rise to tales of things supernatural. There is a large stone called Cailleach-vear (Old Woman of Thunder) on a ridge of hills separating Stralachlan from Glendaruel with descent from it on every side. *Be ir* is the Gaelic for thunder bolt. It is pronounced Ve-ir as in Beinn-ve'ir...the Mountain of Thunder in Appin. Cailleach-vear was said to have a considerable property in cattle. *"When a storm was accompanied with thunder, it may be easily supposed, that such as were tending herds or flocks around that stone, would be much alarmed, would run off, and leave their charge to the mercy of the person who was supposed to produce the storm. If any of the cattle were amissing, Cailleach-vear was accused of having seized upon them, and no further search was made."* (Statistical Account of Scotland Vol 4.)

Gruagachs were the helpful spirits sometimes called Brownies who looked after the cattle. For these services the dairymaids poured an offering of milk each evening onto a clach-na-gruagach...a large stone some of which had a slight cavity...frequently the pouring was accompanied by the rhyme *"Brownie, Brownie, uphold my herds, keep down the 'Guaigean', keep them from the 'Geige'."* If the offering was forgotten the cows would be found broken loose in the corn in the morning. The Gruagachs seemingly were no match for the power of witches since there was a widely practised habit of placing rowan twigs at the byre doors to help protect the cattle from having milk drawn off for witch benefit. Some milkmaids even tied a rowan twig to the cow's tail, and of course the fetter (buarach) used at milking to tie the hocks to prevent the milk pail being kicked over was best made of stallion hair and a strip of rowan twig. (*Carmina Gadelica*) Without the benefit of insights from twentieth century archaeological research folklore linked the ancient circular stone fortifications known as brochs and duns to fairies, ghosts and spirits. It was thought dangerous to approach brochs at night when a strange green light could be seen emanating from them. The Sithichean (fairies) would capture humans and cattle and take them to the Sithein (brochs) which were thought to be entrances to the fairies' country. The brochs were said to be 'as old as the Sithichean' meaning older than man.

A broch and stone huts excavated by A O Curle on a site near Latheron in Caithness led him to consider that a 40 feet (12 metre) long pillared rectangle had possibly been an unroofed cattle shelter where a fire was lit at one end through the night to scare off predators. Other excavations by F T Wainwright in Angus, which exposed a hookshaped souterrain of over 130 feet (40 metres) long at Carlungie dated around 150 AD, left him also contemplating that it had possibly been a shelter for cattle. (*Prehistoric Scotland* by A MacSween and M Sharp 1989.)

Dun Gharsain, or Ghaisin, is the site of a concentric fort long since destroyed at Tobht Ardair in Bracadale Skye. According to Donald MacCuithean from Fearann-an-lethe, Skye, Dun Gharsain was once a famous fairy bower which was destroyed by a man who took away the stones to build folds for his cattle and sheep. "*A light not of earth was seen where their hall had been and a voice not of man was heard in the air vowing vengeance. But no harm came to the man because he had drunk milk from a cow that had eaten the 'mothan'.*"

Mothan, Gaelic for pearlwort (*Sagina procumbens*), was used as a protective charm. In Glenurquhart and Strathspey it protected possessions as well as the person if cheese had been eaten made from the milk of a cow which had eaten mothan.

A story which queries if fairy-flax is the same thing as mothan tells of a lad who asked a fairy sweet-heart "*What makes calves notch-eared?*" to which the reply was "*Because their mother shuns the fairy-flax.*"

Notch-eared calves were thought to be either the offspring of the mythical water-bull or the Crodh-mara...sea-cows. Those sired by the water-bull had both ears cropped as if the upper part had been cut off then the remaining piece slit from the top edge whereas those descended from the sea-cows could have only one or both so scalloped. Several sea-cows were believed to have come ashore in the Obbe area of Harris and also on the shores of the Loscantire (Luskintyre) area Harris. Crop eared calves were superstitiously regarded as being off fairy cows...Crodh Shith...but descriptions of fairy cattle vary from being the dunn hornless of Harris, the speckled also red of Skye, to all colours mentioned in the following rhyme:

Bo na braighe meanbh-bhric
Blarag (brown-star), *donnag* (brownie or brown one),
Ciarag (dusky), *riabhag* (brindled),
Odhrag (dun), *gris-fhionn* (black and white).
Agus an t-adhan (and no distinctive colour).

(*Carmina Gadelica*)

It is interesting that the grazings at Portree and Scorrybreac, Skye, where much sought after Highland cattle were bred were, according to folklore, favoured by the selective crodh-shith.

Curiously the colour white did not feature in the rhyme. Maybe the omission in that source was in some way connected with the fact that Skye had a famous herd of white cattle which were dispersed to the mainland much as the following fairy prediction indicated.

About the year 1365 the powerful Murdo Macleod of Gesto, Skye, found two of his men who were building him a new byre were destroying the nearby Dun Taimh by taking stones from it. He stopped them, explaining that the dun might yet be needed as a refuge so they should take stones from the shore instead. Murdo had not known that this dun was a Sithein...fairy dwelling...and the fairy-folk not hearing his reason for sparing their walls, seeing only that he had saved them were grateful. The story tells how Murdo was summoned to a tryst with them at a green knoll by the sea. There an old member of the Daoine Sithe explained that since Murdo had built his new byre with *"stones that harmed no-one"* they would fill it. The old man then called out of the sea a herd of fifty perfect snow-white cattle. *"These and theirs"* said he, *"shall serve thee and thine for 500 years."* Then the fairy company vanished and the cows lowing gently made for the new byre.

The Gesto cattle were pure white shaggy Highland cattle, large and with magnificent horns just tipped with black.

"As a child I saw what was, I believe, the last of the pure Gesto bulls left in Skye. It was at Tote. He was a most beautiful creature and had just returned (in a thoroughly bad temper) from a prize winning visit to a mainland Show. But the cows were said to be gentle and exceptionally good milkers for cows of Highland blood. There are none left in Skye today. The last of the pure herd known were in Argyll, I was told, at Barguillian, and there may be some there still, but of course the 500 years are now up!" (*Skye: the Island and its Legends*. Otta F Swire)

Many poems, ballads, and songs from the Gaelic culture make mention of cattle. The next extracts reproduced here offer comment on cattle management, or appearance, or behaviour, or varying attitudes held towards the cattle and those tending, thieving, or butchering them.

Also evident in poem and song is the division of labour in the old pastoral communities. Women and girls do the milking and making of butter and cheese in addition to family care; boys do the herding; men do the main providing from deer hunting and tending crops to protecting family and possessions.

There was an old belief that Highlands with some white in their coats were good milkers to be coveted. Whether this was fact later evident in the Ayrshire dairy breed or a folk belief perpetuated by the descriptive flair of the bards delighting in the sound and imagery of "white speckled" instead of "milk cow" is hard to say. However, many remnants of the oral tradition of the Gael easily predate the Ayrshire Breed by a long time and it is fair to assume references to cattle mean Highland cattle unless otherwise described as for example in *"Give thou thy milk my hummle brown"*. The Hummle was a polled Buchan breed now extinct but thought to have come from Norway.

Stemming perhaps from a later period in history red cows also had the reputation of being generous and reliable milkers.

A story in a Hebridean folksong spreads the idea that red-coated cattle from the south were introduced to northern folds by the far-travelled and educated landowning Highland gentry. The song tells of a man who is thought to be a beggar and is spurned by all until he arrives at the door of the goodwife of Arivullin who *"belonged to the race of gentry who had red cattle in the meadows"* and who kindly attended to his needs. If the song predates the creation of the Beef Shorthorn breed the red cattle referred to probably were Highland cattle.

Another Hebridean song tells that dun cattle were held in high regard: *"though she were rude and quarrelsome, dun cattle will get her a husband."* Whitefooted cattle are mentioned in a song from a widow longing to be back on her home ground although no comparative value of the animals is suggested in *"I was in Lewis of the whitefoot cattle, Tis my own land I like better."* (Above three songs are in John Lorne Campbell's *Hebridean Folksongs* 1969)

SONGS FROM THE MACNEILS OF BARRA

A lady with a gifted musical voice and a rare way with cattle worked for 55 years as the head milkmaid with the MacNeills of Barra famed far and wide for their cattle. When Mary MacNeill, (Mairi Raghaill) wanted to retire General MacNeill asked her to sit at the gateway to the fold watching the calves go in and out. "*The eye of Mary daughter of Ranald is putting lustre and fatness on my calves,*" he was wont to say. It was said that Mary could reduce the crossest cow to giving milk to calf and milkmaid. Few of her substantial number of songs remain, most having died with her or being lost when the people of Barra were scattered over northern Canada but of those collected this one mentions coat-colour in the milk cows: "*Ho my little cow, ho my brown cow! Little cow of my heart, dear, beloved, Jewel of the white cows art thou,*" and "*my little brindled cow, dear, beloved, Safe thou wouldst cross the crest of the peaks.*"

A different MacNeill...Catherine MacNeill of Ceann Tangabhall, Barra, gave a song which is probably much older in origin than that for it tells the story of how a widow appealed to St. Columba for help to feed her children because she would be bereft of income if her heifer continued to refuse to suckle its calf. St. Columba gave the widow a new song to sing called *The Charm of The Wild Heifers* after explaining that his skin book of cattle charms had been stolen.

Verse 1: *My heifer beloved, be not alone,*
Let thy little calf be before thee;
See yon bramble bush a-bending,
And bowing down with brambles.

Verse 3: *Coax thy pretty one to thyself,*
Till thou sendest to the fold a herd.
Columba's tending shall be thine behind them,
He made this lilt for thyself.

Verses condemning the calfless cow follow

Verse 8: *The black heifer is reconciled,*
Thou wilt make lowing to thy pretty one;
Thou wilt come home with droves,
Thou wilt quench the thirst of hundreds.

Last verse: *My little black heifer thou! my little black heifer!*
The same lot is mine and thine.
May the little black calf not be lost to thee;
But mine only son beloved is beneath the sea.

(Both MacNeill songs from those collected in *Carmina Gadelica* by Dr Alexander Carmichael 1900)

BARDS WITH EXPERIENCE OF CATTLE

What Burns is to the Lowlands of Scotland Duncan Ban is to the Highlands, was said of Duncan Ban Macintyre, known posthumously as Duncan Ban Nan Oran – Fair Haired Duncan of the Songs. Born in 1724 Duncan Macintyre was gamekeeper to the Earl of Breadalbane working Coire Cheathaich and Ben Dorain and later to the Duke of Argyll in Glen Etive. Hailed as pure untutored genius Duncan Ban could neither read nor write. He came of an oral tradition and carried, it has been calculated, about 6,000 lines in his memory. He did not particularly feature cattle in his works but they were an integral part of the Nature he described for example as in verse 4 of *My Beauteous Corri where cattle wander*:

In yonder ruin once dwelt Mac Bhaidi,
Tis now a desert where winds are shrill;
Yet the well-shaped brown ox is feeding by it,
Among the stones that bestrew the hill.
And fine to see, both in light and gloaming,

The smooth Clach-Fionn, so still and deep,
And the houseless cattle and calves most peaceful,
Grouped on the brow of the lonely steep.
(from the rendering by Robert Buchanan in *The Hebrid Isles*)

Duncan Ban Nan Oran was buried in Greyfriars Church in Edinburgh. There is also a monument to him on the banks of Loch Awe near Dalmally. (M Maclean)

Robb Donn (alias Mackay or Calder) was famed for his eighteenth century poetry and song although he could neither read nor write. He was born in Sutherland in 1714.

He was a cattleman at Balnaceill for first Lord Reay and then Colonel Hugh Mackay and shows concern in his *Song to Winter* for the suffering of ill fed cattle:

How mournful in winter
The lowing of the kine;
How lean backed they shiver,
How draggled they cower,
How their nostrils run owre
With drippings of brine,
So scraggy and cringing
In the cold frost they pine.

According to John MacInnes, *Oran Nan Drobhairean* – (The Drover's Song), is the only Gaelic composition that expressly celebrates the drover's trade in Highland cattle. There are five known versions collected from the oral tradition, all composed after 1746. Donald Stewart's version is:

"The first skilful young men who are brisk and strong and fleet of foot would not arrive empty-handed when they came to seek the cattle. You were ever expert at walking the moors; you were manly, generous, and cheerful; your skin was bright, your appearance was excellent, you who were the ladies' desire.

When you appeared to collect the cows, before the drought of summer had come upon them, you wore not the lowland dress that curbs the vigour of the leg with its fastenings but the kilt and short hose and the splendid, ample plaid that was ever your emblem, nor would you exchange it for any other habit.

At the beginning of May, when the cattle are on the high ground of the cold mountains, calves in plenty will run about the fold, with young girls herding them. Generous men will be there telling stories – I could call on half a dozen reciters of ancient tales generous women will be there doing good, happily, jovially and affectionately." (K J Bonser)

A twentieth century cattleman flexed his bardic tendencies in the following jaunty verse which tells how difficult it is to abhort the friendship that grows between man and beast.

SEUMUS SOUTH OF THE BORDER
Today Seumas went South o' the Border,
I'm thinkin' that's the last straw,
It's nae that he'll nae like the English,
It's jist sic a lang wie awa'.
I got my picture taen wi' him,
When I went tae say my good-byes,
It's maybe jist me, bit I thocht I could see,
A tear in auld Seumas' eyes.

I promised I'd pay him a visit,
But I didna mean 'twid be the morn,
I'll get a' his news, I'll nae speak tae the coos,
In cae they find oot that he's foreign.

I'll definitely go doon an' see him,
When I promised – I really did mean it,
I'll show him his photo, I think a good lot o',
Aince a'body up here has seen it.

Well, Good Luck tae auld Seumas where-ever he is,
I'm sure he'll keep things in order,
An' ye never ken when we'll see him again,
He could be back this side o' the Border.

SEUMAS THE FAVOURITE BULL

He was the famous Seumas
Everybody's friend
Everybody loved him
From here down to Lands End.

From Australia to New Zealand
From France to Timbuctoo
Even then they didna' ken
Old Seumas frae a coo.

So when he'd done his duty
And Seumas had to go
It fell to me to put him on
The float for Oban Show.

And when I saw him in the ring
On the final day
He looked at me
And he shook his head
And he slowly walked away.

I said "Now look here, Seumas
Dinna act sae queer
It's not ma fault you had to go
Just you blame Finlay Weir".

And anyway, its no so bad
'Cause after all the hassle
I'll still be fit to see you
'Cause you're just going to Glamis Castle.

So when the Queen looks in
To see her mother's hame
She'll say "Hello there, Seumas
I know from where you came. "

And next time I see our Liz
She'll gie me a' your news
And she'll tell me how you've settled doon
Wi' a lovely herd o' coos.

(Doug Shewan on Seumas, the Highland bull)

THE POETRY OF BADENOCH

The following extracts are from *The Poetry of Badenoch* by The Reverend Dr Thomas Sinton published in 1906 by the Northern Counties Publishing Company, Inverness, and now out of print.

There are no titles, only Latin numbers, and no music notation is given. Dr Sinton recognises that much of the impact and subtlety and rhythmic flow of the Gaelic language is lost in translation into English but his book also prints the Gaelic versions in full.

Geographically Badenoch spreads around the upper waters of the River Spey, with Culloden and Moray forming the northern boundary, the Cairngorm mountains the eastern, while in the south Badenoch merges with Rannoch and the Drumalban mountains and in the west with Lochaber. The area is understood among the current local populace although not recognised in political registers as one region, shire, or county. Many of the Badenoch ballads were also common to the neighbouring areas. The Reverend Sinton who grew up in Laggan and in the Parish of Kingussie rescued much from impending oblivion with his publication of "this collection of minstrelsy".

References to Women's Work:

Number IV *You found me a maid of low degree*
As I milked the cows beside the fold.
You smashed the coag and you broke the fetter
And you trained me to act a lady's part.

(Part of a song, in which a girl dreaming of a better life addresses her hero.)

Number XLIII *The wee glen abounding in cuckoos, in which rushes*
and mountain down will grow.
There cattle will be found in folds, and fair maidens
tending the new-born calves, and blowing upon
them with their breath.

(Part of the song, number XLIII, of a jilted girl singing from the hillside to the man she still loves as he journeys within earshot.)

Further on in this ballad mention is made of *"dark-grey cows coming up from the foot of Rannoch."* Several farms breeding quality Highland cattle lay in Rannoch, Perthshire; for example Camusericht, and the bard's words suggest that dun Highlands came from Rannoch.

Less typical behaviour from the women is told in the legend related to T. Sinton by the great-grand-daughter of one of the participants.

"Griatach and Caitriona – two young wives – were alone at the sheilings near the head of Loch Pattock, a remote pasture, which now forms part of the great Forest of Ben-Alder. At the dead of night they heard the cattle lowing, and knew that the men of Lochaber had made a foray, and were now in the act of carrying off their cherished fold.

"O! what shall we do?" said Catriona
("O! ciod e ni sinn?" thubhairt Caitriona.)
"We shall do to take them from them, " replied Grace.
("Ni, an toirt bhuapa!" fhreagair Griatach.)

Acting under the directions of this Amazon, they hurriedly took shafts of the churns, and fastening to them every metallic article within reach, the two lone women sallied forth thus armed, and commenced the pursuit of the despoilers. Griatach had a loud, gruff voice, with which she commenced to whoop and haloo in imitation of a body of men, while Caitriona was content to supply the more shrill notes which the women of the sheiling might be expected to contribute to the uproar. They soon overtook the cow-lifters, and the cattle, recognising through every disguise the voices of their mistresses, broke off in all directions. Meanwhile the Lochaber men, finding it impossible to retain their booty in the darkness, and hearing, as they supposed, the voices of enraged pursuers and the clangour of arms, concluded that they had fallen into an ambush, and were fain to beat a retreat for home."

These cattle were in their mountain pastures for the summer months where the temporary dwellings called sheilings housed those tending them. Close to the sheiling was the fold. The cows were milked beside the fold where many a song was crooned. Apart from entertaining or soothing any babies at the sheilings no doubt there were some songs which seemed to achieve a fuller pail (Coag or coggie, see p11) than others. Although Highland cattle are not the only breed to respond favourably to voice music at the milking there is some merit in the belief that they enjoy music and can recognise certain airs.

My mother's story comes to mind here of how she, from a Kingussie family of strictly regular church attenders, found it amusing that her father's dairymaid sang a solemn hymn with great gusto every evening as she milked the cows, capped head buried into their flanks:

"Lord, a little band and lowly
We are come to sing to thee;
Thou art great and high and holy;
O how solemn we should be!"

Rhythmically accentuated by the percussion effect of spurts of milk jetting into the pail the hymn sounded out...

Spurt a **Spurt**-lle **Spurt** and **Spurt**-ly,
Spurt are **Spurt** to **Spurt** to **Spurt** and so on.

The dairymaid's choice of song remains alas a mystery.

Sheiling Songs: (From *The Poetry of Badenoch*)

The following are sheiling songs from Badenoch which make particular mention of cattle:

Number XV *A silken fetter,*
A silken fetter,
A silken fetter's on my heifer dear.

When ropes of straw
Tie the township cattle,
A silken fetter's on my heifer dear.

Whenas there's straw
On the crofters' cattle,
A silken fetter's on my heifer dear.

When Winter comes,
And the straw is scanty,
The crofters' cattle will not rear their young.

But though my barn
Might of sheaves be empty,
I'd raise the foam on my milking coag,

When I shall go
With my lot of heifers,
Ere dawn of day to the Narrow Sheiling-ground;

How big my cheese,
And my churn how heavy,
How broad and yellow is my lot of calves!

Number XVI *My pet of cows is the white-shouldered,*
Nor is the white-head a cow of less worth;
The blessing of a milk-maid and herd-boy, -
Thou wouldst not be troublesome in tending!

Full well is known to me thy mother -
Grey One's daughter, Spottie's grandchild:
*For me how oft hast thou filled a lippie stoup!**
Nor in my darling would there be failing.
* A wooden vessel

Number XIV

The sheiling days were a happy change for some but others felt the pain of an unwelcome separation from dear ones.

Driving the steers, I'm sad at heart,
Driving the steers, and tired;
Driving the steers, I'm sad at heart,
Taking the way alone.

Number XVIII

This ballad is included in full because it is more widely known among English speakers probably than any other sheiling song. Here is an authentic version taken down from a live rendering of Colin's Cattle – *Crodh Chailein* – as it was sung throughout Badenoch, Strathspey, and Braemar in the eighteenth and nineteenth centuries.

"The maiden who composed these verses, is said to have engaged as dairymaid with an elderly couple, whom she accompanied to the sheilings. A son of her employer fell in love with her, and this romantic attachment gave occasion to the song. According to this tradition, Cailean was the name of the girl's master." (Sinton)

Bayley & Ferguson

The music for Chrodh Chailein is given in an extract from *The St. Columba Collection of Gaelic Songs* published by Bayley & Ferguson. The page is reproduced by courtesy of the current copyright holders, Bayley & Ferguson, Glasgow.

Kine of Colin, kine of Colin,
Kine of Colin, my dear;
Brindled mottled and spotted -
Of the heather-fowl's hue.

The lass hath no sweetheart,
And the lad hath no wife;
And the fetter and milk-coag
Are lost on the hill.

The carline is deaf,
The carl's blind of an eye;
They can't see to milk the cattle,
For the grey mist of the rocks.

Colin's kine are my fondlings,
They'll give milk on the heath,
On the top of the mountain,
With nobody near.

On the top of the mountain ,
With nobody near,
With a coag, and no fetter,
No tulchan, nor calf.

The cow of the mistress
Is broad and dark grey, -
A cow to fill milk-coag -
A cow to rear calves.

There's not the match of my cow
In the byre of the King;
Her low's heard in Dunedin,
While herself's in Glenlui.

When evening would come,
And the calves get their milk,
My love will come home
After slaying the deer.

In despite of the keeper,
And though he'd go mad,
I shall be with my love,
In the wee glen of the deer.

Going up through Glen Ei,
And coming in by Glen Dee;
From wee glen to wee glen,
Still pursuing the deer.

From wee glen to wee glen,
Still pursuing the deer;
Where will slumber the hinds,
And the fawns by their side.

There's not the venison I long for,
In Glenshee or Glen Dee;
Nor yet in Glen Tay,
Or the Rough Corries of Dee.

I'll go not to the Birch-clump,
Nor in quest of the calves;
The man with fine checkered plaid,
On the heath waits for me.

Number LXXVII

A criticism of a croft on very poor soil. Verse 1:

"The Wee Field of Whortles! It has scattered my family. It has put my meeting farther than is my way. The white steer has gone, and the black steer has gone. They have all gone since the food came to an end. Wee Field of Ill Fortune! –That I should ever have seen it! The Wee Field of Whortles, – it has gone against me." (Sinton)

Number CXLVI is a powerful lament. Sinton introduced the ballad thus:

"About seven score years ago, the cattle belonging to Captain John Macpherson, tacksman of Blaragie, being let loose on a sunny day in early spring, became frantic with delight at their novel and unexpectedly acquired freedom, and betook themselves to the hills, heedless of consequences. The herd – a young man named Macdonald – followed them as far as Drumochter. While he traversed that bleak and solitary tract which extends between Dalwhinnie and Dalnacardoch, the weather, proverbially fickle at that season, suddenly and terribly changed. A blinding snow-storm set in, and the unfortunate lad never more found his way home. Among those who set out in quest of the lost herd was his true-love. When the body was found in a well, the famished deer were stripping the willow branches overhead. What a wild wail of heart-grief resounds through these verses! The late Principal Shairp of St. Andrews greatly admired this ballad, and an English version from his pen will be found in Glen Desseray and other Poems edited by Mr Francis T. Palgrave. But the text has been collected in snatches from the recitation of a dozen persons and the text I supplied to the Principal was more fragmentary than that given here." (Sinton)

The unelaborated style gives strength to the lines of this moving ballad which came into being because skittish heifers and freak weather conditions combined in a way that shocked the community. It clearly records that when of a mind Highland cattle in the eighteenth century easily travelled upwards of 15 miles in flight even in a frail condition after the winter.

The cattle are only mentioned twice in this thirty-three verse ballad sung by the lost herd's true love.

My heart is as broken
As the fluttering of a little bird;
And my heart is so hurt,
That it will not bear the cotton.
Many an eye was showering,
Between Rannoch and Drumochter.
The Day of Bride's Fair in Spring time
The heifers went in elation.
And I am weary with wandering
The dark hill-side of Drumochter.
Though the heifers were gotten,
The herdsman could not be found

Another story found by Sinton suggests that heifers racing off was not an unusual occurrence in former times. But the fate that befell the careering heifers of Crathie, Laggan, remains unexplained.

"Long ago the cattle belonging to the crofters of Crathie, when away at their summer pasturage were lost in a strange manner. One day they suddenly broke loose from all control, and entered upon that wild race, called in Gaelic dol air theas (going on heat). Up the sloping ridges of the mountains they careered, until they reached the summit of a gorge which overlooks Loch laggan and is named Slugan Coir'nan Gall...The Gullet

of the Strangers' Corrie. Over its cliffs the whole herd wildly plunged, and for many years afterwards, their bones mingled with rocky debris below." (Sinton)

Number LX

Margaret Cameron's song of compliment to Alexander Macdonald, Garvamore, mid-eighteenth century on receiving the gift of a mart includes:

"I went a journey to the fair, and my purse was not according to my desire; but there met me right handsome gentlemen, and they gave me fine assistance in my need.

Young Alister of the beautiful hair, from Garvamore in Badenoch:

Long to thee to be healthy and whole! thou didst make me a gift in the goodly steer.

Thou madest me a gift in the dusky black steer that was lengthy, portly, and well-bred; on which there were two stones of fat, – and for his hide I got a guinea. etc." (Sinton)

Number CXXIV

"And if I be alive for five years, I shall yet see evil retribution on the people who cut the hides off the cattle;

On the folks of red long coats, and on the Argyle Militia,

Ye will yet see an evil condition on the brutes." (Sinton)

These lines, refer to vicious acts of reprisal perpetrated on any cattle the victors found after the Scots were defeated in their last armed uprising against English rule.

The Supernatural:

An unsettling experience in the sheiling of Ruighe near Gaick was recounted to Sinton by one of the children who was present.

"Early in 1799 the winter fodder ran short and the crofter's wife had to take the cattle to the sheiling earlier than usual. When there one of the cows calved. Its strength was failing so badly that the good-wife sent their maid running back to the strath with a key to fetch two sheaves of barley prudently hidden in the cheese press in the barn. This "toothsome morsel" brought back promptly by the speedy Annack saved the cow's life. Later that year Annack's fleet-footedness brought protection to the family in the sheiling. One dark Autumn night Annack, her mistress and family were very alarmed by a terrible confusion of noise outside the sheiling as if it were surrounded by a menacing crowd. When at dawn they ventured to look out there was no trace of the nocturnal visitants. The woman sent Annack to fetch her husband who had to spend every night for the remainder of that season with his family at Ruighe leaving to work in the strath during the day." (Sinton)

Towards the end of that year around Christmastime Captain J Macpherson "The Black Officer" and his hunting party perished in Gaick not far from Ruighe in circumstances attributed to evil forces.

"Captain J Macpherson was an able farmer applying new agricultural techniques successfully in advance of many in Badenoch on his farm of Ballachroan between Newtonmore and Kingussie. His ability to ensnare young men into the armed forces supporting the English king earned him a mean reputation and local rumour spread that he was in league with the devil." (Puck Ross, Crofter, Newtonmore 1995)

The Gaelic fairy folk were mostly thought of as thieving elfin peoples who inhabited green knowes. They could be vindictive and mischief-making and were best avoided if possible.

A fearless hill herd near Newtonmore dealt with his encounter with the wee folk this way:

"Farquhar had searched for his goats in the MonadhLiadhs all day until past sundown. Then he heard low sweet sounds of song. Not far away was a fairy milking deer. Impulsively he let fly an arrow

at this vision. It hit the milk cog, which was of course under the left side of the deer since fairies milk on the sinister side of animals, causing the fairy to call out "Thanks to thee, Farquhar! Clever thy shot. Thine be the fetter, the milk-cog, and milking."

(Tapadh leat, Fhearchair! 'S tapaidh d'urchair, 's leat fhein a'bhuarach, 's do ghogan, 's do bhleoghann.) Farquhar understood the fairy had acknowledged herself to be vanquished – an important point in such encounters – so before he allowed her depart he extracted a promise that she would grant him his first three desires. His first was wealth. Presenting him with the milk cog the fairy promised that as long as a stave of it remained in the possession of his family no evil influence could affect their cattle. Then she directed him to where his goats were."

That concludes the extracts from the *Poetry of Badenoch.*

RITUAL

As the commercial importance of cattle in the Highlands waned so too did the relevance of ceremonies and rituals connected with them.

The fire festivals of Beltane, 1st May, when livestock went to high summer pastures, and Samhain, 1st November, when they returned were observed longest in Lewis, but by the twentieth century had died out completely.

The custom at Beltane was for the community to extinguish all hearth fires and lights then rekindle them with flames from a hill-top bonfire which itself had been lit from flames made by friction of a stick on dry wood using agaric from birch trees to flame sparks. The precise ritual varied across Scotland but in many areas the cattle were driven sunwards around the bonfire to keep them healthy all year. Most areas also prepared an oatmeal based cake, Beltane Bannock, for ritualistic consumption.

The Need-fire ceremony was a ritual performed usually to remedy an outbreak of cattle disease. A bonfire was made as for Beltane but the burning ashes were spread a bit to allow driving the cattle through the smouldering ash, smoke and flames several times. Sometimes the cattle were badly scorched and died from the procedure.

THE CAIRN OF THE HEATHER COW

One heap among several tumuli to the west of a church near Bower in Caithness was mentioned in the late eighteenth century as being *"surrounded by 6 or 7 circles, described at different distances around by large stones set on edge, and seems to be some monument of Druidical antiquity."* (Rev W Smith) It was called The Cairn of The Heather Cow. Enquiries pursued in 1995 by Mr Derek Douglas, Bowermadden, revealed that there are now no stone circles to be seen, that the cairn was thought to have been excavated in the late 1800s, and most interestingly that the name derives from the Norse for the top of the height...**Haethar-Kollr**... nothing to do with cows!

BULL-BAITING

Bull-baiting was a ritualistic sport in the Middle Ages when butchers in England could actually be convicted for omitting to beat the bull. The idea then was that the meat was indigestible and unwholesome unless the bull had been baited and beaten. The practice of bull-baiting was widespread in the south of England, almost unknown in the north of England and virtually unknown in Scotland judging from the difficulty in finding printed information on the subject. There is however a Bull Stone on the village green at Leslie in

Ian Cochrane

Fife. Bull fights and games of skill at an annual Festival there were held until around 1800. Bulls chained to the solid upright stone were attacked in a variety of ways until they died or were killed. The repetition of this process is thought to have worn the deep grooves in the stone that give it a waist. But Fife County folklore literature is silent on what breed of bull was most commonly baited.

HOGMANAY

A ceremony performed on the last day of the year, Hogmanay, derives from the combination of the importance of cattle and the level of superstition in past times. It has lingered on in Scotland in a modified form where preparations are made on the last day of the year for celebrations to commence the minute the new day of the next year begins. The custom of lively parties involving visits to several homes in succession sometimes until dawn, stems from the original ritual which is recorded as follows.

A man dressed in cow-hide visited each house in the community while his followers beat his hide with a staff to which a bit of raw hide was attached. He ran three times sunwards around the house with followers chasing him and beating both the hide and the walls of the house, accompanied by vocal whoops and shouts. Clearly Hogmanay was never a silent affair. When admitted to the house one of the group said *"May God bless the house and all that belongs to it, cattle, stones, and timber! In plenty of meat of bed and body clothes, and health of men may it ever abound!"* Then each stave holder singed the raw hide strip in the hearth fire and applied it to the nose of every person and domestic animal belonging to that house to protect them from disease, witchcraft, and misfortune in the coming year. (*The Golden Bough*, Sir James Frazer, 1890.)

DOUKING AT HALLOWE'EN

A rather slight connection with Highland cattle is to be found in the old apple rite performed since Druid times at Hallowe'en.

Hallowe'en celebrations are still fairly widely practised and generally include apple-douking. The ancient Druidical ritual required cow hair in a ring around a small wooden cross which formed the stirring end of a frothing stick.

First the Druid stirred the water in the tub of apples for each douker whose task was to retrieve an apple by biting into it without any help from hands. After the douking a piper appeared followed by two old women with a churn filled with fresh cream. They whipped the cream with the frothing stick mixing in toasted oatmeal and charms. The doukers then took a spoonful, hoping of course to find a charm. (*The Silver Bough (Vol 1), Scottish Folklore and Folk Belief,* F. M. McNeill)

Mashed potato replaces cream in the twentieth century practice, no frothing stick is necessary and no pipers or Druids turn up.

CATTLE RAIDS

Folklore, ritual, and fact blend in the history of organised cattle stealing in Scotland. A complex moral structure existed concerning whose cattle were 'fair game' to "lift" or steal, and whose ground they could be driven over safely. Breaking the codes of conduct was despised and successful thieving of large numbers of cattle from over 100 miles away held in great regard.

The Gaelic people believed that they, the people, owned the land under a patriarchal administration and that possession was maintained by use of the sword when or if necessary.

When the King gifted lands of Urquhart to the Strathspey Grants the clans who regarded the land as theirs and not for any King to give away raided in 1545 taking amongst a great deal else 1188 great cattle, 392 young cattle, and 525 calves. (J A Symon)

"They are formidable fellows...they are all gentlemen, will take affront from no man, and insolent to the last degree." (D S MacLagan)

Cattle raiders were called Ketherani in the fourteenth century, Cateran by the seventeenth century, and Reivers in the southern and borders territories by the eighteenth century. The term thief was offensive to the Highland raiders as Captain Edward Burt's notes show. He wrote that the morality of cattle-lifting was a vexed question and quoted a Highlander charged with stealing cattle as saying most indignantly

"Common tief! common tief! Steal ane cow, twa cow dat be common tief. Lift a hundred cow, dat be shentilman drovers." (R H Coates)

"William Bane Macpherson when a twelve year old herd boy in 1689 saw a creagh and pursuit on a large scale passing through Badenoch. (creagh = a drove of stolen cattle) On inquiry the lad found out that this herd of about 72 head of black cattle driven by a dozen wild Lochaber men had been lifted more than a hundred miles away in Aberdeenshire and had travelled to within a day's journey from home without any pursuit or attack. A few hours after the Lochaber bound creagh had gone, a well mounted and armed troop of about fifty horsemen appeared. With them were a number of horses carrying bags of meal and other provisions intended as a ransom in exchange for the creagh. The courteous gentlemanly leader signalled William Bane to approach and "minutely questioned" him about the Lochaber men, then the troop set off in pursuit of the cattle accompanied by young William Bane who was keen to see the result of the meeting. It bespoke spirit and resolution in those strangers to seek an encounter with the robbers in their native wilds, and on the borders of that country, where a signal of alarm would have raised a numerous body of hardy Lochaber men, ready to defend the creagh, and punish the pursuers. Towards nightfall, they drew near the encampment of the thieves at Dalunchart, and observed them busily engaged in roasting, before a large fire, one of the beeves, newly slaughtered.

A council of war was immediately held, and, on the suggestion of the leader, a flag of truce was forwarded to the Lochaber men, with an offer to each of a bag of meal and a pair of shoes, in ransom for the herd of cattle. This offer, being viewed as a proof of cowardice and fear, was contemptuously rejected, and a reply sent, to the effect that the cattle, driven so far and with so much trouble, would not be surrendered. Having gathered in the herd, both parties prepared for action. The overwhelming number of the pursuers soon mastered their opponents. Successive discharges of firearms brought the greater number of the Lochaber men to the ground, and in a brief period only three remained unhurt, and escaped to tell the sad tale to their countrymen." (*Inverness Courier*)

Alan nan Creach – Alan of the Cattle Raids – is supposed to have made a raid for every year of his life and three for each of the quarters of a year he was in his mother's womb.

Mac Iain Ghiarr – Short MacIain – was among those who refused to submit to the Earl of Argyll in 1600 or so when their land was taken. Legend tells that they seized an English ship, set up as pirates and carried out cattle raids by sea. (Reader's Digest)

Rob Roy MacGregor was an honest and well trusted agent in cattle dealing for various landlords until his wife was nastily evicted from her home in a cowardly attack by one of them, the Duke of Montrose, in Rob's absence. Rob's instant revenge was to collect Montrose's rents but never pass them on – behaviour that earned him the Robin Hood image of the honourable man who 'robbed the rich to pay the poor'.

The MacGregor clan were, however, notorious for their fierceness and skill in cattle lifting. The Gregor and Chattan Clansmen are thought to have lifted 2,700 cattle from Glen Shee and Glen Isla, and 600 cattle, 800 sheep, and 200 horses from the Colquhouns in the one year of 1602.

ROB ROY, BLACKMAIL, AND THE BLACK WATCH.

Rob Roy himself had such control over many raiders in the shires of Argyll, Stirling, and Perth, that he could guarantee the return of cattle stolen from his customers. His fees for the return of cattle and for their protection developed into a protection racket which became known as **Blackmail**. Some say the word derives from the procedure of being forced to pay with bags of 'meal' for the protection of their black cattle.

In 1724 the government in the reign of William and Mary formed an armed watch to end the cattle raiding exploits throughout Scotland. Six companies of clansmen loyal to the British government were formed and the dark uniform they wore for their duties which often involved night work became known as the Black Watch Tartan. Once enlisted in this regiment being paid by the government the clansmen found they were being posted abroad to fight as soldiers in wars far removed from the well-understood activities of lifting and moving Highland cattle and dealing with the Cateran.

The Black Watch Tartan, known worldwide, is clearly a cultural connection with the native cattle and folklore of Scotland.

REFERENCES

Inverness Courier 1847 (printed in the Domestic Annals of Scotland volume III)

Statistical Account of Scotland Vol 4

Dr. Alexander Carmichael, *Carmina Gadelica*

A MacSween & M Sharp, *Prehistoric Scotland,* 1989

O F Swire, *Skye:The Island and its Legends*

J Lorne Campbell, *Hebridean Folksongs,* 1969

Magnus Maclean, *Literature of the Highlands,* 1903

K J Bonser, *The Drovers* 1970

Sir James Frazer, *The Golden Bough,* 1890

F M McNeill, *The Silver Bough (Vol 1) Scottish Folklore and Folk Belief,* 1957

J A Symon, *Scottish Farming*

D S MacLagan, article in the *Transactions of the Highland and Agricultural Society of Scotland,* Vol II 6th Series

R H Coates, *Travellers Tales of Scotland,* 1913

Readers Digest Association Ltd., *Folklore Myths and Legend of Great Britain*

CHAPTER 10:
HIGHLAND CATTLE SOCIETY PUBLICATIONS

CHAPTER 10: HIGHLAND CATTLE SOCIETY PUBLICATIONS

MINUTE OF THE INAUGURAL MEETING IN 1884

Minute of Meeting of Gentlemen interested in the Formation of a Highland Cattle Society and Herd Book, held in the Highland and Agricultural Society's Show Yard, at Edinburgh, on the 24th July, 1884.

On the motion of The Mackintosh of Mackintosh, The Right Honourable the Earl of Dunmore was called to the chair.

The Chairman, in opening the proceedings, thanked the gentlemen present for responding to the Circular he had issued, inviting them to meet him on the present date, to discuss this question, viz., the necessity of establishing a Highland Cattle Society and a Herd Book.

He was very glad to see so large and influential a gathering of gentlemen present, representing, as they did, some of the great Highland Folds, and he also was able to state that the following noblemen and gentlemen, although unable to be present, had given their adhesion to this scheme by letter, viz., Mr J Anderson, Killin; Mr Anderson of Lochdhu; The Duke of Atholl; Mr Baillie of Dochfour; Mr Balfour of Strathconon; The Earl of Breadalbane; Cameron of Lochiel; The Earl of Cawdor; Sir W Gordon Cumming; Mr J Duncan, Benmore; The Earl of Kintore; Lord Lovat; Mr Malcolm of Poltalloch; Mr Osgood H Mackenzie of Inverewe; Sir Alexander Muir Mackenzie of Delvine; Mr W D Mackenzie of Glen Kyllachy; Mr Mackintosh of Kyllachy; Mr Macgillivray, Ballachroan [*sic*]; Mr Marshall of Callander; Mr A Macgregor, Glenlyon; Mr A Macgillivray, Kingussie; Mr Robertson Greshornish; Mr Robertson, Achilty; Mr P Russell, Warroch; Mr Rollor, Baadhead; Mr Stewart, Bochastle; Mr John Smith, Inverallan.

The Chairman then adverted to the fact that, although there were Herd Books for Shorthorn, Hereford, Polled Angus, Galloway, Ayrshire, and Jersey Cattle, yet their own most beautiful breed, the Highland Breed of Cattle, had no Herd Book. The time had now come to remedy this, and he considered that the names which had already been sent in as favourable to the formation of a Society were sufficient to guarantee success in the launching of the scheme, and feeling as he did that this movement would be of the greatest benefit to all breeders of Highland cattle all over the Highlands of Scotland, he begged to move the following resolution:-

"That a Society should be formed, to be called 'The Highland Cattle Society of Scotland,' the object of which shall be to maintain the purity of the breed known as Highland cattle, and to establish a Herd Book in which to register their pedigrees."

This motion was seconded by Mr Stewart of Ensay, and carried unanimously.

Mr Campbell of Kilberry then moved, "That in order to provide funds for the launching of the said Society on a solid basis, all subscribers of Ten Guineas shall be duly registered as life members, and shall be entitled to every issue of the Herd Book, free of cost, and that the annual subscription for other than life members be 10s. per annum, but members might compound by paying down ten guineas, which would entitle them to the same privileges as life members." This was seconded by Mr Carnegie of Stronvar, who testified to the great advantages that would accrue to Breeders by being enabled, by the establishment of a Herd Book, to register the pedigrees of their cattle, and thus enhance the value of their stock.

Mr Hardie, Lochaline, seconded by Mr Cameron, Mossfield, moved, as a modification, that tenant farmers should only pay five guineas, one half down, and the other half in two years, and the motion, as modified, was carried unanimously.

The following gentlemen who were present then intimated their intention of becoming life members:- Allan, Robert, Glenmore; Baird, John, Knoydart; Brydone, T, Luskentyre, Harris; Campbell, John, Shinness, Sutherland; Campbell, Donald, Mossfield, Oban; Campbell, James, Ormaig; Campbell, John, Kilberry; Campbell, Hector A, Island of Coll; Carnegie, David, Stronvar; Carnegie, James, Aytoun Hill, Fife; Dunmore, Earl of Harris; Forbes, Duncan, Culloden; Hardie, J, Lochaline; Macdonald, Alexander, Balranald, N. Uist; Macdonald, Donald, Tormore, Skye; Macdonald, James, Vallay, N. Uist; Macdonald, Allan, Waternish, Skye; McDiarmid, Duncan, Camusericht, Rannoch; McDiarmid, D A, Killiemore, Mull; Macdougall, J, Ardsheal; The Mackintosh of Mackintosh; Mackenzie, N B, Fort William; Malcolm, John, Poltalloch; Malcolm, J Wingfield, Poltalloch; Malcolm, W Maitland, Auchnacraig, Mull; Martin, W J B, Ri Cruin; Maclellan, Keith, Melfort; Mackenzie, Allan R, yr, Kintail; Middleton, Lord, Applecross; Murray, C J, Lochcarron; Moray, Colonel H Drummond, Blair, Drummond; McGillivray, John, Ballachroan, Kingussie; Reid, Robertson F, Biallid, Kingussie; Shankland, William, Achnacrosh, Lismore; Southesk, Earl of, Kinnaird Castle, Brechin; Stephens, H C, Avenue House, Finchley; Stewart, John, Ensay, Harris; Wood, Herbert, Raasay.

The Mackintosh of Mackintosh then moved that a President, a Vice-President, and an Editing Committee be appointed, and that the first President be the Duke of Atholl, the first Vice-President Mr Malcolm of Poltalloch, and that Lord Dunmore be Chairman of an Editing Committee representing the various Highland Counties to be selected by the present meeting. The following gentlemen were then unanimously nominated as members of the Editing Committee, viz.:

For Inverness-shire – Mainland District – Mr John Macgillivray, Ballachroan. For Skye and Long Island District – Mr Stewart, Ensay. For Perthshire – Mr Duncan McDiarmid, Camusericht. For Argyllshire – Mr Martin, Factor for Poltalloch. For Mull District – Mr W M Malcolm, Auchnacraig. For Ross-shire – Mr Mackenzie, yr. of Kintail. For Sutherlandshire – Mr Campbell, Shinness.

This motion was seconded by the Earl of Southesk, who remarked that foreign purchasers, especially Americans and Canadians, would not look at an animal unless it had a registered pedigree, and that he looked forward to the time when this splendid breed of cattle would take their proper place and command large prices; but that this could never be until a Highland Herd Book was firmly established.

The Chairman, in acknowledging a vote of thanks, congratulated the meeting on the success which had attended its initiation. He stated that they had now formed themselves into a Society, and that with the membership already intimated they would have money enough to start the first volume of the Herd Book, for the preparation of which he would take the necessary steps forthwith.

TITLES OF HIGHLAND CATTLE SOCIETY PUBLICATIONS

Herd Book – ongoing since 1885. Issued to members registering cattle. Back numbers out of print.

Preserving a Noble Breed. Highland Cattle by James Cameron. Issued by the Highland Cattle Society in 1929. Out of Print

Highland Hardiness for Profit – 1946. Out of Print

The Highlander for Thrift and Profit – *circa* 1955. Out of Print

Highland Cattle Today And Yesterday by A McKenzie. Issued by the Society – circa 1950s. Out of Print

Highland Cattle For Hardiness Thrift And Profit – 1975. Out of Print

Highland Breeders' Journal – ongoing from 1961

Newsletters – issued for members since 1983

The Breed That's Not Just A Pretty Picture – Highland Cattle Society Video prepared for the British Food and Farming Year Show in Hyde Park.

Societies have been formed in several countries where Highland cattle are bred and many publish their own magazines, information letters, and instructive videos.

SELECTED ARTICLES FROM HCS PUBLICATIONS*

NOTES FROM JAMES CAMERON IN *PRESERVING A NOBLE BREED*

In 1929 the Highland Cattle Society of Scotland issued a ten page pamphlet written by James Cameron entitled *Preserving a Noble Old Breed – Highland Cattle.*

It contains information under five headings – Historic Survey, Points of the Breed, Temperament and Feeding, Great Improvers, General Notes, and includes a black and white photograph of the 1927 Highland & Agricultural Show Champion An-t-Uramach of Errol and the 1928 Champion at the same Show, Corrina of Southesk.

Salient points made are:

1) Historic Survey

All Highland cattle *"had uniformity of character"* although the mainland stock tended to be bigger framed and more given to variation in colour. *"Until two generations ago the Hebridean stock, which had not been crossed with mainland blood ran largely to black, with some brindles and browns as variations."*

Thomas Bates in England conducted Shorthorn-Highland crossing experiments for about 25 years. He had selected the Highland Breed because it was *"old, fixed in type, and admirably balanced in frame"*, because he admired the breed's *"long hind-quarters and formation of hind leg"* and because he found the breed *"useful in milk production."*

There was a belief in Glenlyon, Perthshire that before 1700 *"a race of white Highland cattle flourished"* there. The nineteenth century Glenlyon cattle included the Dubh Chiar strain blacks with white hair running through their coat, the white bellied Targeal strain, and the Chaisin strain with white heels often accompanied by white tail, but their origins could not be traced. In 1929 a little white on female animals was tolerated but disliked in males; brown "donn" was not officially recognised for registration and reds, yellows, silver duns were very popular for policy parks.

* Reproduced here by kind permission of the Society

2) **Points of the Breed**

At one time bulls were a bit loose-skinned "throaty" at the neck but that fault was more or less bred out. *"In some instances the long quarters which Bates admired have not been maintained and the hind legs are not quite as straight and as broad across the hock joints as they were in the old Taymouth days"* however the general standard has been well maintained, and some advance made in early maturity. There is a generous amount of bone and good sized durable feet in stock of today.

Dock ears are not of any consequence from a practical man's view. They have been seen in the breed for long generations no doubt perpetuated by inbreeding, and are being bred out these days by the use of full eared bulls. Dock ears look as if *"they had been cut across by a ragged set of shears."*

3) **Temperament and Feeding**

"The young Highland bull takes to halter training very easily. No male animal of the cattle kind is so quietly sensible, and the gentle turn is carried on into maturity."

Cows are more suspicious of strangers than bulls but if started young accept a halter well.

Calves born on the hillside can remain timid or flighty in management – calving in byres or boxes avoids this feature.

"Temper and temperament are strongly hereditary" so if possible do not breed from cows of dubious nature.

4) **Great Improvers**

Among the greatest of the improvers of the breed are:

The Stewarts of Ensay and Bochastle, formerly Glenlyon men; the "Old Marquis" of Breadalbane; Mr Charles Stewart, Chesthill; the Dukes of Atholl; Mr John Malcolm of Poltalloch; the ninth Earl of Southesk who *"took to the breeding of Highland cattle during the late 1880s"* after successes in the Aberdeen Angus sphere.

5) **General Notes**

With regard to feeding and breeding animals for summer Shows it is essential to use clean ground, preferably clovery rotation pasture; bran and bruised oats with a little bruised barley and bean meal occasionally are useful condensed foods; give a few turnips as appetisers in winter and spring. The older generation of herdsmen *"made sparing use of linseed cake,"* and found a spoonful of sulphur in mash now and then helped growth of hair.

The Earl of Home and Mr Hugh Morrison of Islay are prominent upholders of the Shorthorn cross.

Highland cattle have been exported to Russia, Canada, the Western States of America, Newfoundland, Argentina, and the Falkland Islands.

In the West Highlands there are still some very good pure-bred females which have not been registered.

PRACTICAL COMMENTS FROM THE JOURNALS

Presented here is a selection of extracts from various articles in The Highland Breeders Journals 1961 – 1990. The points mentioned are personal opinions printed by the Society but not necessarily in line with its views.

1961 in UK: under production of beef and over production of milk.

Requirements of the beef trade are so irregular at present there must be many commercial beef producers wondering what type of animal he should go for.

Beef production requires long-term policy which must aim at giving the public what they want and the first thing they must be given if their custom is to be retained is flavour. This is conspicuous by its absence in too much beef today, and this absence of flavour is often due to immaturity of the animal when slaughtered or lack of marling in the flesh. Marling is the interspersing of small quantities of fat with the lean in the carcase and this produces the best flavoured and most tender meat. (A J K Laing)

The Highland breed suffers from too many enthusiasts and too few practical breeders (A Buchan 1961)

Captain Coutts researched data from the Department of Agriculture farms at Beechwood, Inverness which established that Highland bulls sold to the slaughterhouse after servicing crofting areas are hundredweights heavier than Beef Shorthorn and Aberdeen Angus bulls which did the same job. (1961)

"Its no whit ye hae...but whit ye dae wi whit ye hae...that counts." (Captain Coutts)

The Press is a proper fund of information, good, bad, or indifferent, on beef topics these days. The first of many bold decisions we (Highland cattle breeders) should urgently take, should be:

1 To start treating our Breed as a Beef Breed. In other words, a Breed to produce beef...after all, it is designated as such. . and not treat it solely as a Breed suitable for producing females for crossing with Beef Shorthorn Bulls.

2 To give a great deal more thought to the breeding of the Highlanders, previously this has been given to the crosses. To select with much more vigour, in order to produce better beef-type animals, with better back-ens and broader backs. The butcher never fails to look for those...some of us, I regret to say do.

3 To feed our stots as other stots are fed. . for fattening. This is a most important point, particularly in the first winter of the animal's life when Highlanders grow well, many achieving greater weights than some of the more popular breeds and crosses. In fact, some of the latter could never come to the weights a Highlander can attain at any age. (1962 W H Black, NDA, NDD.)

Animals high in weight-gain ability and efficient food conversion are what's wanted. The pedigree breeder has a vital role to play and can contribute more than he receives credit for in this age of computers and scientific breeding, but he must show awareness of the commercial requirements of modern methods of beef production. A breeder's skill and knowledge of cattle doesn't convert into computer equations...he knows the lines which best transmit uniformity of maximum flesh on hind-quarters and loins. (P Bichan B Sc Agric. 1963)

There's good money in beef for both the commercial and pedigree breeder. It may not be easy to get but it is there for men who know the job, who can interpret present trends and anticipate and provide for future requirements.

The home market not the export sets the pattern for production.

Buyers are more reluctant to buy beef bulls on conformation only. Records of growth rate and feed conversion are expected. Measurement of fat disposition in live bulls is measurable by the Scottish Milk Marketing Board (disolved in 2003/2004).

Bull Beef: a bull calf grows more quickly than a steer and is a better food convertor...prime quality and excellent colour...no strong flavour whatsoever on palatability tests.

The highest quality of beef comes from grass-fed stock.

Grass beef except for the pure beef breeds will continue to decline. Grass has become too expensive for the two year old plus bullock. Nevertheless, much of our highest quality beef will continue to be grass-fed, but the amount will depend more and more on selling and advertising campaigns to increase the luxury quality demand. The real prime "Scotch" has no equal for flavour or tenderness. It is a product for the connoisseur, for the luxury hotel and restaurant and for the butcher with a discriminating customer and a full purse. (J C Leslie OBE MA. 1963)

In a country such as ours, depending to such an extent on imported beef...it is surely economic folly to ignore the full productive capacity of thousands of acres of rough grazings and marginal land...carrying no cattle or inadequately stocked, when they could be carrying considerable numbers of Highland cattle and their crosses. (A J K Laing 1965)

Highland steers have more chuck and less plate-shank beef than other breeds.

They have a smaller carcase but greater ribeye in relation to carcase than Hereford and Highland X Hereford.

The left side is leaner than the right side because cattle get up on the left side.

Weaning age can vary from 7 to 10 months. Weaning weight gives some indication of the milking ability of the dam. Up to weaning a calf is greatly affected not only by its dam but by its environment.

To get the weaning weight:

1 stand the animal square;

2 measure heart girth in inches just behind the front legs and multiply the number by itself;

3 measure from point of shoulder blade to the pin bone point near the tail and multiply again;

4 divide total by 300 to get the resulting weight in pounds avoirdupoise. (1967)

House 7 to 8 month old stirks for their first winter to get them used to eating bruised oats, cobs etc. Give just enough to "keep them going" as too much food up to about 15 months may hinder maximum growth potential expressing itself.

Hand feed Show beasts for 12 to 14 months. Their food graph should rise slowly for the first six months, a good deal faster for the following 3 to 4 months, and rapidly for the last 3 to 4 months. Reduce rate of feeding if there are signs of a belly appearing.

Bulls...steady feeding gives constant growth rate from birth. Feed as frequently as possible with as great a time gap between feeds as is possible e.g. 7am, noon, 5pm, 9pm. Concentrate food must be eaten within 10 to 15 minutes and any left removed. Changes in rations must be made slowly. Feed roughage of a good quality twice daily and 5 to 15 Kg per head of chopped roots once daily.

Steeping concentrates for one day reduces dust aggravations.

Highland calves resist dust pneumonia better than Hereford calves.

Highland cattle have a higher conception rate than most other breeds according to statistics from the Agricultural Research Station in Alberta, Canada, which produced these figures... 79% pure Highland, 70% other breeds, 82% first cross Highland. The geneticist involved in the research considers 20 to 25 cows to one bull is to be recommended.

In Peru Mr H E Gildemeister found that whilst the calving rate in his best herd of some 100 cows with three bulls is 90% to 100%, his herd at the highest altitude achieves only about 75% even with one bull per fifteen cows.

Yearly calving is more regular in Highland cattle if the bull runs with the fold than if using Artificial Insemination.

Cows tend to fight if the bull is not running with them.

Some hold the view that Highlands are more docile than the boisterous Welsh Black and less temperamental than the Galloway. The director of parks for Manchester City said *"Highland cattle are probably the most docile breed of cattle in this country."*

One breeder finds her cattle so tame that not only can she milk a Highland on the open hill, which her Jersey cow will not allow, she has sawn hoofs needing attention without putting the animal in a crush.

In small folds Highlands move more readily when led and called. Being driven from behind can have the effect of making them suspicious.

Home-made crush for first six heifers of novice breeder...

To begin with we built a small fold yard with post and rail fencing. Eventually it had to be raised to 5' 6" in height, for I found that 'Les Girls' could clear 5' with a standing jump. Against one side of the fold, at the corner, and two feet distant, we placed a gate post with a full-sized gate hanging from it and hinged on to this was a much lighter gate that would swing out making a fence two gates in length. The heifer was driven in to the corner so formed, the gate closed upon her and with a stake behind and one above (through two metal guides) she was as fast as though in irons. (1965)

Allow three weeks adjustment period for stock transferred from one area to another. Increased scrutiny on feeding and interaction with other stock during this period is advisable. Some animals adjust very quickly, taking only a day or two to settle after transport and release into unfamiliar territory and stock, while others can take longer. Unsettled behaviour after 3 weeks may indicate a health problem.

Some marginal land such as the machairs in the Outer Hebrides or hill grazings in North Argyllshire can be short of cobalt and copper which will result in cows not conceiving and failing to thrive well.

The acid and phosphate deficient soil in the Cairngorm area has led one breeder to supplying the following winter feeding:

mineral licks, mid-November Kale, January oat straw, hay or silage, and through calving from January till grass is available in April a small feed of draff and bruised oats.

One feeding system applied with success in North West hill territory is:

Cows: silage, Hill cow cobs, potatoes.

Calves: good hay, calf rearing nuts, bruised barley and a little fish meal to maintain steady growth.

Rising 2 year olds: hay or silage only.

Winter feeding in Sussex:

Highlands outwintered in mixed woodland took 7 pounds hay each daily from unlimited supply while others which were outwintered in a field took 13 pounds each daily and did not thrive so well.

One feed per day for outwintered Highland cattle means that they feed then move away to forage or seek sleeping quarters rather than hang about in bad weather conditions waiting for a second feed.

Highland cattle face into the wind and blizzards so that their coats are blown smoothly along their bodies and not parted.

If the breed is to keep its hardy hill characteristics it must continue to live in the hardships and hazards which evolved it in the first instance.

Concern has been expressed that the growing numbers of Highland cattle being bred and reared in city parks whilst maintaining breed numbers might in time contribute to a loss of the all important traits of thrifty adaptability and all weather endurance.

The feed efficiency of the Highland breed is high even under alien control conditions:

73% feeding is for survival;

18% feeding is for milk production;

9% feeding is for formation of the unborn calf.

The size of cow affects the amount of food it requires. (1982)

Steer Finishing Systems

In 1985 Highland cattle breeder J R E Nelson motivated four other breeders to join him in recording simultaneously methods of feeding different small groups of steers from weaning to finishing. Each feeder person would outline his system, rations, cost, targets for finishing and slaughtering in accordance with the following points:

1 finish cattle at or near the farm of birth
2 use stockmen experienced in Highland cattle
3 use small lots up to ten, more than twenty too many for this trial
4 steers to be outwintered
5 slaughtering and marketing to be in the feeder's area
6 investigate elite markets such as Harrods, QE 2 Liner
7 investigate markets for skins and horns
8 at end of trial to finish more cattle on an annual basis or provide breeders with information on successful systems.

The breeders involved, whilst still believing in the aim of the scheme, would not repeat the same methods. They regard the venture as having been limited in its success. To wean, transport to new territory, drench, vaccinate, dehorn and castrate all within one week in order to standardise and co-ordinate the starting points of all participating control-groups was harsh treatment of the livestock central to the scheme and proved counterproductive to its aims. However, expertise in the management of control-groups deepened considerably and any future work will benefit immensely.

Here is a condensed version of the article in the 1988 Highland Breeders' Journal entitled *Highlanders Ltd. A Report by J R E Nelson Managing Director.*

Report from Feeder One

Target: maintain steers outside; feed farm mix of grains and minerals; hay on restricted offer starting 3 pounds daily rising to 5. 5 pounds daily; slaughter at 30 months.

System: First winter: 11 bullocks each received 3 to 5 pounds daily of barley, beet pulp, maize, grains, and minerals (farm mix costing £140 a tonne) plus approximately 5 pounds of hay daily. Summered on the policies.

Second winter: the 6 best bullocks in sheltered field each getting daily feed of 8 to 10 pounds of above farm mix in addition to silage or hay. Sold at 24 months at around 10 cwt. liveweight. The other 5 wintered on the policies with only silage as supplementary feed; summered on the policies; fed concentrates mid October onwards to be sold fat in January.

The only veterinary product used was Ivomec to control lice and lungworm. Highland bullocks do far better outside with some shelter than shut in a shed. The above system results in prime Highland bullocks at 2½ to 3 years old.

Report from Feeder Two

Target: finish at 2½ years since beef is best only after 2 years age; feed outside entire period in troughs on ground sheltered by trees in winter; 10 bullocks.

System: first winter: daily feed per head of 10 pounds silage, 8 pounds turnips, 2 pounds hay, 1.5 pounds Bruised Oats. Cost was £2 a head for 29 weeks...total £58 a head.

First summer: on grass at £1. 60 a head. Cost £35 (approx 22 weeks)

Second winter: 30 pounds silage each daily, £56 for 30 wks.

Second summer: on grass plus daily 3 pounds cake per head; £63

Total cost per steer to include labour and veterinary fees expected to be £265.

Prolonged wet weather and poor quality silage due to wet weather having affected its production caused a need to feed an additional 3 pounds per head cattle cobs for four winter months.

Even with this extra cost the gross profit per head worked out at £87 with the steers having been graded as follows: four at R4L one at R4H, three at O+3. It proved impossible in the local circumstances to sell these steers direct to consumers. There was therefore nothing extra obtained for skins, horns or offal, simply because the facilities for slaughtering on one's own behalf were not available.

Report from Feeder Three

Target: to finish at 18 to 24 months.

Method and comments: 10 calves on arrival early October to be fed 2 pounds each sugar beet pulp per day with hay introduced mid December. From then until late May daily ration per head of 6 pounds sugar beet pulp and 5 pounds hay. Hay phased out late May. Hard feeding continues at grass with beef fattening nuts up to 6 pounds a head daily introduced to replace sugar beet.

Steers in a 20 acre field with run into 10 acres Forestry Commission plantation. Ragwort in the forest caused a setback and ill thrift. Do not castrate or dehorn if selling as fat beef at 18 months or less. Can sell at 18 months if reaching 3. 75cwts. which is 190 Kgs. by December of their first year. A few steers will thrive well if run with cows and heifers.

Report from Feeder Four

Target: to finish 20 bullocks at 30 months.

Method: Feed in whins and trees an average daily ration from 8th October to 22nd April of 10 pounds hay (£20 a tonne), 2 pounds barley (£100 a tonne), 5 pounds draff (£20 a tonne), 3 pounds turnips (£20).

No more of this breeder's system was available at the time the Highland Breeders Journal went into print.

Conclusions and comments: from the recent trial it is clear that it can make sense for individual breeders to finish their own steers **if** –

a the market price for Highland calves is substantially below other stores. (e.g. at 80p/kilo when other calves are making £1. 20) At present this is not the case as there is a strong demand for Highland steers probably for ornamental purposes.

b one of the systems outlined earlier can be adapted to suit the breeder's circumstances e.g. shelter, access to appropriate feedstuffs, knowledge, stockmanship etc.

c a local market for quality Highland beef can be established...hotels, restaurants, friends, neighbours. Also consider the value of liver, heart etc. for dog food £10 to £20 per beast. If marketed intelligently (ie. not dumped on the market) Highland beef can make attractive returns.

There is a market for skins, but it has been difficult to find any tanner who can produce the skin in the soft pliable form that is required.

There is no doubt that well-bred calves, with good conformation and with a good weight at weaning did best. This may sound obvious, but don't expect good results from calves born in July off poor quality parents.

The marketing of horns has some possibilities. Keep the top of the skull and horns. The inner horn will dry out and you will be left with a piece of skull and two outer horns. This can be joined together and finished off with a strip of cured skin, neatly brushed up which makes an attractive curio.

Grading of Highland cattle can pose difficulties. It is generally agreed that lack of conformation is a present weakness of many Highlanders. This can be compounded if grading of Highlanders is taking place alongside continental crosses of strong conformation. With regard to quality outlets for Highland beef there are two problems. The first is the difficulty of guaranteeing regularity of supply and quality. The second problem is that the "quality" market is particularly good at its pricing...it may charge top prices, but it wont pay over the odds for the goods it sells. The premium in Mr Nelson's view is available by selling direct from farm to consumer, cutting out as many middle-men as possible.

BREED STANDARDS

"It is generally agreed that the well-bred Highlander is the most picturesque animal in the Cattle world. Straight above and below, short in the legs, deep in frame, rich and flowing in hair at the proper time of year, varied in colours and singularly dignified in movement...There are two styles of horn in females – the out, slightly forward and upward; and the out, less forward and backwards swirling. In a bull a wide level sweep is best. As the animal approaches maturity, the horns take a moderately forward set and tend to rise, if anything at the tips. . . At the fall of the year and in winter the brow of the well-bred bull or heifer should be like a sporran, with straight flowing hair down to the edge of the nose, and leaving not more than a mere peering opportunity for the eye. Long hair should also fall from the ridge of the neck, the spinal column, and should be abundant down the thighs. A long fringe should also hang from the lower edge of the ears. I always think this is a sign of good breeding. It is of consequence to have a very thick, soft undercoat, or 'vest'. The fact is that I would not have great confidence in a feeding animal that showed deficiency in vest. Towards the end of the summer when calves have cast a good deal of their first coat, they should still show plenty of 'apron' along the low line..." (Written by James Cameron in *Preserving A Noble Old Breed* and quoted by A McKenzie in *Highland cattle Today and Yesterday*.)

Breed standards were set first in print in 1885 in Volume I of the Herd Book. They are reprinted at intervals by the Highland Cattle Society in its newsletters and journals.

extract from HERD BOOK VOLUME I

The Head

Of all the representatives of our British bovine breeds, the Highlander has the grandest and most picturesque head; it is indeed, to his head that he owes his great favour among artists.

As a rule, it is most proportionate to the body of the animal, and is broad between the eyes, while short from the eyes to the point of the muzzle. The forelock between the eyes should be wide, long, and bushy, and any nakedness or bareness there is certain to detract from the appearance of the animal. Some would almost have the hair so wide there as to obscure the eyes, but this in many cases would be allowing one good point to overshadow another. The eyes should be bright and full, and denoting, when excited, high courage. When viewed sideways, there should be a proportionate breadth of the jaw bones readily observable, when compared with the width of the head in front, whilst the muzzle should, when looked at from a similar point, be short, though very broad in front, and with the nostrils fully distended, and indicating breeding in every way. One of the most noteworthy features in a Highlander is, of course, the horns. In the bulls, the horns should be strong, and come level out of the head, slightly inclining forwards, and also slightly rising towards the points. Some, however, do not care for this rise, though any drooping is considered to be a very bad fault when between the crown and the commencement of the curve, as this is generally accompanied by a low weak back. Some, too, are of the opinion that the masculine appearance is slightly detracted from when the horns rise directly from the crown. This, however, can only readily be detected and commented upon when particular animals are brought before experienced judges, as within a Show ring.

As regards the horns of the cow, there prevail two opinions. As a rule, they come squarer out from the head than in the male, rise sooner, and are somewhat longer, though they preserve their substance and a rich reddish appearance to the very tips. The lack of the appearance of substance or "sappiness" about the horns of the male would be very much against the animal in the Show yard. The other taste is that for a female, the horns of which come more level from the head, with a peculiar back set curve, and very wide sweep. A large number of enthusiastic breeders seem to prefer, by comparison, the latter, which gives possibly the more graceful appearance. In all cases, however, the horns of a Highlander, when well set, give the animal a stamp of nobility which causes it to attract the attention of any stranger who might pass heedlessly by animals of other breeds as merely cows, bulls, or oxen.

The Neck and Shoulder

The neck should be altogether clear and without dewlap below. It should form a straight line from the head to the shoulder in the cow, but in the bulls should have that distinct crest common to all animals of the bovine species. This crest should come gracefully down to the roots of the horns, and, being well coated with wavy hair, the masculine appearance of the animal is fully completed. The shoulder should be thick and should fill out greatly as it descends from the point to the lower extremity of the forearm.

Back, Body and Hind-quarters

From behind the shoulder the back should be fully developed and beautifully rounded. Any slight sinking or hollow is most decidedly objectionable. It should also, as in the Ayrshire, be as straight as possible, and the ribs should spring boldly out and be both well rounded and deep. When measured across the hips the breadth should be very great, and the quarters should be exceedingly well developed from the hips backwards. The thighs should also be well developed, and should show great fullness.

Viewed generally the quarters should be square between the hips and the tail, and from between the tail right down to between the hind feet. The legs, both before and behind, should be short and strong, the bones strong, broad, and straight, the hoofs well set in and large, and the legs well feathered with hair. The animal should be set wide between the forelegs, and it should move with great dignity and style, as this is considered to be one of the most reliable evidences of careful and true breeding.

Hair

The hair, of which there should be a great profusion, more particularly on the parts indicated, should be long and gracefully waved, very much as in what dog breeders denote wavy-coated retrievers. To have a curl is to possess a decided fault, and one which has of late years become unfortunately too common in some folds. This has been attributed in some quarters to a growing desire to make Highlanders grow big from feeding them higher and housing them more. At any rate, experience goes far to prove that the more exposed they are the greater the profusion of hair, and the less its tendency to curl. Thus, the reason of the island cattle being always so much better haired than the mainland cattle is owing to their never being housed in winter.

The usual colours are black, brindled, red, yellow, and dun, and there is considerable difference of opinion among breeders as to which is preferable.

In general, as to colour, it may be said that a good herd should possess a mixture – avoiding always all those which indicate unhealthy thrivers. The thickness of the skin, as in all fattening breeds, comes in for a considerable amount of attention, but it has to be borne in mind always that the Highlander has been adapted by nature to withstand great exposure.

The committee of the Highland Cattle Society of Scotland agreed in 1990 that the following colours be regarded as acceptable for pedigree registration in the official society Herd Book: black, white, red, yellow, dun, brindle, parti colour. Parti colour was understood to mean any of the accepted whole colours with substantial areas of white appearing in any pattern.

MANAGEMENT

UPLAND FOLD (extract from *Highland Cattle for Hardiness Thrift and Profit*)

In the area slightly west of Central Scotland the rainfall is high at 80 inches per annum, and the ground is poor. The growing season for grass is short, and this means that one has to hand feed the cattle for six months of the year, from mid-November until mid-May. Gone are the days, we hope, when people thought that Highland cattle lived on "fresh air" – they don't. They thrive on land where other breeds would melt away, and indeed, improve it. Especially if the grass is old and rank, they will crop it down thereby making future growth sweeter, and if sheep are running on the same land, it is much more palatable for them.

Rushes are a menace in my area but when hay was fed it was put on top of the rushes and the cattle ate it and continued down into the rushes pulling the young shoots out and thereby weakening the offending weed.

Before the prices for hay and haulage became so high, hay was bought and the cows fed on it along with cow cobs. An allowance of up to two tons per cow was made and the cobs were fed at the rate of 2 lbs per day for a start, rising to 4 lbs when the cow calved. The cobs are to be highly recommended as they contain the protein and minerals that are so essential to keep the cattle in good heart. The alternative to hay is silage and straw. The latter is also expensive to buy, so where possible silage is made but if it is insufficient, for the first six weeks or so straw and a protein lick are given, and after that silage feeding at the rate of approximately 70 lbs per day. Into this is mixed 1 lb of bruised barley, 1 lb bruised oats per head of cattle, and minerals. The bruised corn and minerals fed in this way rather than in cob form is a new idea, only recently tried for the first time, with, so far, successful results. It does, however, entail more work.

Where one is dealing in small numbers it is still advisable to use hay and cobs, as silage making is a costly business and unless there is a fairly large acreage to crop it would not be worthwhile.

Calving

The time to calve your cows is debatable, as obviously your average winter conditions must play a large part in what you decide to do. Every month from December up until May has been tried, but, perhaps, mid-February to the end of March is the best. Some of the worst weather can be experienced in December and the calves, if they survive the first few hours, spend the next weeks just existing rather than growing, with the result that the earlier calves are very little larger at the end of the day. A good idea to help the calves is a creep feeder. Into this is put bruised oats and calf nuts, the calves pick away at this when two or three months old and it teaches them to eat hand feeding. This is a help in the Autumn when they are weaned as they don't lose condition, and, in fact, take more readily to their winter rations.

If calves are housed inside for their first winter it gives them a better chance to give them a bit of growth. The diet is in no way fancy, it is intended to grow the cattle without making them too fat. They start off on ad lib straw and promax to which is added 1 lb mixed bruised barley and oats. This is changed after two to three months, the bruised corn being increased to 3 lbs per head per day and silage up to 20 lbs each per day, the straw is deleted from the diet at this point.

With these methods cattle have grown to sufficient size for the heifers to go to the bull at two years old, although with some strains this is not always possible.

Testing

Nowadays farming, even if it consists of only a few cows has its rules and regulations, which are laid down by the Department of Agriculture and must be adhered to. The latest test that has to be carried out, is a blood test every year for brucellosis. The other is for tuberculosis and this is carried out every two to three years. For these tests to be done with a minimum of disturbance to the animals and the maximum safety for those persons involved, a crush and catching crate is all important.

Dosing

There are other times too when the crush is used, namely dosing and innoculating or treating for lice. There is a new treatment for lice which has been found to be extremely good. It is an oily substance which is poured down the backbone of the animal in the Autumn and that gives protection right through the Winter and Spring. Regular dosing for worms is another "Must" if your cattle are to remain in good condition. Also if you live in a wet climate there most probably will be liver flukes in the wetter areas and treatment for the prevention of these parasites is advisable.

The adaptability of Highland cattle is well-known, and contrary to some beliefs are very docile if treated quietly and sensibly. Care should be taken not to get them too tame as then they become jealous and a dig in the ribs from a horn half a metre long can be painful!

Over the years I have tried to have my cattle tame enough to put a halter on them out on the open hill, this is a great time saver in an emergency as then the ailing can be removed without having to involve the entire fold.

On the whole Highland cattle are fairly disease free, but the sort of thing that can happen when a cow has been calved for some time, is that the hair on the udder gets wound round the teats (Pics 53, 54 p50) and this unless it is removed quickly results in a badly damaged teat and possibly an irrepairable quarter in the udder. I have had one instance of hair winding round a calf's teeth and causing infection to the gums.

Don't be put off by these warnings, a watchful eye prevents many a future trouble.

LOWLAND FOLD (extract from *Highland Cattle for Hardiness Thrift and Profit*)

Because the Highland Herd Book or Registration Year begins on December 1st, calves born as near to that date have an age advantage over say April or May born calves which is with them throughout their juvenile life, but an advantage which adulthood tends to nullify. Therefore, in order to have calves born about the 1st December – the bull is put with the cows about the beginning of March. Highland cows are excellent mothers and have a very strong protective instinct – accordingly one should approach a newborn calf with care – there should be little need to approach in any case as the cows generally do get on with it themselves, the calves being of medium size, and parturition therefore, quite easy. However, should a problem arise the cow is better taken into a pen or building where she may be restrained for attention. Calving at this time of year, of course, means that calves arrive in all kinds of weather including snow, and very cold wet conditions. Natural shelter is a great thing, where a calving cow can get out of the wind – an old piece of woodland is ideal and even a rough scrubby patch is a big help. In an hour or two the calves are about following mother – but sometimes she will hide them away for a day or two, returning to them only to suckle. The cows are generally fed a maintenance ration (a ration suitable to retain body conditions without improving on it) of silage or hay or roots together with barley or oat straw – and once she calves a compound or cereal is fed in sufficient quantity to maintain a regular milk supply for the calf.

The kind of quantity involved could be as follows:

Daily

30 lbs Silage		5 lbs Cereals
or	10 lbs Barley Straw	or
35 lbs Swedes		2 lbs Cobs

The animals ought, in addition, to have access to a clean water supply and a mineralised supplement should be given, on a free access basis where the cows may use the material when they require it – it should be based on Magnesium and Phosphorus, Magnesium for prevention of Grass Staggers and Hypomagnacaemia, and Phosphorus as an aid to getting the cows back in calf.

When the calves are about two months old they will require some additional nourishment where the mother cannot get at it. This is known as a creep feed, fed where the calves can get peace to take nourishment without a greedy dam eating the lot. Calves will eat ½ – 1 lb of a mixture based on cereal per day. However, once the grass grows this can be stopped as well as the feeding of the cows. Mid-April is about the time of grass growth, but it varies from area to area.

When the female calves are coming up to six months of age the bull should be removed from the herd – most of the cows will have been settled long since and in order not to encourage an untimely interest in their daughters the bull is best elsewhere. He is usually put along with a couple of stots, to quietly graze a paddock. Weaning takes place when the calves are about 8 – 9 months old, in late August early September. Prior to this, creep feeding is again commenced as the grass loses its feeding value and by the time the calves are taken away from their mothers, they will be eating 2 – 3 lbs per day. At weaning they are put straight inside a court – this allows them to settle as they do not see other cattle, but the roaring is deafening as cows look for calves and vice versa.

At this stage several jobs have to be undertaken:

1 Tattoo the calves in order of age with the Herd Letters and Year Serial letter followed by a number. (Tattoos have been replaced by obligatory ear tags)

2 Dose the calves for Lungworm and Roundworm.

3 Spray them over for lice and mange.

After they have settled down the calves are put out to graze again on good re-seeded ground and are fed some cereal in troughs. The complete crop of calves is housed for winter, allowing them:

1 To quieten down.

2 To be handled.

3 To grow on at a stage where growth rate is high, and can be achieved at reasonable cost.

This is the only stage in their whole existence when a roof is over their heads, although the duration of housing varies it would probably be from November to April when they return to grass. While housed they feed on chopped or fingered turnips and hay with 2 – 3 lbs of cereal or Calf Rearing pencils, feed which stands them in good stead all the days of their lives.

Meantime, mother should be back in business with calf No. 2 – a better one than the last.

"Nae man can fetter time nor tide, Nature's cycle in full stride!"

HIGHLANDERS IN SUSSEX BY A. LUMSDEN (extract from *The Highlander for Thrift and Profit*)

Our farm is small, being sixty acres of grassland on a heavy clay soil, and was originally laid out as a stud farm for the family hunters and for my Welsh Mountain ponies. The buildings consist of a range of loose boxes – an implement shed and a Dutch barn and some of the fields have open sheds. In addition there is a wood of twenty acres which is a typical Sussex covert of beech-chestnut-oak-laurel and rhododendron. The staff consists of one man and myself and we are completely self-supporting as we only feed grass and hay. We are attested and up to the present have not had a reactor.

With the exception of one fourteen acre field of permanent pasture which has not been ploughed in living memory, all the fields have been re-seeded with a mixture of Cocksfoot S. 143 Timothy S. 48 Meadow fescue S. 215 and Wild White Clover S. 184. In some fields the seeds were broadcast, in others drilled, and more recently the Cocksfoot has been drilled in rows two feet apart, while the other grasses have been broadcast, and in our experience this combination appears to be the ideal method for our soil, as the Cocksfoot makes greater growth, and in a wet Autumn the poaching of the ground seems to be reduced to a minimum. We aim to hay about twenty acres each year and our average crop since re-seeding has been two-and-a-half tons to the acre.

In December the cows, of which we aim to keep forty, are turned into the wood, and we have found it advisable to run the Highland bull with them as otherwise the cows are inclined to fight. The indispensable male! Hay is fed twice a day from wooden racks and the cattle and ponies are given as much as they will eat. Last winter a careful check was kept on the consumption and it was found that the cattle in the woods consumed seven pounds per day while some outwintered in a field ate thirteen pounds and did not thrive so well. In March the cows return to the fields and some go to a beef Shorthorn bull and the others remain with the Highland bull. Calving commences in March and is completely unaided. As a rule every cow produces a calf each year and they are long-lived, as our best heifer was produced last year by a cow in her nineteenth year. In October the calves are weaned and in November all the cross-bred calves and the pure Highland males are sold, while the Highland heifers are kept for another year and are then either drafted into the herd or sold. At the last sale in our local market the pure and cross-bred calves averaged £32 10s 0d, while eighteen months old pure Highland heifers averaged £65 – prices which compared very favourably with those received for other beef cattle. It is generally supposed that Highland cattle are slow maturing and this may well be the case where they are brought through the winter on a starvation diet, but although our cattle live their lives under almost entirely natural conditions on a natural diet, we find that the heifers can go to the bull at two years of age and the general development is fully up to that of the members of the other beef breeds which have been expensively fed. Our grass is in fact almost too good for the cattle as they seem to prefer a rough pasture, and visitors have remarked that they seem to eat closer than other cattle and to graze right across a field taking the weeds equally with the grass. Our wood, which was a wilderness of brambles and weeds, is a testimony to their grazing habits.

Highlanders certainly look fierce, but in my experience they are fundamentally gentle creatures and become attached to the people they know, although it must be admitted that for a week or two after calving the cows are resentful of strangers and it is not advisable to go between a cow and her calf.

We have not found the horns any disadvantage at feeding time and although my ponies live and feed with the cattle I have not yet had one injured.

I like the cows, but my real affection is for the bulls, who seem to have all the quiet dignity and courage of their Highland ancestry. Our first bull was an enormous fellow called "Ghillie Bheag, " which in Gaelic means "The little man." One day I noticed that he was lying in his field in discomfort and on investigation I found that he had run a steel skewer which had been left behind by the Army deep into his foot. With some trepidation and difficulty I extracted it and then, much to my relief, he followed me home and made himself comfortable in a loose box while I sent for the vet. The wound took some time to heal but he was a model patient and the only trouble he gave was that on being liberated he gambolled like a lamb – all the tons of him – and he smashed a tree which my father declared he had planted himself with much labour.

PREPARATION FOR SHOWING (extract from *Highland Cattle for Hardiness Thrift and Profit*)

Introduction:

Show specimens tend to be bred rather than made. Inevitably one finds that these occur with greater regularity in certain families, where desirable features of an ideal specimen of the Breed show up more frequently, and on research into the pedigree of these families one is sure to find that Champions and prize winners abound through the generations. However, despite this, without the aid of an attentive Stockman, skilled in feeding and the art of having an animal at its peak on a given day, success would be limited.

A. Selection:

1 Select your intended entries in plenty of time for a given Show – an old rule, still true, was to select Highland Show entries at the time of the Fatstock Shows, and Fatstock Show entries at the time of the Highland. This gives some idea of the amount of time required to feed on an animal quietly on a rising plane of nutrition to reach its peak on a given day. (Note: Royal Highland Show – June, Fatstock Shows – November/December)

2 In selection pay particular attention to the following:

a. A Good Head – as broad as it is long with a nice broad muzzle, bright clear eye and evenly matched horns (neither too strong nor too fine).

b. A Good Coat – healthy and with an abundance of hair – selected from a family known to keep its coat in summer heat. Generally speaking, Red is the colour which keeps the coat best – the lighter colours Yellow and White tend to throw the coat in summer and are probably thinner coated anyway with less hair follicles per square inch of hide.

c. Good Sound Legs – with hair cover down to the hoof and not too fine in the bone. The animal should have a smooth walking action, neither throwing nor hooking. The feet would require to be pared to make certain the animal walks squarely on the sole and that the hoof is neat and blocky with an absence of long toes.

B. Schooling:

The Show animal must be halter broken and schooled in what is requested of it in the Show ring. These tend to be:

1 To walk alertly, quietly and yet sedately.

2 To stand smartly with each leg correctly placed.

3 To be quiet enough that a Judge may handle and allow someone to approach from behind.

4 To be able to do all these things with someone else other than the Stockman leading the animal out.

These do not seem a lot but patience and perseverance, and a lot of time goes into proper schooling of the Show animal.

C. Feeding:

Regular feeding at regular times is essential in bringing out an animal for Show. The quality of the material fed must be good and anything which might upset a healthy appetite should be avoided. Feed no more than will be cleaned up in twenty minutes as often as is necessary – maybe four times per day at regular times – as the animal gets to know these times and will look to be fed then.

Everyone bringing out animals for Show tends to have his/her own ideas on what to feed them. Generally a little of what one fancies is said to do good with people and it is the same with animals. Good hay is generally the basis of a ration – with cereal based feed an essential to supplement this.

D. Dressing:

The coat should be clean and with lustre – this can only be achieved by regular attention for:

a. Parasites – the animal to be shown should be dipped regularly with a lice wash. One wash is insufficient as lice eggs are not killed by the wash and a new hatch means re-infestation. Therefore 3 – 4 times.

b. Dirt – the coat should be washed over at least twice before a big Show, the last wash being within the 2 – 3 days prior to the Show. Thorough soaping and sound rinsing are necessary. The animal should be dried artificially or naturally in the sun – and walked to avoid it catching cold while it dries.

c. Grooming – this should be carried out regularly to help quieten the animal, help the lustre of the coat and avoid tangling. A Dandy Brush, Horse Comb and Rake Comb are the tools of the trade, plus patience and the satisfaction of a good job being well done.

The only stumbling block is the Judge who may not like your cattle or likes big ones when you have small ones, or vice versa. Judges have their own ideas but compare fairly what is put before them. Their decision is final and irrevocable and should be accepted without demur or jubilation. One old Herdsman used to say:

"*If you are winning say nothing, if losing say less*"

He may well be right.

Knowing How To Show Your Animals

1 Pick an alert showy animal that carries its head and ears erect, has breed characteristics and lots of eye appeal.

2 Select one which has enough potential to grow out.

3 Smooth, straight topline and shoulders well blended into the crop or girth area.

4 Look for length and depth of line between the last rib and hock bone, as depth indicates the rib eye size.

5 Check the hindquarter for length and depth. Length is determined by the distance from the

hook to the pin bones. For depth, the well rounded deep muscle should carry on down to the hocks.

6 The front and back legs should be pointing straight ahead – not toed in or out.

7 Looking at the back legs from the side – imagine a straight line down from the pin bones to the hock and down the back of the legs.

8 Summing it up, an animal with eye appeal, height and length, breed character and structural soundness with growth potential is the one to prepare for Showing.

9 After you have selected your animal worm and delouse.

Feeding

1 Give your animals a good clean and well balanced feed ration, avoiding fine powdery feed.

2 Show and sale animals should have a clean dry bed. It is easier to keep animals clean daily rather than clean them out after they have become dirty and caked with manure.

3 As a guide, feed 2 pounds of grain per 100 pounds of body weight.

4 Hay may be fed freely at first but later on it may be necessary to cut back in order to avoid developing a hay gut.

5 Salt and minerals may be fed free choice or supplemented in the grain ration.

6 Feed your animals at approximately the same time each day.

7 Watch how your animals clean up their food and remove and discard what is not eaten.

8 Increase or decrease the amount of food you give according to your animal's finish and appetite, keeping in mind the amount of time left to sale or Show date.

9 Breeding stock should be on a good growing ration consisting mainly of oats and good quality hay.

10 To achieve the best results you should have your animal on feed for at least 80 – 120 days before the Show or sale date.

11 Familiarise your animals at home to the feed and bucket you will be using at the Show or sale.

12 Three or four days before the Show cut back to about half the normal feed ration. Feed hay during this period and restrict their drinking.

13 Do not water your animals 2 – 3 hours before loading time. They will travel better and stay cleaner this way.

Handling of Show cattle in general should start at an early age. People tend to leave it until the animals become older and at this point it becomes more difficult on man and beast. If when a calf is quite young (weeks old) it is tied along with the mother without any duress this eliminates a lot of hardship later on as the animal becomes more accustomed to its handler and learns to Show itself properly without becoming nervous.

The washing of animals should not be left until the day of the Show. If possible, wash your animals twice or three times at home. This will not only have them accustomed to the shampooing, but will also enhance their appearance and help their coats in general.

CHOOSING A STOCK BULL

extract from *Some Points to Consider Before Purchasing a Stock Bull* (Angus Mackay)

1 Assess all the cattle in your own fold and look at the features they have in common – both good and bad. Then decide which characteristics you would most like in your new bull such as size, breed character, colour or conformation.

2 Try to spend some time before the sale looking at bulls that will be available, e.g. at the summer Shows, or visit folds of cattle that you particularly like. Look at the sire and dam of any bull that is for sale.

3 Get the catalogue some time before the sale and study the pedigree as there will be some bulls closely related to cows in your own fold.

4 Inspect all the bulls well, if possible when they are being measured and weighed. Also watch the Show carefully. If you are inexperienced watch the judging with an experienced breeder. Don't let the judge influence you too much as he may be looking for points which are not necessarily relevant to your circumstances.
5 Ask the owner or the stocksman of the bulls you have selected anything you want to know about the sire and the dam. Handle the bull yourself to assess conformation and temperament. Also look at any other progeny by the same sire that might be at the sale.
6 Do not hesitate to ask for assistance and advice from a Society fieldsman, Council member or a fellow breeder.
7 When you have bought your bull ask the owner what he has been fed as most of the bulls will be in very good condition and will have to be looked after well when you get them home. Cobs and hay will not do.
Good luck as there is a large element of luck involved.

TATTOOING

Tattooing Instructions (extract from *Highland Breeders Journal*)

Tattooing bulls began in 1943. [regulations for European Union trading invalidated tattooing, and enforced durable ear tag system from 1992]

1 Have the names of all calves and their tattoo numbers written down on paper before starting work.
2 As each calf is tattooed with its appropriate number, etc. score its name off your list and no confusion in numbering can arise.
3 Do not tattoo with two lines of letters or figures in the implement at once.
4 Make sure your tattooing is clear of the ribs in the ear, or that part of the letter or figure which lies in the rib will be illegible in two or three years time.
5 After inserting the appropriate letters and numerals in the tattooing machine, take a stout bit of paper and make a punch to assure yourself that no figure is wrongly inserted in the machine, i.e. upside down.
6 See that the calf to be tattooed is firmly held.
7 Clean the calf's ear; if very waxy use methylated spirits.
8 Rub a little tattooing paste over the lobe of the ear to be punched.
9 If the ribs in the ear are close together make sure that the important part of the letter is clear of a rib, e.g. the top of the letter T and the bottom of the letter L.
10 In making the punch use both hands and be firm.
11 Rub the tattooing paste over the punch holes in the ear, working it well in.
12 When the work is finished, wash all the figures in hot water and disinfect, then dry thoroughly and oil.

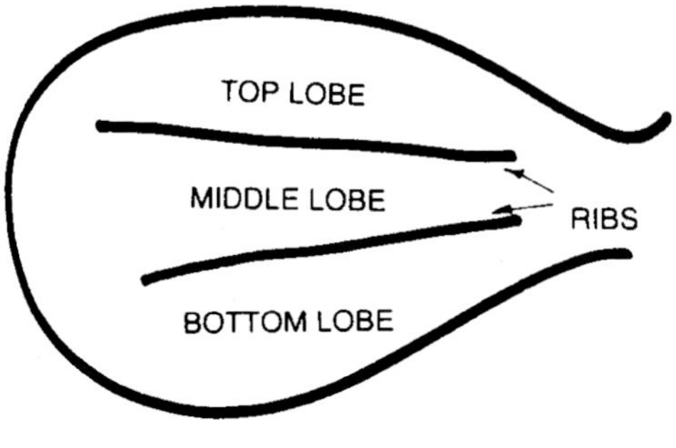

Keep your private herd records up to date with particulars of your animals, e.g. date of birth, name, colour, tattoo and details of pedigree and progeny. If you have no private record start one now. It is worthwhile and will save you no end of trouble.

Finally, make certain that your calves are tattooed without delay – when they are still young enough for you to be absolutely certain which calf belongs to which cow.

MAJOR DISEASES

Enzootic Bovine Leukosis

This disease was first recorded in Britain in 1978 on a proportion of cattle imported since 1967. It is present in most European countries and North America.

Leukosis is the name given to a common tumour condition of cattle, of which two types have been recognised;

1 enzootic bovine leukosis (EBL)

2 sporadic bovine leukosis (SBL)

EBL is an infectious virus disease of cattle causing multiple tumours in the tissues and, in many cases, leukaemia – an increase in the white blood cells. Its infectious nature makes it a herd problem but the clinical disease is rarely seen in animals less than four years old.

Under natural conditions EBL virus affects cattle only, although sheep and goats have been infected experimentally. The virus does not appear to affect man. EBL is a notifiable disease of animals in Great Britain and owners who suspect that their cattle may be affected with the disease are required by the Enzootic Bovine Leukosis Order 1980 to notify their divisional veterinary office either directly or through the local authority or police.

An animal affected with EBL virus may never show clinical signs during its natural life and tumours may not be present at post-mortem. In instances where tumours develop, the disease is characterised by chronic ill health, loss of appetite, progressive loss of condition and general weakness. Lymph glands may be visibly enlarged but painless when handled. The eyes of affected cattle may protrude or have a staring appearance. Affected animals will eventually die. When such signs are seen EBL should be suspected and the local divisional veterinary officer notified.

EBL infection can be confirmed only by laboratory examination of blood or tumour samples.

An animal once affected with EBL virus, whether clinical signs develop or not, is capable of spreading the infection through the herd, particularly when calving or in contact with other bovines of any age or when housed in close contact with other bovines.

About one in five calves born of infected dams is infected before birth. The virus may also be present in the colostrum of infected cows. Calves may be infected from this source and even from the feeding of pooled colostrum derived from one or more infected dams. Infection may also be spread by the transmission of small quantities of infected blood from injections or by other processes which may draw blood such as earpunching, tattooing, dehorning, or biting flies or ticks.

There is no evidence of spread by embryo transfer or AI but the virus could be spread by natural service if the ejaculate contains bloodcells.

There are two main considerations in herd control. Both depend on good standards of management and general hygiene. First the aim should be to keep EBL out of a herd which is free from the disease. The major hazard is the introduction of infected animals either by purchase or by short-term borrowing of animals from herds whose EBL status is unknown. Proposed purchases would be tested before introduction to the home herd; stock movements should be limited to the absolute minimum and contact with neighbouring herds should be avoided.

Where reactors are disclosed within a herd, the local divisional veterinary officer will serve a notice restricting the affected animals to the farm where they must remain either until they die or they are removed under the conditions of a licence direct for slaughter.

Infected animals should be kept in isolations and, when they are sent for slaughter, the isolation premises should be cleansed and disinfected before re-occupation. The entire herd should also be re-tested at an interval of not less than four months. Two consecutive voluntary clear herd tests would provide satisfactory evidence of freedom from the disease.

Owners not wishing to slaughter reactors are recommended where possible, to keep them in buildings or pastures away from the rest of the herd. But where this is not practicable the following measures will minimise the possibility of further spread throughout the herd:

Put reactors into isolation when due to calve and dispose of the afterbirth immediately. Disinfect the accommodation before use again. Remove calves from reactors as soon as possible.

Do not feed calves with milk or colostrum from known reactors. Avoid feeding pooled colostrum.

Avoid prolonged contact between reactors and animals from the remainder of the herd. Control ticks and biting flies.

Cleanse instruments used in connection with earpunching, tattooing and so on after use on each animal.

In any programme of vaccination or treatment involving intravenous, intramuscular, or subcutaneous injection of groups of animals, or any testing involving blood sampling, use a fresh sterilised needle for each animal.

Further advice on EBL in your herd may be obtained from your own veterinary surgeon.

From July 1st 1990 breeding cattle may only be traded between member states of the EEC if they come from herds officially recognised as free from Leukosis.

Officially Brucellosis Free

Cattle exported to European Economic Community and Nordic countries are required to be officially declared free of the disease Brucellosis at a specification higher than that generally used in Britain in 1978.

Cattle which have successfully undergone the more stringent testing are then categorised as OBF meaning Officially Brucellosis Free.

To become OBF a herd has to satisfy the following criteria:

1 It must be a self-contained herd maintained on the same ground and have been accredited under the Accredited Herds Scheme for three consecutive years.
2 No cattle within the herd under the age of three years must have been vaccinated with strain 19 vaccine – and therefore vaccination must not have been a policy for at least three years.
3 Two Brucellosis Herd Tests must be undertaken at six monthly intervals annually, with passes to a higher standard than normally demanded of all animals over one year old.
4 Suitable isolation must be provided on the farm for incoming animals such as bulls which must undergo two successful tests, before joining the herd and then only with the District Veterinary Officer's approval in writing.
5 Do-it-yourself permits are withdrawn from such a herd and official permits must be drawn from the local office of the District Veterinary Officer.
6 OBF cattle must not be allowed to mix with other Brucellosis tested cattle and special sections have to be available at both Shows and Sales.

There are lots of situations where it would be extremely difficult to test bi-annually but there is little to stop the smaller self-contained herd joining the scheme.

By 1984 there were 29 folds of Highland cattle officially brucellosis Free.

IBR, EBL, *L.* Hardjo and EEC Trading

The Single European Act binds all member states of the European Community (EC) to the principle of removing restrictions on the freedom to trade, including trade in livestock, within the Community from 31 December 1992. Prior to that date Member States must have agreed which safeguards to implement in order to best prevent the spread of exotic diseases within the Community. Just as important are the safeguards necessary to ensure exotic diseases are not introduced into the Community as a whole by trade with third world countries.

Many farmers recognise that bought in animals may bring infectious diseases with them. So breeding stock of recognised disease-free status brought direct from the farm of origin are fetching premium prices.

A nationally co-ordinated disease control programme is offered by the Cattle Health Scheme in Britain. It has registers of herds free on one or more of the following three diseases:

Enzootic Bovine Leukosis (EBL), Infectious Bovine Rhinotracheitis (IBR) and *Leptospira* Hardjo Infection (*L.* Hardjo).

***Leptospira* Hardjo**

The Scheme has an advisory programme for herds infected with *L.* Hardjo. It aims to control or eliminate the disease by vaccination and treatment without the need for culling. When first introduced to a herd *L.* Hardjo may cause dramatic losses. More frequently the onset is gradual and less obvious such that within only thirty years or so since it entered Britain about two thirds of the cattle in the country are infected. It is the most commonly diagnosed cause of abortion in cattle in Britain.

IBR

Infectious Bovine Rhinotracheitis is a virus disease which can cause fever, runny eyes and nose, cough, loss of milk, and abortions. Some strains of the virus are so mild that the infection may not be noticed. Other strains are so severe that infected cattle die within a few days. Once an animal has been infected with the virus it can remain a carrier for life. Blood tests can detect carriers, but not which strain of the disease caused the infection. Very common in Britain this virus is less common in much of Europe. Major agricultural events in Germany will only accept cattle officially recognised as free of IBR.

The national Cattle Health Scheme in Britain offers features beyond what any local scheme could handle such as:

1 an agreed and structured programme to achieve a defined health status which has both national and international recognition.
2 allows prospective buyers find herds on the Register which meet their requirements.
3 specially trained veterinary officers with both local knowledge and a nationwide back up service who can provide the farmer and his veterinary surgeon with up to date, authoritative, and unbiased advice.
4 a newsletter to members and their veterinary surgeons with the latest relevant developments.
5 standardised disease monitoring procedures operating to detect any problem promptly.
6 The *L.* Hardjo programme has provision for an annual management review. The health scheme member, his veterinary surgeon, and the local cattle health scheme veterinary officer discuss the disease security of the farm. This allows details of the programme to be tailored to suit the individual farm.

Rules designed to verify and protect the status of the herd must be upheld by every member of the national Cattle Health Scheme, who have to agree to uphold the following obligations.

1 They must protect their cattle from infection from other animals by...maintaining fencing to prevent contact with non-Scheme cattle.

...Maintaining a closed herd wherever possible.

...Quarantining purchased animals and those which come into contact with non-Scheme cattle at Shows etc.

...In the case of *L.* Hardjo, restricting contact with sheep and access to watercourses.

2 Their herds are blood tested at their own expense at regular intervals to demonstrate freedom from infection.

3 They must ask their veterinary surgeon to investigate any illness among their cattle which might be caused by one of the Scheme diseases.

4 They must keep adequate records to show that the herds' security is maintained.

Potential customers from abroad are refusing to consider purchasing cattle whose health status cannot be easily verified, preferring to select only from those farmers who take advantage of voluntary health schemes which are verifiable at a national level.

BSE

Bovine Spongiform Encephalopathy is a new disease of adult cattle first identified in Britain in dairy cows, officially confirmed in November 1986 and made a notifiable disease in 1988. Ban on export followed.

In 1990 the Euroean Community banned import of UK cattle and bone-in-beef carcasses but continued to accept UK calves for veal production.

Cattle are infected in calfhood but due to long incubation period the disease, generally, only becomes evident at 4 to 5 years old. Individual cases have manifested as young as 20 months and at 18 years for the oldest.

By 1995 research had identified a rogue protein in the brain of all cattle afflicted with BSE rather than a new strain of some viral type of infection. BSE is not known to spread from cow to cow and maternal (horizontal) transmission of infection has yet to be proved. Bull semen is thought to present negligible risk of transmission. Conclusive results of transmission through embryo will be available in 2001.

The most likely origin of the disease is thought to have stemmed from the 1980 changes in regulations over the processing of sheep carcasses used in the preparation of Meal and Bone Meal, MBM. The switch from a solvent extraction process to a heat extraction one may have resulted in the inadequately inactivated agent which causes sheep Scrapie entering cattle and calves through their rations of MBM, meat and bone meal usually given to promote fast protein growth.

The incidence of BSE cases was highest among cattle being intensively managed. The less intensive the booster feeding the more likely the cattle will remain free of BSE. Obviously this invites caution about methods of inducing fast weight gain or high condition for Show purposes and endorses the benefits of the natural foraging capacity of Highland cattle to thrive in extensive management systems.

By 1996 only 18 cases of BSE had been identified in Highland cattle and crosses. This amounted to 0.01 percent of the total cases in the UK and was by far the lowest of all the breeds. (figures from S. F. 30/3/96)

In the past major disease amongst cattle in Britain most usually spread from imported stock.

RINDERPEST: there were serious outbreaks of this acute highly infectious virus disease in the seventeenth, eighteenth, and nineteenth centuries. The disease spreads through direct contact from infected beasts, infected byre litter or infected ground. The virus is killed in sunlight and survives about 2 days in the shade.

FOOT AND MOUTH DISEASE: this was first imported into England in 1839 and there have been sporadic outbreaks ever since.

PLEURO-PNEUMONIA: this first appeared in England in 1840; more chronic than rinderpest it spreads by inhalation of infected particles. Infected animals can be carriers for long periods but the disease was eradicated in 1898.

TUBERCULOSIS: this is a chronic cattle disease spread by airborne infection. It is controlled by a successful vaccination programme launched in the 1960s.

ANTHRAX: Until 1886 there were no government measures to restrict the spread of this deadly disease, the spores of which survive in the earth for a very long time, and which is fatal to man.

MURRAIN: an all embracing word for illness in cattle some two to three centuries ago. The word may derive from the Latin "MORI" meaning to die.

Writing in the late nineteenth century George Armatage noted that it is "*an eruptive febrile disease of horned cattle*" very contagious and infectious to man and other livestock; Irish and Dutch imported cattle bring in the disease; Government action was taken in 1745; the period of incubation can be from one to five days when probably a dry husky cough will have been noticed. The animal may be apart from the rest and shivery.

Prevailing causes of murrain (perhaps different from the above description) in 1866 were "*travelling of diseased animals to fairs and markets, on roads, or in steamboats, or railway trucks subsequently used by healthy cattle*". (*Transactions of the Highland and Agricultural Society of Scotland* Volume 1.)

CROSSING HIGHLAND CATTLE

Duncan M Stewart of Millhills, Crieff, is a worldwide authority on Scotch Shorthorn cattle whose Millhills herd, inherited from his father, is one of the oldest and most famous in the world. Mr Stewart has maintained the Shorthorn herd at a high standard and his advice is sought by stockbreeders the world over. He judged the Shorthorns at the 1955 Toronto Royal Winter Fair.

He has, since the end of the last war, become equally noted as a supporter and breeder of Highland cattle whose inherent worth he recognised when he became, with Sir James Denby Roberts, an initiator of the Ben Challum venture, one of the most truly successful of all attempts to put more beef cattle on the Scottish hills. Mr Stewart remains an all-out supporter of the Highland breed as the only sound foundation for this type of beef cattle production.

The Cross Highlander – 1 (extracted from*Highlander for thrift and Profit* 1955 by D. M. Stewart, OBE.)

It is when we come to cattle that the way has been found open for the development of a type based on the straight first cross with our two native hill breeds, the Highland and the Galloway. The cross with these two breeds is made with the Scotch Beef Shorthorn, the former giving what is now an established type known throughout the length and breadth of Great Britain as the Cross Highland. The Galloway, when put to a white bull, produce the well-known Blue-Grey.

Inherited Hardiness and Early Maturity:

Whilst no Shorthorn breeder would ever claim that his cows could withstand conditions acceptable to the Highland cow, it is an established fact that the cross between these two great breeds inherits the best of both worlds and has the hardiness of the Highland and the quick maturing and the fleshing capabilities imparted by the Shorthorn. The practice has therefore grown throughout Scotland, and is gaining momentum in the hill districts of England and in Wales, of keeping the heifers from the Shorthorn-Highland cross and using them as the foundation breeding herd on hill farms. Consider the great advantage. These hill cows, hardy and rugged, can live under any conditions found in this country but – and this is of the greatest importance – they are half Shorthorn and therefore more than half way to being the best beef animals in the world.

Since the decontrol of meat, public demand has shown itself to be highly selective. This means that the producer must all the time look to the quality of what he is producing and at the same time keep a sharp eye on the economic aspect of his production.

He must in fact find the beast that is going to give him the best finished carcase in the shortest possible time. Feeding stuffs must be converted quickly into meat and money must be turned over quickly too. It is no good producing a perfect carcase of meat, be it mutton or beef, if the production is not done in the shortest possible time on the least possible food. Food conversion has been studied carefully in North America and facts have been established which should be given serious consideration by every beef producer in this country. The facts established have proved the Scotch Shorthorn to give the greatest gain in the shortest period when compared with other breeds. In other words, they have been more profitable to feed than any other breed.

Common Ancestry:

The Scotch or Beef Shorthorn has among its valuable characteristics one which may be said to be a breed monopoly – it can transmit its good qualities to its offspring in greater degree than can any other breed. And this power to transmit seems to be accentuated when the Shorthorn bull is mated to the Highland cow. This is probably accounted for by reason of the fact that the Highlander and the Scotch or Beef Shorthorn have, away back in their ancestry, a common parent. At any rate, whatever the reason, there is no doubt that the cross between these two great breeds, the Cross-Highland as it is called, is a beast of great feeding qualities and one which can hold its own with the best in the land.

Crossing (extract from *Highland Cattle for Hardiness Thrift and Profit* 1975)

The Highland cow is the basis of many Cross-breeding Programmes. The most usual is the Beef Shorthorn/Highland Cross – using a White or Roan Bull of the Beef Shorthorn Breed to produce animals of quality and stature capable of being outwintered and with much the same attributes as their dams.These in turn are generally put to an Angus Bull to produce a terminal X animal of superb butcher quality averaging 8½ – 9cwt at 18 months old. Several variations on the above have

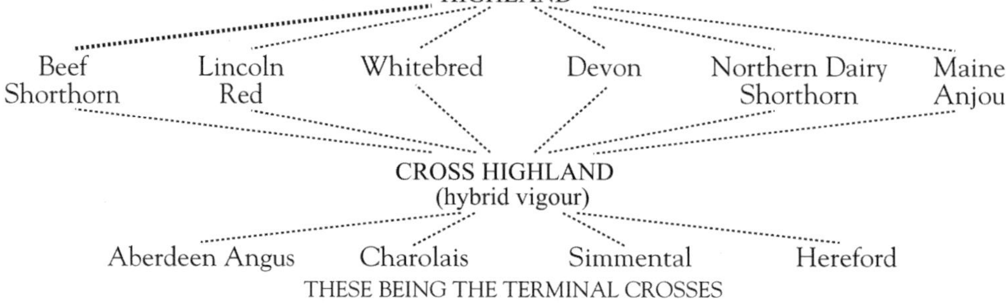

been carried out in latter days, probably due to difficulty in obtaining Shorthorn Bulls of scale. Shorthorn type bulls of other breeds have been used – Lincoln Red, Whitebred and Northern Dairy Shorthorn, Devon and to a lesser extent Maine Anjou. These tend to produce more high standing animals but with perhaps a bit less quality, but still with the qualities passed on from their Highland dams. However, these bigger types are capable of calving down to other terminal X bulls to produce calves for the modern day meat market – Charolais, Simmental and Hereford.

The Place of the Highlander in a Cross-breeding Programme, as seen by a Commercial Farmer (extract from the 1975 *Hardiness Thrift and Profit*)

In my view, the Highland female is the most suitable foundation cow on which to base a herd of outwintered beef cattle in the uplands and wetter areas of Scotland and, probably, much of Great Britain. My objective is to produce a hardy, thrifty cross-bred cow capable of giving me calves that can be carried through to sell fat at eighteen months old and, also, to produce females as herd replacements.

To create and maintain such a herd one must have these objectives always in the forefront of one's mind. Each breeding cow must be assessed, annually, on her merits. I have cast cows after their third calf or because they failed to breed in two years out of five. Equally, I have retained cows until they are sixteen years old.

About 20% of the herd are pure Highland cows, purchased as in-calf heifers at the Society's sales in Oban. These are put to a Beef Shorthorn bull. The bull must have size, be fairly long and be good in the thighs, with sound legs and feet that will carry him on rough ground. The female progeny from this nucleus provides the bulk of the breeding herd with genuine Cross Highlanders and known as such.These cattle retain the hardiness of the Highlander and inherit the well-known conformation and fleshing qualities of the Beef Shorthorn. They have too, that thing called "Hybrid-Vigour". They are long-lived like the Highlander and, given half-decent treatment, breed regularly.

BUTCHER'S BEEF

Mr W Pearson Brown is a breeder of Highland cattle in Yorkshire. He is also a butcher whose services are in demand as a judge at Fat Stock Shows. He has judged at the Scottish National and at the Oban Pedigree Sales. It is from the butcher's angle that he writes this article in support of the Highland breed.

The Highlander as a Butcher's Beast (extract from *The Highlander for Thrift and Profit* 1955 by W Pearson Brown)

I have often been asked what kind of beef they make and I have only one answer. If properly fed there are none better. I think there has been less waste on the cattle of this breed which have been exhibited at our leading Fat Stock Shows than any other breed.

There was the black steer bred at Douglas Castle and exhibited at the Yorkshire Fat Stock Show in 1932. He won first prize and the Lord Strathcona Cup for the best animal of pure Highland Breed; live weight 16 cwt. 70lbs with a dressed carcase weight of 64%. This carcase was a perfect specimen of beef for its size, with not an ounce of waste.

Following this, in 1937, I exhibited a yellow steer, bred by the late Mrs McAlister Hall of Killean, at the Smithfield Club Show at Islington, carrying off first prize and breed champion and third for the best steer in the Show, against all breeds.

Another outstanding animal of the breed, of my own breeding, was the yellow steer exhibited in 1949 at the Smithfield Club Show, at Earls Court. He won first prize in his class, also breed champion. Like his predecessors he produced a carcase of ideally marbled beef, carrying the weight of flesh along the back and down hind-quarters, where it is worth the most per lb.

Although I am a great supporter of pure Highlanders it is the crosses I am chiefly interested in. If we are going to produce store cattle of a beef type from the hills, we must have the Highlander as our foundation stock.The Highland cow crossed with a Scotch Beef Shorthorn bull is the ideal animal for the purpose.

If you have the right cross as I suggest, and wish to have a second cross, perhaps some may wish to use an Angus or Hereford bull. With this I fully agree, as I have slaughtered many of the second cross, about the age of two years, weighing from 9 to 11 cwts. live weight, and producing an ideal carcase of beef, about 62% of their live weight.

EXPORTS

Highlanders Overseas (extract from *The Highlander for Thrift and Profit* 1955)

Prior to the summer of 1954, when Mr T H L Macdonald of Barguillean visited Highland cattle folds in U.S.A., comparatively few people at home in Scotland appreciated that the breed had extended its influence, even in a minor way, beyond these shores.

But Mr Macdonald's visit, as President of the Highland Cattle Society, to the breeders of Montana and the Dakotas, and his official attendance at the annual conference of the American Scotch Highland Breeders' Association received widespread publicity and highlighted the important fact that our breed has been used and appreciated for many years in more than one cattle-rearing country...it will surprise many to learn that Highlanders have been going to America's cattle states for many years, one of the largest earlier importations being in 1922, the importer being Alex Ross on behalf of Walter Hill, Livingston, Montana.

Now, the new Association has registered well over 1,200 head and transferred several hundred head, and with enthusiasts such as Baxter and Lyn Berry, Stanley and Frances Sloan, Ray Carr and others behind the effort, the Highland breed should go from strength to strength in the states mentioned and in others.

There are Highland cattle in Canada also and in Australia, South Africa, Argentina and Czechoslovakia, but next to U.S.A. the strongest footing is in Peru where, 12,000 feet up in the Andes, H E Gildemeister has several hundred head. Mr Gildemeister regularly purchases bulls at Oban and it is interesting to note that he runs three herds each consisting of 100/200 head. This is the accepted South American system and in a recent article Mr Gildemeister described the herds thus:

Herd A – 100 cows and 3 bulls, all pure-bred or imported. This herd reproduces itself from its own females.They produce the stock sires for the other herds.The calf crop has been 90% to 100% average.

Herd B – next in quality, consists of 200 cows and 8 bulls. Bull calves are sold, heifer calves retained.The calf rate is rather lower than in A.

Herd C – the higher the paddocks the lower the calf crop, which drops to 75% while the sires are increased to one per 15 cows as fertility increases.

From 8,000 to 9,000 ft. and often up to 12,000, pasturage is reserved for the Highlanders.

Mr Gildemeister has been able to maintain the true Kyloe in spite of environment and climate.

Exports as mentioned in Highland Cattle Society Publications

(with a few additions from agricultural journals' columns)

1813	One bull and two heifers went to Hudson's Bay Canada from Balnagowan Farm, Inverness-shire. (*Northern Highlands in the 19th Century* by J Barron, 1903.)
1850	Lord Strathcona exported from South Uist to Canada two black, two yellow, two dun females.
1882	Robert Campbell of Merchiston, Canada, returned to Scotland at 74 years of age to buy Calum Riabhach of Athole for export.
1911	Twelve bulls to Newfoundland
1921	Five heifers and two bulls to Wyoming from Mr R Macdiarmid, Corries, Lochawe.
1922	Large importation to America by Alex. Ross for W. Hill, Livingston, Montana, from the dispersal of Miss G Hall's fold at Tangy, Kintyre.
1925	Thirteen females and one bull shipped to Buenos Aires, Argentina.
1926	The bull Fearchar Riabhach of Atholl, and four females from Atholl went to Peru. One bull and four heifers went to the Falklands.
1927	Miss M Lindsay first imported Highland cattle to Canada. Mr R L P Duncan of Pitpointee exporting more Highland cattle to USA, Canada, Falkland Islands. Four cows and one bull went to Falkland Islands. Five bulls from the Duke of Atholl went to Peru for use as crossing sires.
1928	Canadian National Livestock Records began with an import of Highland cattle to Canada.
1929	Four bulls and six heifers went to Saskatchewan, Canada.
1932	Miss Turner, Kilchamaig, sold the animal registered as 3660 for export to Canada.
1946	Two bulls from Ile and Kilchamaig and six Achnacloich heifers went to Peru.
1947	Seven animals from Douglas & Angus estates went to South Africa.
1948	Three cows and two calves bought by J D "Jack" Manke, Edgemont, South Dakota, USA.
1949	Choice draft of unrelated females and one bull went to Queensland.
1950	Brindle bull Calum Ruadh of Achnacloich exported to Australia. One bull from J J Currie, Kildalloig, went to Peru.
1950s	Highland cattle imported to Denmark.
1953	Two bulls and four heifers went to Mr B Berry, South Dakota, USA. One bull went to Miss M Lindsay, Saskatchewan, Canada.
1954	Twenty-one Highland bulls went to the USA in the Autumn – to date the largest importation to any country.
1955	Highland cattle are in Czechoslovakia, Peru, Argentina, Australia, South Africa, Canada, according to an article in *The Highlander for thrift and Profit.*
1956	Thirty-one animals went to the USA.

1957 Two animals from Achnacloich went to Denmark. 40 heifers from Islay went to British Columbia, Canada.

1961 The bull Iain Riabhach of Achnacloich sold in 1960 for export to Canada.

The 1961 Highland Breeders Journals reported the following exports to Canada in 1961:

Two young bulls...Barran Bhuidhe Ile, and Crunair Ile 2nd both registered in Volume 41 of the Herd Book, and six heifers also from Islay and registered in Volume 41 went to A Bruce McLean, BC...Ardtorna Ile 11th, Beaderach Ile 9th, Capleadh Ile 63rd, Capleadh Ile 64th, Eileakach Bheag Ile 8th, Fionnairaidh Ile 17th.

Colonel Oland, Nova Scotia, took Duchess Cora 7th of Cladich 19888, and Baravalla of Ardkinglas 20051.

Mr William Harrington, Cape Breton, Canada, received the bull Torcull of Achnacloich calved 1960, and the heifers Barabal 2nd of Mingary, Donnag 3rd of Mingary, Dossan of Mingary, Rona 1st of Mingary, Ribhinn Dhearg 2nd of Mingary all of which were sired by Viking of Strathallan except for Dossan whose sire was Kinloch of Fordie.

Mr B N Leslie, Ontario, took delivery of the bulls Iain Riabhach of Achnacloich calved 1960, and Crunair Ile calved 1961; the cows Sidonia Ile 37th calved 1957 and Maighdean of Mingary calved 1957, and the heifers Neanach of Mingary calved 1959 and Maighdean 2nd of Mingary calved 1961.

1963 Five Douneside heifers went to Denmark, four red, one brindle. The bull Drambuie of Scone Palace was sold for export to Argentina.

1964 Lachlan of Dalquharran went to Mr J Mutter, Canada.

1965 Highland cattle introduced to Sweden by Mr Rosenorn-Lehn at Rosjoholm's estate. Yeoman of Strathallan, bull, went to Lima, Peru.

1967 Aidan of Ormsary, bull, went to Mr H Carse, Vermont, USA.

1975 In recent years 15 heifers have gone to Sweden. Buyers from Norway and France attended the Ardmenish fold dispersal.

1978 The June Journal in 1978 listed the following exports:

to Sweden: Bhan Og of Scone Palace, Seamrag 13th of Scone Palace, Currac-na-cuthag 11th of Scone Palace, Lady Ruadh 8th of Scone Palace, Cleasach 4th of Scone Palace, Mairi Ruadh 3rd of Balmachree, Ivanhoe of Balmachree,

to France: Barracaid 2nd of Douneside, Baravalla Og 8th of Douneside, Lillian 6th of Douneside.

to USA: Baran 2nd of Douneside, Lileas 12th of Douneside, Lili-a-Gleann 13th of Douneside.

to W. Germany: Seamrag 14th of Scone Palace, Bileag-Bhaite 31st of Scone Palace, Deothlag 14th of Scone Palace, Ida 1st of Scone Palace, Lillian 6th of Scone Palace, Baravalla Laghach 8th of Scone Palace, Lili 10th of Scone Palace, Beinn Bhan of Scone Palace, Coireall 8th of Scone Palace, Lili 11th of Scone Palace.

1979 The Journal of 1979 printed this list of exports:

to France: to M Marcel Guy, St. Sauveur de Bergerac: Domhnull of Harwes 6742,

Caileag of Iomroll 26838, Corinne of Iomroll 26837, Thea of Iomroll 26830, Morven of Iomroll 26833.

to Germany: to Herr Ludwig Doll, 225 Husum-Lund, Federal Republic of Germany: Oganach of Douneside 6769, Barracaid 3rd of Douneside 25367, Oighrig Ruadh Og 2nd of Douneside 26593, Oighrig 7th of Douneside 26583, Eurach Chruinn 12th of Douneside 26582, Dossan Ruadh 22nd of Douneside 25379, Caileag Ghrinn 13th of Douneside 25375, Mairina 6th of Douneside 25366.

to Denmark: to Mr S E R Krause, Glostrup, Denmark: Glenmorangie of Balmachree 6741, Thiona 4th of Iomroll 26832, Capleadh Buidhe of Scone Palace 25997, Deothlag 15th of Scone Palace 26111, Coireal 9th of Scone Palace 26608, Lillian 8th of Scone Palace 26605, Molag Ruadh 5th of Scone Palace 26604.

1980 The Journal of 1980 printed these exports:

to Netherlands: to Beekse Bergen Safari Park, Hilvarenbeek: Catriona Maise Aldannach of Pollok 27658, Morag Caileag Ruadh Aldannach of Pollok 27659, Evelyn of Pollok 25187, Glasghu Oigh of Pollok 26434, Susan Ruadh 2nd of Pollok 25789.

to France: to Mr Currie, White Heather Distilleries Ltd. Abigail of Monkcastle 27814.

to Germany: to Herr Ludwig Doll, Husum-Lund: Leannan Og 10th of Douneside 26580, Mairi 8th of Douneside 26597, Annag 4th of Douneside 26585, Dossan Ruadh 25th of Douneside 26599, Ribhinn 11th of Douneside 26589, Oighrig Ruadh 11th of Douneside 26591, Oighrig Ruadh 12th of Douneside 27279, Princess 19th of Douneside 27283, Mairina 8th of Douneside 27271, Mairi 9th of Douneside 27278.

to Germany: to J Von Schack, Bresahn W Germany: 15 animals from Scone Palace... Bileag Bhaite 40th 27803, Buidhe Og 3rd 27804, Coirneal 11th 27805, Cleasach 7th 27808, Seamrag 16th 27802, Ella Ruadh 12th 27801, An Uiseag 3rd 27798, Cleasach 6th 27294, Bileag Bhaite 39th 27303, Rhonna 3rd 27292, Ella Ruadh 10th 27293, Seamrag 15th 27291, Molag Ruadh 7th 27302, Sidonia 2nd 27301, Barabal Ruadh 7th 27304.

1981 The Journal of 1981 listed these exports:

to Holland: to IR GPA Van Den Eynden, Boxmeer: Ben Loyal of Scone Palace 6,876.

to Denmark: to Copenhagen Parks: Uallach of Commoncraig 6899.

to Denmark: to Herr H Jonsson, Albertslund: Barraidh of Douneside Vol. 59.

to Germany: to Modellbetrieb Sohr Bad Schwalbach, W Germany: 12 animals from Scone Palace...Sidonia 1st 26612, An Uiseag 26614, Deothlag 16th 26618, Bhuidhe Og 1st 26619, Baravalla Laghach 9th 26623, Bileag Bhaite 37th 27285, Lus Mhure 11th 27286, Lillian 10th 27287, Lady Ruadh 9th 27289, Lili 12th 27296, Bhan Og 4th 27799, Sidonia 3rd 27806.

to Germany: to Herr Ludwig Doll, Husum-Lund: 12 animals from Rothiemurchus...

1983 Sixty animals had been exported by June 1983 with another 47 ready to go. Also one bull was to go to Holland and one to Sweden.

1984 The 1984 Journal stated that *"by 1946 there were Highland cattle in Russia"*

1985 93 exports since September 1984 to West Germany, Holland, Canada, USA, and the Middle East.

1986 Four Corriemuckloch heifers went to West Germany.

1988 First Highland cattle imported to Austria in summer 1985 and in 1988 there were 166 breeding animals between 18 Austrian breeders. The first animals went to Mrs L Englhofer's Pirkwiesan Farm in Steiermark.

HIGHLAND CATTLE SOCIETY VIDEO

A video tape was commissioned by the Highland Cattle Society and released in 1984 entitled *Highland Cattle – The Breed That's Not Just a pretty Picture.*
Captain J B Coutts presents the information which is divided into three main sections. The first deals with Breed characteristics and appearance, the second section addresses management of the Breed, while the third presents the Highland Breed as used in many cross-breeding programmes.

PICTORIAL REVIEW IN THREE ARTICLES BY TOM MCLATCHIE, MILLERSTON

HIGHLAND BEEF – AS IT WAS AND SHOULD BE NOW?

First published in the March/April 1984 issue of The Highland Cattle Society newsletter

Since it has been established that the Highland Steers from around 1890 were as large or larger than the Highland Steers of today I have been inundated with requests from home and abroad for statistics and visual proof that this is so. I have compiled statistics taken from papers and journals from that date. The comments are those of the writers of that time.
In 1893 the official average weights were given as Oxen: 17cwts 4 lbs (1,908 lbs) (865 kg), Cows and heifers: 15 cwts 2 qrs 15 lbs (1,751 lbs) (794 kg). Oxen was the name by which steers were known at that time.

The report of the Smithfield Fat Stock Show for 1894 states: "*The animal that the judge liked least the butcher thought most of four carcasses shown.*" In other words the beast not in the prize list killed out better than the prize winners. The carcass of the 3rd prize ox was superior to that of the 1st and 2nd prize animals, every bit of meat was saleable.

Steer "Sandy" around 1900. Date cannot be confirmed but before 1910.
Weights at Smithfield 17 cwts and over were commonly attained at this time.

Norman Reid's Inverness Champion and the black ox killed out at 42.35%, plenty of lean meat, full of nature and plenty of rich fat, ripe and mellow, but not quite so good a carcass as the black ox not quite so full of flesh and the fat was not so mellow.

The splendid big ox Fiorlig 2nd with which Mr Munro won Birmingham was killed by Mr Holton. He cut up at 66.60% and the carcass was full of lean meat nicely marbled and covered by yellow fat. Fiorlig 2nd did not win any prizes at Smithfield. One of the best of all the Highlanders was the red ox Donald owned by Mr Munro but breeder unknown. He got nothing from the judges but at 2 yrs 7 mths old he killed 69.36% carcass to gross live weight and made a nice body of beef well proportioned as to fat and lean.

Pic Ⓐ – A brindle steer bred by the Marquis of Breadalblane K. G. aged 3 yrs 9 mths weighing 16 cwts 37 lbs (1,829 lbs) (830 kg) was the winner of the Breed Championship at the Scottish National Fat Stock Show in Edinburgh.

Brindle bullock aged 3¾ years. Breed Champion Scottish National Fatstock Show weighing 16 cwts 37 lbs

Lord Durham's 3 yr 7 mths ox Langley which was 2nd at Birmingham and commended at Smithfield is warmly eulogised by his butcher. He killed at 64.62% but was an extraordinary cutter full of flesh and very lean in the flanks and brisket. There could be no better butchers beast. Lord Cawdor's Highland Lassie killed at 63.22% and Katie of Balinmore 62. 83%. A heifer which received a very high commendation is Rose of Monkstadt, she showed 64.40% dead to gross live weight and is characterised as the best beef Mr Holton had this season out of the 38 Highland cattle he killed. Another good beast killed by Mr Holton was the Ensay heifer Brandburg Queen at 2 yrs 8 mths killed at 66.97% with an average daily weight gain of 1.3 lbs (0.59 kg). Rose of Monkstadt had the highest daily weight gain of 1.48 lbs (0.67 kgs).

In 1908 Sir Wm Ogilvy Dalgleish's magnificent dun steer won the Breed Championship at Smithfield. At 33 months old he weighed 15¾ cwts (1,764 lbs) (800 kg). Again in 1913 Sir William won the Cup with a 34 month old steer weighing 14 cwts 104 lbs (1,672 lbs) (758 kg).

Errol Candidate XVIII

Highland steers at Douglas. First and third at the Scottish National Fatstock Show 1928.

Around 1920 the averages at Smithfield for a fine class of steers under 3 years was 13+ cwts (1,512 lbs) (686 kg). Average for steers under 4 years was 15cwts 3qrs 181bs (1,782 lbs) (808 kg). Average for a good group of heifers was 13+ cwts (1,512 lbs) (686 kg).

Pic Ⓑ – The brindle steer Errol Candidate XVIII, Sire: An t-urramach, Dam: Fuinary Queen of Errol aged 2 yrs 9 mths 5 days and weighing 13 cwts 30 1bs (1,486 lbs) (686 kg) won the Breed Championship at the Scottish National Fat Stock Show at Edinburgh and also at London in 1924.

Pic Ⓒ – There was a black steer bred at Douglas Castle and exhibited at the Yorkshire Fat Stock Show in 1932. He won the Lord Strathcona Cup for the best animal of the Highland breed, his live weight was 16 cwts 70 lbs (1,862 lbs) (845 kg) with a dressed carcass weight of 64 percent. This carcass was a perfect specimen of beef for its size with not one ounce of waste. It gave complete customer satisfaction.

Scottish National and Smithfield Breed Champion Jock of Leys with his breeder, Sir Francis Walker.

Pic Ⓓ – In 1936 Jock of Leys won the breed championship at both the Scottish National Fatstock Show and the Smithfield Fatstock Show. This was a yellow steer aged 2 years 9 months 19 days and weighing 14cwts 721bs (1,640 lbs) (744 kg) his sire was Duke 2nd of Flichity, his dam was Fearlag Buidhe.

The Reserve Champion at the above two shows was a heifer Daoimon 13th of Stronvar shown by His Majesty the King from Sandringham. This heifer was 43+ months old and weighed 12cwts 591bs (1,403 lbs) (636 kg).

At the Smithfield Fatstock Show in 1937 it was a yellow steer bred at Hall of Killean that won the Breed Championship and stood 3rd for the best steer in the show against all breeds.

During the war years control many 2+ year old Highland Steers were graded weighing between 9 cwts (1,008 lbs) (457 kg) and 11 cwts (1,232 lbs) (559 kg) and producing a carcass of beef equivalent to 58% of their live weight.

It is interesting to note how the killing out % declines with the slaughter liveweight.

These cattle were finished on grass and consumed nothing but what was grown on the farm. I am a firm believer that Highland cattle will respond to good feeding and management as well as any other breed.

The dates I cannot guarantee as accurate. The weights and killing out percentage are as printed in papers or journals. The photos speak volumes.

EARLY HEADS, HORNS & HISTORY OF HIGHLAND CATTLE

First published in the July 1993 Highland Breeders' Journal

For some time now at Shows and sales around the country there has been argument about the trend towards coarseness in the heads of Highland cattle, especially females as compared with the cattle at the turn of the century. With much of this criticism I would agree.

In the following article with illustrations I seek to portray the situation as it existed then and adumbrate my fears for the future of the breed if the present trend is not altered or redirected.

Without doubt the head of the Highland cow or the carriage of the head give that majestic appearance for which they are as a breed renowned. The head deserves the breeder's serious consideration and attention if the present undesirable traits are to be halted or reversed.

Many breeders and biologists believe that the male of the species is responsible for 50% of the genes in their offspring. Genetically this means bad as well as good and since the geneticists cannot (tell) predict the proportion of good or bad genes in the division it is left to the breeders themselves to prove by trial and error the traits that are passed from one generation to another.

1856 award winner in Paris bred by G & JG Smith, Minmore, Ballindalloch. There are still Highland cattle at Minmore at the present time.

Starting with bulls, the earliest example I could find is an artist's impression of the bull that won the honours for the breed at the World Agricultural Congress in Paris in 1856. As this was long before the Highland Cattle Society was formed or the first Herd

Book printed there is no dogma to cloud the horizon. Breeders of that era did their own thing as they thought best and most profitable as any breed can only survive in commerce if it is profitable.

Between 1870 and 1880 the best known and best breeding bulls were Calum Riabhach of Atholl (82) and Donnacha Ban Nan Oran (155).

That in my opinion is the type of bull that could be used to advantage today.

Fear-a-Bhaile of Camusericht (200), Rob Roy 3rd (442) and Lord Dunmore's An-t-Iasgair (13) were the most prominent Show winners of breeders in the 1880s.

Fear-a-Bhaile of Camusericht (200) was a brindle bull used as stock bull at Camusericht, Bochastle, Gordon Hall and Garbole.

Rob Roy 3rd (442) owed his reputation to a unique grandeur, to his form and carriage. Some judges thought his head rather strong.

In 1897 at the Highland Show held in Glasgow Laoch (1260) (see p308) won the President's Medal for the Best Highland Animal for John Stewart of Ensay. He also won the Highland in 1896 and 1901.

Thomas Valentine Smith of Ardtornish won the Aged Class at the Highland and Agricultural Society's Show, Edinburgh in 1893 with Victor 5th (951) (see p308). He also won the prize for the best bull at the Show with Victor 7th (1067) Both were sons of the famous black cow Proisag Dhubh (783) (see p309).

Again in 1894 Valentine Smith won H. R. H. The Duke of York's Medal for the best Highlander with Valentine XI (1160).

On the female side of the breed it was said around 1860, 'The cattle were of a splendid size and bone, remarkably free from coarseness, with soft rich hair. The cows were all very good milkers, had noble heads, the sweep of the horn being most majestic and commanded the enthusiastic admiration of the best judges.' While there is written material around about the famous cows of that era there are very few photographs fit for reproduction.

The first female to be mentioned by name was at the Perth Show of 1861. She was shown as a heifer, calved after 1st January 1859 by the Marquis of Breadalbane, won first in her class and was called Nora Odhar (549).

In 1862 the famous breeding bull Duntroon (177) then a 6 year old brindle, took first prize and Gold Medal for Mr Malcolm of Poltallach at the Battersea International Show.

One writer described Calum Riabhach of Atholl (82) as, 'a bull built on a massive scale, he had a noble masculine countenance, a long deep and wide frame, sappy skin and for all his size and weight he carried himself well up in years with a springy step.'

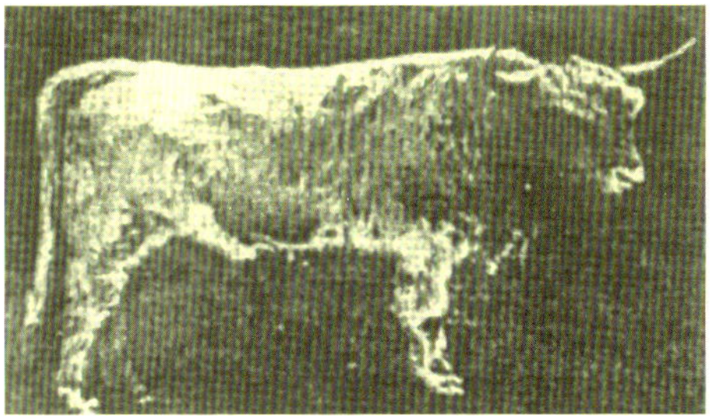

It was written of the bull Donnacha Ban Nan Oran (155) 'he was a light dun colour, had well set horns of great quality and a beautiful brow with soft hair hanging like a sporran, his general shape was good and he stood straight on strong legs, but not specially deep in the rib.'

One of the most characteristic cows at Poltallach was the wide framed robust looking Mhaldag (64) which won at the Dumfries Highland in 1886 as a five year-old against the Ensay cows.

Sgiathach 24th of Ardtornish (4807) (see p310) won the President's Medal. In a choice class of cows there was found no equal for this magnificent black cow. This lovely specimen of the breed was shown to perfection. She has face, back, ribs, quarters and hair of quality.

The cations with the photographs pages 307-310 are taken from the writings of James Cameron about famous Highland bulls and cows at the turn of the nineteenth century.

Ceatharnach Buidhe (719) 'a perfect representation of lordly Highland grandeur when looking one straight in the face. A bull of great massiveness though slack waisted.'

His son Laoch (1260) 'a bull built on the large scale of other days wanting his sire's nobility of countenance but superior in general conformation.'

Victor V (951) a son of Proisag Dhubh (783).

The President's Medal was won at Kelso in 1898 by the Duke of Atholl, K T, with Calum Riabhach II of Atholl (1325). He was the champion two years in succession. 'A prettier or better haired bull has not been seen for at least a generation.'

Calum Buidhe of Atholl, a son of the great cow Te Bhuidhe (1379). 'He has capital hind-quarters but is very near the ground but nevertheless won the Corrimony Cup at Inverness in 1901.'

Victor XXII (1600) born 1889 was another big black bull much talked about for many years.

A bull that won many top awards around this time in the eighteen nineties was King Alaric (1712) bred by the Earl of Southesk and described as having, 'a beautiful head, perfect hair, grand sprung ribs but tapering at the tail.' He is a son of Calum Riabhach II of Atholl (1325) mentioned earlier.

In 1905 and 1906 Lord Clyde (2034) was a winner in his class at Highland & Agricultural Society Shows. He was also Champion in 1906.

Saladin (2067), a three year-old brindled bull who won his class for three years and described as, 'an exceptionally straight stylish bull', remarkably well-bred by Calum Riabhach II and his dam is Lady Sheila (3833) by Ceathernach Buidhe (719)

Calum Ban a Rithist of Farr (2393) is a 'big deep bull with a straight top, lovely quality of substance.' Champion at the Highland Show in 1912.

Morair Inernarin won the medal for the best bull for D M Stewart.

Ribhinn Lurach (1304) and Donnach Riabhach N'Odhar was the granddam of the famous Proisag Dhubh (783).

Te Riabhach (35) probably the wildest headed cow calved within the memory of any Showgoer. (Photo taken at 14 years of age).

Proisag Dhubh of Bochastle (783) at the age of five years won the Glasgow Highland in 1882 and again Aberdeen in 1885. At the age of twelve she won the cup for The Best Female. Her face her head and her backswirling horns were strikingly sweet and of intense Highland character. She was full of quality and had exceptionally good hind-quarters. She was the dam of four black bulls.

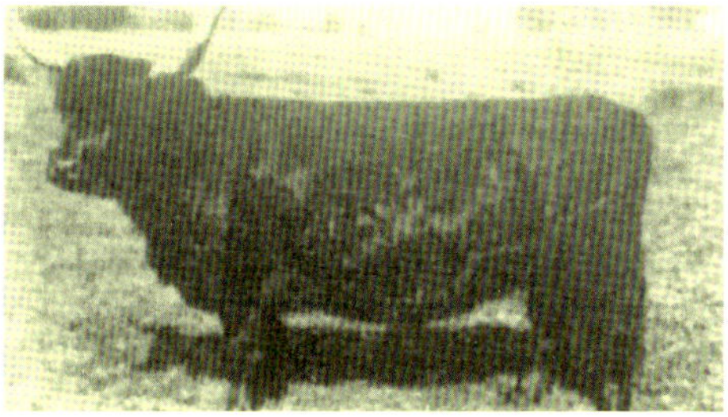

Sgiathach Dubh of Ardtornish (1251) was the dam and granddam of many Show winners.

Ruadh Mhor of Melfort was the first prize cow at the Edinburgh Show in 1893 exhibited by Malcolm of Poltalloch.

Sgiathach 16th (4223) Rhouma (3928) (left) and Laochag Bhuidhe 2nd of Ensay (4290) were first, second and third at the Highland Show at Kelso in 1898.

In 1900 Rhouma (3928) The flecked brindle by Victor V (951) was first. 'She was an easy winner and one of the finest animals of her breed alive.'

Sgiathach 24th (on the right) and Cruinneag 6th three year-old heifers first and second in their class at RHS Stirling in 1902.

The cows made the best class ever seen at the Highland & Agricultural Society Show in 1903. There was no doubt at all about the winner She was easily found in Laochag Bhuidhe 1st (4289) now nine years old and from a very famous tribe. She is a cow of great substance standing close to the ground, made straight and level she stood out as a typical matron and clear winner.

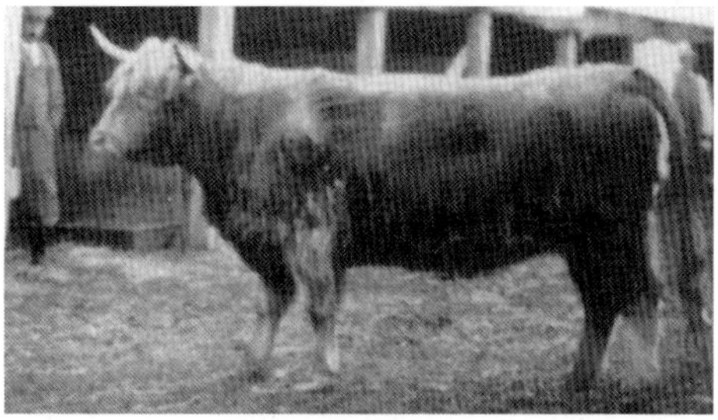

Loachag was a winner in 1905.

In 1906 the females were much better than the males. D. M Stewart was Reserve Champion with Laochag Bhuidhe 4th (6584) a home-bred animal Laochag Bhuidhe 4th (6584) won The Prince of Wales Gold Medal in 1907.

Empress Almira (6933) a dark brindled cow was first in her class at Stirling in 1909.

Fuinary Queen (7705) by Valentine 26th (2212) her dam was the famous May Queen (4795). She is a beautiful short legged cow full of breed character. She has been three times champion at the Highland Shows and is not very likely to be beaten.

For final picture (Stella a three year-old heifer never shown before), please refer to original article in HBJ 36

SOME FAMOUS SHOW WINNERS BEFORE 1939

1 Donnacha Ban Nan Oran 155 (Bochastle Bred); Calved 1875

2 Laoch 1260; Calved 1894

3 Calum Riabhach II of Athole 1325

4 Calum Bhuide of Athole

5 Laochag Bhuidhe of Ensay 6584; Calved 1902

6 Victor XXII 1600; Calved 1903

7 Fiunary Queen; Calved 1906 (Champ Oban 1909)

8 Funery Queen (has split ear)

9 Laochag; Calved 1906

10 Capleadh Ile XVI

11 Calum Ban a Ribhist of Farr 2393; Calved 1908

12 Chevalier; Calved 1909

13 Merlin; Calved 1910

14 Stella 1327; Calved 1910

15 Baran of Camusericht; Calved 1914

16 Capleadh XXIV

17 Proiseag Sgiathach of Garth 9386; Calved 1913

18 Proiseag Sgiathach III of Garth; Calved 1918

19 An-T-Uramach (Ensay Bred) 3050; Calved 1918

20 Ossian Ban of Atholl 3176; Calved 1918

21 Princess Caroline of Southesk 9400; Calved 1918

22 Iarla Buidhe of Atholl 3650; Calved 1922

23 Corrina of Southesk 9824; Calved 1927

24 Merlin IV 3640; Calved 1929

25 Culnadalloch II of Achnacloich 3441; Calved 1929

26 Sweetheart of Achnacloich 10392; Calved 1931

27 Baravalla Smiorail II of Killundine 10636; Calved 1933

28 Ribhinn Ile 10991 (Champ.H&Ag.1938)

1

3

2

4

5

6

7

8

9

10

11

12

13

14

15

16

17

18

19

20

21

22

23

24

25

26

27

28

The Highland Cattle Society of Scotland published a twice yearly magazine in 1961, 1962, 1963, since when the magazine has been published annually entitled *Highland Breeders Journal.*

The Journal contains reports on Agricultural Shows, Fatstock Shows, full details of Highland cattle Sales, Directory of Folds, Stock Bull lists, Obituaries, Address from the President of the Society, and other such membership business in addition to feature articles.

The feature articles from 1961 to 1990 are listed here in two categories:

1 Information on Individual Folds.

2 General Articles.

1. YEAR INDEX TO ARTICLES ON INDIVIDUAL FOLDS

Informative articles featuring individual folds began in 1964.

1964 Douneside
1965 Achnacloich
1966 Islay
1967 Scone Palace
1968 Benmore
1969 Strathallan
1970 Glengorm
1971 Ormsary
1972 Woodneuk
1973 Douglas and Angus Estate.
1974 Leys
1975 Balmoral
1976 No Fold featured
1977 The Glenquoich Fold
1978 Torloisk
1979 Dun Dubh
1980 Trelessick (New Zealand)
1981 Hungerhill
1982 Iddesleigh
1983 Millerston; Douglas; Dun Dubh.
1984 Brand; Pollok; Balinoe; Leys; Blairpark; Woodneuk and Commoncraig; Douglas Estate; Benmore; Tinto.
1985 Ardbhan
1986 Baravalla
1987 Eslington; Austie; Zetland
1988 Thursden
1989 Stichting Cattle
1990 Cullerne; Bungsberg Highlanders

2. YEAR INDEX TO TITLES OF GENERAL ARTICLES

1961 June issue

Our Heritage
Our World Famous Highland cattle Are an Economic Proposition
The Department of Agriculture's Highland Stud.
Highland Cattle in Public Parks.

Is This the Answer to Dwindling Herd Book Entries.
What Kind of Member Are You?
December issue
Can the Highlander meet the present Day Challenge?
Purity and Pedigree
A Review of the Breed in 1961.
Highlander at the Crossroads.
The Breed in North West America
Highland Crosses Provide Barons of Beef.
The Art and Science of Line Stock Breeding.
Highland Cattle for Cross-breeding in Canada.

1962 **June issue**
New Opportunities for an Old Breed.
Intensive Beef Today and Tomorrow.
Letter From Canada (Mr H. O. Rogerson)
Support the Highlander and Confound the Critics.
To Stimulate Breed Interest Bold Decisions Are Urgently Required.
December issue
A Worthy Ambassador
Breed progress in America
Our Heritage
Alien Blood Can Destroy the Highlander.
Mr Michael Noble's Important Appointment
Field Day at Achnacloich and Muckairn
The President Reports on His American Visit
A Tribute to the Highlander
Up Highlanders and At 'Em!
Off the Grass Demonstration Harrogate.

1963 **June issue**
A Breed Resurgence
Important Breed Export to Argentina
Safeguarding Our Heritage.
Revolution in Beef Cattle Breeding
Beef Production and Marketing
Five Heifers Exported to Denmark.
Letter from America
The Vital Role of Breed Societies.
December issue
Beef and Current Matters.
There's Good Money in Beef.
Cross-breeding Experiments at Cladich.
The Potential of the Export Market.
Why the Highlander is Popular in America.
Beef on the Hook.

1964 Highland Bull at AI Station.
Experiences with Highland Cattle
New Stirling venture.
Highlanders in Texas.
The Prime Minister's Farms
Dalquharran Bull for Canada.
Highlanders in Manchester's Public Parks.
Saved from Death...A Poem to Whisky of Strathallan.

1965 The Old Breed.
Beef from the Hills in West Perthshire.
Highland Bull at AI Centre.
Highland Cross Friesian.
Time for Reflection.
A Banner Year for the Breed in USA.
Two Acres and a Cow.
Highland Bullocks Make Good Prices.

1966 Field day at Ormsary
Beef Recording
The Highland Cow as a Source of beef.
What's a Highland
The Highlander at Home and Abroad
At Last
Fold Notes
Dispersals
Thoughts on Testing
Highlanders in Peru

1967 Highland cattle in Canada.
Open Day at Luing.
Highlander from a Butcher's Point of View.
Additional Trophies: W. Pearson Brown and Ormsary.
A Miniature Fold.
Year Round on Grass.

1968 Some Fine Men and Cattle of Another Generation.
Role of the Highlander.
A Tribute to the Late Duncan Stewart OBE of Millhills.
The Tragedy of Foot and Mouth Disease in the Lakeside Fold.

1969 In Retrospect.
Highlanders in New Scotland.
News from America.

1970 Presentation from Canada
Highlanders from Canada
Directory of Herds
Visitors to Oban

1971 Highland Cattle in Die Lage Landen
Highland Fold on Rhum
Devon X Highland Steers
Highland Cattle in The New Forest
Highland Cattle in Canada

1972 Field Day at Achnacloich
Commercial Facts and Figures
Canadian Section...Merchiston Highland cattle
AI Regulations

1973 Highland Cattle on Rhum.
Highland Memories.
The Story of the Snowlander.
Canadian Section.

1974 Life Portraits...a Poetic Oration.
Mothering the Exotics.
Canadian Section.

1975 Gaelic Names of Highland Cattle.
Opportunity for Cattle in West Highlands.
Certificates of Approval.
Canadian Section.

1976 Offchurchbury Dispersal Sale.
Ardmenish Fold Dispersal Sale.
Panel of Judges.
Optimistic After 80 Years with Meat.
Certificates of Approval.
Newsletter on Stichting Cattle.
Canadian Section: Glen Osprey farm Bull Test 1976
Norgrove Registered Highlands

1977 Memories. . Breadalbane Highlanders 1896
In Lighter Vein
Canadian Section: Record of performance Highland cattle on Test in Canada
Touring Some new Folds in East Central Ontario.
Lower Fraser Valley Exhibit.

1978 The Rhum Fold
OBF Brucellosis testing.
Canadian Section: Speech at Mary Lindsay Banquet 1977.

1979 From Highlander to Hook
Corsons...A Mart for the Islands and the West.
A Highland Journey.
Canadian Section.

1980 Thoughts From Abroad.
Highlanders in Sweden.
Floreat DunDubh Dunelmia.
Taking the Highland Road.
The Famous Highland Beef.
I Am A Miserable Highland Bull.
Highlanders in Any Weather.
Canadian Section: Yon Bonny Canny Kine.
Arkell Research Station.

1981 News from France.
The Descent of Scottish Highland Cattle.
Highlanders Enter a New Era of Performance.
Turning Wasteland into Beef
Statistics.
Canadian Section: Koolcairn Fold.

1982 The Famous Highland Drove.
No Decline in Scotland's Native Breed.
The Breed That's Not Just a Pretty Face.
Pictorial Highlights.
Canadian Section.

1983 Centenary
Feeding Young Pedigree Bulls.
The Cattle of Britain...Highland.
Steer Scheme.
Gaelic Names.
Scotch Highlanders.
Canadian Section: Importing from U. K. Highland cattle and Brush Suppression.

1984 Fatstock Shows.
Highland Beef is Best
A View from the Islands.
Highland cattle Exports.
Breed With A Proud History.
Highland Cattle Tour 1955 (poem)
The Highlander Today.
The Steer Scheme.
Douglas Cross-Highland Cattle.
Cattle Who Improve the Scenery While Chewing It.
Robert Henry Jane 1904 –1984 Monksmoor Farm.
Highland Cattle in The United States of America.
Dan Flynn – Massachusetts.
Andana Farms USA.
Highland Cattle in North Central Massachusetts. USA
Highlanders in Australia

Highland Cattle in Denmark.
Highlanders in Sweden.
Canadian Section: Shelterwood Farm.
Covenant Fold.
Cnoc Eilidh
Tell It Like It Is (research on growth High Arrow Fold rates)
Swains Fold
Glen Osprey Farm.

1985 Factors Affecting Liveweight Gain.
Food For Thought.
A View from the Islands.
The Steer Scheme.
EBL Enzootic Bovine Leukosis.
Canadian Section: Centenary Reflections.

1986 From the Highland Breeders Journal of 25 Years Ago.
Crush for Highland Cattle.
Cross-Highland Bullocks.
Canadian Section.

1987 Highland Cattle.
Trip to Mull.
Open Day.
Export Requirements.
Fickle Fluke.
Canadian Section: Highland Cattle in Eastern Canada; Tweed; Alberta Highland Cattle Association.

1988 Highland Cattle in Drenthe.
The Old Rusty Binder.
Feed Conversion Efficiency.
Modern Sheep Dipping.
Successful Adaption. (Thursden Fold)
Canadian/USA Trip Report.
Highland Cattle in Austria.
Salers X Highland.
Ode to Seumas. (p. 260-262 of *A Keen Eye*)
Highlanders LTD.
Highland Cattle in 1919.
American Highlanders.
Highlanders in Sweden 1988
Scotch Highlanders.
Yon Bonny Canny Kine.
Highland Cattle in Schonwalde.

Canadian Section: Keijoasan Fold; The Earlona Connection; Glen Roy Fold; Knowlton Rendezvous; Hardy Highland Cattle; Maple Lea Farm Highlands Go to Brome Fair; Showtime in Yakima; Informal Meeting of 1988; Middle River Site of 1988 AGM; The Long's Point Highland Festival Colorado; 1988 Grand Champion Female Moves to Ontario.

1989 Hyde Park Festival of Food and Farming.
Glasgow Garden Festival.
Fluke Update.
Highland Gains Cheer David.
Highland Cattle for Thrift and Profit.
Hochlandrinder.
Curing a Highland Skin.
Canadian Red cattle Breeders.
Canadian Section.

1990 Importance of Hoof Care.
Organic Highlanders.
Developments in Beef Cattle Breeding.
Fluke Disease.
Oh No! Not Another Bull.
Embryo Transfer.
Bovine Spongiform Encephalopathy.
Belgium: A New Destination.
American Simmental Association's Sire Evaluation System.
Frankfurt: Tier und Tachnik.
Short Sailing Tour Account.
Canadian Section: The Goodwill Connection.

HERD BOOKS
INDEX TO ARTICLES AND PHOTOGRAPHS

The Herd Books form a register of such Highland cattle as breeders wish to record and which the Highland Cattle Society of Scotland consider meet their criteria for the breed.

The format of the Herd Book has varied over the years, at times including articles of interest and photographs of award-winning stock in addition to the regular entries of bulls, cows, heifers, their breeders, the owners, office bearers, any necessary intimations from the secretary of the Society, and errata.

Access to complete sets of these from 1885 is less than straightforward, there being neither a public library in Scotland with a full set nor study facilities in the Society Offices for prolonged perusal of the volumes. Computerised registration data will soon make obsolete the bulky collection of volumes of Herd Books but may retain variants of individual Gaelic names and may not initially facilitate access to the student of pedigrees, so this index of selected contents and appendices may be of some guidance to any engaged in particular research.

Of the 195 breeders and owners of Highland cattle who registered animals in the first volume of the Herd Book 60 were from the Islands, 59 from the West Mainland, 48 from Central, and 28 from Mainland Inverness-shire and the North, of Scotland.

The distribution of Islands breeders/owners was:

Mull – 11, Skye – 7, Islay – 9, The Uists – 16, Rhum – 2, Barra – 1, Jura – 2, Colonsay – 2, Raasay – 1, Harris – 5, Gigha – 1, Coll – 1, Benbecula – 1, Luing – 1.

VOL I – 1885

Lithograph: Calum Riabhach of Athole 82, awarded the Champion Cup as best male of the West Highland Breed at the 1884 Centenary Show of the Highland & Agricultural Society.

Retrospective volume entered bulls only.

The six-and-a-quarter pages of preface give a brief history of the breed mentioning successful breeders and listing guidelines of the accepted points of a well-bred animal.

VOL II – 1887

Photograph: Proisag Dhubh 783 with calf. Bred by and property of J Stewart, Bochastle.

Pedigree cows calved before 1st January 1882 and bulls calved before 1st January 1884.

VOL III – 1888

Photograph: Ribhinn Lurach of Ensay 1304. Bred by and property of J Stewart of Ensay.

In addition to registered bulls, cows, and heifers. Appendices A: Change of Ownership; B: Corrigenda; C: Awards to Highland cattle from 1822 to 1884 inclusive.

List of breeders and owners with names of their cattle.

VOL IV – 1890

Photograph: Ceatharnach 642. Bred by and property of J Stewart of Ensay; Te Riabhach 35 aged 14 years, bred by the Duke of Athole KT, property of the Earl of Southesk KT.

Reprint of the minute of the inaugural meeting of the Society.

VOL V – 1891

Photographs: Lord of the Isles II 781. Bred by the Duke of Sutherland KG. Property of Mr Hume Webster, Marden Deer Park, Surrey. Sgiathach Dubh of Ardtonish 1251 bred by J Duncan of Benmore, property of T V Smith of Ardtonish.

Appendix C: awards to Highland cattle from 1885 to 1891 inclusive.

VOL VI – 1893

Photograph: Ceatharnach Buidhe 719. Bred by and property of J Stewart of Ensay. Awarded firsts at the Highland and Agricultural Society of Scotland's Shows 1891, 1892 and Highland Cattle Society's Cup at Inverness 1892.

Appendix D: Awards to Highland Cattle at the Highland and Agricultural Society's Show 1892.

VOL VII – 1895

Photographs: Valentine XI 1160. Bred by and property of T Valentine Smith of Ardtornish. First as a yearling and won the Duke of York's medal for the best Highland animal at the Highland & Agricultural Show at Aberdeen in 1894. An-t-Iasgair 13 bred by the Earl of Dunmore; property of the Earl of Southesk KT, Kinnaird Castle. Proiseag Ruadh of Poltalloch 3272 and Ruadh Beag VI of Poltalloch 3273 both bred by J Malcolm of Poltalloch and property of Colonel J W Malcolm CB of Poltalloch.

Appendix C: awards to Highland cattle at the Highland & Agricultural Shows of 1893 and 1894.

VOL VIII - 1897

Photograph: Laoich 1260. Bred by and property of J Stewart of Ensay. First as two year old and winner of the President's Medal for the best Highland animal at the Highland & Agricultural Show at Perth 1896.

Appendix C: awards to Highland cattle at the Highland & Agricultural Shows 1895 and 1896.

VOL IX - 1898

Photographs: Calum Riabhach II 1325. Bred by and property of the Duke of Atholl KT. First as two year old. Won President's Medal for best Highland animal at the Highland & Agricultural Show at Kelso 1898. Sgiathach XVI 4223 bred by and property of T V Smith of Ardtonish; Rhouma 3928 bred by T V Smith of Ardtonish property of G Bullough of Rhum; Laochag Bhuidhe II of Ensay 4290 bred and property of J Stewart of Ensay. Winners of first, second and third prizes respectively for three year old heifers at the Highland & Agricultural Show, Kelso 1898.

Appendix C: awards to Highland cattle at the Highland & Agricultural Shows of 1897 and 1898. Prize lists at the Highland Cattle Society's Bull Shows 1892 - 1898.

VOL X - 1900

Photographs: Mac-a-Mhullich 1393. Bred by M Sinclair, Culnadalloch, Connel. Property of D Graham of Airthrey. First as two year old at Highland & Agricultural Show in Edinburgh 1899.

Mairi Bhuidhe of Atholl 4450 and Beauty IV of Atholl 4449 both bred and property of the Duke of Atholl KT, and Lady Clare 3826 bred by and property of the Earl of Southesk KT, placed first, second and third respectively for three year old heifers at the Highland & Agricultural Show, Edinburgh 1899.

Appendix C: awards to Highland cattle at the Highland & Agricultural Show in 1899. Prize lists at the Highland Cattle Society's Bull Shows in 1899 and 1900. General index of animals entered in Volumes I to X of the Herd Book.

VOL XI - 1902

No photograph.

Appendix C: awards to Highland cattle at Highland & Agricultural Shows in 1900 and 1901. Prize lists at the Highland Cattle Society's Bull Shows in 1901 and 1902.

VOL XII - 1904

Photograph: King Alaric 1712. Bred by and property of the Earl of Southesk KT. First as yearling at the Highland & Agricultural Show in Aberdeen 1902, first as two year old at the Highland & Agricultural Show in Dumfries 1903, and medal for the best Highland animal, and Silver Medal for the Best Highland Bull.

Appendix C: awards at the Highland & Agricultural Shows of 1902 and 1903. Prize lists at the Highland Cattle Society's Bull Show 1903.

VOL XIII - 1905

Photograph: Laochag Bhuidhe of Ensay 6584. Bred by and property of D A Stewart (of Lochdhu) Ensay, Obbe (renamed Leverburgh, December 1920). First as two year old at the Highland & Agricultural Show, Perth 1904; first as three year old along with President's Champion Medal for best Highland animal at the Highland & Agricultural Show, Glasgow 1905.

Appendix C: awards to Highland cattle at the Highland & Agricultural Show in 1904 and 1905. Prize lists at the Highland Cattle Society's Shows of 1904 and 1905.

VOL XIV – 1907

Photograph: Lord Clyde 2034. Bred by the late Earl of Southesk KT. Kinnaird Castle, property of the Trustees of Mr Bullough, Meggernie Castle. First as two year old along with Silver Medal at the Highland & Agricultural Show, Glasgow 1905; first as aged bull along with President's Champion Medal at the Highland & Agricultural Show, Peebles 1906, and second as yearling at the Highland Cattle Society Show in Oban 1904.

Appendix B: awards to Highland cattle at the Highland & Agricultural Show 1906. Prize list for Highland Cattle Society's Show 1906.

VOL XV – 1908

Photograph: Saladin. Bred by the late Earl of Southesk KT. Kinnaird Castle. Property of Mr Craig Sellar of Ardtornish. First as yearling at the Highland & Agricultural Show, Glasgow 1905; first as two year old along with Silver Medal at the Highland & Agricultural Show, Peebles 1906; First as aged bull along with President's Champion Medal also Silver Medal at the Highland & Agricultural Show, Edinburgh 1907; first as aged bull at Highland Cattle Society's Show in 1908.

Appendix C: awards to Highland cattle at the Highland & Agricultural Show 1907. Prize lists at Highland Cattle Society's Shows of 1907 and 1908.

VOL XVI – 1910

Photograph: Laochag Iseabal 7396. Bred by and property of D A Stewart (Lochdhu) Ensay, Obbe. First as two year old at the Highland & Agricultural Show, Peebles 1906; first as three year old at the Highland & Agricultural Show, Edinburgh 1907; first as aged cow in milk along with President's Champion Medal for the best Highland animal at the Highland & Agricultural Show, Aberdeen 1908. Appendix B: awards to Highland cattle at the Highland & Agricultural Shows of 1908 and 1909. Prize lists at Highland Cattle Society's Shows of 1909 and 1910.

VOL XVII – 1912

Photograph: Fuinary Queen 7705. Bred by Mr Craig Sellar of Ardtornish. Property of G C Sellar of Ardtornish. Awarded the President's Champion Medal at the Highland & Agricultural Shows of 1909, 1910, 1911.

Appendix C: awards to Highland cattle at the Highland & Agricultural Shows of 1910 and 1911. Prize lists at the Highland Cattle Society's Shows of 1911 and 1912.

VOL XVIII – 1916

Photograph: Chevalier 2548. Bred by the Right Honourable the Earl of Southesk, Kinnaird Castle, property of Col.Campbell of Kilberry, Argyll, V.H.C. at the Highland and Agricultural Show Dumfries 1910; first in Section II of the Highland Cattle Society's Show of 1911; Championship and first as aged bull at the Society's Show of 1915.

Appendix C: awards to Highland cattle at Highland & Agricultural Shows of 1912, 1913, 1914. Prize lists at the Highland Cattle Society's Shows of 1913, 1914, 1915, 1916.

VOL XIX – 1920

Photograph: Righ of Morvern 2605, calved 1910. Bred by G C Sellar of Ardtornish. Property of A G Thom of Canna.

At Highland Cattle Society's Shows awarded first as yearling; Championship as three year old; first as aged bull in 1916.

Appendix A: awards to Highland cattle at Highland & Agricultural Show in 1919. Prize lists at the Highland Cattle Society's Shows of 1917, 1918, 1919.

VOL XX - 1923

Photograph: An-T-Uramach 3050, calved 1918. Bred by and property of D A Stewart of Lochdhu (Ensay) First and Champion at Highland Cattle Society Show of 1920.

Appendix A: awards to Highland cattle at Highland & Agricultural Shows of 1920, 1921, 1922, 1923. Prize lists at Highland Cattle Society's Shows of 1921, 1922, 1923.

VOL XXI - 1928

Photograph: An-T-Uramach of Errol. Bred by Brigadier General J D H Maitland, CMG., DSO. of Errol. Property of the Earl of Home, Douglas Castle. First and Reserve Champion at the Highland Cattle Society's 1926 Show.

Appendix A: awards to Highland cattle at Highland & Agricultural Shows of 1924, 1925, 1926, 1927. Prize lists at Highland Cattle Society's Shows of 1924, 1925, 1926, 1927.

VOL XXII - 1929

Photograph: Culnadalloch II of Achnacloich 3441, calved 1927. Bred by Mrs Maze of Achnacloich. First and Male Champion at the Highland & Agricultural Show, 1928 in Aberdeen.

Appendix A: awards to Highland cattle at Highland & Agricultural Shows of 1927 and 1928. Prize lists at Highland Cattle Society's Shows of 1928 and 1929.

VOL XXIII - 1932

Photograph: An Gille Siobhalt 3520, calved 1927. Bred by D A Stewart of Lochdhu. First and Champion at the Highland Cattle Society's Show 1929.

Appendix A: awards to Highland cattle at Highland & Agricultural Shows of 1929 and 1930. Prize lists at Highland Cattle Society's Shows of 1930, 1931, 1932.

VOL XXIV - 1937

Photograph: An Baidheach of Killundine 3657. Bred by the late A M Lees-Milne, Knock, Mull. First prize, Male championship, and Reserve Supreme Championship at the Highland & Agricultural Society Show, Dundee 1933.

Appendix A: awards to Highland cattle at Highland & Agricultural Shows of 1932, 1933, 1934, 1935, 1936; awards to Highland cattle at the 1935 Show of the Royal Agricultural Society of England. Prize lists at Highland Cattle Society's Shows of 1932, 1933, 1934, 1935, 1936.

VOL XXV - 1940

Photographs: Coinneach Ruadh of Barbreck 3962, calved in 1937. Bred by J P Dalgleish of Barbreck, Lochgilphead First prize and Reserve Male Champion at the Highland & Agricultural Shows of 1938 and 1939. Winner at the Highland Cattle Society's Show of the Craig Sellar Challenge Cup in 1940.

Ribhinn Ile 10991 bred by J G Morrison of Islay, supreme breed champion and winner of first prize and Perpetual Victory Challenge Cup at the Highland & Agricultural Show Dumfries, 1938.

Appendix A: awards to Highland cattle at Highland & Agricultural Shows of 1937, 1938, 1939. Awards to Highland cattle at the Royal Agricultural Show of 1939. Prize lists at the Highland Cattle Society's Shows of 1938, 1939, 1940.

VOL XXVI - 1946

No photograph.

Appendix A: prize lists at Highland Cattle Society's Shows of 1941, 1942, 1943, 1944, 1945.

No Show of the Highland & Agricultural Society of Scotland, nor of the Royal Agricultural Society of England, has been held since the year 1939.

VOL XXVII - 1948

No photograph.

Appendix A: prize lists at the Highland Cattle Society's Shows of 1946, 1947, 1948, and winners at the Highland & Agricultural 1948 Show and the Royal Shows Lincoln 1947, York 1948.

VOL XXVIII - 1949

No photograph.

Appendix A: Awards to Highland cattle at the Royal Highland & Agricultural Society of Scotland Show 1949. Awards to Highland cattle at the Royal (Agricultural Society of England) Show 1949. Prize lists at Highland Cattle Society's Shows of 1949 and 1950.

VOL XXIX - 1950

No photograph.

Appendix A: awards to Highland cattle at the Royal Highland & Agricultural Society of Scotland Show 1950. awards to Highland cattle at the Royal Agricultural Society of England Show 1950. Prize lists at Highland Cattle Society's Shows of 1950 and 1951.

VOL XXX - 1951

Herd Book presented in a new form. Reference in the preface to a pamplet and a brochure on the breed available from the Secretary of the Society. Historical sketch of the Breed. Highland cattle in 1951 by A McKenzie (Scottish Farmer Album) Article by Mr Baxter Berry, President of the American Scotch Highland Breeders' Association. Details of February 1952 Shows and Sales. The Society held for the first time at the Oban spring Bull sales in 1951 a Show and Sale of heifers. Royal Highland Show, Aberdeen, Royal Show, Cambridge, Oban October Sale. Attention of members is drawn to notes on Grading up, Bull licensing, Tattooing instructions. List of registered affixes. Errata.

Photographs and extended pedigrees of Principal prize winners 1951: Aodhair of Mingary 4775, Noinean II of Strathallan 13614, Hamish of Fordie 4766, Dossan Ruadh IV of Achnacloich 13499, Fear Tagraidhe Ile II 4791, Catriona Ile 13724, Uilleam Buidhe of Glenfalloch 4798.

VOL XXXI - 1952

Photograph: Highland cattle, Rothiemurchus. Historical Sketch of the Breed. Article by Mr H E Gildemeister, Peru. Article by MR H O Rogerson. Highland cattle in 1952 by A MacKenzie (Scottish Farmer Album). Details of Oban Shows and Sales October 1952, and February 1953. Secretary's notes "*as from 31 Dec, 1952 the Herd Book is closed to animals being entered directly into the Herd Book after inspection*", Grading up regulations, tattooing instructions.

Photographs and extended pedigrees of Principal prize winners 1952: Adamh of Glenfalloch 4930, Annag of Kildalloig 13543, Corneil Ruadh of Mingary 4771, Uilleam III of Foreland 4820, Calum Og Ile Champion Highland Steer 1952 Scottish National Fatstock Show.

VOL XXXII - 1953

Photograph: Uilleam Buidhe of Glenfalloch 4798 bred by E Lowes Esq. Gravely Sussex. Male champion and Reserve Supreme champion at Royal Highland Show Alloa 1953 and the Royal Show Blackpool 1953. Historical Sketch of the Breed. Royal Highlanders, Establishment of Pedigree Fold at Balmoral. Annual Meeting of the Society 1954. Highland cattle in 1953 by A Mackenzie (Scottish Farmer Album). American Highlanders by THL Macdonald. Oban Shows and Sales October 1953 and February 1954. Secretary's Notes and Tattooing instructions.

The 1953 photographs: Catriona Ile 15498 Supreme champion, Royal Highland; James of Fordie (by 4424); Corneil Ruadh of Mingary 4771 Supreme champion, Oban in 1953; Jack of Fordie Reserve champion Oban 1953; Morag Ile; Ban Righ II of Douglas; Violet V of Strathallan;

The 1954 photographs: Barbara II of Mingary Breed champion Royal Highland in 1954; Gaisgeach of Duart Champion bull Royal Highland 1954; Capleadh Ile XXIV Breed Supreme Champion Royal Show Windsor in 1954 and Reserve supreme champion at Royal Highland Show 1954; Laochan of Douneside Champion Oban 1954; Kinloch of Fordie Reserve Senior champion Oban 1954.

VOL XXXIII - 1954

Photograph: a visit by H. R. H. the Duke of Edinburgh, President of the Royal Highland and Agricultural Society to watch the judging of Highland cattle at the Royal Highland & Agricultural Show, Dumfries.

Historical sketch of the breed. Annual Meeting of the Society. The Cattle of Britain from The Journal of the Ministry of Agriculture 1955. *Looking At Highland Cattle* in 1954 by Ben Coutts (courtesy of Scottish Farmer Album). Details of Oban Shows and sales October 1954 and February 1955. Secretary's Notes and Tattooing instructions. Since 1952 "*No male progeny will be accepted for registration from Appendix B and A animals. A male calf must have both dam and sire fully pedigreed and entered in the Herd Book.*"

Photographs: Anna of Findrack Champion at Oban 1954; John of Severie Breed champion Royal Highland 1954, Champion at Oban Spring 1955; Uallach Ile 3rd Breed champion at Royal Agricultural Show of England and Reserve male champion Royal Highland; Seumas, Breed champion 1954 Scottish National Fat Stock Show.

VOL XXXIV

Report of Annual General Meeting 1956 - charges for 1955 registering heifers to go up; reduction in Assistance Scheme for Show transport expenses. Details of Oban Shows and Sales October 1955 and February 1956, and the Royal Highland and the Royal Shows of 1955. Secretary's notes and tattooing instructions - rules for entering females in the grading up register

Appendix B "*Before inspection animals must be horn-branded if they do not bear any other identification marks e.g. Ministry attestation mark.*"

Photographs: Capleadh Ile XXIV Supreme champion at the Royal 1956; Ailsa II of Findrack Champion Oban October 1955; Boidhchead Dubh II of Braes of Greenock Reserve champion October 1955 Oban; Iarla of Ormsary Champion Oban February 1956; Bratach Dearg of Jura, 1st two year old Oban Feb. 1956; Somhairle of Mingary 2nd prize two year old bull Oban Feb. 1956; Lilli-a-Ghleann of Douneside Supreme breed champion at Royal Highland 1956 and Reserve champion the Royal 1956.

VOL XXXV – 1956

Report of Annual General Meeting 1957 mentioning *"first Englishman ever to be its President – Mr W Pearson Brown, Easingwold"* also that the late Mr Duncan Stewart had through his trustees presented a magnificent trophy to the Society which the council decided should be presented to the female champion at the Society's February Sale. Details of the Oban Shows and Sales October 1956 and February 1957. Secretary's notes and tattooing instructions including further rules about upgrading female cattle. *"Cattle may still be entered on inspection in Appendix B (i.e. females accepted after inspection by a Member of Council as true examples of the pure Highland Breed) but their female progeny will only be eligible for direct entry into the Herd Book if sired by a pedigree bull."* Royal Highland and Royal Agricultural Shows 1956.

VOL 36 – 1957

Report of the Annual General Meeting. Details of Oban Shows and sales October 1957, Feb 1958. Secretary's notes and tattooing instructions. Royal Highland and Royal Agricultural Shows 1957.

VOL 37 – 1958

Report of Annual General Meeting: a new cup to be awarded for the best Highland steer suitable for Smithfield Fatstock Show offered by Mr Lloyd Derisley of Byfleet, Surrey for competition at the Oban sale. There are to be for the first time classes for Highland cattle at the Ayr Agricultural Show and the Great Yorkshire Show in 1960. Details of Oban Shows and Sales Oct 1958 and Feb 1959. Secretary's notes and tattooing instructions. Royal Highland and Royal Agricultural Shows 1958.

VOL 38 – 1959

Annual General Meeting report included that 24 animals had gone to Canada. Details of Oban Shows and sales Oct 1959 and Feb 1960. Secretary's notes and tattooing instructions.

VOL 39 – 1960

Details of Oban Shows and Sales Oct 1960 and Feb 1961. No report of the Annual General Meeting. Secretary's notes and tattooing instructions.

Photographs: Morag Ruadh of Mingary, Supreme breed champion at Royal Highland 1960 and Reserve breed champion at the Royal Agricultural Show 1960; Rannoch of Strathfillan Supreme champion Oban 1961; Pauline of Ardkinglas Supreme champion Oban 1960

VOL 40 – 1961

Secretary's notes and tattooing instructions including *"members are asked to note that the recognised colours of Highland cattle are: Red, Light Red, Black, Light Brindle, Dark brindle, Dun, Silver Dun, Yellow, White."*

Photographs: Princess Ealasaid 6th of Achnacloich 17575 Supreme breed champion Royal Highland 1961; John of Cladich 5626, Supreme champion Oban, March 1961; Lili-a-Gleann of Douneside 16230 Supreme breed champion Oban Spring 1961 and at the Royal 1961; An Ghille Siobhalt of Mingary 5569 Reserve Supreme champion Oban Spring 1961; Nell 2nd of Glen Tanar 19490 Supreme champion Oban in October 1961

VOL 41 - 1962

Secretary's notes and tattooing instructions.

Photographs: Bile Buidhe 3rd of Scone Palace 19592 Supreme breed champion at Royal Highland and Royal Agricultural Show 1962; Diarmid of Achnacloich 5759 Male champion Oban 1962; Lili-a-Gleann 5th of Douneside 19586 Champion female at Oban Spring 1962; Mac-Iain of Mingary 5660 sold for top price at the Society's Spring Show and Sale Oban 1962; Iseabal Bhoidheach 2nd of Mingary 19349 Supreme champion Oban Oct 1962.

VOL 42 - 1963

Secretary's notes and tattooing instructions

Photographs: An Gille Urramach of Mingary 5785 Supreme champion at the Royal Highland 1963; Capleadh Ruadh 6th of Easingwold 20175 Supreme breed champion Royal Show 1963; Colin Ruadh of Glenalmond 5830 Male champion Oban 1963; Sobhrach Og 32nd of Achnacloich 20783 Female champion at Oban Spring 1963; Boidhchead Ruadh of Douneside 20710 Female champion at Oban October 1963.

VOL 43 - 1964

Secretary's notes and tattooing instructions including *"registrations are now accepted for calves got by AI"*

Photographs: Coireall 3rd of Scone Palace 20314 Supreme breed champion Royal Highland and Great Yorkshire Shows 1964; Capleadh Ruadh 6th of Easingwold 20175 Supreme breed champion at the Royal 1964; Ballochmorrie of Ormsary 5736 Male champion Oban February 1964; Seud of Glenquoich 20993 Female champion February 1964 Oban; Priscilla 3rd of Ardkinglas 20801 Female champion in Oban Autumn 1964.

VOL 44 - 1965

Secretary's notes and tattooing instructions

Photographs: Exhibit of Strathallan 5874 Supreme breed champion at Royal Highland and Great Yorkshire Shows 1965; Marlaoch of Douneside 5855 Male champion Oban, February 1965; Dosan Og 12th of Achnacloich 20767 Female champion at Oban Spring 1965; Princess 3rd of Douneside 21070 Female champion at Oban October 1965; Alice 6th of Mingary 21216 Champion Heifer at Oban October 1965.

VOL 45 - 1966

Secretary's notes and tattooing instructions

Photographs: Ruadh Bheg 20th of Balole 21083 Supreme breed champion at Royal Highland Show 1966; Exhibit of Strathallan 5874 Male champion Oban March 1966; Molag 3rd of Strathallan 21152 Female champion Oban March 1966; Sine of Dunach 20944 Female champion October Oban 1966; Peucag 4th of Dalquharran 21815 Champion Heifer October Oban 1966

VOL 46 - 1967

Secretary's notes and tattooing instructions

Photographs: Baravalla Og 2nd of Douneside 21375 Supreme breed champion Royal Highland Show 1967; Carn Mor Dearg of Scone Palace 5937 Male champion at Oban Spring 1967; Bhanna Prionnsa 21st of Benmore 21222 Female champion at Oban Spring

1967; Eva 9th of Ormsary 21346 Supreme champion at Oban in October 1967; Caileag Ghrinn 8th of Douneside 21678 Reserve Supreme champion at Oban October 1967.

VOL 47 – 1968

Secretary's notes and tattooing instructions

Photographs: Corryarrick Lily 20170 Supreme champion and Best Female at the Royal Highland Show 1968; Mairina of Douneside 22009 Supreme champion at Oban in October 1968;

Mairad 2nd of Glenquoich 22232 Female champion at Oban Spring 1968; Ben Alder of Scone Palace 5988 Male champion at Oban Spring 1968; Molag Ruadh 4th of Leachy 22502 Reserve Supreme champion at Oban October 1968.

VOL 48 – 1969

Secretary's notes and tattooing instructions

Photographs: Capleadh Ile 87th 22038 Supreme champion and Best Female at Royal Highland Show 1969; Dosan Og 22nd of Achnacloich 22047 Supreme champion at Oban in October 1969; Ribhinn 9th of Creagan 22175 Female champion at Oban in Spring 1969; Moirreach of Douneside 6048 Male champion at Oban in Spring 1969.

VOL 49 – 1970

Secretary's notes and tattooing instructions

Photographs: Leannan Ruadh 3rd of Douneside 20302 Supreme champion and Best Female Royal Highland Show 1970; Seumas of Ulva 6090 Reserve champion and Best Male at Royal Highland Show 1970; Seumas of Douneside 6106 Champion male Oban Spring 1970; Bhanna Prionnsa 8th of Benmore 22452 Champion female at Oban Spring 1970; Anna 2nd of Ulva 22491 Supreme champion Oban Oct. 1970

VOL 50 – 1971

Secretary's notes and tattooing instructions

Photographs: Boidhchead Og 4th of Douneside 22574 Supreme champion and Best Female Royal Highland 1971; Andie Riabhach of Benmore 6174 Male champion and Reserve Supreme champion Royal Highland Show 1971; Barraiche of Douneside 6148 Champion male at Oban Spring 1971; Cailleach Beag 4th of Ormsary 22552 Champion female at Oban Spring 1971; Oighrig 3rd of Douneside 22580 Supreme champion at Oban Autumn 1971

VOL 51 – 1972

Secretary's notes and tattooing instructions

Photographs: Baravalla Og 2nd of Douneside 21375 Supreme champion and Champion Female at Royal Highland Show 1972; Ben Nevis of Scone Palace 6254 Male champion and Reserve Supreme champion Royal Highland Show 1972; Manus of Douneside 6193 Champion bull Oban Spring 1972; Proiseag 10th of Shenavallie 22738 Champion female at Oban Spring 1972; Bhanna Prionnsa Beag of Benmore 23026 Supreme champion female at Oban Autumn 1972.

VOL 52 – 1973

Secretary's notes and tattooing instructions

Photographs: Lady Ruadh 8th of Strathallan 23217 Supreme and Female champion Royal Highland Show 1973; Ribhinn 6th of Douneside 23131 Reserve Supreme and Reserve Female champion Royal Highland Show 1973; Leodhas of Douneside 6289 Champion and top price bull; Corrina Foil 5th of Leys 23910 Champion female Oban Feb 1973; Myra 3rd of Ormsary 23112 Supreme champion at Oban in October 1973.

VOLUMES 53 - 1974 TO VOLUME 62 - 1983

All contain Cattle entries, Office bearers and Council members, list of affixes, notes on registration, errata, but no photographs, no articles.

VOLUMES 63 - 1984 TO VOLUME 66 - 1987

In addition to content as above since 1974 the secretary's notes assert that the accepted coat colours are RED, BLACK, BRINDLE, DUN, YELLOW, WHITE.

VOL 67 – 1988

in addition to the above as from 1984 the Secretary's notes *"calves born by Fertilised Ovum Transfer (FOT) are to be registered in accordance with Society's Rules."*

VOL 68 – 1989

Secretary's notes include the following about the forthcoming computerisation of the Herd Book:

1 Where the name of an animal is preceded by letters and a number in brackets the animal is registered in the Herd Book of another Society e.g. CHCS- Canada, D-Germany, SW-Sweden, the number being the reference from the relative Herd Book.

2 Where no Herd Book number is given after the name of an animal although the pedigree is known the animal has not been registered in the Herd Book.

General Index

Charles Reid (1837-1929), born in Turriff, was a pioneer of animal photography, overcoming the long exposure times and limitations of camera equipment available. His studies of rural scenes, like this one, sold widely and were displayed in many Victorian drawing roooms and parlours. He travelled widely across the UK from his studio in Wishaw, and was one of Scotland's most successful commercial photograhers.

Index of Named Cattle

The enforced transition from Gaelic to English caused confusion in spelling e.g. Proiseag: little proud one, variations include Proisag, Proisaig, Phroiseag, Prosaig.

Index of Folds and Farms

Prior to individual identification when registered by the Highland Cattle Society with a Fold name and an allocated unique number per animal, Highland cattle were widely known by the name of the farm or land on which they were bred. They were spoken of as stock from, for example Monkstadt, Shinness, Balranald, Cashlie, Ballachroan, Braes of Foss, Urlar, Corrychoillie, Poltalloch, Chesthill, Monachyle, Taymouth, Faside, and many others all had old Highland cattle bloodlines well before the Highland Cattle Society was established in 1884.